A
COMPASS
ON THE
NAVIGABLE
SEA

A COMPASS ON THE NAVIGABLE SEA

100 YEARS OF WORLD LITERATURE

Edited by
DANIEL SIMON

Introduced by
PICO IYER

RESTLESS BOOKS

NEW YORK · AMHERST

Compilation copyright © 2026 *World Literature Today* and the Board of Regents of the University of Oklahoma
Introduction copyright © 2026 Daniel Simon
Foreword copyright © 2026 Pico Iyer

Restless Books and the R colophon are registered trademarks of Restless Books, Inc.

First Restless Books paperback edition February 2026

Paperback ISBN: 9781632064134
Library of Congress Control Number: 2025941102

Publication of this book was made possible, in part, by a Faculty Investment Program grant sponsored by the University of Oklahoma's Vice President for Research and Partnerships and the OU Research Council, with additional funding from the office of the Senior Vice President and Provost and the Dodge Family College of Arts & Sciences.

This book is also supported in part by an award from the National Endowment for the Arts.

NATIONAL
ENDOWMENT for the ARTS
════════════════ arts.gov

Owing to limitations of space, all acknowledgments for permission to reprint previously published and unpublished material can be found on pages 438–442. All efforts have been made to contact copyright holders. In case of inadvertent omissions, please contact Restless Books: publisher@restlessbooks.org.

Royalties derived from the University of Oklahoma's sales of this anthology will be donated to *World Literature Today*'s student scholarship funds at OU.

Cover design by Keenan
Text design and typesetting by Tetragon, London

Printed in the United States

10 9 8 7 6 5 4 3 2

RESTLESS BOOKS
NEW YORK · AMHERST

restlessbooks.org

CONTENTS

PART II: FIRST TAKES ON MODERN CLASSICS, 1926–1975

PART III: BOOKS AS SHIPS

PART IV: FIRST TAKES ON MODERN CLASSICS, 1976–2025

PART V: BOOKS AS LIGHTHOUSES

FOREWORD: THEIR STORY IS OURS

PICO IYER

A STRANGER ARRIVES on your doorstep—in Norman, Oklahoma, say—bearing jewels, spices, stories. She transforms the language that you speak with her lilt; her history sounds like fairy tale. But, no less happily, your stories sound wondrous to her and your life seems a marvel even as you're standing in your home. You're coming to the street you share from opposite corners of the world, yet neither of you can fail to recognize the other's longings, or her fears.

In our Age of Movement, such exchanges can unfold even within a family. My grandparents spoke three languages between them that were all metaphorical Greek to me; my mother and father, from North and South India, respectively, had no words but those of Shakespeare and the King James Bible in common. When my mother told me stories of her girlhood—"Kabul-wallahs" from Afghanistan bringing rich woolen rugs to her home in Bombay while Chinese traders trundled past on bicycles, selling exquisite embroidered cloth—they seemed to belong not just to a different time, but to the pages of a novel. And when my parents moved from my birthplace of Oxford, England, to California, suddenly, at seven, I found myself to be a curious little creature with an Indian face, an English voice, and an American residence.

How blessed I felt! I had three sets of eyes, three ways of regarding every circumstance. I could mix my perspectives, match them, see California with English eyes, England with Indian. My classmates, nearly all of whom had only one culture inside them, seemed to be missing something precious. I could never have guessed then that children today would often be far more multicultured than I am, and that we mongrels would be the honorary citizens of the new millennium, in Sydney and Singapore, Vancouver and Paris.

Every culture—of course—has always had its own literature, but I'm not sure people have ever crossed borders at the rate and scale that we experience now. One soul in seven across the planet is displaced, as we read here, which means that more than one billion people are on the move. A few of us are lucky enough to experience foreign cultures firsthand, and so to see how the wildest dreams of Kew, in Kipling's words, are the facts of Kathmandu; too many others are propelled out of their homes into places they never wished to visit. In either case, a new literature comes to light speaking the truth that few of us can be reduced to a single home, and it's the passageways between cultures that are our new bases and centers of possibility. Guerrero's stories make sense even in Chicago and Lagos's problems now are London's.

Classrooms seldom adapt as quickly as their inhabitants do, however; when I studied literature at college in England, our course ended abruptly at 1832. Even writers born in the U.S.—T. S. Eliot and Henry James—were deemed beyond the pale. Yet only a few years later, the doors and windows of the stuffy old Havisham house of English letters were flung open as migrants from Zanzibar and Pakistan, from Port of Spain and Perth began to stream onto British shores, bringing fresh scents, tropical breezes, new conspiracies into the land and language.

By the 1980s readers were starting to notice that the Booker Prize, awarded each year to the best single work of sustained fiction to emerge from Britain and the Commonwealth, seemed less and less often to go to writers from Britain; the voices that were catching the moment came from South Asia, South Africa, New Zealand, Japan. Salman Rushdie brought the mishmashed language of the streets of Bombay—Hinglish and P. G. Wodehouse and Marathi—into his tales of a liberated London; Kazuo Ishiguro evoked the costs of classic British self-suppression and stoicism by giving us precise descriptions of the Nagasaki where he was born. Timothy Mo delivered a portrait of London in which not a white skin was visible, even as the national dish of Britain was evolving from roast beef and Yorkshire pudding to chicken tikka masala.

Art was being true to a new kind of life: the average person you meet today on the streets of London—or Toronto—was born in a foreign country. Leaders in those countries, as in many others, look nothing like the stately portraits hung along the walls. Even those who never leave home have, as Shuri Kudo writes here, "a thousand countries" within them. My Japanese mother-in-law seldom set foot outside Kyoto. But every time she looked out from her little wooden house, with its tatami mats, to the narrow lane leading up to the fox shrine with 10,000 *torii* gates, she was met by headscarves and saris and turbans and the sound of reggae. An entirely British writer, David Mitchell, effectively announced the arrival of the new millennium by publishing in 1999 a debut novel, *Ghostwritten*, set in nine countries, each of which is in some ways a version of the others.

While my father was studying in England, his classmate V. S. Naipaul began working to expand English literature by crafting a prose cleaner and more rigorous than that of any English writer; around the same time, Naipaul's Caribbean contemporary (and rival and fellow Nobel laureate) Derek Walcott was at once exalting his native St. Lucia and enriching the tradition we knew by recasting *The Odyssey* among the fishermen of the West Indies, hymning them with a sonorous eloquence born of Shakespeare and Milton. By 1992, Michael Ondaatje's *English Patient* was charting a world in which all distinctions dissolve in the desert and simple assumptions of where anyone comes from can be a kind of death. By 1993, when I was asked to write a cover story for *Time* magazine entitled "The Empire Writes Back," international coproductions were increasingly the norm, and magic was already the realism of the day.

As many in this volume remind us, much in the Age of Movement is tragic in both cause and consequence. Exile is never an easy prospect, and too many end up stranded in some no-man's-land between the country they have fled and the one that refuses to accept them. Yes, they can fashion a fresh kind of sensibility, but it is in the service of a story haunted by sorrow and separation. Their stories may be the only things they have.

Yet it is partly because the world remains so divided that World Literature carries such urgency today. At a time when so many are trying to build walls and yank us back into the black-and-white divisions of the past, it's our imaginations—the stories we tell, and the empathy and sense of solidarity they awaken—that help us build bridges and remind us of how much we share. Stories can cross every cultural divide and speak in any language; no one is a foreigner to *Romeo and Juliet*, even though it was written more than four centuries ago in England and set in Verona. Memories can't be confiscated by customs, nor cadences blocked by an immigration officer.

It seems only fitting that the writer who sets the keynote for this volume, Octavio Paz, served as a diplomat for his country, a literal emissary to other lands who brought back their cultural and philosophical treasures to his compatriots; the same was true of Pablo Neruda and Carlos Fuentes. The writers who teach you in the New World may be bringing you a history you barely recognize, if their names are Czesław Miłosz or Li-Young Lee, but their loves and their challenges are as familiar as are our siblings, or our parents.

To see World Literature continue spreading across the globe, taking on new colors at every turn, is thrilling to this lifelong reader. Returning to a classroom recently, for the first time in thirty-seven years, I was startled to register that three of the central professors at my university—Jhumpa Lahiri, Aleksandar Hemon, and Yiyun Li—were all writing in languages not originally their own. How could they not bring something new to the literatures they were expanding, and how could they not speak in ways that were novel, perhaps even emancipating to themselves? When my friends speak of the writers who feel like their secret biographers, the names they cite are not always easy to pronounce: Knausgaard and Ferrante and Bolaño and Murakami. J. M. Coetzee has even begun publishing his novels first in Spanish—as a protest against the hegemony of English—and tried to get his English-language publishers to bring out editions in his almost-mother tongue by translating from his third language.

I feel immensely grateful to be released from my provincialism by such voices, and for the chance to learn from—and about—other cultures as my grandparents could not so easily have done. W. G. Sebald and Orhan Pamuk, Arundhati Roy and Yoko Ogawa extend my horizons and make the world new for me again. Dinaw Mengestu opens up my adopted home with rare mastery and heart, and Edwidge Danticat gives me a Haiti filled with Polish soldiers. Richard Rodriguez, Laila Lalami, Chimamanda Ngozi Adichie allow me, gloriously, to become the inheritor of everywhere, in a music all their own.

It's bracing—inspiring—to recall that World Literature Today has been around for one hundred years; never has writing from the other side of the waters been more necessary or more timely. Why? Because soon after that stranger arrives at your door, one of her children starts to notice one of yours. They're fascinated by their differences, united by all they have in common. Once they join hands, producing a new generation, the world expands a little more, with a whole new culture, a fresh soul who lives farther from simple definitions than ever, promising in her every utterance to remake the ways we see and speak, the ways we live and, in the end, the ways we love.

Pico Iyer is the author of seventeen books, translated into twenty-three languages; his recent bestsellers include *The Open Road*, *The Half Known Life*, and *Aflame*.

INTRODUCTION: A RELIABLE COMPASS

DANIEL SIMON

Magazine [> Arabic *ma<u>k</u>zin* storehouse]
A ship which supplies provisions.[†]

—*Oxford English Dictionary*

IN THE 1820S, Johann Wolfgang von Goethe articulated a nascent vision of literature on a transnational scale. This ideal, which he coined *Weltliteratur*, took root during an era marked by fierce nationalism, imperial greed, coal-driven industrial economies, and astonishing technological change—all of which coalesced when World War I unleashed its destruction upon the world. Just before and after the so-called Great War, this time from an Eastern perspective, Rabindranath Tagore and Zheng Zhenduo tried to harmonize their worldviews with Goethe's Western paradigm as part of a cosmopolitan literary modernism. The Bengali term *viśva-sāhitya*, the Chinese term *shijie wenxue*, and German term *Weltliteratur* all represented attempts to encapsulate the notion of a globe-striding literature even as nation-states rose and fell around the world, sometimes violently.

Writing in their mother tongues, these literati also held something else in common: all three served as editors of leading literary periodicals in their day, and they passionately debated the role of literature in those pages. As was true for books and newspapers, the extraordinary democratization of print technologies in the nineteenth century made the globalization of the magazine form possible. The Gutenberg revolution that began with the invention of the printing press in the mid-fifteenth century had set off seismic shifts in society and religion, ushering in modernity. During the Enlightenment, epochal advances were made in science, technology, and medicine—not to mention literature. Such European prose masters as Rabelais, Montaigne, and Cervantes—along with poets representing geographies as far-flung as Djeli Mamoudou

Kouyaté, William Shakespeare, Sor Juana Inés de la Cruz, Matsuo Bashō, Phillis Wheatley, Mirza Ghalib, Nguyễn Du, and Alexander Pushkin—not only reflected changes happening in the world around them but helped create the world as we know it today. Translations of *The Thousand and One Nights* and *Bhagavad Gita* in the eighteenth century also brought new visions of the world into global circulation. Following Goethe, from the mid-nineteenth century to the fin de siècle, Darwin, Marx and Engels, Nietzsche, Freud, and other thought leaders articulated new theories in science, economics, philosophy, psychology, and related domains that would revolutionize ideas about the human condition.

Enabled by modern print practices, the serial form of the magazine had helped transform the nineteenth-century ideal of world literature into an emerging reality by the early twentieth century. Spurred on by the so-called little magazines, literary modernism would soon reach its apogee in the Paris, London, Berlin, and New York of the 1920s. Virginia Woolf's *Mrs. Dalloway*, Marcel Proust's *Albertine disparue* (*Albertine Gone*), Franz Kafka's *Der Prozeß* (*The Trial*), Alain Locke's *The New Negro*, and F. Scott Fitzgerald's *The Great Gatsby* were all published in that annus mirabilis of 1925, which the BBC once called "the greatest year for books ever." That same year in Paris, the first exhibition of surrealist art debuted, and the Exposition Internationale des Arts Décoratifs et Industriels Modernes gave the Art Deco style its name. In the Berlin-based journal *Zeitschrift für Physik*, Werner Heisenberg and his colleagues elaborated a cutting-edge theory of quantum mechanics.

But literary modernity didn't just happen in the glittering metropolises of the U.S. and western Europe. In his book *Little Magazine, World Form* (2016), Eric Bulson makes a compelling case for little magazines' role in the "globalization of modernism," not only in the 1920s but well into the twentieth century. The story of those editors—Harriet Monroe, Margaret Anderson, Ezra Pound, T. S. Eliot—who served as impresarios of anglophone modernism is well known, but Bulson argues that the material form of the magazine itself helped create transnational—and in many cases oppositional—literary networks "open to writers and critics everywhere." He lists many of the names that little magazines were known by in such places as Japan, India, Uganda, Jamaica, and Argentina, including *rivista, revista, periódico, zhurnal, Zeitschrift, dōjin zasshi, tidsskrift, samizdat*, *folyóirat*, and *patrika*. If the apotheosis of the book, primarily the novel, represented the pinnacle of the Gutenberg half-millennium, the technology of the magazine provided the crucible for world literature's twentieth-century ascendancy in almost every country in the Americas, Africa, Asia, the Middle East, and Europe.

THE LOCAL AND THE UNIVERSAL

> *The world entire is contained inside us.*
>
> —Ilan Stavans, "Is American Literature Parochial?"

In the selections that follow, readers will be guided through an inductive survey of world literature "as it happened" over the last century, as presented in the pages of a little magazine called *Books Abroad*—founded at the University of Oklahoma in 1927—and its successor, *World Literature Today* (*WLT*), over the past century. The essays, poetry, interviews, fiction, and letters gathered here are thematically grouped in three parts: (I) "Books as Maps," (III) "Books as Ships," and (V) "Books as Lighthouses." The reviews in parts II and IV, sequenced in chronological order, present "first takes" on works that, in time, readers would come to regard as modern classics.

The anthology's title, *A Compass on the Navigable Sea*, takes its inspiration from Octavio Paz's 1982 Neustadt Prize acceptance speech, which he delivered at the university's main campus in Norman, Oklahoma. *Books Abroad* editor Ivar Ivask had launched the prize in 1969 as an expression of "American concern for genuine achievement in world literature." The seventh laureate to win the Neustadt award, Paz recalls having encountered *Books Abroad* while he was a college student in the 1930s:

> In those days the literary isolation of Mexico was almost absolute, to the degree that when I read those pages I felt the opening of the doors of contemporary literature in languages other than my own. For a while *Books Abroad* was my compass, and foreign literatures ceased to be for me an impenetrable forest.

Paz, who founded two influential Mexican literary magazines in the 1970s, extends the compass metaphor to imagine the Great Plains as a "navigable sea" for those who might dismiss the landlocked prairies as empty of culture:

> Situated in the center of the United States and surrounded by immense plains, Oklahoma seemed destined due to geographic fate for interior activity and historical apartness. However, the relation of every society with its surrounding physical reality is one of contradiction: men who inhabit a valley climb mountains that separate them from the world, and men of the plains move along the endless expanse as if it were a navigable sea. These are opposite and reversible metaphors: the desert is a sea for the Arab, and the sea is a desert for the sailor. In each case the metaphor is a challenge and an invitation: the horizon remains at the same time a call and an obstacle.

From its base on the U.S. Southern Plains, *WLT* centers its vision of world literature in an Indigenous ethos of rootedness in the land emblematized by the oral traditions of the world's ancient civilizations. Two Oklahoma-born Native writers featured here—N. Scott Momaday and Joy Harjo—offer millennial perspectives in that regard. For Momaday, the vocation of the storyteller is to "speak, listen, and remember"; for Harjo, the land itself embodies "a speaker, a singer, a keeper." From the transnational crossroads that is present-day Oklahoma, the primacy of Native languages extends throughout the Americas. From the Southern Cone of Latin America, nearly six thousand miles to the south, Mapuzungun writer Liliana Ancalao reminds readers that "the land speaks" in its own tongues, despite the imposition of Spanish: "I'm talking about an ancient language and the ignorance of men who mapped a country over a territory full of names, elements, and meanings, silencing it." Of course, that postcolonial legacy persists today, well into the twenty-first century. In its early decades, *Books Abroad*'s focus was conventionally Eurocentric—as the selection of book reviews in part II attests—but the editors gradually expanded the literary map by pointing the magazine's compass to the furthest reaches of the known world.

In addition to geographical specificity, an emphasis on language pervades the anthology. From Anne Carson's translations of Ancient Greek verse to Meena Alexander's musings on the unsayable in poetry, many of the writers featured here offer rich reflections on literature's raw materials, from stories told through images painted onto cave walls to the printed and virtual page. Debates about linguistic autonomy and vernacular expression naturally segue into meditations on the interlingual interplay between migrant and immigrant cultures, as in A. A. Roback's essay on American Yiddish literature. Mauritian writer Ananda Devi offers a prime example of this phenomenon: Telugu, Creole, French, and English all enrich her work.

Arising from preoccupations with language is a persistent emphasis on the power of storytelling in pieces by Aminatta Forna, Natalie Diaz, and others. While stories may be rooted in place and time, what came to be known as the Republic of Letters ultimately transcends geography, mapping a new aesthetic topography over the borders of nation-states. For Elie Wiesel—who first wrote *Night*, his most famous book, in Yiddish—the Holocaust "expelled" Jewish writers from geography into the sanctuary of books. For Aleš Debeljak, in speaking "the language of translation," this sanctuary is created not just by writers, translators, editors, and publishers but by a diverse community of global readers: "With every story read, with every verse quietly recounted, we renew our citizenship in the Republic of Letters." Drawing on the examples of Scheherazade and Lewis Carroll's Alice while reflecting on the recent "Woman, Life, Freedom" protests in Iran, Azar Nafisi—who received her PhD in English from the University of Oklahoma in 1979—evokes an analogous term in her interview that concludes part III: the "Republic of the Imagination."

Indeed, that republic only exists via the work of translators, whom Debeljak calls "the exemplary citizens of the republic of letters." The polyglot Valery Larbaud once famously compared translators to "beggars at the church door" outside the cathedral of world literature. Better, perhaps, to think of them as sextons, those unheralded lumpen literati in charge of maintaining the church's property, whether called upon to ring the bells summoning the faithful to services or—to echo Walter Benjamin's metaphor for translation as *Überleben*—to dig graves for the corpses of writers who hope for a literary afterlife. Ironically, Larbaud's personal wealth gave him the freedom to travel the world, but he also labored in what Kafka called "the pit of Babel" by translating two titans of modernity, Whitman and Joyce, into French. Ananda Devi writes that, in addition to her work as an interlingual translator, she became "a kind of translator of bodies, minds, hearts, in order to fight against the erasure" of "those whom the world rarely listened to." She cites the example of a Mauritian Creole translation of Jean Cocteau's French play *La machine infernale* that connects both the Greek myth of Oedipus and the Hindu myth of Ramayana. "In the history of tongues," asserts the Hindi poet Geet Chaturvedi, "the tongue of the translator is the most selfless, which even fire cannot summon courage to burn."

Within the ambit of this anthology, Momaday completes the circle of geography, language, and translation by offering the examples of *Beowulf, Hamlet*, and Lincoln's Gettysburg Address, all of which rise "to universal significance . . . as story, as poetry, as drama, and as a statement of the human condition, not only of its own time but also of all times." While each writer claims a homeland as part of their origin story, the experience of exile—perhaps *the* defining condition of the modern writer—necessitates a different idea of literary citizenship. In his reflections on American literature, which he calls "the most cosmopolitan, the most universal of local literatures," Ilan Stavans connects what Paz, in his Neustadt acceptance speech, calls the twin poles of Universality and Plurality. "In aesthetic terms," Paz writes, "Plurality is a richness of voices, accents, manners, ideas, and visions; in moral terms, Plurality signifies tolerance of diversity, renunciation of dogmatism, and recognition of the unique and singular value of each work and every personality. Plurality is Universality, and Universality is the acknowledging of the admirable diversity of man and his works." For Stavans, Paz's theorem is exemplified in the "infinite ways of being a writer in America." Throughout the pages that follow, we find writers the world over constantly negotiating the polarities of home and exile, mother tongue and translatability, past and present, local and universal.

FROM THE REPUBLIC OF LETTERS TO A REPUBLIC OF READERS

An angel is there / bringing back love.

—Refaat Alareer, "If I Must Die"

While the emergence of a truly global literature manifests itself in the century (1925–2025) spanned by these pages, less clear-cut is the answer to the question—to echo Meena Alexander's essay that leads off part V— What *use* is world literature? Since 1925, the globe has been convulsed by extremes of ideology (fascism, communism, and other forms of totalitarianism), two world wars and countless millions dead, the Holocaust and other unspeakable genocides, the specter of nuclear war, ongoing settler-colonial violence, terrorism, militarized ethno-states, endless despotic regimes, global pandemics, and climate crisis. A century ago, lynchings in the Jim Crow American South, anti-Semitism in Europe, and every stripe of hate based on race, religion, class, and nationality everywhere made a mockery of the humanist ethos embodied in Enlightenment philosophy. Many of the writers featured here were drawn into the debate over *l'art pour l'art* versus *littérature engagée*, variously emphasizing the autonomy of the aesthetic realm over the necessity of political engagement. As Wiesel notes, "The first crime committed by the Nazis was against language"; indeed, writers in the postwar era fought to reclaim or reimagine humanism's shattered ideals from the terrain of language. Since the eighteenth century, many of the writers who espoused a Republic of Letters did so from the comfort of their salons, debating the finer points of *belles lettres*; after Auschwitz and Hiroshima, many postwar writers insisted that the so-called Republic had rotted from within. Yet the ideal of a true world literature persisted as the emphasis shifted from the lingering Romantic trope of the solitary, inspired genius to the democratization of access represented by an emerging Republic of Readers.

So, from the crow's nest of 2025, looking out toward "the challenge and the invitation" of Paz's horizon, where is world literature headed in the next century? Most of the writers here would insist that circumnavigating the globe is less of a geographical proposition than a temporal one, more of a conical spiral—connecting past and present—than a straight line. At least since the time of Horace, writing in the first century BCE, the primary tasks of the poet were encapsulated in two dictums: to *instruct* and *delight*. Enlightenment, pleasure, or a combination of both can be found in abundance in the colloquy that *A Compass on the Navigable Sea* convenes in its pages. Following a classic lodestar, Nicaraguan/Salvadoran writer Claribel Alegría insists on wielding her pen as a "sword of poetry" while channeling such predecessors as Sor Juana, Percy Bysshe Shelley, Rubén Darío, and Rainer Maria Rilke. Inspired by the "poetry of witness" of Alegría and other writers, Carolyn Forché insists that the testimonial presence of language "incises the page" with both our "infinite responsibility for the *other one*" as well as a sense of sacred radiance. Croatian writer Dubravka Ugrešić also takes up the Horatian theme in her 2016 Neustadt Prize lecture, invoking a Nabokovian storyteller who embodies the roles of both "teacher" and "enchanter." Ultimately, Ugrešić says, writers, readers, and publishers must work together to invest in and preserve "the intellectual, the artistic, the spiritual capital" of literature and the arts against the "latter-day inquisitors" who would burn such vanities at the stake. Both Meena Alexander and Azar Nafisi proclaim that love, truth, and imagination, in the face of violence and death, are humanity's only hope. For Alexander, writing from the tesserae of destruction in New York City after 9/11, writers create works that serve as a counterweight to forces of chaos. And while "seeing beauty amidst iniquity seems a tall order," writes Russian-born writer Anna Badkhen, "I insist we must—otherwise we will not survive our own history of violence, we will stop falling in love and die off as a species."

In his recent book, *World Literature as Discovery: Expanding the World Literary Canon* (2024), the distinguished Chinese comparatist Zhang Longxi makes an eloquent and sophisticated plea to move beyond the perennially Eurocentric canon of world literature to champion a more egalitarian, indeed planetary understanding of global literary production and excellence. In his compelling final chapter, "World Literature and Cosmopolitanism," Zhang insists that reading world literature should defang the varieties of "parochialism, tribalism, ethnocentrism, and narrow-minded nationalism" that poison relationships between and within nations. Zhang's model of cosmopolitan literary citizenship is both ethically driven and future-oriented: "Cosmopolitanism means to cultivate the feeling of a shared, common humanity with strangers, foreigners, or people outside one's own community." Ultimately, such a model obligates us to translate what we learn and delight in into an ethical praxis that enlarges the humanity of others as much as our own. The compass is both a navigational tool and a moral instrument.

Publishing a magazine like *World Literature Today* takes the abstraction of a term like "world literature" and materializes it in the work of the writers featured—and the readers envisioned—in its pages. I hope the materiality of that work, manifested by the selections that follow, will translate into an imaginative republic and ethical praxis that continue to inspire a global vision of literature.

NORMAN, OKLAHOMA, JULY 2025

Editorial note: For more on the history and editorial leadership of *Books Abroad* and *World Literature Today*, a postscript, "*World Literature Today* and World Literature," can be found on pages 431–434.

Every literature will exhaust its vitality, if it is not refreshed by the interest and contributions of a foreign one.

—JOHANN WOLFGANG VON GOETHE (1828)

A
COMPASS
ON THE
NAVIGABLE
SEA

PART I

BOOKS AS MAPS

OCTAVIO PAZ

Translated from the Spanish by Lowell Dunham

IN ALL LANGUAGES there are limpid words which are like air and the water of the spirit. To express such words is always marvelous and furthermore necessary, like breathing. One such word is *gracias*, thank you. Today I pronounce it with joy. Also with the awareness of being the object of a happy confusion. The truth is that I am not very certain of the value of my writings. On the other hand, I am certain of my literary passion: it was born with me and will die only when I die. This belief consoles me. The jurors were not completely mistaken in awarding me the Neustadt Prize for 1982: they wanted to reward, in my case, if not excellence, then obstinacy. . . . I shall not say more about my feelings. I am no more than the incidental (or accidental?) cause, and so what should count, however deep my gratitude, is not my person but the significance of the Neustadt Prize. It is worth reflecting upon this for a moment.

Situated in the center of the United States and surrounded by immense plains, Oklahoma seemed destined due to geographic fate for interior activity and historical apartness. However, the relation of every society with its surrounding physical reality is one of contradiction: men who inhabit a valley climb mountains that separate them from the world, and men of the plains move along the endless expanse as if it were a navigable sea. These are opposite and reversible metaphors: the desert is a sea for the Arab, and the sea is a desert for the sailor. In each case the metaphor is a challenge and an invitation: the horizon remains at the same time a call and an obstacle. In the domain of literary communication, Oklahoma has overcome isolation and distance through a series of exemplary initiatives.

The first was the founding of the journal *Books Abroad* in 1927 by Roy Temple House. I remember how many years ago, when I was studying for the bachelor's degree and was beginning to discover literature for myself, a copy of the journal came into my hands. In those days the literary isolation of Mexico was almost absolute, to the degree that when I read those pages I felt the opening of the doors of contemporary literature in languages other than my own. For a while *Books Abroad* was my compass, and foreign literatures ceased to be for me an impenetrable forest. *Books Abroad* no longer exists, not because it has disappeared but because it has been transformed, enlarged, and rejuvenated. Under the energetic and intelligent editorship of Ivar Ivask, a poet who himself is a lucid and intrepid literary explorer, the review has grown. It is now called *World Literature Today* and has become an indispensable periodical for all those who want to keep up with contemporary literature on a worldwide scale. I stress the word *worldwide*, which must be understood literally: *World Literature Today* is not dedicated only to the analysis of literature from the major European languages, but it also follows with genuine and admirable sympathy, not lacking in rigor, the development of letters in the so-called minor languages. It is no secret that these languages are often rich in notable works and original talents.

Following the example of *World Literature Today* and inspired by it, there have emerged during these last few years other activities which exhibit the same universal calling. One of these activities has been the series of symposia which are convened periodically at the University of Oklahoma honoring writers in Spanish or French. In these conferences critics from both the Americas and from Europe participate, and the papers and discussions represent, in many cases, essential contributions in the field of contemporary Hispanic and French literature.

Another manifestation, no doubt the most important to date, has been the establishment in 1969 of the Neustadt International Prize for Literature. In many countries there exist national literary prizes to single out a writer in a common language of several nations. On the other hand, there are very few literary prizes indeed which are truly *international*. Among these a place apart is occupied by the Neustadt Prize. Two characteristics lend it a unique face: the first is that each jury is composed of critics and writers belonging to different languages and literatures, which means that it constitutes an *international* body, as international as the prize itself; the second characteristic is that the jury is not permanent but instead changes from one prize to the next—that is, every two years. These two characteristics translate into two words: *Universality* and *Plurality*. Due to the first word, the prize has been awarded to poets and novelists in Italian, English, French, Polish, Spanish and Czech; due to the second word, Plurality, we find among the laureates not only writers of different languages but also of different literary and philosophical persuasions. In aesthetic terms, Plurality is a richness of voices, accents, manners, ideas, and visions; in moral terms, Plurality signifies tolerance of diversity, renunciation of dogmatism, and recognition of the unique and singular value of each work and every personality. Plurality is Universality, and Universality is the acknowledging of the admirable diversity of man and his works.

Considering all this, in the convulsed and intolerant modern world we inhabit, the Neustadt Prize is an example of true civilization. I will say even more: to acknowledge the variety of visions and sensibilities is to preserve the richness of life and thus to ensure its continuity. Hence the Neustadt Prize, in stimulating the universality and diversity of literature, defends life itself.

MEXICO CITY

Born and raised in Mixcoac, part of present-day Mexico City, Octavio Paz (1914–1998) was only nineteen when he published his first collection of poetry. In 1945 he began working as a diplomat for the Mexican government in such metropolises as Paris, Tokyo, Geneva, and Mumbai. Paz delivered this acceptance speech upon receiving the Neustadt Prize at the University of Oklahoma in 1982. He went on to win the 1990 Nobel Prize in Literature.

Lowell Dunham (1910–2001) was a longtime professor of Spanish at the University of Oklahoma. His honors included the Order of Andrés Bello, First Class, granted by the Venezuelan Academy of Language.

WANDERING BIRDS

(2021)

SHURI KIDO

Translated from the Japanese by Tomoyuki Endo & Forrest Gander

A thousand countries in myself—
There's something that precipitates to the very bottom of such a feeling.
Is everything just an image,
or is this only a wasteland where images overflow,
and become a language?
There is a sound you can hear
only when your body grows older and more tranquil.
And yet, can it be called "a sound"?
It's more a smell
than a sound.
People die,
just as the dead die,
and then, those who died twice
die three times,
and they seem to fill "afterdeath."
As such, in regions where water is abundant,
human life and death aren't separated out.

Odor of snow.

In the margin, going paler and paler,
where not even one line has been written,
an empty sky has already collapsed.
(After that, 500 years pass)
And in the second line, not yet written,
a water rail begins to chirp.
From where the chirp merges with the sky
(another 300 hundred years pass)

a river begins,
offering the gods an entrance,
as if remaining in place,
      you stop where you are,
      reflecting on yourself,
      dancing,
      going mad.

And the gods are already gone.

The breast-like mountains
sink below the misty, gloomy air.
The mountains are so low,
clouds, like a dog's tongue, lap at them.
The skies are so low,
the river gets much colder.
Sticking your hand into the flow
you cleave the stream into two
currents that come clear as life and death.

Around here,
when you ask the name of a tree,
what you'll hear is "It's a tree."
Yes, that's a tree.
Yes, that's a mountain.
Yes, and this is water.
"Here in this place,
there are more badgers and foxes than people.
You may see a human
who is not human
who is some hirsute creature
disguised,
and if you see some part of its body
is transparent,
you'll know for sure it was once human."

Well, is that a human?
It may be I miss the living.

The thousand countries within me—
appearing from nowhere,
and uttering nothing: this is my father.
Sitting upright with her legs folded
and smiling unselfconsciously,
my mother.
Every night, the illusion passes,
leaving a sliver of pain;
wandering birds chirp sadly,
not given to fly anywhere else.
The birdsong carries up to the clouds,
tomorrow it will snow.

Shuri Kido (b. 1959) has been a prominent member of the Japanese poetry scene for more than thirty years. He has published essays on literature and Buddhism as well as translations of Ezra Pound and T. S. Eliot into Japanese. His book of poems in English, *Names and Rivers*, was published in 2023 by Copper Canyon.

Tomoyuki Endo is an assistant professor at Wako University in Tokyo with a focus on American and Japanese literature.

A multidisciplinary writer and translator, Forrest Gander is the recipient of numerous awards, including the Pulitzer Prize and the Best Translated Book Award. His most recent book is *Mojave Ghost*.

ALL GEOGRAPHY IS WITHIN ME: WRITING BEGINNINGS, LIFE, DEATH, FREEDOM, AND SALT (2018)

EDWIDGE DANTICAT

1

THIS PAST JUNE I was in Haiti in part for the opening of a library in a southern town called Fond-des-Blancs. Fond-des-Blancs, which literally means "The Fountain of the Whites," is mostly known for being home to a large number of people of Polish lineage, the descendants of soldiers from a Polish regiment that switched alliances from the French armies they were fighting alongside in nineteenth-century Haiti to join the Haitians in their battle for independence from France in 1804. The mutinous Polish soldiers who ended up settling in Fond-des-Blancs were the only whites and foreigners who were granted Haitian citizenship after Haiti became the first Black republic in the Western hemisphere in 1804.

The library we were there to celebrate had been started by a nonprofit called Haiti Projects, which was run by an acquaintance of mine whose mother is American and whose father is Haitian. The opening-week program included writing workshops and conversations with writers. I took part in a conversation and writing workshop with the Haitian novelist and short-story writer Kettly Mars. Our moderator, a Haiti-based educator named Jean-Marie Théodat, asked each of us to read both the beginning and the end of one of our short stories, then explain to the group of twenty-five or so eager teenagers why we had chosen to begin and end that story the way we had.

If you have ever spoken to a group of teenagers, you know how intimidating it already is to explain anything to them, but this was a bit extra-intimidating for me. It is much easier to explain or elaborate on an ending than a beginning. For endings, you can always say that it ended *this* way because it had begun *that* way. Or it ended that way because something popped up in the middle that led me there. Beginnings have a much bigger burden and are often less clear.

In the beginning was the Word, the Good Book tells us. And perhaps the Word—or the Words—was, were . . .

Once Upon a Time,

Il était une fois or

Te gèn yon fwa or

Krik? Krak!

I feel the same dilemma right now while trying to trace the geography, or cartography, both internal and external, that has brought me from my own beginnings to this moment.

Once upon a time, a little girl was born in Haiti during the middle part of a dynastic thirty-year dictatorship. Her parents were poor, though maybe not as poor as others. My parents didn't get very far in school because their parents could not afford it. My mother was a seamstress. My father, a shoe salesman and a tailor.

When I was two years old, my father left Haiti and moved to the United States to look for work. Two years later, my mother joined him and left me and my younger brother, Bob, in the care of my aunt and uncle in Port-au-Prince.

One of my earliest childhood memories is of being torn away from my mother. On the day my mother left, I wrapped my arms around her legs before she headed for the plane. She leaned down and tearfully unballed my fists so that my uncle could peel me off her. As my brother dropped to the floor, bawling, my mother hurried away, her tear-soaked face buried in her hands. She couldn't bear to look back.

If my life were the short story I was asked to explain the beginning of in that writing workshop with the teenagers in Fond-des-Blancs, this might have been my chosen beginning, the most dramatic one I can remember. After all, as the French-Algerian writer Albert Camus wrote, a person's art is "nothing but this slow trek to rediscover, through the detours of art, those two or three great and simple images in whose presence his heart first opened."

Since I was too young to remember my father leaving Haiti for the United States, my mother's departure was one of the first images in whose presence both my heart and my art first opened, an art and a heart that suddenly expanded beyond geographical confines and also made me realize that one can love from both near and far.

In Haitian Creole when someone is said to be "*lòt bò dlo*," on the other side of the water, it can either mean that they've traveled abroad or that they have died. My parents were already *lòt bò dlo*, on the other side of the waters from me, before I fully even knew what that meant. My desire to make sense of this separation, this *lòt bò dlo*-ness, is one of the things that brought me to the internal geography of words and how they can bridge distances.

One way I used to communicate with my parents was through letters. We spoke on the phone once a week while sitting in a telephone booth, where we had a standing appointment every Sunday afternoon, but we also communicated through cassettes that we sent back and forth with people who were traveling between New York and Port-au-Prince. We wrote letters too. Every month my father would send us a half-page letter composed in stilted French to offer news of his and my mother's health as well as details on how to spend the money he and my mother wired for my and my brother's food, lodging, and school expenses.

When my parents' letters and cassettes found their way to me from Brooklyn to Port-au-Prince, I again realized how words—both written and spoken—can transcend geography and time. My mother could tell me stories—once upon a time—in my mind. And I knew, because she later told me this, that she was imagining every day of my life, then whatever indispensable thing I needed to know, only she could tell me. The way she imagined my life in her absence was sometimes better and sometimes worse than what was actually happening to me at ages four, five, six, seven, eight, nine, ten, eleven, and twelve, but we were constantly alive in each other's imagination. And because my mother did not write letters and because I did not ever want to forget the things I wished my mother were telling me, the stories I wish she were telling me, I tried to write them down in a small notebook I made from folded sheets of paper bound together by thread. In that notebook, I also sketched a series of stick figures, which were so closely drawn that they almost bumped each other off the page. But mostly I wrote stories, which I later found myself elaborating on. Stories like one of the first prose poems I would write years later and call "Legends."

"Legends" is about a desire, a hunger, I had developed both in my parents' absence and, much later, to tell stories. "Legends" is about a little girl who is dreaming of telling her immigrant mother a story. It's also about a mother who works in a sweatshop in the United States while dreaming of telling stories to her daughter back home in Haiti.

> Once, upon an endless night,
> I dreamed of telling you a story,
> Of pleating you a tale out of my breath
> And carving it into your flesh with my hair.

I imagined that my parents wanted to tell me stories because they were worried that I would forget not just them but the geographies within both me and them. I imagined they wanted to tell me what in Creole we call *lejann*, stories about night women, women with wings of flames who want to draw you out of your bed. Stories about three-legged horses rising at full speed to either snatch or rescue children who had lost their way.

I also imagined that they wanted to tell me what it was like to work in a sweatshop where they might or might not pay you at the end of the week because you're undocumented. Or how the immigration police might come and raid your workplace at any time and take you to a detention center to await your deportation. I imagined that they wanted me to know even before I stepped foot in the United States that the streets were not littered with gold.

> Once, while cradling someone else's child in my arms,
> Standing at a kitchen stove
> Stirring a soup for the child's hunger,
> I dreamed of telling you a story.
> A story that rains with salt.
> I am telling you to open your mouth,
> And catch as much of the salt as you can.
> The salt sizzles on your tongue.
> And suddenly you understand
> That this story is all I know,
> And that this story is all I have.

I often tell people about this salt by way of a question I am asked quite often. *Who taught you to write?* I always say that my best writing teachers were the storytellers of my childhood, who were not readers at all—and some not even literate—but who carried stories like treasures inside of them. In my mother's absence, my aunts and grandmothers told me stories. They told me stories in the evenings in the countryside, or when the lights went out in the city, or while they were doing my hair, or while I was doing their hair. This too is another possible beginning. These stories that were told to me in such intimacy by women like the ones the great writer Paule Marshall called kitchen poets. The kitchen poets in my life are also the *poto mitan*, the middle pillars of my beginning as a writer, because they taught me that no story is mine alone, that a story lives and breathes and grows only when it is shared.

2

I moved to the United States in 1981 at age twelve to join my parents soon after cases of acquired immunodeficiency syndrome (AIDS) were first discovered in the United States. The Centers for Disease Control named four groups at "high risk" for the disease: intravenous drug users, homosexuals, hemophiliacs, and Haitians. Haitians were the only ones solely identified by nationality, in part because of twenty or so Haitian patients who'd shown up at Jackson Memorial Hospital in Miami. Suddenly, every Haitian was suspected of having AIDS. At the public junior high school where my parents enrolled me, some of the non-Haitian students would regularly shove and hit me and the other Haitian kids, telling us that we had dirty blood. My English as a Second Language class was excluded from a school trip to the Statue of Liberty out of fear that our sharing a school bus with the other kids might prove dangerous to them.

But I also had a wonderful teacher at this junior high school, a Haitian exile named Raymond Dusseck. Mr. Dusseck was part of my beginning in the United States. Mr. Dusseck built science, math, and ESL lessons around games and songs to help us begin speaking in our new tongue. He taught us English songs that were full of stories, starting with the African

American national anthem. I remember being enchanted by James Weldon Johnson's beautiful lyrics:

> Lift every voice and sing,
> Till earth and heaven ring,
> Ring with the harmonies of Liberty . . .
> Let us march on till victory is won.

I was eventually mainstreamed from ESL to a regular English class, where my English teacher, an African American woman named Mrs. Wright, asked me to write an essay about my first Thanksgiving. I wrote that I was looking forward to eating the "golden" turkey, which I thought was rather original. Later I would be horrified by my cliché, but she told me I had a great writing voice. Lift every voice, indeed.

In high school, I had a history teacher named Mr. Casey who taught an elective Black history class during our lunch period. I wrote an essay for that class about wanting to be a writer, and Mr. Casey loaned me a book called *Black Women Writers (1950–1980): A Critical Evaluation*, which was edited by the African American poet, writer, and dramatist Mari Evans. It was in that book that I discovered, among others, Paule Marshall, Alice Walker, Audre Lorde, June Jordan, Gayl Jones, Sonia Sanchez, Gloria Naylor, Nikki Giovanni, Toni Morrison, and Zora Neale Hurston, who would become some of the great literary loves of my life.

They were not only part of my new beginning as a writer, but they, along with the great Haitian writers I began reading in New York, writers like Marie Vieux Chauvet, Jacques Roumain, Jacques Stephen Alexis, J. J. Dominique, Ida Faubert, and Dany Laferrière, gave me a place to stand.

"Give me a place to stand," the Greek mathematician Archimedes is believed to have said, "and I will move the earth." But how can we move the earth when all seems to be against it? I asked myself then and ask myself that now. Can words, language change some of the worst conditions we face, especially in situations that seem insurmountable?

The day that Donald Trump was sworn in as president of the United States, I went to hear the Alabama-based poet Ashley M. Jones read from her book *Magic City Gospel* at my local bookstore in Miami, a city that is home to one of the largest foreign-born populations in the United States. In his inaugural speech, Trump had repeatedly invoked "the people" and said, "And this, the United States of America, is your country," but it was hard to believe that he meant to include my Black and Brown neighbors, friends, and family, many of whom came to America as immigrants. Trump's speech was dark, rancorous. Political language, like poetry, is rarely uttered without intention. Afterward, I wanted to fall into a poet's carefully crafted, insightful, and at times elegiac words.

At the bookstore, I listened as Ashley M. Jones read a poem called "In the beginning there was sound":

> After I was born,
> I cried for three months straight . . .
> *Alive*, I said.
> *Pain*, I said.

Later that same week, some writer friends and I, along with dozens of others, rallied in front of Miami International Airport to protest Trump's executive order barring all refugees, particularly those from seven predominantly Muslim countries. At the airport rally, we carried signs, like mine, that said "No Human Being Is Illegal." A woman held one that read "Immigrants Are America's Ghostwriters." Another woman had simply scribbled on a piece of cardboard the word "No."

Throughout the rally, my thoughts kept returning to the late Gwendolyn Brooks and some lines from her ode to the singer, actor, and activist Paul Robeson:

> we are each other's
> harvest:
> we are each other's
> business:
> we are each other's
> magnitude and bond.

Once again, I was seeking a new beginning in words.

How far do we have to go through to provoke new beginnings? Does it take the image of children in cages, cell phone videos of policemen and women shooting Black men, women, and children in the back?

What does the artist do to move the world? I want to say we can begin by bearing witness. Not everyone is comfortable with the term *witness*. But no matter what term we use, it means, to me, being as Henry James said, "one of those on whom nothing is lost."

In a 1984 *New York Times* interview, James Baldwin had the following exchange with the writer Julius Lester:

"Witness is a word I've heard you use often to describe yourself. What are you witness to?" Lester asked.

Baldwin, answering in the simplest terms, said, "Witness to whence I came, where I am. Witness to what I've seen and the possibilities that I think I see."

Witness is not just where I began but also where I want to end up as a writer. This is the kind of writer I would like to be. Sometimes we cannot fully move the world, but it can move us with its vastness, its expanse, its limitlessness, its geography or geographies, its beginnings and endings, its injustices, and *lòt bò dlo*-ness.

A few weeks ago, a friend I was talking to about this week told me that I should talk about love. I started considering all the things I could possibly have to say about love, but then I realized that, without sounding too lofty here, that every word I put down on paper is in some way an act of love. And I'm sure that I am not the only writer for whom this is true.

I also started thinking about what James Baldwin wrote about love in *The Fire Next Time*. In that essay, he talks to us about the geography of love that is potentially within us all. "Love takes off the masks that we fear we cannot live without and know we cannot live within," Baldwin wrote. "I use the word 'love' here not merely in the personal sense but as a state of being, or a state of grace—not in the infantile American sense of being made happy but in the tough and universal sense of quest and daring and growth." Yes, that kind of love is also part of my beginning.

So along with this particular kind of love, I decided instead to also talk about the geographies within me, starting with my beginnings.

3

After Zora Neale Hurston's mother, Lucy, died and she was forced to leave her home and travel to places previously unknown to her, she wrote in her autobiography, *Dust Tracks on a Road*, that she realized that she was suddenly forced into "the beginning of things" and that "all that geography was within me. It only needed time to reveal it."

All that geography was within me. It only needed time to reveal it. I love this line so much that sometimes I misquote it as "All geography is within me. It only needs to reveal itself."

When, after graduating from high school in Brooklyn, I had yet another beginning and became a student at Zora Neale Hurston's alma mater, Barnard College, I felt as though her ghost was shadowing me. This new and unexpected geography—Barnard and Zora—was now within me too, along with all the others from my past and the possibility of other geographies in the future. Like reading and writing, this type of geography can take you away and bring you back, internally and spiritually, back to the source, back to the ground from which you had been wrestled away.

Zora's ghost was also shadowing me in the car in March 2014 after my mother had been told by her doctor that she had terminal ovarian cancer. At a red light, where I stopped for too long, my mother spoke up for the first time since we'd heard the news and warned, "Don't suddenly become a zombie." My mother was telling me not to lose my good sense, to keep my head on my shoulders, but it popped up in my mind that a motherless Zora had gone to Haiti to study zombies.

When we got home from the doctor's that day, my mother made us each a small cup of coffee that she sprinkled with salt. According to Haitian folklore, one way zombies can be liberated from their living death is by eating salt. People who suddenly receive terrible news are also given salt, in coffee for example, to help ward off the *sezisman*, the shock, so that we are able to pick ourselves up and keep moving.

This salt is for me the source of all forceful beginnings and the source of all freedom. We are here because in some way we were given the salt. For some of us that salt is *words*. For others, it is *paint*. For others, it is *music*. For others, it is God. For some it is simply the ability to survive.

When I first came to this country, I remember being shocked that salt was powdery white. In my household in Haiti, we would often buy rock salt in the market, and it often looked like little crystals or small pebbles, which were unevenly shaped and had dark streaks either on the surface or inside. You always had to wash the crystals before putting them in food, and even after you washed them they looked more gray than white. This is the salt I imagined those seeking their liberation wanting to be fed.

This type of salt shows up in another part of "Legends":

> And what was that Sleeping Beauty,
> If not a zombie?
> And what was it that gave her freedom
> From the sleeping sickness,
> If not the taste of salt on the prince's lips?
> Let no one tell you that it was the man's breath itself.
> Everyone knows—or Manman knows—that it was the salt.
> It is always the salt that wakes the dead.
> And brings the children home.

This home for me is first and foremost the page. And the page is both full of death and free of it. Full of death because a trail of bodies from the Middle Passage lies behind me in the sea that made the first kind of salt I ever knew.

"The sea is salt," Zora Neale Hurston wrote.

"The sea is History," Derek Walcott wrote.

The sea has been part of both our beginnings and our endings.

The story whose beginning I chose to explain to the teenagers at the library in Fond-des-Blancs is from my 1995 short-story collection *Krik? Krak!* and is called "Children of the Sea." It is about a group of Haitian refugees who are trying to reach the United States by boat, like so many refugees and migrants have been trying to reach so many shores, lately including European shores.

I began the story the way I did, I told them, with lines borrowed from a Haitian proverb: "Dèyè mòn gen mòn." Behind the mountains are more mountains. The story begins with "They say behind the mountains are more mountains. Now I know it's true." I began it this way because that story had reminded me that some people's potential new beginnings can also lead to their end. Writing that story had reinforced for me the idea that the page—my writing home—has to also be free from death because creating anything, be it words, images, song, and dance, means that we believe in immortality, that we believe we can survive, even on the other side of the waters, even *lòt bò dlo*.

You never know a person until you've eaten salt together, Toni Cade Bambara writes in *The Salt Eaters*. And this week we have all had the privilege of eating salt together, by yes, breaking bread together, but also with the words we have spoken, the songs we have sung, the ways that we have moved our bodies through these dances that have come to us, both ancestral memory and more recently acquired knowledge. And for this I do not have enough words to say thank you. So, I will offer my gratitude in the voices of those who came before me, with all my honor and respect (Onè, Respè).

Mèsi anpil, anpil. Thank you.

MIAMI, FLORIDA

Haitian-born writer Edwidge Danticat (b. 1969) was named the 2018 laureate of the Neustadt International Prize for Literature. Her 1996 novel, *Krik? Krak!*, was a National Book Award finalist, and her 2019 short-story collection, *Everything Inside*, won the National Book Critics Circle Award for Fiction. She currently teaches at Columbia University.

BLESS THIS LAND (2019)

JOY HARJO

Bless this land from the top of its head to the bottom of its feet

From the arctic old white head to the brown feet of tropical rain

Bless the eyes of this land, for they witness cruelty and kindness in this land

From sunrise light upright to falling down on your knees night

Bless the ears of this land, for they hear cries of heartbreak and shouts of celebration in this land

Once we heard no gunshot on these lands; the trees and stones can be heard singing

Bless the mouth, lips, and speech of this land, for the land is a speaker, a singer, a keeper of all that happens here, on this land

Luminous forests, oceans, and rock cliff sold for the trash glut of gold, uranium, or oil bust rush yet there are new stories to be made, little ones coming up over the horizon

Bless the arms and hands of this land, for they remake and restore beauty in this land

We were held in the circle around these lands by song, and reminded by the knowers that not one is over the other, no human above the bird, no bird above the insect, no wind above the grass

Bless the heart of this land on its knees planting food beneath the eternal circle of breathing, swimming and walking this land

> *The heart is a poetry maker. There is one heart, said the poetry maker, one body and all poems make one poem and we do not use words to make war on this land*

> Bless the gut labyrinth of this land, for it is
> the center of unknowing in this land

Bless the femaleness and maleness of this land, for each holds the fluent power of becoming in this land

> *When it was decided to be in this manner here in this place, this land, all the birds made a birdly racket from indigo sky holds*

Bless the two legs and two feet of this land, for the sacred always walks beside the profane in this land

> *These words walk the backbone of this land, massaging the tissue around the cord of life, which is the tree of life, upon which this land stands*

Bless the destruction of this land, for new shoots will rise up from fire, floods, earthquakes and fierce winds to make new this land

> *We are land on turtle's back—when the weight of greed overturns us, who will recall the upright song of this land*

Bless the creation of new land, for out of chaos we will be compelled to remember to bless this land

> *The smallest one remembered, the most humble one, the one whose voice you'd have to lean in a thousand years to hear— we will begin there*

Bless us, these lands, said the rememberer. These lands aren't our lands. These lands aren't your lands. We are this land.

And the blessing began a graceful moving through the grasses of time, from the beginning, to the circling around place of time, always moving, always

---

Born in Tulsa in 1951, Joy Harjo is an internationally renowned performer and writer of the Muscogee (Creek) Nation. The recipient of multiple awards and honors, she was named the 23rd Poet Laureate of the United States in 2019. *Weaving Sundown in a Scarlet Light: Fifty Poems for Fifty Years* appeared in 2022.

THE SILENCED LANGUAGE

LILIANA ANCALAO

Translated from the Spanish by Seth Michelson

ALTHOUGH IT WAS only one hundred years ago, it seems to my generation like some mythical age. The Mapuche could roam freely across their territory and communicated with the elements of the *mapu*. Mapuzungun means "language of the land." The land speaks. All its beings have language, and the Mapuche know it.

Mapuzungun was the first language, and it was taught and learned in optimal conditions. In the shade of elders, new saplings grew, a perfect green preceding the rituals, near the water.

The women would sing their *tayüles*, which transmitted power, and the pride of being who one is was not a philosophical question.

But the death that has crept toward the First Peoples of the Americas since 1492 left no stone unturned in the south. The war for the desert, the *winka* raids, signaled military defeat and the occupation of territory by the Argentine state. "The end of the world" took place one hundred years ago.

Mapuzungun became the language for expressing pain, the language of despondence during the divvying up of men, women, and children as slaves. The clandestine whisper in the concentration camps. The language of solace among prisoners of war. The language for thought.

It was the language of the long road of exile, the distance of banishment. Of the harsh march of our great-grandparents to reservations, *ka mapu*.

Our grandparents were sent to rural schools and made bilingual by force. But however banned by the schools, where teachers shamed children for their home language, Mapuzungun endured. The language of the land was in the air of orality; Spanish in the writing crossed out in workbooks.

Linguistic anthropologists, *ka mollfunche*, tried to write it. They created dictionaries and grammar. Just as they tried to trap the territory within barbed-wire fences, so, too, did they try to trap the sound of Mapuzungun within Western graphemes.

Within our community, the politics of shame wreaked havoc. Mapuzungun became a stigma, the mark of inferiority of those admitted by force to the capitalist system as cheap labor.

Perhaps the elders made a decision to stop teaching it. Could they get together? Did they speak in Mapuzungun of the future? Maybe they simply went silent, determining their knowledge to no longer suffice, that the saplings could manage better without them in this new world of constant threats, stigmas, accusations, smirks.

Mapuzungun was the language of conversation of the elders, the language for summoning the elements in the intimacy of dawn. The language of defense. Of silence. The city offered work and study to the saplings. Our parents arrived monolingual, without *ngillatun*, without Mapuzungun, exchanging the natural cycle of time for work hours and school calendars.

And we entered local schools, bearing our faces and surnames, without any language for which to feel ashamed, with Spanish as our one and only tongue, without history or memory.

I'm talking about *Puel Mapu* and the history of my family, which is the history of so many families, and which explains the loss of our language as mother tongue by the majority of my generation. I'm talking about an ancient language and the ignorance of men who mapped a country over a territory full of names, elements, and meanings, silencing it. I'm talking about what we lost. All of us.

All of us who were born without knowing the names of every plant, every stone, and every bird of this land.

I woke in the middle of a lake. In gasps I tried to give thanks but didn't know the words. They hadn't been taught to me. I found in poetry in Spanish the possibility to express something of the profundity that flooded me. And god's nostalgia, which is to say a cosmovision, carried me down the path to recovering his language.

On the 500th birthday of the discord, we began to emerge from the brush, and with each step we returned closer to our roots, making ourselves visible. We'd say *Mapuche ta iñche* to recognize ourselves and repair the damage they'd done to us bit by bit.

Mapuzungun is the language of the recovery of pride, the language of the reconstruction of memory.

The conditions for teaching and learning our language are ever more difficult because as time passes, the elders bearing our knowledge die. The federal government should push a linguistic politics to accelerate and support with resources the process of recovery of our language. A process of recovery to include not only orality but also our adoption of writing and of the creation of methods for teaching and learning our language as a second language.

To learn it is to travel a path of amazements. My heart swells each time I explain that in Mapuzungun, besides the singular and plural, there exist the dual pronouns *iñchiu*, meaning "we two"; *eymu*, meaning "you two"; and *fey engü*, meaning "them two." Pairs give balance to our cosmovision.

I learn and practice the words for summoning and serving the elements. I live in the city, where I have a profession and struggle not to succumb to Western individualism: *Kishungenelan* is the teaching given us by the elders.

I think and write in Spanish and later translate it clumsily into the language that seduces me with its immense, deep blue.

COMODORO RIVADAVIA, ARGENTINA

GLOSSARY

mapu: land
zungun: speak, language
che: people
tayüll: the sacred song of a family lineage
winka: strange, foreign, enemy
ka mapu: distant land
ka mollfunche: foreign people, of a different blood
ngillatun: propitiatory ritual

Puel Mapu: land of the east, actually Argentina

Mapuche ta iñche: I am Mapuche

Kishungenelan: I am not guided by myself alone

Liliana Ancalao (b. 1961) is a member of the Mapuche-Tehuelche Nankulaven community in the Patagonian province of Chubut in southern Argentina. She is a leading Mapuche poet, and her academic investigations of Mapuche culture and Indigenous music are similarly acclaimed.

Seth Michelson is a poet, translator, professor of poetry, and a 2018 NEA Literature Translation Fellow. His awards include an NEA Fellowship, the International Book Award for poetry, and an Anna Davidson Rosenberg Award.

ESCAPE FROM SUPERSTITION   (1931)

GEORGE BERNARD SHAW

MY KNOWLEDGE OF Schnitzler's work is not exhaustive. From what I know of it I class him with those writers of the latter half of the nineteenth century who had lost its illusions and broken its superstitions without ever escaping from it into the twentieth. To be a freethinker or a freelover in those days was exciting, hazardous, and illusorily momentous. Nowadays all that seems only a hopelessly old-fashioned Bohemianism, Victorian and pre-Karl Marx. It has for the moment no message except for fogies and Fundamentalists—survivals from 1865 who are still shocked by Darwin. But when the nineteenth century and the twentieth pass into distant perspective, probably Schnitzler, Brandes, Turgenev, and the rest of their school will be seen in a juster proportion to those who have played them off the stage, some of whom will by then be quite forgotten. I was in that position until I was twenty-five, and retain a certain affection for them still.

George Bernard Shaw (1856–1950) was an Irish playwright, critic, and political activist. He wrote more than sixty plays, including *Man and Superman* (1902), *Pygmalion* (1913), and *Saint Joan* (1923). He was awarded the Nobel Prize in Literature in 1925.

FORUGH FARROKHZAD

Translated from the Farsi by Sholeh Wolpé

All my being is a dark verse
that repeats you to the dawn
of unfading flowering and growth.
I conjured you in my poem with a sigh
and grafted you to water, fire, and trees.

Perhaps life is a long avenue
a woman with a basket crosses every day;
perhaps life is a rope
with which a man hangs himself from a tree,
or is a child returning home from school.

Maybe life is the act of lighting a cigarette
in the listless pause between lovemaking,
or the vacant glance of a passerby who tips
his hat and says, *Good morning!*
                    with a meaningless smile.

Perhaps life is a choked moment where my gaze
annihilates itself inside in the pupils of your eyes—
                    I will mingle that sensation with my grasp
                    of the moon and comprehension of darkness.

In a room the size of loneliness,
my heart's the size of love.
It contemplates its simple pretexts for happiness:
the beauty of the flowers' wilting in a vase,
the sapling you planted in our garden,
and the canaries' song—the size of a window.

Alas, this is my lot.
This is my lot.
My lot is a sky that can be shut out
by the mere hanging of a curtain.
My lot is descending a lonely staircase
to something rotting and falling apart in its exile.
My lot is a gloomy stroll in a grove of memories,
and dying from longing for a voice
that says: *I love your hands.*

I plant my hands in the garden soil—
I will sprout,
                    I know, I know, I know.
And in the hollow of my ink-stained palms
swallows will make their nest.

I will adorn my ears with twin-cherry sprigs,
wear dahlia petals on my nails.
There is an alley where boys who once loved me still stand
with the same tousled hair, thin necks, and scrawny legs,
contemplating the innocent smiles of a young girl
swept away one night by the wind.

There is an alley my heart has stolen
from my childhood turf.

A body traveling along the line of time
impregnates time's barren cord,
and returns from the mirror's feast
intimate with its own image.
This is how one dies, and another remains.

No seeker will ever find pearls from a stream
                    that pours into a ditch.

I know a sad little fairy who lives in the sea
and plays the wooden flute of her heart tenderly, tenderly . . .
A sad small fairy who dies at night with a kiss
and is reborn with a kiss at dawn.

Forugh Farrokhzad (1935–1967) was an Iranian poet and filmmaker. Her published works include *The Captive, The Wall, Rebellion, Reborn,* and *Let Us Believe in the Dawn of the Cold Season.* She broke with many traditional conventions and exercised an immeasurable influence on modern Iranian poetry.

Sholeh Wolpé is a recipient of the PEN/Heim Translation award and the Lois Roth Persian Translation prize, as well as the author of numerous collections of poetry, plays, translated books, and anthologies.

BUILDING A SCHOOL IN NICARAGUA

MAX FRISCH

I AM GRATEFUL—as I wrote in my letter some months ago—very grateful, and I have to tell you in a few words: grateful for what? . . . Your country spoiled me quite a lot: thirty-five years ago, with a Rockefeller Grant that gave me the chance to live in New York and San Francisco over one year (on a modest standard, but free to write every day or night). Some other recognitions followed, recognitions by American academies and American universities, and today this final decoration.

I think my ambivalence, in regard to your great country, has its origin not in personal frustration; my criticism is not an expression of personal resentment. That means it certainly is not what some like to call *Anti-Amerikanismus*. It only concerns my criticism of politics wherever politics becomes inhuman-inhumane. That's what it's all about, and I am grateful for your generous understanding. I also thank you for your kindness in traveling from Oklahoma to Zürich; your visit here, ladies and gentlemen, is an honor for our town. Dafür danke ich als Zürcher.

As to the money, you know my decision to support with these funds a nonmilitary organization in Nicaragua, a nonprofit organization. It is a Swiss group of younger volunteers working there for development, which means aid to the people of Nicaragua in their long and painful struggle for independence. Two of those volunteers, Maurice Demierre and Yvan Leyvraz, were killed last year. Compared to the one hundred million U.S. dollars for military equipment on the other side, my support is very modest indeed—twenty-five thousand dollars—but it is said to be sufficient for one of the projects presented by the Asociación de Trabajadores del Campo: a school in a village with sixty farm families who want their children to learn the alphabet. The place (so I have been informed) is not far from the region where the terrorists known as contras are using their U.S. military equipment to destroy bridges, power plants, homes, et cetera, hunting down farmers with gunfire and killing civilians from time to time before escaping across the border to Honduras, where they are trained by US advisers.

The name of the modest project: Escuela Santa Emilia. The construction time: six months, assuming that the contras do not launch a sudden attack. It will be a simple building for three classes: Escuela Santa Emilia.

ZÜRICH, SWITZERLAND

Swiss novelist and playwright Max Frisch (1911–1991) was named the 1986 laureate of the Neustadt International Prize for Literature for an exceptional body of work, including his 1957 novel *Homo Faber*, the 1961 play *Andorra: Stück in zwölf Bildern*, and 1980 novel *Man in the Holocene*. He delivered his Neustadt acceptance speech at a ceremony in Zürich.

MIA COUTO

Translated from the Portuguese by Paul Fauvet

IT IS A GREAT HONOR to receive this award. I am saying this not just as a simple formality. It is a deeper feeling. The importance of this award goes far beyond the work of a particular writer. What we are celebrating here, in Oklahoma, year after year, is more than literature. With the Neustadt Prize we all praise the cultural diversity of our world and the cultural diversity of each one of us. That is crucial in a moment where personal and national identities are constructed like fortresses, as protection against the threats of those who are presented to us as aliens.

This prize is important for the relations between our worlds, which seem to be situated not only on different continents but on different planets. Despite all diplomatic and political efforts, a considerable reciprocal ignorance still prevails between Mozambique and the United States of America. We tend to assume this remoteness as natural, given the physical location of our countries. However, we must nowadays question what is presented as "normal" and "natural." There are, indeed, other reasons that lead to our mutual lack of knowledge. And those reasons have nothing to do with geography.

We have a common struggle for freedom, democracy, and independence. We share a past and a present of resistance against injustice and discrimination. But in the quest to affirm the uniqueness of our nations we have created, without knowing, a reductive and simplistic vision of the other, and of ourselves. We suffer from a narrow and stereotyped vision of a multicolor reality. We are only able to recognize one cultural dimension of reality. We have fallen into the temptation of the "Single Story" against which Chimamanda Ngozi Adichie so eloquently warned us.

The Neustadt Prize has the merit of promoting dialogue between cultures and creating bridges where there is distance and, worse than that, mere indifference.

It's good to know that literature can help build neighborhoods in a world which imagines that the proximity between cultures is totally resolved by technological solutions.

Dear friends, I am the second son of a Portuguese couple forced to emigrate, trying to escape from the fascist regime in Portugal. Each night, my mother and my father told me stories. They thought they were getting us to sleep. In fact, they were producing a second and eternal birth.

What fascinated me was not exactly the content of those tales. As a matter of fact, I can't remember a single one of those stories. What I remember, first of all, is having my parents just for me, next to my bed, next to my dreams. More than anything I remember the passion that they found in the invention of those stories. That intense pleasure had a reason: using words, they could travel and visit their missing homeland. They could erase time and distance.

In that very familiar and domestic moment, the very essence of what is literature was present: a chance to migrate from ourselves, a chance to become others inside ourselves, a chance to re-enchant the world. Literature is not only a way to affirm our existence. It is a permission to disappear and to allow the presence of those who seem to be absent.

We Africans come from a long and painful narrative to affirm our nations and our singular identity. I am afraid that, although historically necessary, part of the nationalist discourse has become a burden that prevents us from being plural, available to be others and to travel inside other lives. That availability is the essence of literature. And the essence of our humanity.

I come from a nation that is regarded as one of the poorest in the world. I don't know how poverty is measured, but many of the African languages spoken in my country do not have specific words for saying "poor." To designate a poor person, one uses the term *chissiwana*. This word means "orphan." A poor person is someone who lives without family and without friends. He is someone who has lost the ties of solidarity.

This other poverty, born of solitude, is more widespread than one might think. Never before has our world been so small, so simultaneous, so instantaneous. But this speed has not solved our solitude. Never before have there been so many roads. And never before have we made so few visits. What could bind us together would be the desire to tell and to listen to stories.

There are many hidden dimensions of the art of writing. A few years ago I experienced an episode that showed me a different meaning of what I do as writer.

It happened in 2008, in northern Mozambique in a coastal village called Palma. It's a remote region, without water, without electricity, in the middle of the savannah. I had finished my day's work as a biologist, and I was in the shadow of my tent, when a peasant came and called me. *Come here*, he said. *Come and see a man who's been killed.* I went into the darkness, and I followed the old man along a path in the middle of the bush. *How did he die?* I asked. And the man replied: *He was killed by a lion. That lion is still nearby. And he's going to come back to fetch the rest of the body.* I returned hastily to the tent, with no wish to see whatever he had to show me.

I closed the zipper of the tent, knowing how inadequate this gesture was as protection. A short distance from me lay a corpse ripped up by a lion, and a wild beast roamed nearby like a murderous shadow. During my professional life, I have worked for many years in regions where there are still dangerous animals. But I didn't know how to deal with a situation like that. I remember that the first thing I did was to switch on my small flashlight and begin writing in my notebook. I was not describing what was going on, because I didn't know, nor did I want to know what was happening. The truth is that until daybreak, I was busy writing in order not to be overcome with fear.

That fear was a primitive feeling, a memory of another time, in which our fragility was more evident. I am an urban man, born and raised in modernity. I had no defense against a fear that was more ancient than humanity itself. I gradually realized that the wild creatures were not lions but the monsters that have dwelt within us for centuries.

Only later did I understand; I wasn't really taking shelter in the tent. I was taking shelter in fiction. I was creating a story like someone making a house not just to live in but to erase reality. Without knowing it, I was beginning to write a novel called *Confession of the Lioness*.

But another one of my novels served as the basis for the choice of this prize, the novel *Terra sonâmbula* (*Sleepwalking Land*). This book speaks of a dramatic moment in the history of Mozambique. For sixteen years we suffered a civil war, which killed the economy and crippled the country.

Those sixteen years of conflict left a million dead out of a population of eighteen million. In its intention, violence is opposed to the art of telling stories: that intention is to dehumanize us, a dehumanization achieved in various ways. We were living in a kind of absolute solitude: isolated from hope, incapable of turning the present into a treasure trove of stories. We were all alone, the dead and the living. Without a past, without a future, without stories. The present was only worthwhile insofar as it was born to be forgotten.

Terra sonâmbula was the only book I found painful to write, because it was written during the war, at a time when I was also besieged by despair. For months I spent sleepless nights visited by friends and colleagues who had been killed during the conflict. It was as if they came knocking on the door of my insomnia, asking to live in stories, even if they were lies or just a way for me to fall asleep.

I remember that once, after one of these sleepless nights, I came out of the building of the biology station where I was working and sat on the beach. And I realized that there, very close to the breaking waves, was a whale which had decided to come and die on the beach. Then I saw people arriving hastily at the beach. In an instant they rushed together at the dying animal to hack chunks from it, ripped to pieces with the greed of a hunger of centuries. It had not yet died, and its bones were already shining in the sun. Little by little, I came to think of my country as one of those whales coming to die in agony on the beach. Death had not yet come, and yet the knives were already stealing chunks of it, each person trying to take as much as possible for himself. As if that were the last animal, the final opportunity to grab a meal. I went back to my room weighed down by an incurable sadness. On that early morning I wrote the final chapter of my novel. Two months later, when I was delivering the text to my publisher, the news arrived of the peace agreement.

When the peace agreement was signed in 1992, we thought that revenge and the settling of scores would be inevitable. But it didn't happen like that. People decided on a kind of collective amnesia. The reminders of violence were cast into a pit of oblivion. We know that this oblivion was false. A war is impossible to forget. But we wanted the war to forget us.

Mozambique's experience showed how literature can play an active role in the construction of peace. Fiction and poetry do not cause the guns to fall silent. But they can reconcile us with the past, no matter how painful it might be. Fiction and poetry can help reconquer our inner tranquility and promote reconciliation with others. By means of stories, these others were freed from the condition of demons. I can say with pride that poets and writers have helped to rehumanize my country.

Unfortunately, it is not so much stories that unite humanity. What unites us today, in all countries, on all continents, is above all fear. The same feeling of abandonment and insecurity brings us together everywhere. There are no great or small powers that are safe from fear. We live the same anguish faced with the other transformed into an enemy. We all live in a small tent surrounded by the threat, real or imaginary, of a beast in the dark wanting to devour us.

The fear that rules us is, in large measure, nourished by the profound ignorance we have of one another. Literature can be a response against the invitation to fabricate fear and mistrust. Literature and storytelling confirm us as relatives and neighbors in our infinite diversity.

Dear friends, it is very gratifying to know that the next laureate is an African as well. We know that the Neustadt Prize is not limited by the author's geographical origin; the only issue is the quality of his or her work. This means that Africans are imposing themselves on the international scene without recourse to any paternalistic criteria. In truth, for some years now, we African writers are freeing ourselves from a literature dominated by a desire to affirm our identity. Formerly, we felt a historic and psychological need to demonstrate that we were as able as others. This period of affirmation made sense after centuries of cultural and historical denial. But today we are more free to act without fulfilling our function as the Other.

A new generation of Africans is more and more free to act as universal writers. They feel free to write about any subject, in the language they choose. Our new literature is now less afraid of the accusation of not being faithful to genuineness, or not respecting the so-called "tradition." We are producing a literature that is free from having to show its Africanness as a kind of passport to be accepted.

Many of our young writers are using literature to denounce the arrogance, corruption, and nepotism of some current political leaders. But more than that, they are busy producing good literature. And they know that there are as many Africas as there are writers, and all of them are reinventing continents that lie inside their very selves. This is not a quest that is exclusively ours, as Africans. There isn't a writer in the world who doesn't have to seek out his or her own identity among multiple and elusive identities. In every continent, each person is a nation made up of different nations.

Dear friends, the Neustadt Prize is announced as follows (and I quote): "This is the first international literary award of its scope to originate in the United States and is one of the very few international prizes for which poets, novelists, and playwrights are equally eligible."

I would like to thank the Neustadt family, the University of Oklahoma, and *World Literature Today* for the open and all-embracing conception of this initiative. The format of this celebration reveals a concern not to reduce the event to an award ceremony alone. In this way, justice is done to the principle that what is important are books and not so much their authors.

One of the merits of this prize is that it is guided by criteria devoted exclusively to literary quality. I present myself to you not as a representative of a place, of an ideology, of a religion. But I will never forget those who give meaning to my writing, the anonymous people of my country. Some of those Mozambicans—who are, together with me, author of my books—do not know how to write. Many don't even speak Portuguese. But they are guardians, in their everyday lives, of a magical, poetical dimension to the world that illuminates my writing and gives delight to my existence.

It would be an injustice not to mention here the people who have given my presence here their support: The first of these people is Gabriella Ghermandi, the member of the panel that proposed me as a candidate. Without her, I would not be here. I would not be here if it weren't for my longtime translator, David Brookshaw. A translator is a co-author and should appear on the covers of books, and his presence in this ceremony is totally justified. Accompanying me is my wife, Patricia, who is my primary inspiration and my first reader. Present with us is my daughter, Luciana, and she represents here my other children, Madyo and Rita. No prize can prove stronger than the delight we have in seeing ourselves born in our own children. To them I owe this feeling of lived eternity.

I shall end by reading a poem I wrote some years ago. I remembered these verses when I discovered that the emblem for this prize was an eagle's feather. This symbolic representation is a metaphor for writing that seeks to have the lightness of wings. I shall ask David Brookshaw to read this poem, in his own translation.

IN SOME OTHER LIFE I WAS A BIRD

I preserve the memory
of landscapes spread wide
and escarpments skimmed in flight.
A cloud and its careless trace of white
connect me to the soil.
I live with the heartbeat
of a bird's wing
and plunge like lightning
hungering for earth.
I preserve the plume
that remains in my heart
as a man preserves his name
over the span of time.
In some other life I was a bird
in some other bird I was life.

The author of more than twenty books, including novels, poetry collections, and essay collections, Mia Couto (b. 1955) was born and raised in Mozambique. He wrote poetry for the anticolonial political movement FRELIMO during its overthrow of Portuguese colonial rule in 1975. Couto was awarded the Neustadt International Prize for Literature in 2014.

Paul Fauvet has worked as a political analyst, editor, and English-language communicator at the Mozambique News Agency (AIM) in Mozambique since 1980.

THE CITY OF THE WALKING FLOWER (2021)

SALMAN MASALHA

Translated from the Hebrew by Vivian Eden

HERE, ON THE watershed of the winds, between reality and imagination, between the utopia of the celestial spheres and the doom of the underworld, stands Jerusalem. The city is a pile of stones that separates sea from sea, tomorrow from yesterday, the green from the desert, and, above all, the sacred from the profane. It is like a broad cosmic-political terminal, the starting line for the competitions in which participants race to other places, other times. Here in Jerusalem, and in the four corners of the earth, the descendants of Moses, Jesus, and Muhammad jostle one another on the track, taking part in an Olympics of the evil spirit that knows no rest. They are all poised, crouching to the ground in awe of the holy, waiting for the starting gun in order to defeat gravity.

When I was a child, Jerusalem was inextricably linked in my imagination to the apocalyptic day of the great dash forward, from which there is no return. The scenario, including the instructions issued by the official sitting on a raised platform in the dome of the sky, was determined in advance and minutely detailed. In the play of the End of Days, mortal actors have no freedom to improvise. They must play the roles determined for them, with complete faith and no reservations or questions, such as *what if, maybe, nevertheless*. According to the scenario, the Jews are destined to destroy the Muslim mosques in Jerusalem. Because of the support the primarily Christian West gives the Jews and the Jewish state, the Muslims will retaliate by rising up and destroying the Christian churches. The West's reaction will be swift: it will gather its armies to conquer the K'aba. And thus, in an uncontrollable chain reaction, a great world war will break out: the Apocalypse. Eventually, the Messiah will come and bring a new world order, entirely different from the one we have now. As a child, I never imagined fate would call me to rub shoulders with the inhabitants of this city, nor did I conceive of the possibility of living in what was destined to be the eye of the storm at the End of Days.

In the year 1690 there also lived someone who thought the End of Days was happening before his lightless eyes. No one knows his name, and chances are no one ever will. A man from Aleppo, 'Abd al-Ghani al-Nabulsi, arrived that year in Jerusalem. He prayed there, strolled through its markets, met its people, and as is the habit of many pilgrims, put his impressions down in writing. One day he went out to a hill west of the city walls. The hill served as a Muslim cemetery, and the graveyard still exists in the center of Jerusalem in the Mamilla quarter. His guides related that here, at the edge of the cemetery, someone once dug a grave and, within the grave, found a Muslim man sitting and reading the Qur'an. The man from the grave addressed him and asked what had happened, whether the Hour, the End of Days, had come. The digger, frightened by what he saw, fled for his life. However, after a while he returned to the place, accompanied by other people, and found no trace of digging or the man in the grave.

Nearly two centuries later, someone else thought the End of Days was near. In 1874 a Dutch woman came to Jerusalem; the citizens called her the Dutch Princess. She decided that it was not enough to dream. She wanted to anticipate the practical needs of the Redemption and the End of Days. Therefore, she embarked upon the construction of a building that was to serve as a huge hostel meant to accommodate the 140,000 Children of Israel who would remain alive at the End of Days. The place she selected was none other than that same plot west of the Muslim cemetery in Mamilla. The man from the grave in the previous story is of the Children of Ishmael, but had his luck been with him, he might have been able to lodge in a five-star hotel as the "Shabbes goy" (a Gentile who performs household tasks prohibited to Jews on the Sabbath) for the surviving Children of Israel. The Dutch Princess ran out of money and never completed her project, which shows that even in the business of the End of Days, the earthly marketplace reigns.

Independence Park now stands on that site. Like many of the gardens in the Holy Land, it represents the Garden of Eden and, by extension, the expulsion. So, throughout the years, the people of Jerusalem, the living and the dead, dwell there in expectation of the Day of Judgment. Jerusalem is slowly borne above the earth's surface, as if the stone of the city were not the same stone, as if the wind were not the same wind, and as if the people were not the same people.

Jerusalem is unlike other cities. It has laws of its own. For example, the laws of physics do not apply here. The city of Jerusalem is borne above the earth's surface by supreme metaphysical forces, and any attempt to descend with it to the firm ground of reality—to the street, the café, the noise of the buses, the municipal garbage—leads to the crashing of dreams soaked in the holiness of the End of Days and fantasies sprinkled by divinity. Therefore, the city is famous for its syndrome, the Jerusalem Syndrome. Anyone who strolls through the streets is likely to encounter people whose dreams have all shattered on the ground of reality in this strange city. Where else in the world is there a city with a syndrome all its own?

Jerusalem is best kept in the cellars of the imagination. It is recommended, and perhaps desirable, to write about it, especially poetry. The city does right by poets. It provides them with an abundance of color, images, and metaphors. However, it is not a good idea, perhaps it's even dangerous, to break it down into small details. Reality could hit you in the face, and dealing with this will be difficult. All of Jerusalem's inhabitants are strangers, yet she does not welcome strangers. Here, strangeness has a hierarchy. I, too, am a stranger in Jerusalem, and it does not welcome me either. But what am I, a mere mortal, compared to the many days through which so many mortals have passed?

During the 1870s, about a hundred years before I came to Jerusalem, a man from Damascus named Nu'man al-Qasatili came to the city gates seeking progress and openness. The Damascus of those days looked to him like the epitome of backwardness, so he set out for what he imagined to be the city of lights. He did not find the city of lights, of course, but he immortalized his impressions in a chronicle of his journeys through the provinces of Greater Syria. He noted that there were about forty thousand inhabitants in the city at the time. The natives were a minority in Jerusalem. The rest were a motley of strangers: Jews, Muslims, and Christians. The majority of the city's inhabitants had arrived there from distant places, beyond the sea and desert. Today the population of Jerusalem is more than four hundred thousand souls. The inhabitants of today are new strangers, or the descendants of yesterday's strangers. The strangers of today are the fathers of the strangers who will be born here. Gradually, it becomes clear that strangeness is an inseparable part of the city. The strangers who have settled in the city enjoy when strangers come to visit. They wait expectantly for the visitors because they provide a significant part of their income, as al-Qasatili says. Those who have already settled in Jerusalem do not love the other strangers who have already settled here, but all of them want the strangers' money, that is to say the tourists, because that is how they earn their living.

Who builds whom? Does man build a city in his image, or is it the city that builds the man? This question may seem simple, but with respect to Jerusalem, it is not. Cities built along the coast take their character from the sea. They face the sea and draw serenity from it. The cycle of the waves beating endlessly on their shores pervades them with a sense of life without end. In Jerusalem, too, there is a cycle, but it is the cycle of a volcano, and you never know when it will explode. There is also a sea near Jerusalem. But in this Jerusalem sea, you always lie on your back with your eyes looking up toward heaven. You needn't lift a finger in order to float because Jerusalem's sea always pushes you upward. You can sink only into hallucinations of other places and other times. Any attempt to stand with your feet on the ground, to be in reality, demands a supreme effort, and in many cases it demands a lot of tears, and not always because of the salt of the Dead Sea.

As I told you, I was not born in Jerusalem. I came there in the seventh decade of the twentieth century to join the congregation of strangers that inhabit it. Jerusalem is ultimately a city of eternal strangers. The connection to the city is not a connection to place, but rather a connection to time. The connection is not to stone, object, or anything earthly, but rather to moments, feelings, experiences. And Jerusalem, as opposed to many cities, has too much time, too many moments, and too much past. And with so much past in Jerusalem, it is hard to see the future, because the future of Jerusalem always pulls toward the past. The people of Jerusalem walk through it with their eyes stuck in the backs of their heads and their faces eyeless. This is perhaps another reason why the people of Jerusalem frequently fall down in the street. Every movement in it, even the smallest, leads to a wound. Every stone you turn over in this city could be hiding a scorpion because, as the tradition has it, Jerusalem is a golden chalice full of scorpions. The Jerusalem of yesterday, today, and presumably tomorrow sits on the watershed of the winds, between the desert and the mountain. It is a mixture of Hebron and Warsaw. Two seas battle for it, the Mediterranean Sea to the west, and the Dead Sea to the east. A sea of life and a sea of death, exactly like its history. Though it seems, more and more, that it is turning its back to the West and not dwelling in the East. It pulls toward the past, to Creation. Too much past has passed in Jerusalem, and in a place where the past is so dense, it is hard to see the future.

And at that very place in Mamilla, al-Nabulsi writes, he saw something wonderful. He noticed a plant the size of a finger, green in color and with a flower. The plant had two arms, four legs, and a small red head with a white tuft on top. It also had a reddish-pink tail with vertebrae, and this plant was alive and walked on its legs. Hope hides in al-Nabulsi's legend. The day will come when not only the Torah will go forth, but the flowers of Jerusalem will begin to walk freely on its earth. I have been living in Jerusalem for a number of years now, and I pass by this place often. Every time, I examine the ground, hoping to see that walking flower. However, in the meantime, I make do with other walking flowers, which I have been seeing for years. They have arms and legs, but not their own. These are the arms and legs of the girl who makes the rounds at night, selling flowers in the bars of Jerusalem.

JERUSALEM

Born in al-Maghar, an Arab town in the Galilee, Salman Masalha (b. 1953) has lived in Jerusalem since 1972 and holds a PhD in classical Arabic literature from the Hebrew University. He writes in both Arabic and Hebrew and translates into both languages. The author of numerous volumes of poetry, his articles, columns, poems, and translations have appeared in newspapers, journals, and anthologies in both languages.

Vivian Eden holds a PhD in translation studies from the University of Iowa. The author of a book of poetry and numerous articles, she mainly translates from Hebrew. Her day job is at *Haaretz*'s English edition.

JANE HIRSHFIELD

Sixth Extinction
It took with it
the words that could have described it.

Obstacle
This body, still walking.
The wind must go around it.

Biophilia
Most of us hungry at daybreak, sleepy by dark.
Some slept, one eye open, in water.
Some could trot.
Some of us lived till morning. Some did not.

A chancellor of the Academy of American Poets and member of the American Academy of Arts and Sciences, Jane Hirshfield (b. 1953) is a poet, essayist, and translator. Her most recent book is *The Asking: New and Selected Poems* (2023).

ELIZABETH BISHOP

THE NIGHT BEFORE I LEFT BOSTON to come here, I had dinner at a Chinese restaurant. I thought you might be interested in hearing the fortune I found in my fortune cookie. Here it is. It says: YOUR FINANCIAL CONDITION WILL IMPROVE CONSIDERABLY.

However, I don't want to express my gratitude *only* for the "improvement" in my "financial condition," grateful as I am for that. Mr. Ivask has selected a poem called "Sandpiper" to be printed on the program today, and when I saw that poem, rather old now, I began to think: Yes, all my life I have lived and behaved very much like that sandpiper—just running along the edges of different countries and continents, "looking for something." I have always felt I couldn't *possibly* live very far inland, away from the ocean; and I *have* always lived near it, frequently in sight of it. Naturally I know, and it has been pointed out to me, that most of my poems are geographical, or about coasts, beaches, and rivers running to the sea, and most of the titles of my books are geographical too: *North & South*, *Questions of Travel*, and one to be published this year, *Geography III*.

The first time I came to Norman, Oklahoma—in 1973—it was the farthest I had ever been inland in my life. I enjoyed myself very much on that first visit, and of course I am enjoying myself on this second, and very special, visit. I find it extremely gratifying that, after having spent most of my life timorously pecking for subsistence along coastlines of the world, I have been given this recognition from so many different countries, but also from Norman, Oklahoma, a place so far inland.

BOSTON

Nominated in 1976 by both John Ashbery and Marie-Claire Blais, Elizabeth Bishop (1911–1979) was the first woman to be awarded the Neustadt International Prize for Literature. Widely considered one of the most important poets of the twentieth century, Bishop was Consultant in Poetry to the Library of Congress (1949–50), won the Pulitzer Prize for Poetry (1956), and received a National Book Award (1970).

OKLAHOMA (1965)

TOMAS TRANSTRÖMER

Translated from the Swedish by May Swenson with Leif Sjöberg

I

The train stalled far to the south. Snow in New York,
but here we could go in shirtsleeves all night.
Yet no one was out. Only the cars
sped by in flashes of light like flying saucers.

II

"We battlegrounds are proud
of our many dead . . ."
said a voice as I awakened.

The man behind the counter said:
"I'm not trying to sell anything,
I'm not trying to sell anything,
I just want you to see something."
And he displayed the Indian axes.

The boy said:
"I know I have a prejudice,
I don't want to have it, sir.
What do you think of us?"

III

This motel is a foreign shell. With a rented car
(like a big white servant) outside the door.
Nearly devoid of memory, and without profession,
I let myself sink to my midpoint.

Editorial note: Tranströmer took the train from Chicago to Tulsa and drove
around eastern Oklahoma in 1965.

Tomas Tranströmer (1931–2015) was a Swedish poet, psychologist, and translator.
He won the 1990 Neustadt Prize and the 2011 Nobel Prize in Literature.

May Swenson (1913–1989) was an American poet, playwright, and translator.
During her lifetime, she received many honors, including a Guggenheim Fellowship
and the 1981 Bollingen Prize.

MARGHERITA

ROBERTO CARRETTA

Translated from the Italian by Stiliana Milkova

MARGHERITA WAS tiny and hunched. She had light eyes, and always—summer or winter—wore a shawl she kept closed on her chest with her hand, as if clutching a necklace. She lived in a small place under the low porticoes of the city hall, a place that seemed the lair of a wood fairy.

One day, she asked me where I came from.

"Turin . . . ," she repeated with a sigh, squinting her eyes. "I was in Turin once . . . right after the war. Many houses bore the signs of bombing and many were no longer there. . . . Trams went through the streets—trams are old animals and modern machines—they scared me a little."

She had never seen the sea, so I promised to take her there.

We left early in the morning one weekend.

During the trip she remained silent until we entered the tunnels.

She was agitated. Every now and then she mumbled something to herself.

"Margherita, are you all right?"

"Yes . . . you know, I am thinking of my husband, years ago in the mines . . . it must have been terrible. I was young, it hurt to be apart, I didn't understand the mines . . ."

Finally, after the last mountain, the sea stretched out before us. While we slowly walked down toward its gray-blue expanse, she covered her eyes and asked me to stop.

She opened her hands, freeing for a moment her gaze, then closed them immediately. She did this for some time.

"It's so big that I can only look at it bit by bit."

The last time I saw Margherita she was stretched out on a big bed—she seemed swallowed by the blankets. Only her face peeked out, her eyes a faint gray, almost colorless, like the eyes of a newborn.

All of a sudden she covered them with her hands and repeated this "peek-a-boo" of hers, then she smiled at me.

"Poor thing," her relatives said. "She's turned into a child."

TURIN, ITALY

Roberto Carretta (b. 1963) is a contemporary Italian philosopher, writer, and translator who lives and works in Turin. He has published books and short stories, and translated works by Aldous Huxley, Guy de Pourtalès, and Robert Darnton into Italian.

Stiliana Milkova is a Bulgarian-born translator and professor of comparative literature and literary translation at Oberlin College. She edits the online journal *Reading in Translation*.

DID GABRIELE D'ANNUNZIO INVENT FASCISM?   (1938)

CARLO SFORZA

IN FRANCE during the Revolution all the extreme Jacobins adopted in the cafés a pseudo-Roman style. How many "patriots" christened themselves Brutus, only to become plain Jacques and Paul the very morning after Thermidor! A great many of the most rabid of the Jacobins and members of the Convention were the product of ecclesiastical colleges and had been brought up on Roman heroes. They believed that the "noble style" could be nothing else than declamatory; simple and sensible in their ordinary relationships—see their private letters—they became insufferable as soon as they mounted the hobbyhorse of their Roman reminiscences.

In Italy the "Roman" mania took two forms; in the past, especially in the seventeenth and eighteenth centuries—the Baroque period—it was extolled by the Jesuits, who judged it more prudent to shunt young men off in the track of the innocuous dead than in the direction of that powerful and dangerous idea which would have been—no more and no less than—Italy.

The great blast of the Risorgimento had dispersed this old miasma. But the war of 1914–18 left in its wake, to a certain extent everywhere, and especially in Italy and Germany, a new category of white-collar proletarians, who saw themselves as troubled wreckage in a society in which capitalism and the world of the workingman seemed equally hostile to them. In Italy the greatness of our Middle Ages, in which all is disorder and life, was necessarily incomprehensible to their limited capacity; just as the generations of the Risorgimento, with all their human generosity, were incomprehensible to them.

By a strange paradox, it was Gabriele D'Annunzio, whose lyric richness had been so splendid, who became the poet and the prophet of all these pathetic misfits. It was he who was the real inventor of fascism.

Even in his poetic expression the man had never become the prisoner of any theory; he had been, successively, a superman with Nietzsche and a compassionate anarchist with Walt Whitman; a decadent with Barrès and a primitive with Claudel. (Pedants have sought in his poems echoes of other poets; as a matter of fact D'Annunzio's lyric torrent is so powerful that it transformed everything at the very source from which he took it; only his reminiscences of Claudel are at times recognizable—that is because Claudel is too completely Claudel.)

Literary glory never seemed to D'Annunzio a prey quite worthy of his talons; and that is the secret of his conduct after the War; even before the War, although he was one of the most famous Europeans, he always envied men of action; but, unfortunately, to act meant, to him, not to act for an ideal—as it did to a Mazzini and a Garibaldi. D'Annunzio was a pathological leftover from the Renaissance, lost in the wave of democracy which swept over Europe from 1890 to 1920. The psychological confusion of the after-war must have seemed to him his great opportunity. Moreover, in the Renaissance itself (his books prove it) he never lifted his eyes to a Michelangelo, nor even to a Machiavelli; his man was Cesar Borgia, with the *bellissimi inganni* of his ferocious individualism.

When in 1919 D'Annunzio seized Fiume, what drove him on was not the idea of preserving the Italian character of the unfortunate Adriatic city (whose occupation by the French immediately after the armistice constitutes, in my opinion, the greatest psychological blunder France has been guilty of in her dealings with Italy); what he thought of, and immediately, was a coup aimed at the whole of Italy; for him, Fiume was to be merely a springboard.

D'Annunzio was too intelligent and too subtle to believe in this adulterated wine of *romanità*—the heritage of Rome. But he took advantage of all these springs of action, because he felt that they were more within the imaginative grasp of the petite bourgeoisie embittered by the after-war, and it was from this class that he recruited his volunteers. It was he who, at Fiume, invented that "Roman salute," which has now become also the "German salute," and which he, overlooking its implications, copied from some statue or fresco, forgetting that, in Rome, the *cives* greeted each other by shaking hands, and that only slaves made the sign which has been adopted by the subjects of Mussolini and Hitler.

But behind the enormous stage setting of Fiume, D'Annunzio's ideas were not altogether theatrical; when I became minister of foreign affairs he wrote me several times from Fiume in the effort to enlist my support for his designs. He knew that immediately after the war, I had been alone in my contention that Turkey had not been conquered; that it was childish to talk of its partition, a fond dream in which the Big Four at Paris had indulged; he knew that my short stay at Constantinople after the armistice had made me many friends among the Musulmen, and he proposed to me, in mysterious phrases, that I should arrange an understanding between Mustafa Kemal (whom he admired) and Italy, with the idea that this alliance should seize the Balkans and from that point of vantage, terrorize Europe.

Aside from what I shall not call the madness—What *is* madness?—but the anachronism of his ideas, what displeased me the most in all these messages from D'Annunzio was that I never felt in them the slightest true and filial love for our Italian fatherland, nor the least spark of fraternal love for our people. On one occasion, to tempt me, he was so childish as to promise me some odes in which my name was to have "defied the centuries." (One juncture at which the littérateur, with his frivolous gifts, got the better of the budding man of action.)

It was D'Annunzio who invented those dialogues with the crowd, which fascism later on found so useful at the Piazza di Venezia at Rome.

"To whom shall Fiume belong?" D'Annunzio called down from the capitol balcony.

And the mob of volunteers who had invaded Fiume thundered from below:

"To us!"

And the poet-dictator:

"And Italy?"

And the mob, once more:

"A noi!" (To us!)

This "to us" gave the key to the real love of D'Annunzio for the fatherland, a love of possession, not a love of devotion and sacrifice.

The fascist conquest of Italy, which came three years later, was nothing, after all, but a gigantic repetition of the mad and romantic enterprise of Fiume—the tame following up of D'Annunzio's brilliant pioneering.

I had wished, when I was in power, to make of Fiume a happy little *Civiltà libera* (free city) which, attached geographically to Italy, assured of its age-old Italian identity, would have realized and symbolized—in its magnificent harbor (one of the most beautiful in Europe)—the most fruitful economic entente between Italians and Slavs, without neglecting the broadest hospitality to Hungarians and Austrians. Fascism, come into power, rejected all such conciliatory measures and preferred to them the empty glory of annexing the *houses* of Fiume—houses soon to be without souls—since that annexation killed with one blow, one fatal blow, the life of the port; its vast quays are deserted today. Fascist Fiume truly deserves the title of one of D'Annunzio's works, *La Città Morta*.

Over the tomb of the poet who was never satisfied with his literary glory (and that constitutes for me his greatest praise) one may truly say that it was not the Italy of Mussolini which annexed Fiume, but the Fiume of D'Annunzio which annexed Italy—I mean, of course, Fascist Italy.

PROVENCE–ALPES–CÔTE D'AZUR

Carlo Sforza (1872–1952) was an Italian diplomat and antifascist statesman who went into exile during the Mussolini era and became a major figure in post–World War II foreign affairs. He authored several books, including *Makers of Modern Europe* (1930), *European Dictatorships* (1931), and *The Totalitarian War and After* (1941).

IF I MUST DIE   (2023)

REFAAT ALAREER

If I must die,
you must live
to tell my story
to sell my things
to buy a piece of cloth
and some strings,
(make it white with a long tail)
so that a child, somewhere in Gaza
while looking heaven in the eye
awaiting his dad who left in a blaze—
and bid no one farewell
not even to his flesh
not even to himself—
sees the kite, my kite you made, flying up above,
and thinks for a moment an angel is there
bringing back love.
If I must die
let it bring hope,
let it be a story.

Refaat Alareer (1979–2023) was a professor of world literature and creative writing at the Islamic University of Gaza and the editor of *Gaza Writes Back: Short Stories from Young Writers in Gaza, Palestine* (2013). He was killed by an IDF airstrike on December 6, 2023, along with his brother, nephew, his sister, and three of her children.

IMAGINATIVE LITERATURE IN THE AGE OF SCIENCE   (1962)

CHU YO-SOP

THE MEMBERS of the Korean Center held several meetings to find out the definite meanings of terms such as "Age of Science" and "Imaginative Literature" and the probable reasons why such a subject had been adopted for this year's Congress. Some suggested that "Age of Science" should mean, not only the technology or mechanism, but also modern life itself; the intellectual, rational, materialistic, objective and realistic life contrasted with the emotional, irrational, romantic, subjective, vital, and intuitive life. Others said the adoption of this particular subject might have been prompted by the fact that from 1957 the utilization of atomic energy has turned, in part, toward the peaceful prosperity of mankind, and by the fact that the scientists have launched man-made satellites successfully into outer space. The fuller knowledge of outer space, I am sure, would influence the life of the peoples on earth with a new hope, and at the same time widen the scope of the writers' imagination.

Still others said that our discussion should be centered on the problem of how we, the creative writers, can cope with a certain particular phase of the age of science that made mass communication extremely easy and very popular. I really fear that, due to the too widely spread mass communication, the individual is losing his own independent mind-ideas, and is becoming a mere mouthpiece of the mass-mind: the mass-mind which might be controlled by a few strong-willed and cunning men whose motive might be detrimental to individual freedom of thought. There is a fear also that Science is becoming God over man, and the highly skilled scientists are becoming like the priests of the Dark Ages in Europe. If this is to be the real case, we need another Renaissance. And there is a pressing need for the revival of Romanticism in order to release the human imagination that would transcend bodily fear or discomfort. No matter how highly science may develop, only to fall into hands whose aim is to destroy or enslave mankind or construct a hell on earth, as long as the spirit of romanticism and humanism prevail we will never be bound to see the gruesome future societies described by Aldous Huxley or the late George Orwell.

Scientists are only discoverers and inventors, while literary writers are creators: creators of hope. And hope, however meager it may be, makes man brave. There are many episodes that tell how hope made desperate people courageous enough to conquer their misfortunes. I will relate only one example. When beaten and lost troops, hungry and thirsty, were desperately wandering on a bare and rocky mountain, they were on the verge of collapsing or going insane. An officer who had an imaginative mind invented a lie by saying that he happened to know the topography of the area and was sure that there was a vineyard on the other side of the peak. Upon hearing him, every soldier's mouth watered so that it relieved him for a while and gave all the soldiers hope and strength to march on. Who knows, there might be a vineyard just around the corner?

If man's ultimate aim is the pursuit of happiness, the physical comfort provided by scientific inventions alone cannot quench the thirst for spiritual happiness. Imaginative literature, I believe, is one of the best means to satisfy spiritual hunger. While the scientists are trying to conquer the moon by the use of scientific tools, we Koreans who have lived quite happily in a world of imagination rather than that of reality or science, our native Shamanism having been enriched by Taoism and Buddhism imported from abroad, have lived on the moon for centuries in our imagination. The following popular folk song that has been sung from generation to generation ever since our ancestors began to love Li Po, the greatest Chinese poet of the eighth century, came to my mind last night as I was sitting on a bench along the Main River. I saw the full bright moon coming up. It had a magic power to transform me into a little boy, and I could not help but hum the folk song:

> Moon, moon, moon, the bright moon,
> The moon with which Li Po played.
> On the moon there stands a cinnamon tree.
> I'll cut the trunk with a golden hatchet.
> Trim the branches with a jade hatchet.
> And build a grass-roofed hut with only three rooms

Where I'll live for a thousand and ten-thousand years,
Serving my dear parents.

While the scientists keep on trying to conquer the moon by the use of their scientific tools, or some more aggressive ones try to claim it as their new territory, we, the Korean people, have lived and will keep on living a humble, filial, and peaceful long life on the moon.

SEOUL

One of modern Korea's "most versatile men of letters," Chu Yo-sop (1902–1972) wrote poetry, fiction, and essays; edited the journal *Shindonga*; and served as head of the Korean Literary Translators Association. His story "Mama and the Boarder" was reprinted in *The Penguin Book of Korean Short Stories* (2023).

SEVEN MARYS (2006)

LI-YOUNG LEE

Father John,
I have seven Marys.
What am I to do?

Ancient when I was born,
each sings to me in three colors: Blue,
wishing, and following the river.

Growing younger while I die faster
every year, they speak to me
in four languages; Thinking, dreaming,
drowning, and guitar.

And one never knows what to do with her hair.
And one rocks me in and out of moonlight.
One cauterizes broken wing joints with black honey.
And one lifts my heart
onto the weighing pan opposite hunger.

Seven Marys, Father, and one
sets me on her lap and opens a book
and moves her finger from word to word

while I sound out evening's encrypted sentences.

And one is the book itself. A book,
yet not a book,
but a house called *Day*.

Seven, Father John, Marys, Father John,
the fulcrum, the eye, the heart enthroned, the dove
without person, homing.

And I can't tell the one who's always looking ahead
from the one who's always looking behind,

the one who's late for everything
from the one who's quick to remind me:

Be ever beginning.
At time's brim, abreast
of that dream
whose wake is each flown act, word,
wish, the stars, their dust,
who stays too long at childhood's window
leaves earth's shadow unsung.

Seven Marys, Father John, seven laughing Sarahs.

One to kiss my mouth and one to tie my hands.
One to build the pyre and one to assure me:

Don't be afraid. Find yourself
inside good-bye, one with life,
one with death.

Seven mothers, their backs turned,
walk ahead of me forever.

Sisters dancing, they're the hub
of all that wheels,
all that joins or comes asunder.

Rachels underneath my bed, they decide
the fate of my sleep.

Bells tolling my solitude,
they're seven zeroes
trumping every count.

Lure, slaughter, feast,
blood in the throat,

fire at the whispered gate, the song
that keeps leaving, they're seven wings
stalking my voice,

they're seven dragons marrying seven sheep
with their heads bent down
by seven enormous crowns.

Marys, Father, Rachels and Sarahs,
and I can't tell one from the other.

Is it Rachel who sings to remember the flood?
Is it Sarah who sings to forget it?
Is it Mary making my bed?
Which one can tell me
the shape of my destiny?

Born in Jakarta, Indonesia, to Chinese parents, Li-Young Lee (b. 1957) has received the Delmore Schwartz Memorial Poetry Award, the Lamont Poetry Selection (now the Laughlin Award), and an American Book Award from the Before Columbus Foundation. Lee's other honors include fellowships from the National Endowment for the Arts, the Lannan Foundation, and the John Simon Guggenheim Memorial Foundation. He lives in Chicago.

YIDDISH WRITING IN AMERICA (1934)

A. A. ROBACK

WHILE EVERY nook and corner of American literature is being searched and explored, every bit of gossip examined and dwelt on, there is one section of it, at least, which has been wholly neglected in American literary circles, in spite of the vitality and lustiness which it has been exhibiting on its own territory. I am referring to Yiddish literature, the literature of the two million American Jews who have not yet strayed from the cultural fold of their people. The Jews are paradoxical in more than one way, both actively and passively. They are ubiquitous, mix with all other peoples. You meet them in every walk of life, even in church, yet their cultural life remains as much hidden from the view of the average American as the Buddhist gospel.

If the Yiddish literature of which I speak here were a foreign importation, its unfamiliarity at least could be understood. It so happens that American Yiddish literature is, in a sense, flesh of America's flesh and bone of America's bone. Having been produced on American soil, even if it does not always portray American life, it must necessarily represent, in some degree, the American viewpoint. Moreover, a large part of the younger Yiddish literature does depict American life and is even identified with American ideals. Epic poems like I. J. Schwartz's *Kentucky* and *George Washington* are surely part and parcel of American literature, even though they are composed in Yiddish. The line of cleavage between the American literature and the English seems to be a geographic demarcation and not a linguistic differentiation. When Isaac Raboy tells about life on the prairies, and Moyshe-Leyb Halpern apostrophizes the sidewalks of New York, they are essentially contributing to the literature of America in a language which is spoken in America.

The foreign elements of American literature (from the linguistic angle) have not yet been done justice to. Not only is it a desideratum to investigate the racial influences of Theodore Dreiser and H. L. Mencken, Joseph Hergesheimer, Louis Untermeyer, Ludwig Lewisohn and Stephen

Vincent Benét, Alfred Kreymborg and Carl Sandburg, but the very foreign adjuncts which have crept up in this country among the various racial units (German, Polish, Lithuanian, Italian) should receive at least a modicum of attention. Yiddish literature is superior in one respect to the other adjuncts in that it is no mere hangover or moribund survival of an established literature in Europe, but is a full-fledged literature able to stand on its own feet and possibly leading in the world federation of Yiddish literatures, which extends from Soviet Russia to South Africa and from Canada to the Argentine.

Until very recently, Yiddish America still looked to Russia and Poland for its beacons. The three giants of Yiddish letters, Mendele Mocher Sforim, Sholem Aleichem, and I. L. Peretz, all died within two years of each other and all three during the World War [I]. The epigones, Sholem Asch and Abraham Reisen, had already emigrated to America, where they served to magnify the galaxy of writers and poets that had already formed during the latter part of the nineteenth century.

Yiddish literature in America is scarcely fifty years old. Fifty years is certainly not a long period historically considered, only a generation and a half. In these five decades a powerful press has been established which numbers even today, with the tendency toward assimilation and the restriction in immigration, an array of half a million readers. Yiddish journalism, from the very beginning, found a fruitful soil in the United States, where the fugitives from Russian tyranny and persecution could both satisfy their craving for knowledge and at the same time learn from the articles in their newspapers how to ameliorate their economic condition.

The outsider little realizes how vast an edifice American Yiddish literature is. Not only does it comprise some hundred newspapers and periodicals, several hundred plays, collections of poetry by the scores, novels by the hundreds, but even a library of essays, scientific works, books of criticism, treatises on music (harmony), excellent memoirs, art—in short, all that goes to make up the literature of a cultured people.

It was in America that the first history of Yiddish literature was written, that the first history of the Yiddish theater was published, and, what is more, that the first adequate Yiddish translation of the Bible appeared, an undertaking of twenty years by the poet Yehoash (Solomon Blumgarten), who, together with Morris Rosenfeld, dominated Yiddish poetry for a generation. In this connection, it is noteworthy that Yiddish poetry flourished in the United States more than anywhere else. The earlier tendentious notes of David Edelstadt and Morris Winchevsky, which called the workingmen to combat for better social conditions and a more equitable economic system, gave way to the more lyric strains of the reflective Yehoash and the impassioned Morris Rosenfeld, in whom the national tendency blended with the personal. Rosenfeld, too, complained of the sweatshop which prevented him from seeing his child awake, but he was no agitator. Among living Yiddish poets in America today, H. Leivick perhaps stands out because of the lofty conception of his *Golem*, a mystic play in verse, which has been rendered into English as well as into several other languages. This pillar of contemporary Yiddish literature, until his recent retreat to a sanitarium for tuberculosis, was compelled to work as a paperhanger for his daily bread.

The novel and the short story have not fared so well as poetry, strange as it may seem. With Sholem Asch residing in Paris, the number of good Yiddish fiction writers reduces itself to Joseph Opatoshu, Jonah Rosenfeld, Lamed Shapiro, and Isaac Raboy among the older men, and Leivik Chanukoff and Baruch Glassman among the younger set. David Pinski, whose reputation as a dramatist resounded far and wide in non-Jewish circles, has recently entered the domain of the novel, bringing out his *Noah Eden's Generations*, first as a serial in Yiddish and subsequently in book form in English. The book is a sort of *Forsyte Saga* on a restricted scale, but bristling with conflicts not only between the old and the new, but between two divergent civilizations in different parts of the world.

The Yiddish theater, founded about fifty-five years ago in Romania, flourished on the East Side more than anywhere else in Jewry because it served as an agency both for amusement and self-development, and furthermore its program was not impeded by oppressive government measures as in Russia or by the poverty of the masses. It was here that great actors like Jacob Adler, David Kessler, and Max Morrison began to thrive, and it was here that Jacob Gordin undertook to reform the Yiddish drama; but his productions were not American either in spirit or in content. Leon Kobrin and Zalmon Libin were the first to write on American Jewish subjects: life in the tenement houses of the lower East Side, problems between immigrant parents and the children weaned away from them by the environment. They were, and are still, the "presentialists," i.e., those who react to the present environment, as compared with David Pinski, Peretz Hershbein, and others of a higher caliber who hark back to the past, in some cases the remote past.

When we ask ourselves whether the American Yiddish writer is more akin to the older Yiddish writer or to the non-Jewish American writer of today, we find the question difficult to answer. For the younger American Yiddish writer, the surroundings are distinctly American, the environment is a Jewish figuration against a multicolored American background, but the spirit, nonetheless, the conception, the Weltanschauung is rather Jewish—not that one can speak of an American or Jewish point of view of poetics, as if dealing with political parties, but rather in the sense that the composite picture of Yiddish writing and the synthetic makeup of American writings do not coincide. Yiddish fiction written in this country, let alone that of the Old Country, will not appear in *Liberty* or the *Saturday Evening Post*. Similarly, Yiddish readers, even of the less-educated classes, will not take a fancy to the stories printed in the average American magazine. At the same time, the American reader will read a translation of Chanukoff's *Submarine Z-1* without being aware that this is not a novel originally written by an American writer, a circumstance which is not possible with the works of the classical Yiddish writers.

The word *extinct* suggests the most vital question of all: what prospect is there of Yiddish literature surviving in the New World? This question has been posed and debated back and forth for more than a quarter of a century. Indeed, it was the author of the first history of Yiddish literature, Professor Leo Wiener of Harvard, who prophesied its disappearance. It was long before there was any notion of restricting immigration and certainly when there was no anticipation of an economic debacle such as we are experiencing, that Wiener, with reference to the Yiddish theater in America, wrote: "It is very doubtful whether the Jewish theater can subsist in America another ten years" (*History of the Yiddish Literature in the Nineteenth Century*, p. 242).

A whole generation has passed since these words appeared in print in 1899. For two decades the gates of America had been practically closed to Yiddish-speaking newcomers, and to boot, within the last two years, the Yiddish theater, together with Broadway's White Way, has been undergoing a most critical period which bids fair to stifle the creative impulses of dramatic talent as well as the ambitions of producers, directors, and actors. With all these handicaps and drawbacks, both general and specific, it is estimated on the basis of actual box office receipts that in the first half of the 1931–32 season alone, consisting of twenty weeks, the Yiddish-speaking public in greater New York paid over three-quarters of a million dollars in admission fees, which means that the receipts for the entire season would aggregate well over a million dollars in greater New York—only one, although of course the largest, Jewish center.

Prophets of doom are just as often wrong as prophets of boom and probably for the same reasons. Both see before them a regular slope, either uphill or downhill, and mistake the probable trend for an absolute certainty. Prophets of conditions involving human relations all too frequently are prompted by too much self-confidence and wishfulness, on the one hand, and too little knowledge of psychological laws and historical events on the other. When Professor Wiener predicted that 1909 would usher in the finale of the Yiddish theater, it was probably because he himself was preparing to bid adieu to Yiddish literature.

CAMBRIDGE, MASSACHUSETTS

Born in the Russian Empire (now Poland), Jewish American psychologist, philologist, folklorist, and educator Abraham Aaron Roback (1890–1965) immigrated to Montreal with his family in 1892. After graduating from McGill University, Roback received his MA and PhD from Harvard. From 1949 to 1958 he served as chair and professor of psychology at Emerson College in Boston. As an indefatigable promoter of Yiddish, Roback compiled a 10,000-volume Yiddish library for Harvard.

GIFT

CZESŁAW MIŁOSZ

Translated from the Polish by the author

A day so happy.
Fog lifted early, I worked in the garden.
Hummingbirds were stopping over honeysuckle flowers.
There was no thing on earth I wanted to possess.
I knew no one worth my envying him.
Whatever evil I had suffered, I forgot.
To think that once I was the same man did not embarrass me.
In my body I felt no pain.
When straightening up, I saw the blue sea and sails.

BERKELEY, 1971

Czesław Miłosz (1911–2004) was a Polish American poet, writer, translator, and diplomat. He won the 1978 Neustadt International Prize for Literature; in nominating Miłosz for the prize, Joseph Brodsky called him "one of the greatest poets of our time, perhaps the greatest." Miłosz also received the 1980 Nobel Prize in Literature.

J. M. G. LE CLÉZIO

Translated from the French by Julia Luisa Abramson

IT IS IN READING that I first found evidence of alterity. First it was in my childhood reading of the collected issues of the *Journal des Voyages* from the years 1850–70, a present from a friend of my grandfather who bore the astounding name of Claudius-Veran. I read the journals as if they were about current news; they presented the world as a mystery to which the key must be found: unreal, ghostly Africa, where the other—the African—always wears a mask, stripped of humanity, belonging to the animal kingdom. Yet I had known Africa, at the age of eight, during a trip to the Ibo country, where I met my father for the first time, doubtless the only traveling I had ever done. Fortunately, the imperialist fantasy of the *Journal* was exorcised by the reserve of emotions, intuitions, recollections that the real Africa had given me—the smell of the earth after tropical rains, the vault of the forests on the road to Abakaliki, the mountain where gorillas lived near Obudu, the steppe scattered with giant termitaries around Ogoja, on the bank of the Cross River.

Those were the last days of colonial society, its terror and banality. Day after day, the voice of the BBC spread news of the extortion of the leopard-men in the Congo and of the Kikuyu in Kenya. Soon rebellion would come to Morocco, war to Indochina and Algeria.

Very early on, I got the feeling that the principal function of books was not to distract but rather to take the measure of things. Doubtless I will never be able to locate exactly the memory of reading *Don Quixote*, *Treasure Island*, or *Lazarillo de Tormes* knowing nothing of literature; the books spoke inside me then, in my own language, as if they were my own memory. I paid more attention then to the woodblock prints illustrating the old editions, to the drawings by Tony Johannot or Gustave Doré, to the engravings in the Hetzel edition of *Twenty Thousand Leagues Under the Sea*.

The world's mystery cannot be found through exploration; mystery resides rather in the world's imaginable power. During the time I am remembering, there still appeared in the Atlases (*The Advanced Atlas of Modern Geography* by Bartholomew) immense "frozen regions" and rivers such as the upper Xingu that disappeared into stippling toward the source. Jack London, Jean Malaurie, P. E. Victor, Colonel Fawcett were the last explorers: those who brought the stuff of dreams back for children, growing close to and distantly witnessing their own savage beginnings. On the eve of an era of exploitation, on the morrow of one of the greatest crimes organized by modem society, must we not believe in savage man, in the wolf-child, in the lost world of some valley in New Guinea, so that we may exorcise fear, racial hatred, the sterilization of the police city?

THE INFINITE LIBRARY

Later, when my father returned from Africa, I discovered a universe of reading in books which had returned to us through the play of inheritances, having belonged to my great-grandfather Sir Eugene, a judge on the Supreme Court of Mauritius. They were the only treasure I will ever find.

All of those books were fabulous, bearing my ancestor's spindly signature on the first page. They were bound in leather, decoratively stamped in gold, at once dreadful and attractive in their Second Empire cases. It was those books which gave me a feeling for the strangeness and familiar force emanating from printed volumes. Once opened, the books offered up their nourishment, and even as a child (I was between ten and fourteen years of age) I could partake of it.

Aside from the great classics—Horace, Lucretius, Rabelais, Goethe—and the Romantics—Hugo, Heredia, Vigny, Longfellow—it was the extraordinary travel narratives which influenced me more than anything else I read or experienced. I will cite a few of the titles, not in the order in which I read them, but according to their arrangement on the bookshelves devoted to them and reverently inventoried by my mother.

Shelf 1: *Souvenirs de la Réunion* (1853); Bory de Saint-Vincent, *Voyage dans les quatre principales îles de la mer d'Afrique* (1804); Tombe, *Voyage aux*

Indes Orientales (1810); Marchand, *Voyage autour du monde* (Year VI of the Republic); Cook, *Voyage aux Mers du Sud*; Duchesne, *Atlas du répertoire des plantes utiles et des plantes vénéneuses du globe* (1840); the *Voyage* by François Leguat (1708); and a little book which immediately set me dreaming, *Un project de république a l'Ile d'Eden (L'Ile Bourbon)* by the Marquis Henri du Quesne, published by Sauzier in 1887.

Shelf 2: Abbé de Caille, *Voyage au Cap de Bonne-Espérance* (1763); La Bourdonnais, *Mémoires* (1751); Souchu de Rennefort, *Histoire des Indes Orientales* (1668); Luillier, *Voyage aux Indes* (1762); Dubois, *Voyage aux îles dauphines* (1674).

Shelf 3: Le Gentil, *Voyage dans les Mers de l'Inde* (1777); De Laval, *Voyage de François Pyrard de Laval* (1679); De Flacourt, *Histoire de Madagascar* (1661); *Relations véritables et curieuses de l'isle de Madagascar et du Bresil* (1651); Drury's *Madagascar* (1807); Lacombe, *Voyage à Madagascar* (1840); Abbé Rochon, *Voyage à Madagascar* (1801); *Voyage de Benyoski* (1761); Le Vaillant, *Voyage dans l'intérieur de l'Afrique* (1750); Haussman, *Voyage en Chine* (1847); Dumont d'Urville, *Voyage au Pôle sud* (1842); Marco Polo, *Le Livre des merveilles* (1865); Billard, *Voyage aux colonies orientales* (1825); *Voyage de l'Arabie heureuse* (1716); Prince Roland Bonaparte, *Voyage en Insulinde* (1884); Régnon, *Madagascare et le Roi Radama* (1865).

Shelf 4: Albert Pitot, *L'Île Maurice* (1810); Charles Grant, *History of Mauritius* (1801); Milbert, *Voyage pittoresque à L'Île-de-France* (1901); Adrien d'Epinay, a manuscript titled *l'Île de France* (1901); Bojer, *Hortus Mauritianus* (1837); D'Unienville, *Île Maurice* (1885); Bernardin de Saint-Pierre, *Voyages à l'île Maurice et La Réunion* (1773); Pierre Poivre, *Voyages d'un philosophe* (1794); Charles Baissac, *Étude sur le patois créole mauricien* (1880); Matou, *Les Guêpes mauriciennes* (1861); Pajot, *Simples renseignements sur l'île Bourbon* (1878).

ON THE ISLAND AS MYTH

In principle, to grow up in a culture is to accept all of its limitations. Yet it is possible that literature exists uniquely to force us to transgress such limits. If French literature is a territoriality, how can one conceive of Rimbaud alongside Racine, Péguy next to Radiguet, Saint-Exupéry with Nelligan? Can all of Proust be summed up as the simple exploration of a zone in Greater

Paris, of membership in a certain community? If I thrill at hearing the sound of the bell which sets off memory's movement at the moment Swann pushes open the garden door, is it not because there exists another territory, drawn in language? Literature brought me liberty. Was it indeed inconceivable to be French, raised in the almost military discipline of a provincial lycée during a postwar period hesitating between civil republicanism and monarchic Catholicism, and at the same time troubled, haunted as if by a dream of an island so distant (in an era in which chartered flights did not exist and an airmail letter took a week to reach us from Mauritius via London and Paris) that it seemed stricken, not with unreality, but with unknowability and immoderation? An island to which we did not go. An island on which nobody imagined taking a vacation, damned as it was by memories of slavery, malaria, and cyclones. An island like the moon, an island like Eden, an island from which we had been irreparably and definitively excluded, and which persisted all the same as a hidden motive, nostalgia, reference, memory. Reading, instead of the *Figaro* or the *Times*, the *Mauricien-Cernéen* (a paper founded, it was said, by the one whose signature had been scratched on the first page of the books I read), and evoking, at every turn, like a vain litany, names familiar and strange: *Euréka*, *Moka*, *Curepipe*, *Vacoas*, *Mon Désert-Alma*, *Pamplemousses*, *la montagne Ory*, *le Pouce*, *le Pieter Both*, *le Morne Brabant*. Names I could not share with anybody else in Nice, just as I could not share this useless knowledge of the Creole names for things and people; the soft speech of the islands with its singsong accent must be hidden on pain of being a white Negro in a land of exile.

An island where, in the end, people tread as on an open book.

THAT EXOTICISM IS IMPOSTURE

Conrad, Kipling, Haggard, Loti, Segalen searched less to express disorientation than wandering, the impossibility of being entirely oneself (unique, logical). Through writing they lived what the adventuress Isabelle Eberhardt had experienced in her life, having wanted, she said, to possess Africa, and having been possessed by Africa. Likewise Delacroix, Gauguin, or the photographer Curtis, fixing on his plates the last free moments of the North American Indians.

Exoticism is a contemporary plague. It is ballast—"margaritas"—the smooth glass pearls that the conqueror Cortés solemnly exchanged for the gold necklace decorated with fish and shellfish offered by Moctezuma's ambassadors as a gesture of welcome, or the trinkets that the Dutchman Peter Stuyvesant gave to buy the island of Manhattan from the Indians. What territory would we exchange for our illusions? The plague is always the same, the conviction that the world may be sold and consumed, that it is but the object of our leisure, desire, desecration. The appetite of the affluent has surely never been greater. Swelling, it needs ever more salt, pepper, sex, and blood. Thus it conceals its own impotence, its failings in imagining the other.

But the world cannot be bought. It evades those who want to possess it. Humanity's great innovators were nomadic, living not off accidents but rather in relation, and they trespassed at every turn on territoriality's bounds. Turner, Van Gogh, Matisse, De Staël did not explore strange foreign lands, only captured elements of them: light, fleeting sensation; they were possessed by these.

ANYWHERE OUT OF THIS WORLD

The other, the *here-beyond*, is not at the antipodes, not overseas, not in the past. It is next door, in the eye of the octopus, in the dog's nose, in the tree's fluid skin, in the sandy desert, the ocean's movement, the slight trembling of a dreaming cat.

What differentiates an Emberá Indian of the Panamanian forest ("An Indian, just a man," said Michaux) from an inhabitant of the modem metropolis's glacial solitude is not intrinsic value. There are as many assassins and rapists, as many villains and hypocrites, in the one place as in the other. What differentiates them is not clothing or custom, is not dietetic or cosmetic, is not prettiness or ritual. It is more that the one has kept, the other lost. Bare feet on our earth-mother, lying down in warm cinders among our grandparents' bones, we unite dreams with myths, we eat and drink of history and anoint our skins with memory.

Modernity's paradox is to give us the world and at the same time to exile us from it. Knowledge, television reports, sociological investigations should have freed us from all certainties. Instead we have become impervious to intelligence, incapable of mysticism or trance. More than anything we dread suffering and death, and we close our eyes before the greatest crimes perpetrated against children in Africa, Latin America, the East, the Near East. We hate blood, and difference—be it only vestimentary—frightens us. In the name of rationality, we have closed ourselves behind our borders, and we have invented new demons possessing the face of the other. We have become dogmatic even in our tolerance. We are ready to go to war against those who do not think, do not pray, do not judge as we do, but we say nothing of the slavery to which poor countries have been reduced, nothing of border closings, nothing of abandoning the elderly and dissembling death.

At times something stirs. The conformism and tactical forgetfulness encysting us ruptures sometimes, cedes before the pressure of the real. Something reaches us through foreign words, Ainu songs, ancient Tahitian myths, Sufi tears. Something continues to be born, in Quevedo's poetry or in Rimbaud's, in Swift's tales, in Kabyle songs, or vibrates in our very core in the magical voices of Nat King Cole or Mahalia Jackson. We hear lessons taught by travelers and children. Light shines, we perceive the world cracking and, beyond, true silence.

NICE, FRANCE

Born in Nice, France, Jean-Marie Le Clézio (b. 1940) has published over forty works since the early 1960s, including short stories, novels, essays, and children's books. In 1997 he was the Puterbaugh Fellow at the University of Oklahoma, and he received the Nobel Prize in Literature in 2008.

Julia Luisa Abramson is an associate professor of French at the University of Oklahoma.

POETRY AS WONDER, DESIRE, RAGE, AND MEMORY: A CONVERSATION WITH NATALIE DIAZ (2020)

SHOOK

SHOOK: You've spoken before about how you came to poetry through your family, and through your mother in particular, "even though she was denied poetry." I too devoured my mom's *Reader's Digests*, and I feel like I learned my respect for language, for the power of the word, from my family, from their respect for the Word. I'm interested in your earliest beliefs about language, about how your mother gave you poetry.

NATALIE DIAZ: We live on our Mojave homelands and see the land's stories all around us. We don't name things after the white men who "discovered" our land—we name things for what has happened there, the ways we interacted with the land in that place. For example, here Pach Karawhe (the Man of War) tried to lift the mountains but dropped them, and now the peaks are crooked and Mojaves are fallible; here is 'Avii Hukyaampve, where Pach Karawhe taught the people, many of whom were still in their animal form, to shoot arrows and other arts of war; here is 'Aha Kulooh, or the name for where our California village is located now, and it tells you that before the dam was built, this is where the river broke loudly against the bank.

My mother is a storyteller. She comes from this Mojave land and community of story. She has a limitless imagination and lexicon—she could have gone to college; she could have done anything. Instead, she took care of her father when he was sick, then her family after her father died. Then she took care of us. When I was a child, I was anxious and always worried about everything—I still am. My mother often rocked me to sleep reading me stories. She let me read anything I wanted—I read everything in the house, including the *Reader's Digests*, a faux-leather-bound Old West encyclopedia set from a raffle, my grandmother's Danielle Steel novels. My mom is one of the funniest people I know, while also bearing a lot of weight and carrying many wounds. That's the nature of language for me, that it holds within it all that has happened—to the earth, to the body, to the heart and mind, and also holds in it what we might shape or be shaped by in the future.

Once, when I saw she had pulled out the giant black pot speckled with millions of distant white stars, which I called the galaxy pot because it seemed to have an infinitude of depth, a galactic capacity, I complained that we were eating beans again! My mother never addressed my complaint; never explained the beans were free on WIC, which I had thought was a kind of money up until then; didn't address that the beans were connected to the fact that our electricity was shut off (the stove was gas) or that she was boiling water in the same pot for our baths that month. Instead she told me that beans wouldn't give you gas if you chewed them more thoroughly. She launched into what seemed like legit science to me at that age—she was very serious, and I was interested in the experiment, eager even to eat beans that night. I spent the next several years eating my beans three times more slowly than my siblings. I'd miss out on seconds because I was still eating my first bowl, thoroughly chewing, invested in the hypothesis. That's what poetry is like to me—it's the gift of a bowl of bright beans and intestines of bright gas when the family and the house is on the brink of collapse.

SHOOK: As I was considering what I wanted to ask you, I was thinking about other contemporary American poets, and my mind snagged on the phrase "American poetry." As a translator of numerous Latin American poets, I'm often frustrated by the exclusionary definition of what it means to be "American." But it's actually much worse than just that: the imposition of America's very name meant the genocide of this land's Native inhabitants, and with it an extermination of so many of their poetries and languages. Do you consider yourself an American poet?

DIAZ: I'm lately spending a lot of time thinking about all the ways I have been prophesied in America. The incredible currency of identity in what is American poetry—how it makes you poor or rich in what seems to me to be arbitrary moments of categorization. How easy it is to subscribe to what is American poetry and then to prescribe it for others. The argument about why we should revere Walt Whitman. That Marianne Moore worked at Carlisle Indian Industrial School and lauded the school's military leader for his great work at killing the Indian to save the man.

As well, I'm more and more unsatisfied and uncomfortable with the acronyms WOC and POC, American, contemporary, and categories such as emerging and mid-career. I am in the middle of my life on earth, and I am patient with my work. I have just completed my second book. I have had "success" by American poetry standards, and yet I might never have however many books it will take for them to categorize me as mid-career. I've had several careers—professional basketball player, linguist, poet, professor, and who knows what next. This is what I mean by arbitrary. I focus on this category because it is a symptom of the same structure we turn to as we tell people what (not who) they are in the relationship of nation. Also, the crazy reality that race is our grandest and most employed definition while many Americans don't seem to know what race is.

American poetry is as careful a design as a reservation is, as the MFA program is, as any wall or checkpoint. What to do about it? I don't know. The part I am most concerned with is not what they are doing but what I let happen. What have I agreed to become because they told me it was who I was? I'm as much a part of the structure. I don't know how to engage the questions cropping up around what is American or contemporary-American or joyful-American or rigorous- or political-American. I'm a little lazy in the question—a little out of shape on how to ask it. It will require some intensive and uncomfortable training and practice for me to put myself in the right condition to ask it in the ways I feel I must.

SHOOK: How did *Postcolonial Love Poem* come together? To me it reads as a very tight book, a cohesive whole, populated by recurring images from the natural world—water and snakes, skin and hands—and concerns. To what degree did you conceptualize it in its present form?

DIAZ: This book is all itself, because it is all the things I am in wonder, in desire, in rage and anger, in imagination, in memory. Some readers won't be able to hold all of the poems in the book at one time—they will immediately begin to edit me down, to try to shape me and the book to fit their projections of identity or poetry. The book is myriad, because I am myriad. But this book is the book that only I can write—I say that not in any poetical-hierarchical way, but in the energetic way that I need to feel in me in order to maintain my relationship to poetry and language. I thought of the book as a movement of bodies, of life energy, of lexical energy. I thought of the language and the poems as my own body and the way it loves or is loved, the way it wounds or has been wounded. I think of it as a little door of light in my sternum that leads to a labyrinth of blood and water and earth that leads to a dark cave behind my heart where there is another door of light—that is how I put it together.

SHOOK: Throughout the book, you often employ a biblical diction, the Song of Songs–like "rose-horned rams" of a lover's hips, for example, from the title poem, and deploy biblical references. What relationship does the Bible have to your work? What about faith more generally?

DIAZ: I am Catholic and also Mojave. The ritual and ceremony of the Catholicism I grew up with is very linked to the ways we believe as Mojaves, the ways we ceremony and practice. The two ways of living are in relationship, in futuristic ways and in colonial ways. I think a lot about the ecstatic, which to me is very connected to the quantum world-ways my people believe—everything is an energy, and my body is a small gesture in the movement of that energy.

I'm also interested in the etymology of the English language—as well as the etymologies of my Mojave words, which feel different in that they have not evolved away from the earth and its nonhuman life. These etymological meditations often revert to religious or mystical stories. In regard to my own faith, my beliefs and practices are shaped like my desert—I understand the brutality of the world as well as I understand its will to live and ability to flourish. They are shaped like the river inside me. I try to understand my autonomy in relationship to who and what is around me, so that I don't drink while another thirsts, and that is hard in the U.S.

I believe in the beloved, that I can also be one as I love one. I go to mass and feel my life there. I walk out on my land or dunk into my river four times and feel my life. I guess I am not so sure about faith, and more wondering about what I need to do in order to make the kind of world I'd like to be a small part of. I'm always a little worried about writing these things down because they tend to sound a little self-help. Maybe what I mean is that I believe language is not the body but what might make the body act, and I wish that I will always be ready to act.

SHOOK: It's easy to see how *Postcolonial Love Poem* dialogues with the poets who authored its epigraphs, from Harjo to Spillers, Rihanna to Sor Juana. What other poets or books do you think you're in conversation with?

DIAZ: My first poets were Lorca and Borges, and they were given to me by my first lover, along with Amichai and Darwish. Amichai and Darwish were my introduction to Palestine, which I consider a sister-land. Sor Juana was the first woman I read. I came late to Native literature, and in a way I am glad I did. It was lucky for me to search a little for myself before I found the ways I could be and also subvert what America projects onto Native writers. I consider the "conversation" to be one of listening, rather than believing my work is "like" these writers'. Lately I am trying to be quiet and to listen generously to Dionne Brand, to my friend Roger Reeves, to Alejandra Pizarnik, to Kamau Brathwaite, to Nikky Finney.

SHOOK: I'm interested in how your relationship with the Mojave language—both as a speaker and as a language preservationist—influences your poetry in English. (Tangentially, do you ever write in Mojave?)

DIAZ: I don't write fully in Mojave. I am not sure Mojave exists yet on the page. Of course, it can, it can do anything—*jajaj*, that was spoken like a true Mojave! I mean to express that Mojave exists in me beyond the page, whereas English came to me with its own page. I think my relationship to Mojave, my experience with both absence and loss, have let me be more careful with English—by careful, I mean tender and also wary. I know what English thinks of me. I know its limits in thinking of me. It is a gift to have a language that English is too small for, since I have a life that English thinks is small.

Natalie Diaz (b. 1978) is Mojave and an enrolled member of the Gila River Indian Tribe. She is the author of two poetry collections, *Postcolonial Love Poem* (2020), winner of the 2021 Pulitzer Prize, and *When My Brother Was an Aztec* (2012). The Maxine and Jonathan Marshall Chair in Modern and Contemporary Poetry at Arizona State University, she directs ASU's Center for Imagination in the Borderlands.

Raised in Mexico City, poet, translator, and filmmaker Shook founded the nonprofit publishing house Phoneme Media in 2013 and received a 2017 NEA Translation Fellow for their translation of Conceição Lima's *No Gods Live Here* (2024). Shook is a fellow of the Los Angeles Institute for the Humanities at the University of Southern California.

THIS WILL BE THE LAST YEAR   (1942)

VICTORIA OCAMPO

SAN ISIDRO, ARGENTINA, SEPTEMBER 30, 1942

YEAR AFTER YEAR we have been waiting for a word of appreciation (mind! We don't mean praise) from you. It has come at last. After so much silence it sounds too good to be true. We are indeed very happy to hear that you like *Sur*. It has been a great struggle to keep it afloat for twelve long years. Often I have said to myself: "This will be the last year. It is too silly to loose money, and time, and temper for nothing." And there I go on loosing . . . as if I could not stop.

All that I can say is that your letter gave us a most unexpected joy. We are most anxious to get in touch with you, people of the North of our America. And now more than ever. Friends here told us that we, Argentines, are not "en odeur de sainteté" up there (the North seems always to be somewhere up and the South somewhere down).

I should like that misunderstanding to come to an end, because it is a great mistake. A mistranslation of our true feelings; a misstatement of our true thoughts. And many others mis this, and mis that.

I shall perhaps go to USA in the fall, as *you* say, no?

En attendant I will send as soon as possible the article on *Sur*. I don't know yet if I will have time to write it myself. In any case, I hope it will be good enough to be OK'ed by you. We will try hard not to bore your readers and sprinkle generously with humor, pathos and drama every sentence.

If my english is not what it ought to be, please excuse me. I hope it is, at least, clear.

Victoria Ocampo (1890–1979) was an Argentine writer, translator, intellectual, and the author of more than a dozen books. Her work included translations of William Faulkner, D. H. Lawrence, and Albert Camus. She is best known for founding the prestigious literary magazine *Sur* in 1931.

AT THE EDGE OF BORGES (1971)

JORGE GUILLÉN

Translated from the Spanish by Ilan Stavans

> *I owe the discovery of Uqbar to the conjunction of a mirror*
> *and an encyclopedia.*
>
> —*Ficciones*, "Tlön, Uqbar, Orbis Tertius"

Let us dream, soul, let us read!

Among figures and signs
Let us dream—in memory—
Chess, alchemy, kabbalah,
Palimpsest, labyrinth.

Vast garden: library.

Listening, conversing
With faqih, with astrologer
To accumulate a language
Where one might live far away.

Mysterious encyclopedia!

Jorge Guillén (1893–1984) was a Spanish poet and member of the Generation of '27. After being arrested during the Spanish Civil War in 1936, he went into voluntary exile in the United States. Following the death of Franco, he returned to Spain in 1978.

Ilan Stavans is the Lewis-Sebring Professor in Latin American and Latino Culture at Amherst College and publisher of Restless Books.

ORHAN PAMUK

Translated from the Turkish by Maureen Freely

I HAVE BEEN writing for thirty years. I have been reciting these words for some time now. I've been reciting them for so long, in fact, that they have ceased to be true: for now I am entering my thirty-first year as a writer. I do still like saying that I've been writing novels for thirty years. Though this is a bit of an exaggeration. From time to time, I do other sorts of writing—essays, criticism, reflections on Istanbul or politics, and speeches for wonderful events like this. But my true vocation, the thing that binds me to life, is writing novels. There are plenty of brilliant writers who've been writing much longer than I, who've been writing for half a century without paying this much attention. There are also the great writers to whom I return again and again, Leo Tolstoy, Fyodor Dostoyevsky, and Thomas Mann, whose careers spanned more than fifty years. So why do I make so much of my own thirtieth anniversary as a writer? I do so because I wish to talk about writing, and most particularly novel-writing, as a habit.

In order to be happy, I must have my daily dose of literature. In this I am no different from the patient who must take a spoon of medicine each day. When I learned, as a child, that diabetics needed an injection every day, like most people, I felt bad for them; I may even have thought of them as half dead. My dependence on literature must make me "half dead" in the same way. When I was a young writer, especially, I sensed that others saw me as "cut off from the real world" and so doomed to be "half dead." Or perhaps the right expression is "half ghost." I have sometimes even entertained the thought that I was fully dead and trying to breathe life back into my corpse with literature. For me, literature is medicine. Like the medications that others take by spoon or injection, my daily dose of literature—my daily fix, if you will—must meet certain standards.

First, the medicine must be good. Its goodness is what tells me how true and strong it is. To read a dense, deep passage in a novel, to enter into that world and believe it to be true—nothing makes me happier, nothing binds me more to life. I also prefer it if the writer is dead, because then there is no little cloud of jealousy to darken my admiration. The older I get, the more convinced I am that the best books are by dead writers. Even if they are not yet deceased, to sense their presence is to sense a ghost. This is why, when we see great writers in the street, we treat them like ghosts, not quite believing our eyes as we marvel from afar. A few brave souls approach the ghosts for autographs. Sometimes I remind myself that these writers will die soon, and that once they are dead, the books that are their legacy will occupy an even higher place in our hearts. Though of course this is not always the case . . .

If my daily dose of literature is something I myself am writing, it's all very different. Because for those who share my affliction, the best cure of all, and the greatest source of happiness, is to write a good half page every day. For thirty years I've spent an average of ten hours a day alone in a room, sitting at my desk. If you count only the work that is good enough to be published, my daily average is a good deal less than half a page a day. Most of what I write does not meet my own standards of "goodness." These, I put to you, are two large sources of misery.

But please don't misunderstand me: a writer who is as dependent on literature as I am can never be the sort of superficial person who will find happiness in the beauty of the books he has already written, nor can he congratulate himself on how many books he has written or what these books achieved. Literature does not allow such a writer to pretend to save the world; rather, it gives him the chance to save the day. And all days are difficult. Days are difficult when you don't do any writing. They're difficult when you cannot do any writing. The point is to find enough hope to get through the day and, if the book or the page he is reading is good, to find joy in it, and happiness, if only for a day.

Let me explain what I feel on a day when I've not written well, if I'm not lost in a book. First, the world changes before my eyes: it becomes unbearable, abominable; those who know me can see it happening to me, too, for I myself come to resemble the world I see around me. For example, my daughter can tell that I have not written well that day from the abject hopelessness on my face in the evening. I would like to be able to hide this from her, but I cannot. During these dark moments, I feel as if there is no line between life and death. I don't want to speak to anyone, and anyone seeing me in this state has no desire to speak to me either. A milder version of this despair descends on me every afternoon, in fact, between one and three, but I have learned how to treat it by reading and writing: if I act promptly, I can save myself from a full retreat to my corpse.

If I've had to go a long stretch without my paper-and-ink cure, be it due to travel, an unpaid gas bill, military service (as was once the case), political affairs (as has been the case more recently), or any number of other obstacles, I can feel my misery setting inside me like cement. My body has difficulty moving through space, my joints get stiff, my head turns to stone, my perspiration even seems to have another smell. This misery can only grow, for life is full of punishments that distance a person from literature. I can be sitting in a crowded political meeting, or chatting with my classmates in a school corridor, or eating a holiday meal with my relatives, struggling to converse with a good-hearted person whose mind is worlds away or else occupied by whatever is happening on the TV screen: I can be at an important "business meeting," making an ordinary purchase, making my way to the notary, or having my picture taken for a visa—suddenly my eyelids will grow heavy, and though it is the middle of the day, I'll fall asleep. When I am far away from home, and therefore unable to return to my room to spend time alone, my only consolation is a nap in the middle of the day.

So yes, the real hunger here is not for literature, but for a room where I can be alone and dream. If I can do this, I can invent beautiful dreams about those same crowded places, those family gatherings, school reunions, festival meals, and all the people who attend them. I enrich the crowded holiday meals with invented details and make the people themselves even more amusing. In dreams, of course, everything and everyone is interesting, captivating, and real. I make the new world from the stuff of the known world. Here we come to the heart of the matter. To write well, I must first be bored to distraction; to be bored to distraction, I must enter into life. It is when I am bombarded with noise, sitting in an office full of ringing phones, surrounded by friends and loved ones on a sunny seashore or at a rainy funeral—in other words, at the very moment when I begin to sense the heart of the scene unfolding around me—that I will suddenly feel as if I'm no longer really there but watching from the sidelines. I'll begin to daydream. If I'm feeling pessimistic, I can think about how bored I am. Either way, there will be a voice inside me, urging me to "go back to the room and sit down at the table." I have no idea what most people do in such circumstances, but it is this that turns people like me into writers. My guess is that it leads not to poetry but to prose and fiction. This sheds a bit more light on the properties of the medicine I must be sure to take every day. We can see now that its ingredients are boredom, real life, and the life of the imagination.

The pleasure I take in this confession, and the fear I feel when speaking honestly about myself—together, they lead me to a serious and important insight that I would now like to share with you. I would like to propose a simple theory that begins with the idea that writing is a solace, even a remedy, at least for novelists like me: we choose our subjects, and shape our novels, to suit our daily daydream requirements. A novel is inspired by ideas, passions, furies, and desires—this we all know. To please our lovers, to belittle our enemies, to speak of something we adore, to delight in speaking knowledgeably of something about which we know nothing, to take pleasure in times lost and remembered, to dream of making love, or reading, or engaging with politics, to indulge in one's particular worries, one's personal habits—these and any number of other obscure or even nonsensical desires are what shape us, in ways both clear and mysterious. These same desires drive the daydreams of which we speak. We may not understand where they come from, and we may not understand what our daydreams signify, but when we sit down to write, it is our daydreams that breathe life into us like a wind from an unknown quarter. One might even say that we surrender to this mysterious wind like a captain who has no idea where he's bound. . . .

But at the same time, in one part of our minds, we can pinpoint our location on the map exactly, just as we can remember the point toward which we are traveling. Even at those times when I surrender uncondition-ally to the wind, I am able, at least according to some other writers I know and admire, to retain my general sense of direction. Before I set out, I will have made plans, divided the story I wish to tell into sections, determined what ports my ship will visit, what loads it will carry and drop off along the way, estimated the time of my journey, and charted its course on the map. But if the wind, having blown in from unknown quarters and filled my sails, decides to change the course of my story, I will not fight it. For what the ship with full sails seeks is a feeling of wholeness and perfection. It is as if I am looking for that special place and time in which everything flows into everything else, everything is linked, and everything is aware of everything else. All at once, the wind will die away and I will find myself becalmed in a place where nothing moves. I'll sense that there are things in these calm and misty waters that will, if I am patient, move the novel forward. . . . What I most long for is the sort of spiritual inspiration I described in my novel *Snow*. It is not dissimilar to the sort of inspiration Coleridge described in his poem "Kubla Khan." I also long for inspiration to come to me (as poems do to Coleridge and to Ka, *Snow*'s hero) in dramatic ways, preferably in scenes and situations that might sit well in a novel. If I wait patiently and attentively, my dream comes true. To write a novel is to be open to these desires, winds, and inspirations, to the dark recesses of our minds and their moments of mist and stillness.

For what is a novel but a story that fills its sails with these winds, that answers and builds upon inspirations that blow in from unknown quarters and seizes upon all the daydreams we've invented for our diversion, bringing them together into a meaningful whole—a story? Above all, a novel is a basket that carries inside it a dreamworld we wish to keep forever alive, and forever ready. Novels are held together by the little pieces of daydreams that help us, from the moment we enter them, forget the tedious world we long to escape. The more we write, the richer these dreams become; and the more we write, that second world inside the basket becomes broader, more detailed, more complete. We come to know this world through writing, and the better we know it, the easier it is to carry it around in our heads. If I am in the middle of a novel and writing well, I can enter easily into its dreams. For novels are new worlds into which we enter happily through reading, or even more by writing: novelists shape them in such a way that they can carry the dreams they wish to elaborate, and with great ease. Just as they offer happiness to the good reader, so, too, do they offer the good writer a solid and sound new world in which he can lose himself and seek happiness at any hour of the day. If I've been able to create even a tiny part of this miraculous world,

I feel happy the moment I reach my desk, my pen, and my paper. In no time at all I can leave behind the familiar, boring world of the everyday and step into this other, bigger place to wander freely, and most of the time I have no desire to return to real life or to reach the end of the novel. This feeling is, I think, related to the good reader's response upon hearing that I am writing a new novel: "Please make your novel really long!" I am proud to boast that I hear this a thousand times more often than the bad publisher's entreaty: "Make it short!"

How is it that a habit made from a single person's joys and pleasures can produce a work that interests so many others? Readers of *My Name Is Red* like to recall Şeküre's remarks to the effect that trying to explain everything is a sort of idiocy. My own sympathies in this scene are not with Orhan, my little hero and namesake, but the mother who is gently poking fun at him. But if you will permit me to commit another idiocy, and act like Orhan, I'd like to try to explain why dreams that work as medicine for the writer can serve the same purpose for the reader: because if I am entirely inside the novel and writing well—if I have distanced myself from the ringing phone, from all the troubles and demands and tedium of everyday life—the rules by which my free-floating heaven operates recall the games I played as a child. It is as if everything has become simpler, as if I am in a simpler world where I can see into every house, car, ship, and building because they are all made of glass, because they have begun to tell me their secrets. My job is to divine the rules and listen: to watch with pleasure the goings-on in each interior, to step into cars and buses with my heroes and to travel about Istanbul, visiting places that have come to bore me to tears and seeing them with new eyes, and in so doing, transforming them; my job is to have fun, be irresponsible, because while I'm amusing myself (as we like to say of children), I might just learn something.

An imaginative novelist's greatest virtue is his ability to forget the world in the way a child does, to be irresponsible and delight in it, to play around with the rules of the known world—but at the same time to see through his freewheeling flights of fancy to the deep responsibility that will later allow readers to lose themselves entirely in his novel. He might be spending the whole day playing, but at the same time he carries the deepest conviction that he is more serious than others. This is because he can be looking directly into the center of things the way that only children can. Having found the courage to set rules for the games he once played freely, he senses that his readers will also allow themselves to be drawn into the same rules, the same language, the same sentences, and therefore the story. To write well is to allow the reader to say, "I was going to say the same thing myself, but I couldn't allow myself to be that childish."

This world I explore and create and enlarge, making up the rules as I go, waiting for my sails to fill with a wind from an unknown quarter and poring over my map—it is born of childlike innocence that is at times closed to me. This happens to all writers. A point arrives when I get stuck, or I will go back to the point in the novel where I've left off some time before and find that I am unable to pick it up again. Such afflictions are commonplace, and I may suffer from them less than other writers: if I can't pick up where I left off, I can always turn instead to another gap in the novel; because I've studied my map very carefully, I can begin writing in another section of the novel. This is not so important. But this autumn, while I was grappling with various political matters and running into the same problem, I felt as if I'd discovered something that also casts light on novel-writing. Let me try to explain what I mean.

The case that was brought against me, and the political quandaries inside which I then found myself, turned me into a far more "political," "serious," and "responsible" person than I wanted to be. A sad state of affairs, and an even sadder state of mind—let me say it with a smile. This was why I was unable to enter into that childlike innocence without which no novel is possible . . . but this was easy to understand, it didn't surprise me. As the events slowly unfolded, I would tell myself that my fast-vanishing "spirit of irresponsibility," my childish sense of play and childish sense of humor, would one day return, and that I would then be able to finish the novel I'd been working on for three years. Nevertheless, I would still get up every morning, long before Istanbul's other ten million inhabitants, and try to enter into the novel that was sitting unfinished in the silence of midnight. I was exerting myself because I so longed to get back into my beloved second world. After exerting myself greatly, I'd begin to pull bits of the novel I wished to write from my head, and I'd see them playing themselves out before me. But these were not from the novel I was writing—they were scenes from an entirely different novel. On those tedious, joyless mornings, what passed before my eyes was not the novel on which I'd been working for three years but an ever-growing body of scenes, sentences, characters, and strange details from some other novel. After a while, I began to set down the fragments of this other novel in a notebook, and I noted down thoughts that I had never before entertained. This other novel would be about the paintings of a deceased contemporary artist. As I conjured up this painter, however, I found myself thinking just as much about his paintings. After a while longer, I understood why I'd been unable to recapture the child's spirit of irresponsibility during those tedious days. I could no longer return to childishness, I could only return to my childhood, to the days when (as I described in *Istanbul*) I dreamed of becoming an artist and spent my days doing one painting after another.

Later on, the case against me was dropped, and I returned to *The Museum of Innocence*, the novel on which I had already spent three years. Today I am planning this other novel that came to me scene by scene during those days when, unable to return to childishness, I returned instead to the passions of my childhood. But this experience taught me something important about the mysterious art of writing novels.

I can explain this by taking "the implied reader"—a principle put forward by the great literary critic and theorist Wolfgang Iser—and twisting it to my own ends. Iser created a brilliant reader-oriented literary theory. He said that a novel's meaning resides not in the text, nor in its context, but somewhere between the two. He argues that a novel's meaning emerges only as it is read, and so when he speaks of the implied reader, he is assigning him or her a special role.

When I was dreaming up the scenes, sentences, and details of another book, instead of continuing the novel I was already writing, it was this theory that came back into my mind, and what it suggested to me was this: for every unwritten but dreamed and planned novel (in other words, my own unfinished novel), there must be an implied author. So I would only be able to finish that book when I'd become that book's implied author. But when I was immersed in political affairs, or—as happens so often in the course of normal life—my thoughts were too often interrupted by unpaid gas bills, ringing telephones, and family gatherings, I was unable to become the author implied by the book in my dreams. During those long and tedious days of politicking, I could not become the implied author of the marvelous book I longed to write. Then those days passed, and I returned to my novel, just as I had so longed to do, and whenever I think how close I am to finishing it, I feel happy too (the novel is a love story that takes place between 1975 and the present, among the rich of Istanbul or, as the papers like to call it, "Istanbul society"). But having come through this experience, I have understood why, for thirty years, I have devoted all my strength to becoming the implied author of the books I long to write. This may be important to me because I only want to write big, thick, ambitious novels, and because I write so very slowly. It is not difficult to dream a book. I do this a lot, just as I spend a great deal of time imagining myself as someone else. The difficult thing is to be your dream book's implied author.

But let's not complain. Having published seven novels, I can safely say that, even if it takes some effort, I am able to become the author who can write the books in my dreams. Just as I've written books and left them behind me, so, too, have I left behind me the ghosts of the writers who could write those books. All seven of these implied authors resemble me, and over the past thirty years they have come to know life and the world as seen from Istanbul, as seen from a window like mine, and because they know this world inside out and are convinced by it, they can describe it with all the seriousness and responsibility of a child at play.

My greatest hope is to be able to write novels for another thirty years, and to use this excuse to wrap myself up in other new personas.

ISTANBUL

Turkish novelist, essayist, and screenwriter Orhan Pamuk (b. 1952) was the University of Oklahoma's 2006 Puterbaugh Fellow and won the Nobel Prize in Literature later that year. His books have been translated into more than sixty languages.

An author, translator, and professor of English and comparative literary studies at the University of Warwick, Maureen Freely has served as president and chair of English PEN.

PART II

FIRST TAKES
ON MODERN CLASSICS

1926–1975

RED CAVALRY (1926)

ISAAC BABEL

General Budjonny is the almost mythical figure who led the Cossack cavalry for Soviet Russia and swept Poland with terror. In the thirty short sketches assembled into this volume, passing moments of this war are preserved. The Cossacks, madly gallant and beastly cruel, appear in their more tender moments as well as at their worst, together with the whole scenario of a war wherein heroes, after having besmeared themselves with blood, make love to an old woman (or beat her) to get a few onions to appease their hunger. They quarrel, die, make love, complain, tell stories in a century that makes use of Fount-le-Roy's armored airplanes and the wireless, in the primitive naïveté in which their ancestors did the same under Taras Bulba. The author is one of the few who never talk, but create; whether his creation be the son of a rabbi, the last prince of an old dynasty, dying amidst the starving peasants he led, or a poor woman who tries to traffic with salt, and who curses the Soviets wherefore she is duly murdered. A book which should be translated into English—though it would doubtless be suppressed.

WALTER KIEN, JULY 1928

Reviewed in the German, which was translated from Russian by Dimitrij Vmanskij; *Budjonnys Reiterarmee* was translated into English by John Harland in 1929.

STEPPENWOLF (1927)

HERMANN HESSE

The human and wolfish natures of Harry Haller are so actively hostile toward each other that he longs for such sufferings as will make him rejoice in death. Then come idealized sordid contacts with jazz and demi-mondaine society, the bewildering fury of which helps bring him to his senses by way of a fantastic dreamland. Until that moment Harry calls himself the "Steppenwolf" who has strayed into a strange, non-understanding, reactionary world of pseudo-art and practical culture, that is no culture at all. He likes himself no better than he does the world, all of whose vices he represents. Although realizing that the "Bürger" best maintains his ego by virtue of social safeguards, the Steppenwolf scorns all compromise and will never exchange his life for that of a Philistine opportunist. At the cost of his ego he prefers to live in intensely heroic fashion, a foolish Don Quixote whose real service is not appreciated by a ridiculing and ridiculous bourgeoisie society. At the end the problem of the ego is solved—one feels that—and one hopefully suspects that something more pleasant, more universal, and more balanced may now come from the pen of Hermann Hesse.

W. A. WILLIBRAND, JULY 1928

Reviewed in the German; *Der Steppenwolf* was translated into English by Basil Creighton in 1929.

GYPSY BALLADS   (1928)

FEDERICO GARCÍA LORCA

García Lorca has given us eighteen longer or shorter groups of poems, each one dedicated to one of his friends. The last three are labeled *Tres romances históricos*; and all of them live up to the title of the book. With one exception the eight-syllable "romance" verse has been used. Revista de Occidente has put out this volume with characteristic attractive finish, while the author has not only caught well the form of the ballad, but has thoroughly imbued his verses with what strikes one as the real "gitano" spirit. Many of the lines haunt one long after reading them.

CONY STURGIS, OCT. 1929

Reviewed in the Spanish; *Primer romancero gitano* (1924–1927) was translated into English by Langston Hughes in 1951.

JENNY   (1929)

SIGRID UNDSET

This volume represents a hasty response to the demand of a startled French public which awoke to find itself without a translation of Sigrid Undset's works when she was acclaimed as the Nobel Prize winner of 1928. There remains little to add to the tributes which have poured forth in her honor. Portrayed with keen psychological insight and unshrinking realism, *Jenny*, the embodiment of feministic revolt, will rank in modern literature as the third erotic sister of *Madame Bovary* and *Anna Karenina*. It is to be hoped that the publishers will speedily complement this volume with a translation of *Kristin Lavransdatter*, which, written after Madame Undset's conversion to Catholicism, emphasizes the spiritual values that are so unknown to Jenny.

ETHEL LYONS, JULY 1930

Reviewed in the French, which was translated from Swedish by Gaston Bataille; *Jenny* was translated into English by William Emmé in 1921.

TALA   (1938)

GABRIELA MISTRAL

This collection of poems is remarkable for a number of reasons. In the first place, it represents the latest, most mature work of a writer who is, possibly, Latin America's greatest woman poet, and who here exhibits an art that deepens with an ever-deepening humanity. This for the poetic heft and content. Externally, the volume takes on an added significance by reason of the fact that, through an arrangement with Victoria Ocampo, of *Sur*, the proceeds of the book are to go for the relief of Basque Catholic orphans, victims of Franco-Hitler *Schrecklichkeit*. The poems throughout have a fire which, one cannot help feeling, owes much to this dedication of purpose. A third feature of *Tala* is the author's notes to various pieces, in which she reveals the high degree of aesthetic awareness that guides her expert hand.

SAMUEL PUTNAM, WINTER 1939

Reviewed in the Spanish; *Tala* has not yet been translated into English.

THE CASTLE   (1941)

FRANZ KAFKA

It is extremely gratifying to see the Muirs' impeccable translation of Kafka's principal work reprinted after having been out of circulation for eleven years. *The Castle* is one of the world's works of imagination, despite the fact that superficially it deals with the rather pedestrian story of a poor devil of a land surveyor who, lured by the promise of a job, comes from some remote province only to learn that it is all a mistake, and ending his quest, alas, servant to a schoolmaster. This bitter joke is played against a background of such mystery and suspense that the reader is embezzled into a fascinating maze of guessing and evocation.

Kafka's tale is told with utter simplicity and realism, and the avalanche of *a posteriori* interpretations that has piled around this pristine creation would surely have amused and amazed him. Max Brod, for instance, sees in *The Castle* a grand tragedy of metaphysical forces: "two manifested forms of the Godhead (in the sense of *The Cabbala*), justice and grace," etc., and brings to bear Kierkegaard's *Fear and Trembling*. Kafka is a writer who should be read before being read about. His works have many facets, but most of his critics see in them only themselves, as Thomas Mann does when he compares Kafka with Tonio Kröger. As someone once said of Cervantes, he had several things in his mind when he wrote, but unfortunately most of his commentators do not have that faculty. And Kafka should be read in his entirety (surely no one who had read his short stories—*The Metamorphosis* or *The Hunger-Artist*, for instance—could possibly describe him as a "religious humorist").

This new edition of *The Castle* contains a brief homage by Thomas Mann. Edwin Muir's introduction to the first American edition has been put at the back, but otherwise no changes have been made. Brod's postscript to the first edition, quoting one or two deleted passages and promising a supplementary volume of *The Castle*'s unfinished final chapters, remains buried at the end of the book, quietly, as if eleven years of waiting had not gone by since the promise first was made.

ANGEL FLORES, AUTUMN 1941

The Castle was translated from the German by Edwin and Willa Muir.

THREE RUSSIAN POETS   (1944)

PUSHKIN, LERMONTOV, TYUTCHEV

"Good translations of poetry are extremely rare. Good translations of Russian poetry into English are almost nonexistent," justly remarks the jacket of this profitable little volume. Its further declaration that "these selections from the great Russians (are) versions which succeed in being exceptional English poems in their own right," is also true—often if not always. Lines like

> *Deep in the desert's misery,*
> *far in the fury of the sand,*

from Mr. Nabokov's version of Pushkin's *The Upas Tree*; even such whole stanzas as

> *Heavy and near the sky had seemed.*
> *But now the stars are rising high;*
> *they glow and with their humid heads*
> *push up the ceiling of the sky,*

from Tyutchev's *Nightfall*; such phrases as

> *. . . a remnant of blue smoke*
> *spread to bright trees repainted by the*
> *rain—*

are certainly as thrillingly faultless as the most untrammeled original verse. If there are a good many lame lines among the lithe ones, we still owe the translator a debt of gratitude for showing us how satisfying Russian poetry at its best can be. Mr. Nabokov has added a short biographical comment on each of the three poets, and couched as they are in his characteristic *pince-sans-rire* prose, those comments are not mere footnotes but stand on their own sturdy legs.

An extraordinary item is the retranslation from Pushkin's Russian version of a scene from Christopher North's 1816 play *The City of the Plague*. How much of the new English version is due to Pushkin and how much to the other poet Vladimir Nabokov, is unknown to the reviewer, but a comparison of North and Nabokov is an object-lesson in the mutations of the Muse since the days of Keats and Shelley.

ROY TEMPLE HOUSE, WINTER 1946

Three Russian Poets was translated from the Russian by Vladimir Nabokov.

THE STRANGER   (1946)

ALBERT CAMUS

Let us brush aside the shibboleth Existentialism, and the tremulous impressive shades of Kierkegaard and Heidegger. Albert Camus is himself, and he demands to be appraised on his own merits. In his Sisyphus, he has given a quasi-Pascalian conception of the Absurd: man is greater than the absurd world that crushes him, for he is conscious of its absurdity.

In this case, which is absurd, Meursault or the world? Meursault, a modest clerk in an Algiers firm, seems as commonplace as Duhamel's Salavin. But Salavin is haunted with a desire for saintliness. Meursault has no inclination to conform, no urge to rebel. He is completely alien to our conventions. Because he is a stranger, because he does not react in the expected way, this quiet inoffensive being is considered as a monster. Implicated in a crime through the merest chance, he appears as the born criminal, and is condemned. He has one sudden flare of anger, as though he would at least like to reason out his absurd situation; but he soon relapses into his placid submission. He will be killed as cattle are slaughtered, without understanding and without caring. No saint, no genius, no hero, no martyr: an elemental man, not endowed with the mimetic impulse to pretend. But there can be no action without acting. To count in the world, you have to play a part. Because he could not act, because he was purely himself, Meursault was nothing.

I cannot suggest all the philosophical implications of this brief tale. It is written with the classic purity of André Gide; and it can be read with the same interest as a Simenon.

ALBERT GUÉRARD, SPRING 1947

Reviewed in the French; *L'étranger* was translated into English by Stuart Gilbert in 1946.

MEMOIRS OF HADRIAN   (1951)

MARGUERITE YOURCENAR

Only by stressing and straining the accepted criteria for classification by literary genres could this complexly constructed and yet beautifully integrated miscellany be listed as a historical novel, although the author herself refers to her remarkable piece of writing as such. The work has won her the 1952 Prix Femina, a well-deserved distinction; in fact, an even more prominent recognition would seem in order to sanction the value of this outstanding document. If it were to be compared at all with similar attempts like, for instance, Thornton Wilder's *The Ides of March*, it would for quite some time remain ahead of an ever more crowded field.

Impressively well written, the work combines the features of poetized and dramatized biography and the philosophical essay, the latter owing much to insights of "modern" psychology and sociology. It is presented in the form of a fictional letter addressed by the ailing emperor to his successor, followed by a fictionized account of the life and rule of one who knows after the doctor's verdict that his time has come to "entrer dans la mort les yeux ouverts." Widely read on her subject, displaying every evidence of solid and brilliant scholarship, the author quite legitimately takes advantage of the poet's privilege of subjective interpretation. She does not hesitate to introduce unhistoric persons and to lead historic ones to climaxes unauthorized by historic facts.

The result is the beautifully conveyed and bewitchingly convincing "inner truth" of the hero, distilled into his essence as an utterly humane man and efficiently wise ruler. Here is as attractive a picture of the "good tyrant" as ever projected. Yourcenar's Hadrian becomes the embodiment and symbol, the sum total of the conflicting human poles of virtue and vice, striving and resignation, progressiveness and conservatism. He is as aware of his own and his world's potentialities as of their limitations, and movingly endowed with the gift for spiritual transcending of the barriers of nature and society.

ERNST ERICH NOTH, WINTER 1953

Reviewed in the French; *Mémoires d'Hadrien* was translated into English by Grace Frick in 1954.

THE LOST STEPS   (1953)

ALEJO CARPENTIER

Alejo Carpentier is a Hispanized Frenchman who has spent most of his adult life in Cuba and Venezuela. He is the author of two other novels, one dealing with Afro-Cuban traditions and another with Haiti. His third and best, *Los pasos perdidos*, is based on an actual trip he took to unexplored regions near the headwaters of the Orinoco. The book has a semi-documentary flavor plus a sophisticated intellectual texture. The leading figure, in flight from civilization, tries to find himself in the depths of man's past.

Carpentier has meditated upon the meaning of culture and civilization and brings a rich and varied background to this adventure in time. Throughout the book runs a secondary theme, an investigation into the meaning and history of music. The author has re-created the jungle and primitive peoples sensuously and colorfully with the perceptions of a poet. There is violence in the book, as well as atmosphere and intellectual interest. *Green Mansions*, as it might have been written by André Gide, is not an exact comparison, but it serves as an image to suggest the character of the writing. An unusual and provocative novel which ought to be translated into English.

H. R. HAYS, SPRING 1956

Reviewed in the Spanish; *Los pasos perdidos* was translated into English by Harriet de Onís in 1956.

WAITING FOR GODOT   (1954)

SAMUEL BECKETT

This beautifully printed little volume is a "Tragicomedy in Two Acts" originally written in French by Samuel Beckett, an Irishman, one-time secretary to James Joyce, who here assumes the delicate pleasure of translating himself into his native tongue. Beckett's personal transplantation to France has the force of a literary gesture. *Waiting for Godot*, for example, shows the world in exile, waiting for the deliverer of a safe return. But desire for return has been corroded by long helplessness and lethargy; so the world is made up of tramps and madmen—of boredom, cruelty, horror. Nothing happens. "They do not move" is the final stage direction. And the Kafka world remains transfixed.

HARRIET ZINNES, SUMMER 1955

PEDRO PÁRAMO   (1955)

JUAN RULFO

Here is something out of the ordinary, a "stream of consciousness" work with picaresque eddies and skin-prickling supernatural ripples. The reader swims, floats, is dragged into depths of old memories, is thrown into the maelstrom of a world apparently that of the earthbound dead. Indeed, in the middle of the story the main figure, Juan Preciado, dies; thereafter, there is a psychic identification of father and son, with interest centered on the father, Pedro Páramo. This odd biography of a *cacique* vividly describes the interwoven lives of the humble people under his tyrannical rule. The underdeveloped literary ability dimly seen in Rulfo's collection of short stories, *El llano en llamas y otros cuentos*, leaps full-grown before our interested gaze.

Rulfo has succeeded in concocting a style all his own. Throughout the often poetic prose descriptions are found love of nature and a constant recurrence of the water motif. The "crossed narrative" technique keeps the reader engrossed—when those conversing are the dead in their graves! The setting is Comala, a town "as hot as though it were at the gates of Hell; indeed, many who go to Hell return to Comala for a blanket." This novel cannot be lightly read; vaguely posed questions furnish food for thought. Rulfo's work is one of the best which has come our way recently, and it provides a refreshing change. Mechanically speaking, the edition is excellent.

ALBERTA WILSON SERVER, SUMMER 1956

Reviewed in the Spanish; *Pedro Páramo* was translated into English by Lysander Kemp in 1959.

THE TIN DRUM   (1959)

GÜNTER GRASS

This ambitiously conceived, lengthy novel has apparently produced a commotion in German literary circles and caused a frowning reaction from the representatives of *Wirtschaftswunder* mentality. But any charge of sensationalism, blasphemy, or cult of the decadent fails to consider the work in its totality.

This trilogy is unmistakably a postwar novel; not because the third book takes us to reconstructed Düsseldorf, but because of its spirit, perhaps best linked to existentialist skepticism. Grass's anguish takes on the shape of a drum on which he beats out the senselessness of human behavior and the delusion of historical significance. Oscar Bronski-Mazerath, the eternally three-year-old drummer, refuses to grow up into a world inhabited by his Polish-German family in Danzig and especially the larger world, made up in succession of an imperialistic bourgeoisie, *Freistadt* Danzig mercantile spirit, Nazi storm troopers, Polish lancers charging gallantly against tanks, the elusive *Endsieg*, Russian occupation, black marketeering in West Germany, *Aufbau*, and middle-class prosperity, American style. From his unique position Oscar the drummer records with ironic detachment how stupidity, savagery, empty traditionalism, and the seven deadly sins are perpetuated from one generation to the next, abetted by political, social, and religious institutions.

Grass's all-pervading ironic mood is sustained by the skillful manipulation of unconventional syntax, daring imagery, and choice of vocabulary, revealing the poet beneath the prose writer. Like any great novelist, he possesses the gift to breathe life into his creations, presenting full-blown, at times fantastic, yet always convincingly human characters who propagate their follies and disillusion. *Die Blechtrommel* is a *Dichtung* that will fascinate the attentive reader.

H. E. LEWALD, AUTUMN 1961

Reviewed in the German; *Die Blechtrommel* was translated into English by Ralph Manheim in 1962.

TOWARDS UNIVERSAL MAN   (1961)

RABINDRANATH TAGORE

This is a selection of eighteen essays from the pen of the man who can be considered the culmination of India's renascence, translated from the original Bengali by eminent Indians. Poet, novelist, short-story writer, dramatist, artist, musician, educationalist, political, economic and social reformer, philosopher—Tagore exemplified the Renaissance Man. This volume has been issued by the Tagore Commemorative Volume Society of New Delhi in collaboration with the Ford Foundation, on the occasion of the Master's hundredth birthday anniversary. The selections, which concentrate upon Tagore's thoughts on contemporary social problems, emphasize his role as one of India's leading social pioneers. The notes comment briefly on the background to each of the selections. This invaluable contribution to our knowledge of Tagore's works is a result of the selfless exertions of the Tagore Society and its associates, under the leadership of Bengal's distinguished scholar—now the Indian Minister for Culture and Scientific Research—Professor Humayun Kabir, with the eminent author Bhabani Bhattacharya as the editor and chief translator.

ERNEST BENDER, AUTUMN 1961

A HOUSE FOR MR. BISWAS   (1961)

V. S. NAIPAUL

With *The Mystic Masseur*, Naipaul won the John Llewellyn Rhys Memorial Prize for 1957; with *Miguel Street*, the 1961 Somerset Maugham Award.

This novel—the lifetime of one Mr. Biswas—is a panorama of East Indian family life in Trinidad. Mr. Biswas feels stifled by orthodoxy, poverty, and the duties of family relationships. Marriage increases the same by a dreadful ratio. Each way he runs, to books and writing, to losing himself in love-play, to asserting his place in the family, turns out to be another trap. From these incredible pressures and despite a mental breakdown, Mr. Biswas struggles to success—ownership of a home. He has refuge.

Naipaul gives dignity and beauty to what would seem to the casual observer a bizarre conglomeration of cultures. Little can be indicated of the depth and sparkle, compassion and irony that flows so sweetly from this pen. It is the work of a young genius.

LEONA BELL BAGAI, AUTUMN 1962

REQUIEM   (1963)

ANNA AKHMATOVA

The history of this booklet of verses reminds us, in part, of Pasternak's *Doctor Zhivago*: it also appeared only in the West and was passed over in silence in its homeland. Unlike Pasternak's novel, however, these verses reached the West "without knowledge and agreement of the author," as their publisher, the Association of Russian Writers Abroad, in Munich stresses.

The author, Anna Akhmatova, is the oldest Russian woman poet (born in 1889). She developed creatively in the first two decades of this century, which sometimes are called "the Silver Age of Russian poetry." At the same time as the Symbolist, there was then a multitude of poetic currents and experiments, later extinguished by the October catastrophe. Akhmatova herself belonged to so-called Acmeism, a literary movement led by N. Gumiliov, her husband, shot by a Soviet punitive squad in 1921.

Fourteen small poems, united by the title "Requiem," constitute a reflection of the terrible Thirties, the time of the most cruel police license and terror. [. . .] The Stalinist theoretician of the Party line in literature and arts, A. Zhdanov, subjected Akhmatova as well as her work, in his speeches, to savage and humiliating criticism as "vicious and unnecessary to the Soviet people." Soon afterward her son was arrested. [. . .]

Akhmatova's *Rekviem* reflects the tragedy of many thousands of other Russian women, suffering the loss of their nearest ones. So writes Akhmatova about it in the preface to the booklet:

> In the terrible years of the Yezhov terror I spent seventeen months in the prison lines in Leningrad. It happened that once someone recognized me. Then a woman with blue lips standing behind me who, of course, had never heard my name, broke loose from the insensibility so typical of us all and asked silently (we all whispered there):
>   —You can describe this?
> And I answered:
>   —I do.

Akhmatova kept her promise. She transmitted the experiences of the other women, standing "in the terrible cold and in the heat of July" under the walls of Kresty, the prison of Leningrad. [. . .]

The tragedy of the fourteen poems of the collection, written in this classically clear language, warmed by the spiritual expressiveness, so uniquely mastered by Akhmatova, is sharply felt by the reader. However, this tragedy is not only in the pain of those who survived; inwardly the poetry is directed in general toward the innumerable victims of the Stalinian terror over whose memory the official Soviet "rehabilitation" of our days passes in silence. This is, probably, also the reason why the booklet could not appear in the homeland of the author who dared so convincingly to recall these nameless victims by her poetical "Requiem aeternam dona eis . . ."

LEONID D. RZHEVSKY, SUMMER 1964

Reviewed in the Russian; *Rekviem* was translated into English by Stanley Kunitz with Max Hayward in 1973.

ONE DAY IN THE LIFE OF IVAN DENISOVICH   (1963)

ALEKSANDR SOLZHENITSYN

This photostat enables the Western Russicists to acquire the text, now out of print, published in the Moscow review *Novyj Mir* in November 1962. Two English translations are already available (*One Day in the Life of Ivan Denisovich*, 1963), between which this reviewer slightly prefers Ralph Parker (Dutton edition) over Max Hayward and Ronald Hingley (Praeger). Thanks to a greater simplicity of Solzhenitsyn's diction, the translators' haste does less harm to his work than it caused, not so long ago, to Pasternak's *Doctor Zhivago*.

The Western world, used to and long since tired of the German concentration camp literature, will hardly discover, on the strictly literary level, much more, if anything, new in the no doubt talented Russian writer's first book than it had found in the best Western works of this thematical inspiration. Yet Solzhenitsyn, in his presentation of a single day in the life of a victim of Communist justice, shows an admirable artistic restraint that makes this immensely important and consequential document a work of art.

There have been other books dealing with the Soviet camps published in the West—though literarily inferior to Solzhenitsyn's—but none of them appeared in the Soviet Union. It would be a great step forward, even for the Western reader, if this tale should help him to realize once again the value of freedom, as it will not fail to show to millions of Russians.

ROBERT VLACH, SPRING 1963

Reviewed in the Russian; *Odin den' Ivana Denisovica* was translated into English by Ralph Parker in 1963.

A SEASON IN THE CONGO   (1966)

AIMÉ CÉSAIRE

Most festivals have their little scandal or commotion. In the fall of 1965, during the twentieth "Week of Sacred Music" at Perugia, a small political disturbance was created around *Requiem for Lumumba* (a secular, Brechtian composition by Paul Dessau, on a text by Karl Mickel, prologue by Sartre), thus guaranteeing it a success which, some critics say, was not fully deserved artistically. In 1966 Césaire published the play *Une saison au Congo*, then rushed to Dakar to be a judge at the Festival of Negro-African

Cinema. There seems to be a thread connecting those three separate and little-known events, which students of Africa might explore with profit. It is sufficient to state here that *Une saison* is of musical and cinematic structure and could also have been titled *Requiem pour Lumumba*.

Our century has produced few political heroes; excepting Churchill, modern mythology and hagiology have included only those men who died prematurely, generally by assassination: Jaurès, Lenin, Albert of Belgium, Trotsky, Gandhi, Kennedy—and Lumumba. This is an old historical pattern which has become quite pronounced in modern times; longevity, especially political, carries the price of cult-destruction: witness Stalin, Mao, or De Gaulle. Patrice Lumumba has remained, for many westerners, a shadowy, ambivalent figure, but for the Negro-African circle, its allies and its sympathizers, Lumumba is the African hero par excellence. Césaire's play follows, in a linear and episodic fashion, Lumumba's life from shortly before the Independence of the Congo to his death. The core is the Passion of the Martyr, "martyr" being used here both in the ordinary sense of "sufferer" and in its etymological meaning of "witness." For Césaire's Lumumba bears witness to an impassioned vision of Africa. Behind the speeches of the modern leader lies a poetic, almost bucolic conception of Africa. The Congo here is not "a region of the mind" (Graham Greene) but a vast area of the heart.

Césaire operates in several registers: still-unfinished history, Patrice the man, Lumumba the visionary, fact and symbol, all mix and interact. For many westerners there will be difficulties, even losses, in following the play, because our knowledge of African affairs is inadequate. To some extent Césaire, as he had done in his *Toussaint Louverture* and his splendid *Tragédie du Roi Christophe*, for Haitian history, here calls our attention to African history. At the very least we will rethink Lumumba and his world, our world. [. . .]

Above all, Césaire is a poet, the finest "de langue noire." His *Saison* obviously derives its title from Rimbaud's *Season in Hell*, but does not, simplistically, equate the Congo with Hell. It poetizes it, through a diversity of styles, meters, and structures: prose poetry, comic alexandrines, native chants, which result in a vigorous entity full of planned confusion, unified at the top by the poet's lyricism and conviction.

The play, composed like a score, has three acts and twenty-eight short scenes set in many locales; it is unconcerned with practical considerations of staging. To my knowledge it has not been performed. It is not, in fact, exciting reading unless one supplies the sounds and sights in one's mind and envisions patterns, group movements of *ballets africains* quality. This is not so much a play, or even *engagé* total theater, as it is a script for a film that, someday, someone might make, and show in Dakar.

EDWIN JAHIEL, SUMMER 1967

Reviewed in the French; *Une saison au Congo* was translated into English by Ralph Manheim in 1969.

ONE HUNDRED YEARS OF SOLITUDE   (1967)
GABRIEL GARCÍA MÁRQUEZ

García Márquez's literary reputation to date has been built on four works presenting various facets of life in Macondo, an imaginary town in the coastal region of the author's native Colombia. More complex and extensive than its predecessors, *Cien años de soledad* chronicles the activities, also in Macondo, of many generations of the Buendía family. The intense inner conflicts of the characters and their struggles against a hostile environment constitute a vast synthesis of social, economic, and political evils which plague much of Latin America. Although the plot remains firmly anchored on Colombian reality, what lends distinction to the novel is its scintillating, explosive style, its flights of fantasy, and its occasional black humor.

The story ends with the tempestuous love affair between the two remaining Buendías, the scholarly Aureliano and his aunt, Amaranta Ursula, who dies after giving birth to a baby with a "cola de puerco." The newborn infant's death (caused by an army of voracious insects) portends the final blow of fate which strikes Macondo in the form of a hurricane just as Aureliano deciphers the lines from a manuscript: ". . . las estirpes condenadas a cien años de soledad no tienen una segunda oportunidad sobre la tierra."

The title refers to the state of mind of the protagonists whose irrational single-mindedness leaves them both frustrated and alienated. It seems that in a society lacking in solidarity and meaningful communication one is condemned to live in solitude and to engender monsters with "colas de puerco."

Cien años de soledad is a novel of extraordinary literary merit. Its brilliant imaginative portrait of a society on the verge of chaos is both moving and significant.

GEORGE R. MCMURRAY, SPRING 1968

Reviewed in the Spanish; *Cien años de soledad* was translated into English by Gregory Rabassa in 1970.

O THE CHIMNEYS: SELECTED POEMS, INCLUDING ELI, A VERSE PLAY   (1967)

NELLY SACHS

Other than some samples in journals, this is the first major publication in English of Nelly Sachs's poetry. It is fortunate that English and American readers can now become acquainted through a bilingual edition, so beautifully and competently produced, with about half of her work. Nelly Sachs fled to Sweden in 1940 and survived by putting into words what happened to her people. She is a great Jewish poet, even greater in range than Else Lasker-Schüler and Gertrud Kolmar.

In his introduction, Hans Magnus Enzensberger calls attention to her basic imagery: flight, dust, butterfly, metamorphosis. He also very aptly describes her "greatness" as something that can neither be outlined in terms of, or compensated by, fame. There is anonymity in her greatness. She assumed, in her Swedish exile, quite consciously the voice of those no longer able to speak. Thanks to her great poetic gift and to the depth of her despair, this process was miraculously reciprocated: a nameless mass of victims are no longer unnamed and unsung because her poetry exists.

Her verse is—there is no other way, for a brief comment, to set it off against contemporary poetry—very unliterary (not only because of its principal subject matter which allows of no artificial or "literary" treatment) and thereby very unartistic. Although several poems are masterpieces of lyric poetry in themselves, this quality is to Nelly Sachs quite obviously irrelevant. Her entire *œuvre* is the overflow of her creative anguish and imagination. Thus it becomes inexhaustible, and individual interpretations will hardly ever explain its mystery. Much has been written about its cabalistic nature, about this poet's *ars combinatoria*. It is certainly true that Judaic philosophical and literary tradition have influenced and, at times, even borne this work; yet this must be seen merely as a backdrop and not as a method, just as little as the terms "simple" and "complex" will make much sense in the face of her poetry.

The publishers are to be congratulated on their decision to include the original German text. Nelly Sachs's work is not what is sometimes called untranslatable; perhaps this is so because she quite naturally eschews verbal bravado and syntactical trickery. Still, there are translations and translations. All the English texts in this selection are acceptable. Hamburger's are, in my opinion, by far the best. He consciously and modestly remains, as far as verbal sophistication is concerned, that infinitesimal step behind the original, thereby permitting the original, as it were, to reap all the honors; yet, unobtrusively and convincingly, Hamburger points out—in the language of translation—that these honors are richly deserved.

RICHARD EXNER, SPRING 1968

O the Chimneys was translated from the German by Michael Hamburger et al.

SEASON OF MIGRATION TO THE NORTH   (1969)

TAYEB SALIH

Salih's novel is a mosaic portrait of Mustafa Sa'eed, an Oxford-educated Ethiopian. Settings oscillate between the now of Effenti's (the narrator's) small Ethiopian village and the past of Sa'eed's life in London. Effenti, a government official educated abroad, puts together the puzzle of Sa'eed's crowded and violent life from Mustafa's own account and the variously colored accounts of other Africans and Englishmen. A progressively intense involvement in the meaning of Sa'eed's past unifies the fragmentary, unchronological presentation.

A melodramatic portrait emerges from the fragmentary accounts: Mustafa Sa'eed the culturally displaced African, caught between two cultures; Sa'eed the supreme egotist and calculator; Sa'eed as political economist, supporting all-Arab unity. And, hinted at and then rendered pages later in exotic detail, Sa'eed the seducer and murderer. One climactic revelation gasps about Sa'eed's violent affair with Jean Morris. The Arab stabs this young Englishwoman between the breasts while making love.

Effenti's brooding and suspenseful accumulation of details about Mustafa Sa'eed climaxes in garishly rendered glimpses of violence linked to sex. And the narrator's mounting involvement is signaled by his love-lust for Sa'eed's widow, and, following her violent death, by his penetration into Sa'eed's secret study, where he pours over Sa'eed's personal library and writings. The heavy exotic symbolism underlying this pattern of quest, mystery, violence, and sex lends little credence to the portrait of Sa'eed. Thirstings after the oasis of love, bloody sunsets, the image of the caravan, and "seeds of contagion" are examples of Salih's purple prose. And the narrator's ultimate involvement with Sa'eed as alter ego, that is, Effenti's vacillating attempt to drown his sorrow, literally, at the end—this is incredible.

DENNIS R. PASSMORE. SUMMER 1970

Season of Migration to the North was translated from the Arabic by Denys Johnson-Davies.

THE SUNS OF INDEPENDENCE (1970)

AHMADOU KOUROUMA

One of the best novels ever to come out of Black Africa, with an accent of complete authenticity blending with epic grandeur, *Les soleils des indépendances* totally captivates the reader. It does not have an axe to grind, neither negritude, nor anticolonialism, nor any political ideology. It simply and forcefully tells a human story, that of Fama Doumbouya, a fallen Malinké prince (the author also is a Malinké), who has lost everything but his pride, "health and food he had (praised be Allah!), but heart and soul were wilting away . . . under the harsh suns of independence." The novel throbs with life and swarms with the whole gamut of colors, noises, and smells of Africa. Contrasting the old and the new, it follows its hero from the capital city, where he is humiliated and useless, to his native village in the bush, where he is still a king, and through the suffering and injustice of detention camp back to the bush again, where Fama dies, the victim of both colonialism and independence, the last of a long dynasty, after a frustrating, inglorious life.

The novel is a rich fresco of African traditions and beliefs, a sort of *Mondo Cane* complete with marabouts, marketplace vendors, beggars, animal sacrifices and superstitions, masks, initiation and fertility rites, dances, funeral feasts, and endless palavers. The obvious sociological and anthropological values are enhanced by the unusual literary quality of this unique book. Most of the story is told from Fama's point of view, also from that of Salimata, his barren first wife. The narrative is steeped in oral African tradition, which establishes direct contact with the audience.

From the start, the novel bursts with refreshing images, as if translated from Malinké into French, sayings and proverbs that are the authentic voice of Africa, snatches of folk tales as old as the hills. The occasionally twisted syntax does not shock but renovates the language, and has great appeal to jaded tastes. The puzzling strangeness of chapter headings is another charm, like riddles, or minute poems in their own rights. A dynamic vitality runs through the constant flow of images taken from everyday life and from the animal world. One can also sense repressed violence and, above all, the powerful stream of life, even when rotting under the harsh sun of indifference, stupidity, or greed, the "suns of independence." One can only applaud the Canadian review *Etudes Françaises* for having awarded Ahmadou Kourouma a well-deserved literary prize.

DANIELLE CHAVY COOPER, AUTUMN 1970

Reviewed in the French; *Les soleils des indépendances* was translated into English by Adrian Adams in 1981.

ANOWA   (1970)

AMA ATA AIDOO

Anowa, both the title of the drama and the name of the tragic heroine, is the poignant story of a beautiful nineteenth-century Ghanaian girl's search for meaning. Confused by the traditional importunities of her domineering mother and her own restless, inexplicable yearnings, Anowa marries Kofi Ako, a local ne'er-do-well from a prominent family, and flees her Yebi homeland. With Anowa's manlike capacity for work and Kofi's obsession for money, they establish a lucrative trading arrangement with the white traders on the coast. However, in spite of their newly acquired wealth, their marital bliss begins to wane. Continually plagued by the thought of her estranged family, her barren womb, and the Farouk-type existence of her husband, Anowa begins to behave quite strangely. Finally, unable to find emotional fulfillment or satisfaction, she employs the permanence of self-inflicted release.

A drama in three phases, *Anowa* is simple in form and structure. Like Thornton Wilder's Stage Manager in *Our Town*, the Old Man and the Old Woman, called Being-the-Mouth-That-Eats-Salt-and-Pepper, are used to relate setting, to provide a different point of view, and to moralize upon the characters and their actions. These two personable storytellers, together with the simplicity that pervades the realistic settings, the earthy dialogue, and the dimensional characters, serve to heighten the impact of the tragic theme and its universal implications.

BOB DE MUNBRUN, SPRING 1971

FAMILY TIES   (1972)

CLARICE LISPECTOR

Centering as a rule on a single individual at a single moment in time, making frequent use of inner monologue in a profound analysis of the emotional atmosphere of that moment, the short stories of Clarice Lispector provide classic examples of existentialism in literature. Each of her protagonists is unique and totally isolated in his or her (usually her) experience of a universe hostile, or at best indifferent, to human—and animal—kind; while there is no explaining the situations in which the individuals find themselves, their responsibility for the consequences of their actions is clearly recognized. This collection shows the author at her best: the intenseness with which she concentrates on the subjects of her narratives cannot be successfully sustained in a work of novel proportions. The English translation, by Giovanni Pontiero, is eminently readable, as is his introductory essay.

R. E. DIMMICK, AUTUMN 1973

Family Ties was translated from the Portuguese by Giovanni Pontiero.

INVISIBLE CITIES   (1972)
ITALO CALVINO

Returning from each of his missions for Kublai Khan, Marco Polo gives Kublai the account of some fifty cities, each bearing a woman's name. The emperor of the Tartars listens with "curiosity and attention," though he does not believe the wonder of everything he hears. For instance, Marco describes Zenobia, a city located on dry land but built on very high piles; Armilla, where houses have no walls, ceilings, or floors, which is made by a "forest of pipelines" suspended in the air, and where nymphs and naiads abide; Eutropia, a country of many empty cities, so that when its people get bored with one, they may move to another and change everything—house, street, work, wife, parents, children, friends, et cetera; Ottavia, the cobweb city, hoisted over an abyss and tied to the tops of two mountains with ropes, chains, and gangways; Eusapia, whose citizens, in order to avoid the pain of passing from life to death, have built an underground replica of their city.

For the *Tarocchi* (1969), Calvino wrote "Il castello dei destini incrociati," a fable of knights who meet in a castle at nightfall. They are mute, and in order to communicate with each other they use the tarot pack. With each disposition of the cards, a knight narrates the story of his life. The fable is written according to the ethnological-structuralist principles of V. I. Propp and C. Lévi-Strauss, for it becomes clear that by combining the cards in different ways many lives, including the reader's and the narrator's, can be read into it. It seems to me that this fable foretells *Le città invisibili*. Since he does not know the language of Kublai Khan, Marco Polo is a "mute informer" who gives his account by "pantomimes . . . gestures, jumps, shouts of marvel or of horror . . . with objects which he pulled out of his knapsacks . . . disposing them . . . as pieces of chess." Later, "when Polo learned the language of the emperor or the emperor learned Polo's language," his essential information, expressed in words, was followed by "mute comments" in gestures. But at the end, chess becomes Polo's language. In fact, on returning from his last mission, he finds the emperor waiting for him with a chessboard, and he is asked to describe the cities visited "only through the use of chess."

Thus Calvino, a modern fabulist, creates an imaginary world where the reader playing a chess of the imagination can transmogrify cities and lives and live in a world open to all sorts of variations. *Le città invisibili* is a map of the cities of the souls, which, as Kublai Khan says, are "states of mind, states of grace, elegies."

MICHAEL RICCIARDELLI, SUMMER 1973

Reviewed in the Italian; *Le città invisibili* was translated into English by William Weaver in 1974.

THE FACTORY SHIP AND THE ABSENTEE LANDLORD   (1973)

TAKIJI KOBAYASHI

During World War I Japan suffered from numerous labor disputes, while some segments of the country appeared to prosper greatly. The nation's quick rise to international power was achieved, in fact, not without certain evils, which were found especially in the factories and farmlands. By 1917 progressive ideology had grown so much in Japan that the Russian Revolution was welcomed by many people. Some used literature to further advance the ideology. Understandably, the government tried to suppress such thoughts and activities.

The Factory Ship, generally regarded as the best "proletarian" novel of the period, was written in 1929 by Takiji Kobayashi, then a local bank clerk, who had studied economics and reached his manhood during the second decade of the twentieth century. Because of the subject matter and its treatment, the book was banned immediately after its publication and not republished in its complete form until after World War II. The work dealt with the frustrating life of laborers on a factory ship which, under the heavy guard of the Imperial Japanese Navy, processed crabs in the northern sea near Russia. There is a description of the Russian embracing the Japanese after having inspired them to engage in sabotage.

The Absentee Landlord is based on an incident in 1926, when exploited tenants protested against their landlord and won their cause. The novel, incorporating newspaper articles, various reports, and political slogans, is like a documentary with an urgent sense of social appeal. This technique was new in Japanese literature and now reminds the reader of Dos Passos's *U.S.A.*

Frank Motofuji of the University of California, Berkeley, has admirably brought these important works to the eye of Western readers. *The Cannery Boat*, an anonymous translation of *The Factory Ship*, which was published in 1933, was sadly incomplete. The new translation, based on an unabridged version, is extremely readable, having few technical flaws. The introductory essay by the translator offers a rare glimpse of the life of Takiji and the political and social conditions in which Takiji lived. This book has been accepted into the UNESCO Collection of Representative Works.

JAMES R. MORITA, SPRING 1974

The Factory Ship and *The Absentee Landlord* were translated from the Japanese by Frank Motofuji.

SELECTED POEMS   (1973)

MAHMOUD DARWISH

Tumors as symbols do not capture the attention of the Palestinian poet Mahmoud Darwish. Wounds do. And the colossal wound, of course, is Palestine—sad, captivating, real. The major images in Darwish's work draw their sustenance from the Palestinian setting and experience, from the dusty roads, the olive trees, the jasmine patches, the martyred sons, the beautiful women, the bleeding orphans, the torturing exile.

The poems translated here are selected from *Birds Without Wings* (1960), *Leaves of the Olive Tree* (1964), *Day at Night's End* (1968), *My Beloved Wakes from Her Sleep* (1969), and *The Sparrows Die in the Province of Galilee* (1970). These are Darwish's major efforts to date, and they are impressive for a man born in 1941 in Galilee. They impress, not only by the well-defined imagery and tonality that energize them, but also by the delicate allusions to the Christian and Islamic experience that inform them, by the brilliant use of irony as an obbligato, and by the power lurking in Darwish's poetic voice and revolutionary message.

Ian Wedde and Fawwaz Tuqan combined their efforts in producing a splendid volume. It seems that Tuqan, the Arab, did the literal translations and Wedde, the Britisher, cast them into poetry—very fine poetry indeed. Although such central images as those of wounds and martyrdom do not emerge as taut, they do remain tantalizing. Rare are the images that can be captured in translations without a loss of force.

The book opens with an excellent introduction to the Palestinian poet, the one-time journalist for the Communist party in Israel and the winner of the 1969 Lotus Prize awarded by the Soviet Writers' Union. As a poet of the Palestinian nation in exile, Darwish left Israel after the 1967 War and expatriated himself among the persevering refugees, the bold fedayeen, the angry intellectuals. His poetry captures the dilemma of these castes and transcends that dilemma with a unifying ideology of a struggle for personal and national identity.

Unfortunately, the book is less than elegantly designed; one poem inches next to another, creating a "poetry jam" of sorts. Too many decent poems end up choking the page. A little white space here and there would have given the work a measure of aesthetic relief.

SUHAIL IBN-SALIM HANNA, AUTUMN 1974

Selected Poems was translated from the Arabic by Ian Wedde and Fawwaz Tuqan.

THE CONSERVATIONIST (1974)

NADINE GORDIMER

The most important character in Nadine Gordimer's sixth novel is a corpse. An African has been murdered on a wealthy South African's weekend farm; the police, who do not care enough to investigate properly, merely bury the body in a shallow grave. At the end of the novel a powerful cleansing flood washes it free, and the African farmworkers restore it by a decent funeral to its rightful place in the African soil and in the consciousness of the people. This nameless corpse haunts the novel and its protagonist, an industrialist named Mehring. He cannot quite forget its presence and feels vaguely indignant at the callous attitude of policemen who cannot be bothered with murdered Africans because they cannot regard them as persons under a rule of law; but he cannot react positively to the situation because he is too involved in his own worldly success and moral complexities.

Mehring is "the conservationist." He values his farm as a refuge from the world of commerce, and he has all the appropriate attitudes toward farming properly, preventing erosion and planting trees. But he lacks an organic relationship to his land because his link to the future is tenuous. His teenage son, who may be homosexual, abandons South Africa to go to live in New York with his mother, who has divorced Mehring. At the same time Mehring is haunted by memories of his lost mistress, who plagued him with her liberal clichés and finally had to leave the country, and by a rather morbid preoccupation with young girls. Inevitably, the reappearance of the corpse shatters his confidence in himself as a weekend farmer, and he flees abroad on business while his African foreman goes about the honorable business of conducting the funeral that Mehring is too much the white "baas" to conduct himself.

Mehring is no tragic hero, but Gordimer's vision is essentially tragic. The terrible beauty of the land and the innate and patient wisdom of the Africans remain after Mehring's supreme confidence crashes to earth. But Mehring is not an evil man: the pathos of his condition is that he possesses the power to do everything except to be finally human. The moral complexity of Gordimer's vision of Mehring accounts for the rather opaque style of the novel, though that style is characteristic of much of her longer fiction. At the same time she quotes between some of her chapters brief passages from the legends of the Amazulu of South Africa, which in their clarity and simple dignity serve as appropriate commentaries on the tangled web of Mehring's predicament.

The Conservationist is a major achievement by South Africa's most distinguished resident novelist.

ROBERT L. BERNER, SUMMER 1975

DEATH AND THE KING'S HORSEMAN   (1975)

WOLE SOYINKA

Sacrifice, leadership, duty, death, and the delights of the flesh are topics which Soyinka has written about before. But he has (notoriously) not written about the colonial period. The fact that *Death and the King's Horseman* is set in Nigeria during World War II may lead some to regard it as Soyinka's play about colonialism. It is not, although Soyinka eloquently evokes the demanding and ennobling virtues of Yoruba society and examines their betrayal.

Soyinka has conflated a number of historical events in order to bring into coincidence the war, a royal visit, and the intervention of colonial forces in the (attempted) ritual suicide of the King's Horseman at Oyo in 1946. The result is a drama replete with processions, disguises, role-playing, ironies, contrasts, and, realized with Attic decorum, the attempted ritual suicide. The straw men in the Residency are poorly stuffed; their idiom and relationships do not convince. But, though disconcerting, this is not entirely a disadvantage, since they are only the smug silhouettes before which Elesin, the King's Horseman, dances toward "the abyss of transition."

Elesin fails to die at the appointed time. This is partly because of white intervention, partly because of his sensuality, and partly because he commits "the unspeakable blasphemy of seeing the hand of the gods in this alien rupture of this world." He is in the tradition of Soyinka's richest characters, the Bale and Oba Danlola, put in a position akin to that of Achebe's Ezeulu, and he finally salvages some honor in the manner of Othello. Elesin brings to life—infectious, individual life—thoughts about the responsibilities of leaders and the way in which "the world [was] set adrift and its inhabitants . . . lost."

Eyre Methuen has sensibly sacrificed some niceties of printing in the interests of economy. A text of great subtlety in which Soyinka both consolidates and innovates is available for less than one pound.

JAMES GIBBS, SPRING 1976

PART III

BOOKS AS SHIPS

THE TONGUE OF KUMĀRAJĪVA (2016)

GEET CHATURVEDI

Translated from the Hindi by Anita Gopalan

KUMĀRAJĪVA LIVED in the fourth century. The man who rendered the first known Chinese translations of the Buddhist sutras from the Sanskrit and local Pāli. Extensive translations. It won't be an exaggeration if we say that of antiquated history, he was only the greatest known translator. (Although there had been many translators before him, their names could not reach modern times. Even if they reached, they would be little known.)

It is said that his translations were so authentic, so very faithful to the original, so tightly coupled to the truth that when he died and was being cremated, the entire body burnt and became ash, but his tongue withstood the flames and did not burn.

With that tongue then Kumārajīva had, orally by virtue of spoken words, translated the sutras into Chinese.

After all these years, reverse translations of the translated texts are taking place. The original Sanskrit-Pāli treatises have been lost for good, but in the Chinese all of that has survived. Today we get to learn many things about Buddha based on English and Hindi-Sanskrit translations from Chinese.

So the tongue of Kumārajīva is present in much of what we know about Buddha today. Despite that, we know nothing about Kumārajīva. In the history of tongues, therefore, the tongue of the translator is the most selfless.

The tongue of the translator, which even fire cannot summon courage to burn.

You kill the truth, the translation of truth will come forth. You destroy the translation, still the tongue-sized piece of truth will persist. Eagerly-restlessly, hopping and bouncing, it will continue to speak its words.

Geet Chaturvedi (b. 1977) is one of the most widely read authors in contemporary Hindi literature. He has authored twelve books, including *Simsim*, which was long-listed for the JCB Prize for Literature 2023, India's richest literary award. His works have been translated into twenty-four languages.

Anita Gopalan is a translator and PEN/Heim grant recipient. Her translations from Hindi include Geet Chaturvedi's *The Memory of Now* (Anomalous Press), *Simsim* (Penguin Random House), and *The Funeral*, featured in Deep Vellum's *Best Literary Translations 2024* anthology.

WHEN DOGS COULD TALK:
AMONG WORDS IN A STATE OF GRACE   (2007)

N. SCOTT MOMADAY

MY FRIEND, the late Vine Deloria Jr., once chided me for remarking too often a time when dogs could talk. I had to admit that he was probably right. I had discovered that Kiowa elders used this formula to indicate something that had happened far back in time. This or that happened a long time ago *when dogs could talk*. It seems to me a charming and appropriate expression. It is the kind of thing that reveals more and more of itself in the fullness of time. *That*, by the way, is a mystery which distinguishes the oral tradition, and it is a foundation of language itself. Language seems always to exceed itself, and certainly it exceeds our grasp of it. We know that a certain province of experience is ineffable, that there are limits to what language can express. But the fact is, we have no inkling of what those limits might be. Lewis Thomas has told us that we are at the beginning of language. I suspect that to be true.

One evening some years ago, when my eldest daughter was two or three years old, she came to me and asked, "Daddy, is it tomorrow yet?" The question still haunts me. All these years later, I do not have the answer. But what I do have is the awareness that my daughter had come upon a very great moment in the development of her mind and curiosity. And she had shared it with me. The answer that I did not have at hand would come to her eventually in the maze of language and experience, as it had come to me. The struggle for meaning is for all of us to live with—and it is a lifelong struggle—and it is won or lost on a field of words. Language is an element, like the air, in which we live our daily lives.

I have a wonderful German shepherd. He is descended from the wolf, like every other dog in the world, but his descent is a single step. Even to his yellow eyes he resembles his wild forebear. When I look into his eyes I see the fabric of the primordial, the very face of origin. I talk to him. He seems to talk back, but not exactly in my language, not in that artificial system of sounds and symbols that my species fashioned into a superlative invention that, more than any other thing, defines the human being. He talks in the oral tradition, with silences, body language, eye contact, facial expressions, moans and growls and yelps—and of course the great semaphore of his tail.

It is no wonder that dogs should figure in the long story of man's presence on the planet. Their tenure is the same, or it is so closely alike as to be indistinguishable. There might have been a dog in the Garden of Eden, and if the serpent could talk, so could the dog. And it is no wonder that the blood memory of man should extend to a time when dogs could talk.

My first encounter with language was in an oral tradition. I have been a student of oral tradition a longer time than I can tell, and I have taught oral tradition in the classroom for nearly forty years. As a writer and, especially, a poet, language, down to the conceptual symbol of the word, fascinates me. The oral tradition is the most vital, yet the most neglected, dimension of language that I know.

What *is* the oral tradition? In the simplest sense it is language at the level of the human voice, language in the absence of writing. Most of us cannot conceive of that dimension because we inhabit a written tradition and cannot exceed its bounds. I am speaking of this society and this preeminent language community of English speakers, readers, and writers. In my teaching career, all of my students have been literate. That is, all of them could read and write in one or more languages, and none of them belonged exclusively to an oral tradition. In this context one might assume that the oral tradition is dead or dying. And yet the late Peter Farb, whose book *Word Play* is a useful introduction to oral tradition, tells us that more than half the population of the world does without writing at this moment in time. The oral tradition, then, is a universal expression of language, commensurate with the origin and development of language itself.

What are the origins of oral tradition? I suppose that we must consider that moment in which the human brain and the human vocal mechanism coincided on the scale of evolution, and man was first able to utter the sounds of intelligible speech. The formula became speak, listen, and remember. That formula, by the way, remains the cornerstone of oral tradition. It is not so with writing, in which the component of the memory, especially, is greatly diminished.

We can say, I think, that the oral tradition is as old as language itself, for the one cannot exist without the other. This symbiotic relationship enables us to name ourselves and the things around us, to tell stories, to compose poems. We are told that writing is about six thousand years old. As compared to the oral tradition, that is a mere moment in time. Thus we know something about the origins of writing, and we have the record of the printed word in the great books of the world. One cannot exaggerate the importance of that record. There is no such record of the spoken word, of course, and we can only guess at the magnitude of that loss. Nevertheless, we have something like a fossil record of the oral tradition in English, say, as we have in other languages, and we have the evidence of its persistent life in literature, even in our own time.

The place of oral tradition in literature is secure and timeless. In large measure this observation is obvious, but let me point to three works that encompass the greater range of English literary experience. *Beowulf* is the oldest extant epic poem in the English language. It is generally considered to be a distinguished model of oral tradition in almost every respect. As story, as poetry, as drama, and as a statement of the human condition, not only of its own time but also of all times, it rises to universal significance:

> The Geat people built a pyre for Beowulf, stacked and decked it until it stood four-square, hung with helmets, heavy war-shields and shining armour, just as he had ordered. Then his warriors laid him in the middle of it, mourning a lord far-famed and beloved. On a height they kindled the hugest of all funeral fires; fumes of woodsmoke billowed darkly up, the blaze roared and drowned out their weeping, wind died down and flames wrought havoc in the hot bone-house burning it to the core. They were disconsolate and wailed aloud for their lord's decease. A Geat woman too sang out in grief; with hair bound up she unburdened herself of her worst fears, a wild litany of nightmare and lament: her nation invaded, enemies on the rampage, bodies in piles, slavery and abasement. Heaven swallowed the smoke.

Hamlet hardly requires justification here. Of all the plays of Shakespeare, it is arguably the most accomplished and the most imaginative. In no other work do we see ourselves, our history and possibility, our audacious bid for immortality, more clearly. It is no wonder that the greatest writer in the English language should be a playwright. Shakespeare's language is the language of speech. The instrument of his genius is that of the human voice. It is on the stage that we see the oral tradition fully realized in our own time. Every performance is unique. Every movement of the actors, every intonation, every nuance, every silence carries the weight of meaning:

> HAMLET: Why, look you now, how unworthy a thing you make of me. You would play upon me, you would seem to know my stops, you would pluck out the heart of my mystery, you would sound me from my lowest note to the top of my compass, and there is much music, excellent voice, in this little organ, yet cannot you make it speak. 'Sblood, do you think I am easier to be played on than a pipe? Call me what instrument you will, though you fret me, you cannot play upon me.

The Gettysburg Address, like *Hamlet*, was written before it was spoken, but its vitality too is that of speech. In the deepest sense, it must be heard to be believed. Those fortunate enough to be in Gettysburg on that November day in 1863 were present at one of the truly profound performances of oral tradition in human history. For it was not less than revolutionary, what Garry Wills has called "the intellectual revolution contained in those fateful 272 words":

> It is rather for us to be here dedicated to the great task remaining before us—that from these honored dead we take increased devotion to that cause for which they gave the last full measure of devotion—that we here highly resolve that these dead shall not have died in vain—that this nation, under God, shall have a new birth of freedom—and that government of the people, by the people, for the people, shall not perish from the earth.

If we can imagine a time when dogs could talk, we must imagine a time when language was intensely creative, full of power and magic. To the extent that the deepest belief in the efficacy of language survives, it survives in the oral tradition. In *Beowulf*, or in the Book of Job, or in the Navajo Prayer from the Night Chant, the language of story is the language of poetry, plain, exalted, and oral. It is the language of surfaces rather than symbols, faceted like the bright prisms of the dragon's hoard.

Apollo—not the god but the dog—twitches in his sleep, and in his dreams he talks to me. He tells me of wonderful things, of a grandmother who suckled the founders of Rome, of a grandfather who conversed with Francis in the olive groves of Umbria, of one in whose dying eyes Aldo Leopold beheld a fierce green fire. I listen, and I am enchanted. I am returned to a time when dogs could talk, and I dwell among words in a state of grace.

JEMEZ SPRINGS, NEW MEXICO

Born in Lawton, Oklahoma, N. Scott Momaday (1934–2024) was a Kiowa novelist, short-story writer, essayist, and poet. His novel *House Made of Dawn*, awarded the Pulitzer Prize for Fiction in 1969, is considered the first major work of the Native American Renaissance. A fellow of the American Academy of Arts and Sciences, Momaday received the National Medal of Arts in 2007.

YELLOW GERANIUM IN A TIN CAN (1940s)

NÂZIM HIKMET

Translated from the Turkish by Randy Blasing & Mutlu Konuk

The prisoner Halil
closed his book.
He breathed on his glasses to clean them,
    gazed out at the orchards,
        and said:
"I don't know if you're like me, Suleiman,
But coming down the Bosporus on the ferry, say
    making the turn at Kandilli,
    and suddenly seeing Istanbul there,
or one of those sparkling nights
    of Kalamish Bay
        filled with stars and the rustle of water,
or the boundless daylight
    in the fields outside Topkapı,
or a woman's sweet face seen on a streetcar,
or even the yellow geranium I grew in a tin can
    in the Sivas prison—
I mean, whenever I meet
    with natural beauty,
I know once again
    human life today
        must be changed . . ."

Poet and playwright Nâzım Hikmet (1901–1963) is considered one of the most important Turkish writers of the twentieth century. Hikmet wrote *Human Landscapes from My Country* (the source of the text here) while serving a thirteen-year prison sentence during World War II.

Randy Blasing and Mutlu Konuk received an NEA Translation Fellowship for their translation of Hikmet's *Human Landscapes from My Country* (1982).

ARE YOU THE COLONELS NEVVY?   (1935)

EZRA POUND

RAPALLO, MAY 1, 1935
ANNO XIII, VIA MARSALA 12-5

DEAR MR. HOUSE:* Thanks for copy B/A/ recd. I dont quite make out whether you are deliberately avoiding the problem of CONDITIONING. By which I mean, whether you are facing the fact that 80% of all PRINTED matter, for the past 100 years has been affected BY ECONOMIC factor, pressure direct and indirect, conscious and unconscious. Not only authors have distorted their expression in order to please and succede, but they have grown into it.

And not in belles lettres alone. Biologists working to find remedy for pellagra, that shd/ be cheaper than food.

I also don't make out whether England is "abroad" or whether you mean to accept the hideous blanketing of all living thought, that has been practiced by the genius [Henry Seidel] Canby for 25 years.

He even confessed to puffing reputations because it wd/ be too depressing to admit that there werent first grade writers in each decade or every crop.

At any rate there is considerable element of LIVE thought that I do NOT find represented in B/ Abroad Spring issue.

Is this intentional, and part of policy, or merely due to difficulty of getting information re/ less advertised, and less commercialized European publications?

I mean do you WANT to be more effective/ or do yr/ endowers insist on damping down and restricting the current?

Is there anyone on yr/ staff who cd/ and wd/ read foreign periodicals if same wd/ exchange with you? do you mean to establish a coherent and comprehensible set of critical values, or simply to catalogue? and to have yr/ cataloguing done (restricted) by a certain grade of writer, who accepts a certain kind of "authority" and do you insist on dilletantism?

*   are you the Colonels nevvy?

Dr. House replied as follows: "We recognize a certain justice in Mr. Pound's strictures. But our original aim and the conditions under which we must work render it necessary to 'catalogue' rather than 'establish a coherent and comprehensible set of critical values,' and doom us to a degree of what Mr. Pound considers dilettantism. And as for the suspicion that our current is damped down and restricted by 'endowers,' we can only ejaculate a fervent prayer that a dilettante Providence will send us a few 'endowers,' even if they should insist on damping down our current a little" (*Books Abroad*, Summer 1935). [*Editorial note:* American diplomat Edward M. House, known as "Colonel House," was an adviser to President Woodrow Wilson.]

Considered one of the most influential English-language poets, editors, and translators of the twentieth century, Ezra Pound (1885–1972) was best known for *The Cantos*. After he supported fascist causes during World War II, the U.S. government arrested Pound for treason in 1945. Declared mentally ill, he spent a dozen years in St. Elizabeths Hospital before returning to Italy in 1958.

AMERICAN SHORT FICTION AND WORLD STORY: THE FORM READ ROUND THE WORLD (2010)

ALAN CHEUSE

WE'LL NEVER KNOW when the first preclassical rhetors or Homers sounded their earliest invocation to the Muse on the air of antique Greece. That event is lost to us in time, and only some gifted fiction writer can give us a hint of what that moment out of the prehistoric past may have been like.

Living here in history full-blown as we do now, we can confirm some facts about the origins of a much more recent literary form—the modern short story. We know that on such and such a date in the early nineteenth century, the editor of *Blackwood's* magazine in Edinburgh published a story by Edgar Allan Poe, thus bringing to the potential reading public of England, Europe, and America the first of a long line of commercial fiction. Slightly older than Poe, New Yorker Washington Irving had in 1819 published his "Rip Van Winkle" in the first volume of *The Sketch Book of Geoffrey Crayon, Gent*, a hardcover collection of tales, and a year later, in a subsequent volume of this same series, he brought out "The Legend of Sleepy Hollow." Hawthorne published his early tales in book form as well. James Fenimore Cooper published his first novel that same year.

But of all these American writers it was Poe, bent with his raving genius, his drinking problem, and his money problems, who determined to eke out a living from publishing short fiction in small commercial magazines, some of which he eventually edited. He worked at this labor some decades before Europeans such as Gustave Flaubert and later Guy de Maupassant had settled on the short-story form as a vehicle for making art that coincided with popular entertainment. More than half a century after Poe's death, the young Russian physician Anton Chekhov began publishing his first humorous sketches in Moscow literary magazines and, subsequently, a long string of short prose fiction about everyday life that most American writers identify as the model of the modern "art story." Ironically, our man Poe arrived at the form decades before.

Here it might be wise to stop for a moment and meditate on the brevity of the history of the modern story. It's a blink of the eye compared to the long gaze of the epic. Ever since the advent of the Homeric epics with their anecdotes and tale-like narratives within the larger poem, what we call "tales"—accounts or brief narratives of an event, sometimes delivered with imaginative flair—as opposed to stories, have been in plentiful supply, from the Bible to Chaucer to Boccaccio. In those brief narratives embedded in narrative poems, the source remains self-evident—all belong to the overall narration. In Boccaccio, we read tales recounted to us by the narrator. Folktales come to us out of that great mist we think of, because it is easy to do so, as the popular culture of the time.

What distinguishes all this traditional short fictional narrative from the modern short story? The nature of the artwork itself. The anecdote, the fable, the folktale—all would entertain us and, ultimately, call our attention to some moral problem or founding event in what we take to be the world of gods and history. The modern story writer, from Poe onward, seeks to create a work of short fiction that, like a lyric poem, has no immediate tie to the culture in which the writer works or to the history of his or her time. All reference to the everyday world comes by way of analogy only. The art story, as I would like to call it from here on out, is a discrete creation that possesses its own aesthetic, by which it stands or falls. We connect it to actual life in the same way we do a poem or a painting—as I mentioned, by analogy.

Looking at this from another angle, we can see that simply identifying the modern short fiction maker as a writer propels the genre into a new realm. All the myths and brief anecdotal narratives from Homer onward through the late Greek and early Roman period (except perhaps for a maverick work of prose narrative such as given us by Apuleius) clearly belong to a larger story. All else that's come before it has its root in myth or history or theology or (in the case of Boccaccio), as we get closer to our own age, what we might identify as anthropology or sociology or psychology. These older tales and stories seem to have an end other than the satisfaction of pure aesthetics—whether it is to prove a point about morality or history or the lives of city people trapped in a country setting during a time of plague.

Poe changes the direction of short narrative. He takes what otherwise might be the traditional "tale" and transforms it into a prototype of psychological fiction. Taking a cue from his own aesthetic for making poetry, he writes stories whose goal is entertainment at the highest level—stories that he hopes will serve as beautiful creations in and by themselves. His mystery stories, or his so-called ratiocinative fiction, also keep to a singular form, with the end in mind of immediate entertainment. Pieces such as "The Fall of the House of Usher" work beautifully in themselves and as illustrations of the aesthetic Aristotle holds up as a standard in the *Poetics*—the dramatic work that moves from establishing a goal to struggling to attain that goal to the final recognition or revelation.

If we hold that up as a standard, we can see that much of European short fiction before Chekhov does not always keep to the highest level or form. Once he moves from his early comic sketches into the realm of his psychological studies—taking the cue from his training as a physician, I would call them "clinical" studies—of human desire and the attempt to achieve some desired goal, Chekhov presents us with a full-blown paradigm for the modern short story. James Joyce learned from him as did, in America, Sherwood Anderson, William Faulkner, and Ernest Hemingway. I don't know any other major art form except perhaps modern dance that matured so deeply withm the span of a hundred years. From Poe to Hawthorne to Flaubert to Maupassant to Chekhov and back to the United States, the modern short story came into its full growth.

American story writers know this legacy of the art story as opposed to the popular story, though now and then, in golden periods of American publishing, the two varieties of story have overlapped. The art story, as received in the United States by Anderson and Hemingway from Chekhov himself (in translation), and Chekhov by way of James Joyce, is a discrete creation that, like a poem, is linked to reality by means of analogy rather than literal truth, or, as Marianne Moore puts it in a poem about poetry, good short fiction presents us with "imaginary gardens with real toads in them. . . ." To put it another way, in a world in which the ones and zeros of information flood over us more and more each day, short fiction remains an art of the analogue.

Though at the beginning of his career Ernest Hemingway was much more in debt to Sherwood Anderson than he ever wanted to admit, the pair of them clearly owed their aesthetic sense of how the short form works to that line going back to Joyce and Chekhov. Hemingway, the genius of the modern story in English, passed this legacy along to literary cultures around the world.

Allow me to make some large judgments here. By the post–World War II period, a short-story revolution swept around the world, making it clear to writers from Finland to China and points in between that the art story stood as the full-blown expression in the short form of what any serious modern writer believed about his or her aesthetic. In some places, say, New Zealand, when Katherine Mansfield began to work, the writer's goal was to create a story in the spirit of Joyce and Hemingway. In other parts of the world, say, in Egypt or Iraq, the aesthetic news about the gold standard of the modern short story came by way of a generation or two of European writers who owed their aesthetic sense to Hemingway, Joyce, and Chekhov. Graham Greene, mentor of the watershed Indian story writer R. K. Narayan, invoked Chekhov when first recommending him to his publisher in England. Hemingway could not be far behind.

The question of "influence" is always a vexed one. Critics can always come up with a fine writer who claims never to have read the masters whom we think of when we read him. Raymond Carver, the modern American master of the short story, always found himself a bit bemused when told by younger writers that he had influenced them heavily. "Read the people I read, Sherwood Anderson and Hemingway," he would say. "You should look to them, not me." So while influence is a vexed question, it is also a subtle problem.

Read, for example, some of the stories we have collected for you in this issue of *World Literature Today*, and you can easily sense the shape and form of the short story that has come down to the current generation of fiction writers over all the generations from Hemingway and Joyce and Chekhov. Even if some of the writers have not read any of these writers—difficult to imagine but always possible—they have read, and clearly will have found use in, the work of writers who have. I know this sounds tautological, but the freedom of the contemporary short story evolved in much the same way that modern Western political revolutions evolved—if not directly from the American Revolution, then from subsequent revolutions, such as the French Revolution, that looked to the American event as epoch-making.

That's how I see the Hemingway short story, as epoch-making, with, to use Ezra Pound's valuable paradigm from his *ABC of Reading*, Chekhov as the inventor and Hemingway as the master of the form. The shock wave of Hemingway's mastery reverberating around the world, with undertones and deep resonances of Chekhov, has brought us to where we stand today, as readers and writers alike.

Or where we sit, holding this issue of *World Literature Today* in our hands, about to enjoy a sampling of the fictive worlds conjured up by nearly a dozen writers from around the globe, all of whom work with the modern model of the art story, all of whom hope to meld the modes of entertainment and wisdom into a singular narrative line. Some read thoroughly in the modern narrative tradition, hewing to a clear storyline, as in, for example, Sri Lankan writer Ru Freeman's "First Son" and Canadian-born writer Alix Ohlin's "The Cruise." Others, such as Cuban American writer Ana Menéndez in her beautifully dreamlike "You Are the Heirs of All My Terrors" and Benjamin Percy in "The Roof People," produce visionary variations on the straightforward tradition. From the steamy streets of Kuala Lumpur to African beaches to Europe's thoroughfares, families and errant ghosts, lovers and neighbors, poets and fugitives make up the crowded population of these worlds. As diverse as they are, these stories point up that serious fiction writers accept the legacy of the modern short story and brilliantly turn it to their own purposes, which means, ultimately, that they turn it to our purposes—aiding and abetting our desire to know the intricacies of national differences and to participate, at the same time, in the kinship of common earthly concerns.

WASHINGTON, D.C.

The author of five novels, five collections of short stories and novellas, a memoir, and a collection of travel essays, Alan Cheuse (1940–2015) was also an editor, professor of literature, and longtime NPR book commentator. He taught creative writing at George Mason University for more than thirty years. This essay introduced the "International Short Fiction" issue of *WLT* (September 2010), which he guest-edited.

RITE OF BAPTISM (2024)

PÁDRAIG Ó TUAMA

If you pass, know that you will have no say
about what happens.

Some of our people will hate you as they hate themselves.
You must create a life
without giving them all your life's attention.

Some people will delight in destroying you.
Some will strike you. Some will choose
others as their favorites.

Some have been waiting for you for generations;
circling, like hunters, round your little heart.
Of course they don't know you.

This truth will set you free,
eventually. But only after you've forgotten this.

You haven't learnt to fly yet, have you?

Somebody will love you.
Somebody will hurt you too, but you know that already.

We offer you little in the way of certainty;
just that the country you live in will not always be that country.

There is a lot you'll need to suffer.
Remember: help is a howl and an imperative.
    Nothing to be ashamed of.

One way or another, shame
can teach you what nothing else can teach you.

One way or another.

Your body is an event
and you'll spend decades unpacking what's happened.

Here are some things we cannot guarantee you:
guarantees, or history's purity.

Here is what we can:
A platform on which your past can make or break
depending on how power is conceived.

There is no such thing as the past.
Just stories of the past poorly re-enacted.

And nobody knows where the past begins—
in the beginning it was all a dream, not a story.

Remember: you must believe
some of this.

Born in Cork, Pádraig Ó Tuama (b. 1975), an Irish poet with interests in language, violence, power, and religion, is the host of On Being's *Poetry Unbound*. His latest collections, *Kitchen Hymns* and *40 Poems on Being with Each Other: A Poetry Unbound Anthology*, both appeared in 2025.

KAMAU BRATHWAITE

First I must acknowledge the totem honour you accord me in bringing
me here for this most prestigious of literary awards. As I keep on
saying, I had *no idea* this kind of thing was going on behind my back.
You meet in camera and unexpectedly publish me the picture you have
so darkly selected. The names of my colleague previous winners, the
names of those in consideration with me this year—the whole thing is
so awesome it has me walking, like a certain musician, on eggshells

What all this says is that there are still some places in the world
where writers & their writing are taken seriously, our work focussed
and treated w/respect—and at the end of the evening we're
even handsomely *paid* for it; presented w/this silver feather as a
reminder of responsibility—somewhere one senses also an arrow
pointed at the heart of any personal presumption—& there will
be later even a subtle kind of festschrift erected in our honour

IS ALTOGETHER TOO MUCH! But I not complainin. We complain
enough about "neglect." Here at least & at last are dedicated people
putting our poems where their hearts are: Neustadt, *WLT*, Oklahoma!

And all this, haltering as it is, is to sincerely thank you on behalf of my
muse, my muses & on behalf of the Caribbean—for here is a person
from these small islands far south of here who has been brought all
these prairie miles of North American heartland to this crossroads
of the "Trail of Tears" for this honour by an African brother a further
10,000 miles away (I refer to Kofi Awoonor, my colleague-fellow poet &
Neustadt advocat who unfortunately cd not be here w/us this evening)
and who now that he is here, recognizes, as he hopes to show in the
second part of this thanks-tune, that he was always on the way here—
that the Prize is the occasion, almost the xcuse—but not the DNA of the
business; that there is time & spaces shared by our three landscapes—

Antillean, OklaHOMEan, African—
in which he recognize his poem

I'll speak about this in the second part of this Acknowledgement

What I want to end w/here is a plea for continued conversation
among ourselves. In a world of increase & increasing materialism—
trailer-loads of it along the information superhighway—we,
as livicators of this special art of vision/writing, dreamer/
saying, are much reduced; in danger, some of us, of becoming
petitioners not practitioners—dependent upon grants; upon,
as Tennessee Williams long ago warned, the generosity &/
or kindness of strangers; estranged as many of us are from
our villages, our oumforts, from our own zodiacs

And almost as a desperate response of counter-insurrection, it wd
seem, instead of SHARING more w/each other, we pull apart into
our own script/ure, into the precise particular bleeding of our own
individual tick-hearts, into our own deconstructions, for goodness'
sake; so that the possible Global Village (Ogotemmellian as this
may be) is on its way towards the Global Ghetto; and even as

artists (assuming that you will agree w/ me that there is a special
grief, a special GIFT, a special plomb in being this) we allow
Ourselves to be divided—or worse, to remain divided—by race
by age by class by colour by gender by preoccupation of the
stampen ground; producing therefore more heat than light,
more artifice than art beat & far more argument than Sphinx

And I'm not saying this because I'm xpected to
SAY SOMETHING

on an august day in September such as this, but because the constant I
wd even say consistent fabric & praxis of my work has been to connect
broken islands, cracked, broken words, worlds, friendships, ancestories
& I have seen the sea outside our yard bring grain by gentle grain out of

its granary, coast upon coast, & then in one long sweep of light or night,
take all away again A poem tree of tidalectics. A strange 12-branching
history of it which I leave you wit
from Newstead to Neustadt

*

haltering the landscapes of the wind

The place I grow in—the underside of the leaf of my childhood—
like the other & inner slide of the sea into which I am born—is call
Newstead, the hoom & heart of that miracle village you must know by
now as Mile & Quarter (MyLann Quarter) [*Barabajan Poems*, 1994].
Here is open canefield caneland snuggled by the darker colour of
trees, time, green waters of vegetation flowing around the islands
of hills, Brevitor caves, windmills, great white houses (yr horses)
on the horizon among more lime, more trees & our warm sleepy
cooking-smoke villages in the shallow valleys of sound. And at the
centre of this is this house of the ancestors, Newstead, which is
quietly preparing itself for the Neustadt Prize in a similar landscape
of spirit & spirits sixty years later on, on the other side of the wall

I bring you therefore a very special greeting of the most intimate
recognition. I in a sense am sent to return to myself what you both
give me: speech, shafts of canelight, a green silver feather, my
ancestories coming to be born here again: planter & slave, Ogoun &
buffalo, Newstead & Neustadt spiritdances of the native crossroads

And because this is such a special something in such an awesome
silence of such sound in which to rise this evening & celebration
THANK YOU for these thousand years brought to this brief account
of visibility in this time & in this town & w/this tongue, I wish w/
yr permission & w/as much aplomb & care as I can limp & limbo up
to & pour a brief libation at the foot of the several trees of me/mory
I growing see here in these beautiful landscapes where the umbilical
chords of my voice, I suppose we will have to call it that—book, bell,

trigger, treasure of metaphor—have been placed all along the curved
tale & tails of my journey by my mother & father & sisters & my ancestor
   brother & Bob'ob the Ogoun carpenter & Grannpa & Esse & Fillmore
   and "all the aunts & uncles" & Queen Victoria & the Sistine Chapel &
Oshogbo & Hounsi Twenefor & Stephen Dedalus & Stephen Agyemann
   & Boukman & W. B. Yeats & Sycorax & Oya & Agamemnon dead [. . .]

COW PASTURE, BARBADOS / NEW YORK CITY

Kamau Brathwaite (1930–2020) was a decorated Barbadian poet, historian, and
essayist known for his work on Caribbean identity, culture, and history. After he
earned his PhD in philosophy from the University of Sussex in 1968, Brathwaite
spent his life teaching around the globe. Brathwaite received the 1994 Neustadt
International Prize for Literature.

DELIRICA X (2018)

SALGADO MARANHÃO

Translated from the Portuguese by Alexis Levitin

A madman sniffing
at the moon
captures instances of you.

(Captured in his cymbal-clashing soul.)

A madman who can sing.

And over what comes spilling forth
in mantra and nectar,
there is a flame:

hidden in your folded
nakedness.

Neon words linger
as everything flows from resplendent
solidity.

And everywhere, forever,
fire, water, time, and breath
exclaim.

Salgado Maranhão (b. 1953) is the leading Afro-Brazilian poet of our era. His work has twice received Brazil's most prestigious award, the Prêmio Jabuti, and he himself has been awarded two doctorates *honoris causa*. In addition to nineteen books of poetry, he has written song lyrics and made recordings with some of Brazil's leading jazz and pop musicians.

Alexis Levitin's fifty books in translation include Clarice Lispector's *Soulstorm* (1989) and Eugénio de Andrade's *Forbidden Words* (2003). He has published five collections of poetry by Salgado Maranhão: *Blood of the Sun, Tiger Fur, Palavora, Mapping the Tribe,* and *Consecration of the Wolves.*

WORDS MANIFESTED AS LIGHT (1988)

RAJA RAO

I AM A MAN OF SILENCE. And words emerge from that silence with light, of light, and light is sacred. One wonders that there is the word at all—*Sabda*—and one asks oneself, where did it come from? How does it arise? I have asked this question for many, many years. I've asked it of linguists, I've asked it of poets, I've asked it of scholars. The word seems to come first as an impulsion from the nowhere, and then as a prehension, and it becomes less and less esoteric—till it begins to be concrete. And the concrete becoming ever more earthy, and the earthy communicated, as the common word, alas, seems to possess least of that original light.

The writer or the poet is he who seeks back the common word to its origin of silence, in order that the manifested word become light. There was a great poet of the West, the Austrian poet Rainer Maria Rilke. He said objects come to you to be named. One of the ideas that has involved me deeply these many years is: Where does the word dissolve and become meaning? Meaning itself, of course, is beyond the sound of the word, which comes to me only as an image in the brain, but *that* which sees the image in the brain (says our great sage of the sixth century, Sri Shankara) nobody has ever seen. Thus the word coming of light is seen eventually by light. That is, every word-image is seen by light, and that is its meaning. Therefore the effort of the writer, if he is sincere, is to forget himself in the process and go back to the light from which words come. Go back where? That is, those who read or those who hear must reach back to their own light. And that light I think is prayer.

My ancestors and, yes, the ancestors of some of you or of most of you who speak the English tongue, came from the same part of the world thousands of years ago. Was it from the Caucasus or the North Pole? One is not certain yet. They spoke a language close to my own language and close to your language. There is in America a remarkable dictionary called the *American Heritage Dictionary*. It offers almost a hundred pages (at the very end) of the Indo-European roots of many of our words. Most of you are of European origin. At least your thinking has been conditioned by European thought. There is thus a common way of thinking, an Indo-European way of thinking, between us, so that we are not so far from each other as we often think we are. And beyond the Indo-European way of thinking in Asia, Africa, Polynesia, is *that* same human light by which all words become meaning. Finally, there is only one meaning, not for every word, but for all words *where* the word, any word, from any language, dissolves into knowledge. It is only there at the dissolution of the sound of the word or of the image of the word that you say you understand. And *here* there is neither you nor I. That is what I have been trying to achieve. That I become no one, that no one shines but It.

Many good things have been said by distinguished speakers—about me—this evening. But I want to say to you in utter honesty: I would like to be completely nameless, and just be that reality which is beyond all of us who hear me—that reality which evokes in me you, and I in each one listening to me this evening, that there be no one there but light. And it is of that reality the sages have spoken. The sage is one, someone beyond the saint. He is no one. He is the real seer. In fact, we are all sages, but we don't recognize it. That is what the Indian tradition says. In the act of seeing—that is, of the seer, the seen, and the seeing—in seeing alone is there pure light. Where this comes from, nobody can name. I once asked Dr. Oppenheimer, the scientist, who told me his hands were soiled by the atom bomb: Have you ever seen an object? And he answered: Never. If a scientist like Dr. Oppenheimer says he has never seen an object—yet I am hearing him say what he has in all honesty declared—it is that level of knowledge I would like to reach from where I truly write. It is to that root of writing I pay homage. The Neustadt Prize is thus not given to me, but to That which is far beyond me, yet in me—because I alone know I am incapable of writing what people say I have written.

AUSTIN, TEXAS

Raja Rao's semi-autobiographical novel, *The Serpent and the Rope* (1960), established Rao (1908–2006) as one of India's finest prose stylists and won him the Sahitya Akademi Award in 1963. He received the Neustadt International Prize for Literature in 1988.

MARIO VARGAS LLOSA

Translated from the Spanish by Nick D. Mills Jr.

THE NOVEL is the Cinderella of the literary genres of Latin America. Considered subversive by the Spanish authorities (and indeed it was), the novel was banned during the colonial centuries and did not come to life until the nineteenth century, after independence had been achieved. Once born, the novel in Latin America suffered a precarious infancy, except in Brazil, where the work of Machado de Assis endowed prose fiction with a dimension which would not be attained in Spanish America until the twentieth century. In Spanish South America, the most representative works up to the end of the nineteenth century were mere echoes of French, English, or, at worst, Spanish writings. Our "romantic" and our "realist" novels dramatically reflect the colonial temper of the Latin American novelist of the last century whose gaze remained firmly fixed on Europe. Naturally predisposed to assimilate the themes, techniques, and styles of the European masters, the early novelist refused to recognize the literary worth of his own American reality. The most notable nineteenth-century Latin American novel, *María* (1867), by the Colombian Jorge Isaacs, is little more than an opportune adaptation of Bernardin de Saint Pierre's *Paul et Virginie*. The prose fiction which Latin America inspired prior to 1900 gave the singular impression that Latin America was a continent of "whites": Indians, Blacks, and mestizos were incorporated into the novel only during the last decades of the nineteenth century, and even then they were little more than picturesque and distant elements, indistinguishable from the flora and fauna which served as the framework for the action of the novel. Even while essayists such as Sarmiento, González Prada, or Martí, and poets such as José Hernández rediscovered Latin America and enriched our language, giving it an autonomous personality distinct from peninsular models, the novel remained an imitative and submissive genre, stripped of originality and creative inspiration.

After imitating Europe, the Latin American novelist attempted to photograph the reality that surrounded him: folklore replaced mimicry. From invertebrate cosmopolitanism, the Latin American novel evolved to aggressive provincialism. This tendency, initiated by the Peruvian Clorinda Matto de Turner, was given new impetus by the novel of the Mexican Revolution, and it achieved its highest expression with such writers as Mariano Azuela, Alcides Arguedas, José Eustasio Rivera, Ricardo Güiraldes, Rómulo Gallegos, and Ciro Alegría. Historically this represented a step forward, a tapping of the conscience of autochthonous reality, a willingness to reclaim the indigenous and mestizo cultures and, through them, to find national identity. And in some cases it represented a political awareness of the social problems of the continent, problems such as agrarian feudalism, the selfishness of the oligarchic castes, and imperialistic penetration. However, from a literary point of view, the primitive novel confused creation with information, art with artifice. As is well known, good novels cannot be written with good intentions alone. Freed from the domination of the anecdote based on European models, the primitive novelists nevertheless remained bound by the methods of composition and the narrative language of the writers of Europe, principally the naturalists. Painstaking in the description of landscapes and picturesque customs and manners, purists in the portrayal of nature, extremists in the use of the vernacular in dialogue, Manichean in the presentation of social conflicts, the primitive novelists present a view of reality that is at best vividly colorful but which is nevertheless decorative and superficial. The primitive novels are valid geographical testimonials, important documentaries, but their aesthetic significance is nevertheless slight. Although they are enlightening with regard to historical and social reality, the primitive novels do not succeed in creating an autonomous and sovereign world of their own. The quality of a novel is not measured by the greater or lesser degree of correlation between the story and its real-life model; rather it is measured by the story's intrinsic power of persuasion, by its ability to impose itself upon the reader as a living and coherent reality *in and of itself*. In other words, the authenticity of a story is not dependent upon its plot, but rather upon the means by which the plot is embodied in a particular written form and in a particular structure. The failure of the primitive novel is to a great extent the result of the disdain which its authors demonstrated toward the strictly technical problems of artistic creation. The parochial horizon of their vision, their epidermic notion of man, did not emanate from the themes which they adopted but rather from their incapacity to express these themes in a language and a structure sufficiently functional to elevate them to a universal plane.

The creative novel is thus a relatively recent phenomenon in Latin America. Only within the last twenty years has narration come to occupy the same plane of dignity and originality that the poem and the essay had already achieved previously (in general, the theater continues to flounder in a primitive state). Writers such as Borges, Onetti, Fuentes, Carpentier, Guimarães Rosa, Cortázar, and García Márquez have not only put our novel, bluntly speaking, on an equal footing with even the best of other countries; they have in addition made the narration of the 1920s and '30s appear in comparison to be as anachronistic as that of the nineteenth century. Curiously enough, the qualitative changes experienced by Latin American fiction during the postwar period parallels a certain stagnation of the European and North American novel which, after a period of notable splendor—culminating in the works of Joyce, Proust, Kafka, Faulkner—lost its impetus and was either debilitated by formalistic experiments (the French nouveau roman) or else languished in passive conformity with tradition (the current English novel). This fact has undoubtedly contributed to the popularity abroad of the new Latin American novelists ("new" in a literary sense, not generational, since the ages of these novelists range from thirty to sixty years). However, the principal reason behind the acceptance that our narrative has achieved is not of external origin but rather is essentially a result of its own maturity.

And what constitutes this maturity? Thanks to the new writers, it consists primarily of a thematic shift in the axis of Latin American fiction from nature to man. Man's problems, his nightmares, and his ambitions are the essential themes of this fiction, rather than the pampas, the plateaus, or the cane fields, as was the case in the primitive novel. "Indigenous" themes have not been excluded but have been intensified and framed within a perspective that is no longer regional but rather universal. The literary worth of Guimarães Rosa's *Grande Sertão: Veredas* and of Juan Rulfo's *Pedro Páramo* does not reside in the fact that both novels accurately describe the rural worlds of Minas Gerais and of Jalisco, but rather in the fact that, drawing on firsthand knowledge of life in these regions, the authors have created *additionally* worlds which are sovereign and autonomous, worlds endowed with their own significance and mythology, and with the verbal persuasion that allows readers of any country or language to recognize themselves and identify with the characters that populate this fictional world. Just as the Bolivian or Paraguayan reader has little difficulty identifying with a Mr. Bloom and empathizing with his Dublinesque odyssey, so also can the reader from Norway or Finland live vicariously the life of the "yagunzo" Riobaldo and share in his adventures as a highwayman of the sertão. This is possible because, regardless of differences in time and place, both characters express two equally complex paths that human destiny can take.

In addition to becoming "more human," the new Latin American novel has expanded its concept of reality. In the primitive novel, reality consisted solely of geography and history; nature and social concerns delimited its field of action. The new novelists have incorporated into fiction other dimensions of human existence, such as imagination and dreams; and themes of fantasy have invaded the short story as well as the novel. In the case of Miguel Asturias these new thematic devices do not exclude the more traditional themes exploited in the Latin American novel. Asturias blends the two in a curious baroque symbiosis in which social protest and political satire alternate with the evocation of indigenous myths, witchcraft, and magic. Hypercivilized surrealist prose, composed of unexpected associations and nourished by the free flow of subconscious images, is the instrument that Asturias utilizes to reconstruct allegorically—with varying degrees of success—the most primitive of worlds. Jorge Luis Borges, another major representative of the literature of fantasy, adopts techniques diametrically opposed to those of Asturias. His fiction contains nothing that is spontaneous or irrational; everything is the result of intimate knowledge and of maximum intellectual effort. His working materials do not consist of indigenous traditions or social protest, but rather of literary myths, philosophical systems, metaphysics, and the concept of time. Borges is the writer who best symbolizes the end of Latin America's inferiority complex vis-à-vis Europe. Previously, there was a tacit agreement among our writers that certain themes were taboo, beyond their capabilities: how could they possibly traverse the same paths as a Valéry, an Eliot, or a Gide? The great themes of Western culture were considered untouchable; they were the exclusive domain of the European writers. Borges was the first to expose this fallacy and to demonstrate that a Latin American intellectual could also make original statements concerning Shakespeare or Goethe, and conceive credible stories set in the Middle Ages or Turkey.

In the case of some Latin American narrators—Julio Cortázar, Gabriel García Márquez, and José Lezama Lima, for example—themes of fantasy have not replaced the purely realistic ones but rather coexist with them, often in the same work. This fusion of objectivity and fantasy, of myth and history, of dreamed experience and lived experience, crystallizes in literary worlds in which the mysterious and unusual do not destroy objective reality; they are not open doors to mental escape. Quite the contrary; they embody the most urgent problems confronting contemporary man, illuminating those problems with heretofore unknown perspective (the best examples of this are *Rayuela* and *Cien años de soledad*). Lezama Lima's only novel, *Paradiso*, is, in addition, interesting for its "backward" exoticism: it does with Europe and Asia what the surrealists did with Japan; what writers such as Paul Morand or Joseph Kessel did with Africa, Latin America, and Asia; what Pierre Louÿs and Marcel Schwob did with ancient Greece. Just as the exotic worlds in the works of these authors served to mold a "European" interpretation or a superficial "European" view of exotic reality, in the same way, in *Paradiso*, the history, the literature, and the thought of Europe and Asia are exploited by the author as nothing more than decorative motifs or pretexts to construct a monumental fable of truly American origin (perhaps it would be more correct to say of "Antillean" origin).

Just as the countryside was the immutable setting of the primitive novel, the city is the permanent setting of the creative novel. Among the new novelists there are impassioned interpreters and inventors of cities. The first novel by Carlos Fuentes, *La región más transparente*, is a biography of the author's own Mexico City; it is a meticulous study of its human types, of its dramas and frustrations, of its myths, and of the concerns and the ideological battles which are waged within its confines. On the other hand, the novels of José Donoso bring about a confrontation between ruffians and aristocrats in a poetically conceived Santiago which has been stripped of its middle class, a Santiago in which everything collapses in a prolonged and elegant neurosis. And in the demented Caracas of the novels and short stories of Salvador Garmendia, all but the most cruel and sordid of human experience has disappeared. In *Sobre héroes y tumbas*, by Ernesto Sábato, Buenos Aires appears as a kaleidoscope of images that emanate at times from historical reconstruction, at times from direct observation, and at times from hallucination. On the other hand, other writers have invented cities: Juan Carlos Onetti sets his stories in a gray and nebulous Puerto de Santa María on the Río de la Plata; and García Márquez sets his in a mythical tropical hamlet, Macondo.

The primitive novel conformed to a prototype: the predominance of landscape over the individual, of content over form, of objective life over the subjective. Its language was impressionistic and rhetorical, its technique was naturalistic. All of the primitive novels were more or less successful variations of this same prototype. On the other hand, it is impossible to establish a common denominator for the creative novel in which the most heterogeneous themes, purposes, styles, and structures compete with one another. But beneath this diversity, which is the novel's greatest asset, there is one central and unifying element: an awareness of form, an artistic impulse. The new Latin American novelist recognizes that his success or failure as a creator will be decided not by the themes he selects, nor by the emotions or obsessions he expresses, but rather by the formal elements—words and structure—that are adopted to develop those themes, emotions, or obsessions. In the final analysis, the maturity of the Latin American novel signifies the achievement of aesthetic independence. The Latin American novelist now explores not only untapped areas of reality with a view toward transforming them into literary myth, he also explores language. Not only does he invent characters or situations, he likewise invents new narrative techniques. In the case of writers such as Guillermo Cabrera Infante, Severo Sarduy, and Carlos Fuentes in his last novel, *Cambio de piel*, this increasing concern for narrative form has been translated into works which are above all linguistic experiments, novels whose heroes are not men but rather words. This inclination toward aesthetic originality which characterizes the new Latin American writer obviously should not be construed as a return to provincialism or as a total denial of Europe. On the contrary, the curiosity and the interest that exist in Latin America with regard to the new tendencies in narration in the rest of the world are perhaps even more intense than in the past. The one difference is that now the Latin American novelist no longer imitates: he assimilates, he adapts, he modifies, he discriminates and puts to use those imported models that are most consistent with his own literary objectives. Communication has replaced subordination, mutual exchange has replaced dependence. For the first time, literary influences do not operate in only one direction: it is no longer surprising to detect in the works of young European writers a resemblance to the work of Cortázar, or to discover in the pages of *Tel Quel* of Paris that a French essayist repeats as his own the literary opinions that Borges formulated ten years ago.

Nevertheless, the preceding is not sufficient to explain the principal difference between Latin American narrative and what is written today in the rest of the Western world. There is nothing unique about the fact that our novel has substituted man for nature as the central concern; that it has expanded its perception of reality to include the social and the cultural, the imagined and the dreamlike; that the city has become the setting of the story; or that the Latin American novelist has recognized the irrevocable importance of form in the creative process. These developments signify nothing more than that our novel has arrived at a stage of development which had been achieved years ago in Europe and the United States. The circumstances that have stimulated the development of the Latin American novel are of a varied nature, most of them having already been pointed out by the critics. From a literary point of view, the Latin American writer considers himself a "professional" in the most flattering sense of the word, while his predecessors were rather like dilettantes or amateurs. The latter exercised their talent as creative writers while at the same time pursuing careers as politicians, diplomats, merchants, or adventurers. On the other hand, the contemporary authors are, first and foremost, writers. A vocation embraced in an exclusive and all-encompassing way should logically produce more vigorous and lasting fruits than one which is exercised only on Sundays and holidays. From a social point of view the growth of the Latin American cities in the last twenty years, a growth which has proceeded at a staggering pace, has contributed to the creation of a heretofore nonexistent reading public. This same phenomenon is also partly responsible for the establishment of new publishing firms.

Half a century ago, writers in most of the Latin American countries did not write novels for the simple reason that there was no way to publish them: a short story or a poem at least had the advantage of fitting into the Sunday edition of the newspaper. Emir Rodríguez Monegal feels that World War II, which interrupted for several years the importation of European novels into Latin America, should also be included among the factors that stimulated the advance of our prose fiction. The void caused by the war forced the reading public to turn its eyes toward "indigenous" writers, thereby discovering that an Argentine or a Mexican novel could be just as attractive as an Italian or French one. There is a good deal of truth in this observation. I remember, for example, that fifteen years ago, in Lima, the attitude with which my university friends and I confronted a new novel was summarized by the following prejudiced formula: "All Latin American novels are bad until they prove themselves otherwise; all French and North American novels are good until they prove themselves otherwise." The attitude of Peruvian youth today is still prejudiced, but in the opposite sense: they await the appearance of the most recent work of García Márquez or of Carpentier with the same impatience that we awaited new works by Sartre or Camus.

In addition, there is a different type of factor which seems to me to be just as important—if not more so—as previous ones in explaining the qualitative change in Latin American narration in the last few years. It is advisable to examine this in detail because, without a doubt, it is on the basis of this factor that the primary difference between today's Latin American novel and the novels of Europe and North America can be traced. It is neither a literary nor a sociological factor; rather it is a historical one. Unlike poetry or drama, whose origin coincides with the origin of all civilizations, the novel is the most "historic" of all literary genres to the extent that it has a definite place and date of birth. This disinterested verbal representation of human reality that portrays the world at the same time that it denies the world, that recreates by destroying; this subtle murderer of gods that we call the novel, perpetrated by a man who serves as a substitute for God, was born in the West, in the high Middle Ages, when faith was dying and human reason was replacing God as the instrument for understanding life and as the guiding principle for the government of human society. Malraux has commented that Western civilization is the only one which has slain its gods without replacing them with others. The appearance of the novel, that deicide, and the appearance of the novelist, that substitute for God, are to a certain extent the result of that crime. Since the time when the novel of chivalry transposed in fiction the medieval castle which the winds of the Renaissance had already begun to erode, the novel has continued to represent a curious attempt at historical recuperation and exorcism, and it has achieved its most glorious heights when the reality that inspired it was on the verge of apocalypse, when the society that served as its source and paradigm was dying. Rescuer and verbal gravedigger of an epoch, the great novelist is a kind of vulture: the putrid flesh of history is his favorite nourishment and has served to inspire him to his most audacious undertakings. The literary worlds of a Tolstoy, of a Proust, or of a Kafka are monumental verbal images that have been inspired by societies in periods of decadence immediately preceding historical collapse. Like the moribund Spanish Middle Ages which produced the turbulent stories of Amadís, Palmarines, and Tirant lo Blanch; and like the condemned Russia in which Tolstoy and Dostoevsky were reared; and like the anachronistic Deep South which supplied Faulkner with the raw material for the invention of the saga of Yoknapatawpha County, Latin America is today a continent that is changing its skin, that is becoming the subject rather than the object of history. The impetuous explosion of novels that have welled up within its breast is the parting gesture of a dying continent.

Of course, this relationship between the historical evolution of a society and the refinement of its novelistic expertise cannot be measured with scientific precision; it is not as rapid a process as it might appear when described with such brevity. What I have described above is a predominant tendency and not a dogmatic formula. This tendency may be defined by asserting that the most propitious moment for the development of prose fiction is when reality ceases to have precise meaning for a historic community because the society's religious, moral, or political values, which once provided the foundation for social life and the master key for perceiving reality, have entered upon a period of crisis and no longer enjoy the faithful support of the collectivity. As a result, great novels normally do not appear in times of revolutionary fervor when the entire society is united behind one great cause. Not a single outstanding novel was written during the French Revolution, or during the Russian Revolution, or during the wars for independence in either North or South America, or during the Chinese Revolution. Great novels never appear in these moments of optimistic exultation, of hope and faith in a country's destiny; rather they appear in the preceding period when the erosion of the old order permits the community to perceive only confusion and chaos in the reality that surrounds them.

This crisis of faith that accompanies the decay of historic reality, this skepticism toward the guiding values of the world, which is the most overt symptom of the decomposition of a society, curiously enough awakens an increasing receptivity, an appetite, an intense need for fiction, for narrative images that are capable of creating a new reality inherently different from the one in which it is no longer possible to believe. God is assassinated and the cult of the impostor begins; reality is distrusted and faith is sparked in reality's verbal manifestations. It is as if these reserves of faith which had been withdrawn from the real world were, in compensation, redirected toward the novels which the ruins of this world engendered. This is the phenomenon that is currently taking place in Latin America. The Latin American countries today are experiencing the most disturbing crisis in their history. All agree that one period is closing and that another, for better or worse, will soon open up; but no one has the courage to face up to the reality of today. Nevertheless, the narrative images inspired by this offensive reality which all despise have been received with greedy enthusiasm, with unprecedented credulity. Not only are novels circulating in greater numbers (previously, an Argentine, Chilean, or Colombian novelist could expect to sell only 1,000 copies if his work were a success; now an edition of 20,000 copies is not exceptional); but also the novelist has become a popular figure whose picture appears in newspapers and who is met in the streets by autograph seekers.

Of course, this social phenomenon has a literary counterpart: at a moment when circumstances are favorable to the novel, the same gratuitous transference of faith on the part of readers toward the novel serves at the same time as a stimulus for the author in his creative activity; it is what compels him to assume his role as a substitute for God through undertakings increasingly more daring and ambitious. The abundance of these better novels which are stimulated by the confidence of a whole community is itself a result of the unlimited confidence with which they were created. The quality of a novel stems, above all, from its power of persuasion. This power is only as great as the confidence (not the intelligence, or the ingenuity, or the skill) with which the novelist executes the creative act. And the societies in crisis are precisely those in which the literary vocation has adopted an almost religious and messianic character. These societies are the ones that have inspired the most daring and total novels ever conceived. The novels of stable societies which are inspired by a historic reality that is not threatened by an imminent radical change—that is to say, by the type of reality which is still sustained by the confidence of the society—tend to be characterized by a stamp of irony, by formalistic games, by either excessive intellectualism or cynical nihilism. These characteristics reveal an attitude of rejection by the artist when confronted by reality. The author does not dare pretend to be God, he does not compete with reality on equal terms, he makes no attempt to create worlds as vast and complex as the real world. He has no faith in his own powers, and such an enterprise seems to him both absurd and naïve. To a certain extent he is right: all novelistic projects that crystallize in a work of art involve a large dosage of both madness and innocence. The novelist in a stable society takes refuge in brilliance, in formalistic sophistication, and he proclaims that the function of the novelist is not "to compete with the Civil Code" but rather to create new techniques and to reinvent language.

   This, I think, is the basic distinction that exists in our day between the best representatives of the Latin American novel and the best representatives of the European and North American novel. The differences of form, content, and purpose that separate them are a consequence of a more profound difference, historical rather than literary, a difference that is related to the evolution of the respective societies. The historical reality, the framework of experiences within which the Latin American novelist writes, is a reality threatened with extinction. This perspective is traditionally the one which has nurtured the illusion—naïve, demented, but nevertheless formidable—of wishing to recapture with fantasy and words the total image of a world, of seeking to write novels that express this total reality not only qualitatively but also quantitatively. To this devilish and unrealistic impulse we owe the existence of such novels as

The Human Comedy, The Man Without Qualities, or *Ulysses,* novels which represent the highest achievement of European literature. The same holds true today in Latin America with works such as *Los pasos perdidos, Rayuela,* or *Cien años de soledad.*

The European or North American novelist in our day rarely attempts to write a "total" novel. The crises that agitate their societies are different from those that are currently disrupting Latin American society. The former affect only the surface or marginal strata of historical reality; the foundations of that reality remain essentially untouched. This reality, which is still thought to be viable, does not awaken the same "total" rejection which compels today's Latin American novelist to attempt to "totally" replace reality with "total" novels. Quite the contrary: the historic reality currently found in Europe and North America evokes only mocking withdrawal and condescending criticism from the writers of those areas, postures which are translated into novels at times brilliant but nevertheless modest and skeptical, and at times luxuriously gratuitous. What is involved here is a profound difference, but at the same time it is provisional and precarious. Latin America will not continue to languish indefinitely, nor will the European countries and the United States always be able to assimilate their inherent historical contradictions. And these changes will undoubtedly be reflected in the novelistic production of the respective countries. Likewise, a period of historical stability and its corresponding narrative modesty will one day arrive in Latin America. Edmund Wilson boasted several years ago of never having been interested in the Latin American novel. I wonder if he would repeat today with the same conviction this somewhat abrupt remark.

LONDON

Peruvian novelist, journalist, and essayist Mario Vargas Llosa (1936–2025) was only thirty-four when he wrote this essay but had already received the Rómulo Gallegos Prize and written such fictional masterpieces as *La ciudad y los perros* (1962) and *Conversación en la catedral* (1969). In 2010 he was awarded the Nobel Prize in Literature.

Nick D. Mills Jr. was an instructor in Spanish at the University of Oklahoma. He later became director of the Andean Center at the University of New Mexico.

ODE TO AN ACTOR (2023)

PABLO NERUDA

Translated from the Spanish by Jacinta Candelaria

I don't remember
at what age
in your autumn,
I saw you
for the first time
onstage,
thespian
in Plato's
cave:
the curtain went up
and you appeared
as an implacable idol.
I recognized
your naked gesture,
the clarity of your hands,
your tenacious drive,
your circulatory peace,
although I knew
that,
facing you,
it wasn't you
I saw
but
a spirit,
a ghost,
the divine breath.
Who are you?
Prophet,
politician,

liar,
buffoon,
impostor,
the voice of everyone,
ancestral image
of our ancestors,
light and darkness,
yes and no.

When you are others,
you are an exalted
version of our heart,
a copy
without original,
myth of the archetype
of the type
that is
the primordial man.

Since then,
each time I see you
performing
Uncle Vanya
you announce another version
of condemnation
and opprobrium.
And the more I look at you,
the more I want to
admire you.

Laugh
and
cry and kiss,
say
and suffer and love,
but don't die.
You are emptiness,
echo
of the echo
in the emptiness
of our being.
You
are the thundering
that names us
and, by naming us,
grants us life
without dismissing
the wisdom
of our mistakes
on the road
of the thunder
of our truth.

Like a magnet,
from all
the town corners,
the
people
are shaken up,
magnetized,
unfolded,
following your
footsteps,
your wave,
your cloud,
your splendor,

the strident song
of the discord
you pretend,
Shakespeare
behind
Shakespeare,
the subterranean thread
of your emotion
awaking
in our soul
the painful
sound
of solidarity.
Around
you,
we are a single song
and know that with authenticity
the arduous fight
is sustainable,
because
truth
is a mask.

In the plenteousness
of your spacious
life,
grant us gestures,
shudder,
coherence,
let us be
a better
version of
who we
are.

Who are you?
Soldier,
lieutenant,
Prospero,
Tartuffe,
baker,
poet,
human.
Life is short
and theater
distracts us.
You are
the Segismundo
who clamors
for freedom,
who doesn't exhaust
his strength
in the battle

for a
better world.

Dream of us,
actor,
for with you
we shall dream
our better
face.
Dream of us,
for your advice
and attention
are our mirror
and salvation.
Because waking up
makes it possible
to be witnesses to pain.

Pablo Neruda (1904–1973) was a Chilean poet, diplomat, and politician. He wrote political manifestos, historical epics, surrealist poetry, and autobiography, among many other genres. He was awarded the Nobel Prize in Literature in 1971. "Oda al actor," upon which this translation is based, is a fictional original inspired by Neruda's odes.

Jacinta Candelaria is a heteronym for Ilan Stavans.

PAAVO HAAVIKKO

Translated from the Finnish by Philip Binham

THE WRITER MUST WORK ALONE. In a small country he can do this with the reassuring knowledge that his readers are few and close at hand. A writer from a small country and a small linguistic area is at once confined and free. He cannot, indeed he need not think of anything wider than his own environment. He can even be free of popularity, for which he hardly has any use. He is left with very few excuses. He cannot be destroyed by money or fame or the lack of either. All that he is left with is the naked truth of how he sees himself, his potential—and literature.

It is easy to write when one knows that the significance of writing is in the work itself, in the examination of eternal issues. The inevitable consequence of this work is the realization that the only significant problems are those to which there are no answers or solutions. They must be examined constantly; they contain the limits of the possible and of human capacity. Only through the unanswerable questions can the world be depicted, constantly, unendingly.

Thus literature is always philosophical and always moral. It asks what is right in the final count, knowing that there is no reply. But it asks and it seeks, and it cannot be shackled by laws, social systems, technology, or business.

Using all the rich patterns in the world, literature constructs a form in which the following things can be found: the question of injustice and justice, the movement of events in the world, and darkness. The reader is invited, he is given an opportunity—but he may walk past if he will. It is the writer's lot to go on working, in the dark, in motion, free, alone, available. The value of this work is not in immutable, established classics; it is not in any completed book; it is in the endless work itself, the endless effort to remain free and unbound. It is said that art brings nations closer together, since through art they come to know each other. Many work toward this end. I believe that it is much more important for art to bring a man closer to himself. If a man knows one person—himself—he is closer to others than if he knows many people by name, including himself.

The idea of art as a bridge between nations goes with the optimistic belief that everything can be solved in the long run, that problems were made to be solved. This may hold for practical problems. Real problems were not made to be solved but rather to be borne with, lived with, in all countries and seasons, as time passes and changes the terms of life.

The writer has no expert help or institution as surety or support. He has only himself. There is no alternative. Everything else in developed societies is already so guaranteed, subsidized, secured, reliable, and isolated from all reality—science is so exploited and subjected—that there is no alternative left but the individual, set adrift and free.

The writer needs a measure of attention and recognition. He must fight to obtain it. At the same time he must fight against turning or allowing himself to be turned into an institution, who must think of everything, including next year's income. And though I use the word *writer*, I do not wish to differentiate between this activity and the battle each individual must fight. This battle too lasts only one lifetime: it begins in medias res, it ends in medias res; it is final and inevitable.

The only meaningful freedom is that of the individual. Every system desires to offer every other kind of freedom except this one. Every organized society tends toward increasing organization: arranging, caring, protecting, and guaranteeing. Every system, regardless of ideology, wishes to distribute the optimum amount of good to everyone. No system believes that man cannot endure so much good, and every system believes that all problems were made to be solved. Here is the source of the happiness and destruction of systems and political institutions alike.

To an outsider's eyes, America is a uniform, closed concept; it symbolizes a dream, and goals. Coming here as a European, I am aware that Europe is too incoherent for anyone to explain. There can be no comprehensive image of it, except that it is disrupted and broken. And Finland, a remote corner of Europe, is even less comprehensible. It is one of Europe's few neutral countries between East and West. Many think it is merely an all-too-small country in quite the wrong place to exist, if only in the light of recent European history. In the form that it does exist, it is a relic from a bygone age when there were still small, separate principalities in Europe. I am not trying to sell any conception or description of what the country is. It has been difficult enough even for European statesmen to fathom during a whole lifetime. All I can say, without resorting to a false comparison, is that in the light of historical wisdom, the Finns evidently have not had the sense to draw the correct conclusions about the price it is worth paying for freedom. This small nation has never set a price on freedom; it has merely paid, and for this reason it has received an excessive return on its absurd investment.

Winner of the 1984 Neustadt International Prize for Literature, Paavo Haavikko (1931–2008) is considered one of Finland's most influential writers. He published his first collection of poetry in 1951 at the age of twenty. His novels, poetry, and dramatic works are known for their modernism, experimentation, and innovative form.

Philip Binham translated works by Paavo Haavikko, Veijo Meri, and other Finnish writers. He taught at the Helsinki School of Economics.

ILAN STAVANS

I HAVE NO INTENTION of rehearsing yet another diatribe against the Swedish Academy's Nobel committee in Stockholm, which, as is well known in U.S. publishing circles, hasn't awarded its prize in literature to an American writer since 1993. A few years back, Horace Engdahl, a member of the academy, justified the rejection by stating—famously— that Americans are "too isolated, too insular," and that we "don't really participate in the big dialogue of literature." Expectedly, the response from our quarters was fast and furious: the Nobel in literature, the most outspoken decried, has become irrelevant. How else to explain the fact that obscure European honorees keep on being chosen while brilliant craftsmen like John Updike and Philip Roth are ignored? One of the literati was even quoted as offering to "send Engdahl a list" of American writers worth reading.

We may wish to rationalize the rejection in a number of ways. We could pretend, for instance, that we don't care a bit since the Nobel is only about sales, whereas good literature is . . . well, about being good. Or we could argue that it is dangerous to align the Nobel, and litera-ture in general, across national lines. Think of Isaac Bashevis Singer, who got it in 1978. Is he an American writer? Singer was a refugee from Poland who came to the United States when he was already thirty and who wrote most of his work not in English but in Yiddish. How about Joseph Brodsky, who was born in Russia—or better, he was born into the Russian language? The only true country a writer can claim is the language in which he writes.

In any case, the Nobel is supposed to celebrate individual talent, not nationality, which in and of itself is an amphibious concept. Ever heard of Pearl Buck, the American Nobelist of 1938? Well, Buck wasn't an American through and through. She lived almost her entire life, up until the publi-cation of her enduring novel *The Good Earth*, in China. At least two new biographies of Buck have been published in the past decade, and several of her books remain in print and widely read. But the Chinese have a stronger claim on her than we do. To fashion her as an American to boost the Nobel list smells of utilitarianism. In addition, the Nobel committee in those days was still laboring under the edict of Nobel's will about "idealist" literature. Now take Jorge Luis Borges, who unquestionably should have received the prize, especially given that no Argentine has ever been selected. Yet his reputation, mind you, is intact without it; and I'm not sure Borges would have liked to have been awarded the Nobel because he was an Argentine, since the adjective made him uncomfortable. All this to say that good literature is never good by committee.

Of course, generalizations are always dangerous: Engdahl's argument that American literature is "too isolated, too insular," that it is reluctant to "participate in the big dialogue of literature," are broad strokes that make him look like a baseball player trying to hit a fastball in the dark. Could these arguments begin to encompass the diversity of American literature? How about looking beyond the realm of American fiction to poets such as Richard Wilbur, W. S. Merwin, Charles Simic, and Robert Pinsky, all of whom have been active translators and very open to extraterritorial influences? Even if we stay with fiction, the same claim could be made about the provincialism of Orhan Pamuk, Mo Yan, Herta Müller, José Saramago, and almost any other recent Nobel laureate. Naguib Mahfouz focused only on Egypt, Imre Kertész on Hungary, and so on. The trick, obviously, is to understand the tension between the local and the universal, the microcosm and the macrocosm, which is what Gabriel García Márquez did with Macondo and William Faulkner—that most "provincial" of North American writers—with Yoknapatawpha. There is actually no such thing as "the American writer"; instead, there are infinite ways of being a writer in America.

One should also think of the U.S. writers who are read abroad and ask why they are read so widely there and not here (for example, Richard Powers in Germany, Paul Auster in France and Japan). Or one might ponder the evidence that among the most stylistically interesting things done in American writing today are Mark Danielewski's "ergo-writing," Chris Ware's graphic novels, and the fledgling nature of "multimedia literature" on tablets, led by such newfangled approaches as *Electric Literature*.

And yet, to generalize, as Engdahl does, is an essential human disposition. To abstract, to simplify is the mind's way of dealing with a vast universe of infinite possibilities. Without abstractions there is no thought, for to think is to condense, to synthesize, to sum up—to make sense. At any rate, I truly don't care, as I said, about the Nobel per se; what I'm attracted to is the kernel of truth behind the rejection, if such a kernel is indeed tangible. For, as far as I'm concerned, the statement is dead on: American literature *is* parochial, although I'm not sure this is a quality that distinguishes us and our literature from other nations and their respective literatures. By the same token, American literature could be described as the most cosmopolitan, the most universal of local literatures. By virtue of the fact that we are an immigrant nation, we have more "foreigners" (myself included) involved in shaping our bookshelf than any other country on the planet. Plus, when American authors write immigration and financial collapse stories set in the United States, aren't they writing about world concerns, considering the common theme of contraction following an arms-wide-open welcome (Sweden's a good example) and worldwide financial crises (Ireland, Greece)?

The argument for parochialism isn't difficult to prove, though. There has been a plethora of recent analysis offering some context, including Pascale Casanova's volume *The World Republic of Letters*. In a country like the United States with a population of over 315 million, the place of literature among us is risible. It is true that as a nation we don't participate in the big dialogue of literature *among ourselves*. Our literary writing is done by a small elite mostly for its own sake. The average American, ages fifteen to sixty-five, barely opens a single book a year. Still, the number of books published in the United States in 2012, according to Bowker, was 400,000, 55 percent of which were self-published. In other words, production far outstrips the demand: we manufacture books but don't do much with them afterward. Along the same lines, our bookstores appear to be on the verge of collapse, although this too is a double-edged sword since Amazon.com has created an entire new way of selling books. Bookstores in European countries have been propped up by laws that don't allow discounting, which is why there are no bookstore chains in France and Germany.

American literature is taught in colleges, which accounts for a large number of book sales. Interestingly, as William Chace reasoned a couple of years ago in the *American Scholar*, statistics show that in the past twenty years the number of English literature majors in universities in the United States had dropped by 50 percent, down to only 3.7 percent of college graduates, while the number of MFA programs has skyrocketed. On the changing nature of literary readership, it is sometimes said that undergraduate reading mainly focuses on "transgressive" literature (mainly non-WASP). This means that figures like John Cheever go unread. Conversely, Epictetus was broadly read in British schools in the nineteenth century. Perhaps this explains the concept of a funnel shape to literary reading, with the distant past at the narrow end. In any case, nobody seems to care too much that the place of literature in the United States is vanishing. We're transitioning from the traditional print book to e-books even though, again, this truism is questioned by the leveling off of e-book sales in recent years. Besides, storytelling in America is probably more alive today than ever. Our days are filled with tales we tell one another; it's simply that literature is no longer the conduit. Movies, TV, the internet, and video games have displaced it.

American literature is parochial because America is solipsistic. This isn't to say we don't travel. Actually, travel is a national sport among the middle class. We're in cars traversing the country, and, money permitting, our curiosity leads us to visit other societies. But travel for us is by definition a complacent endeavor. Americans only go to safe, secure places where the food and accommodations guarantee that we still feel at home. Therein lies the key to our parochialism: it is an illness of abundance. There is much to see and means to achieve it. Yet we fail to venture beyond secure confines because we are afraid of getting lost. Loss is about the lack of control, and we love to be in control. In our literature, we embrace the exact same approach: we love when our fiction shows us foreign lands but only if those lands are friendly to Americans; and when they aren't, we want the characters to make it safely home. For home is what we're all about: its security, its durability.

How do we define home? As the absence of foreignness. The easiest way to show the degree of parochialism in American literature is to point to the allergy we have toward foreign languages. We never listen to popular songs in other languages. And notwithstanding the popularity of films like Mexico's *Like Water for Chocolate* and Germany's *The Lives of Others*, we tend not to like movies with subtitles. If a successful movie is made in French, for instance, we'd rather wait for the Hollywood remake. In general, translation makes us uncomfortable, even though this country is a Babel of languages, with more than one hundred languages spoken just within one school district in Los Angeles or Queens. On TV, we only like foreign series like *Downton Abbey*, which are made in England and satisfy our obsession with class difference. Sure, the show is a hit in other countries as well, from Sweden to South Korea. Still, nothing in the original language from Italy, Germany, and Turkey is likely to make it to our screen. This aversion is equally apparent in literature: only 3 percent of what's released by American publishers is in translation, in contrast with close to 45 percent in several European countries. Yet American publishers brag about being the world's primary seller of foreign rights. As a result, the exposure the United States has to foreign literature is minuscule. A country as vast as ours is really an island.

None of this says anything about American literature as such. To what extent is the fiction we consume narrow-minded? We are somewhat more forgiving with nonfiction, endorsing investigative writing dealing with war zones and other "problem" sites. We like that type of nonfiction if it is about American policy or about American genius understood in the broadest sense: our capacity to make the world a place we can recognize. But let's stick to fiction. Even when our writers travel abroad, like Jay McInerney or Jhumpa Lahiri, it is to follow an American character on foreign soil. That anchor allows for all sorts of explorations: ignorance, courage, self-knowledge. What matters is that one of us is always receiving an epiphany.

Look at Philip Roth, our perennial Nobel candidate and a writer I admire profoundly. His oeuvre is a tapestry of American motifs: male insecurity, the voracious dream of success, the collapse of public trust. . . . Roth is a cosmopolitan in that he ventures outside our own confines: to London, Prague, and Israel. His Newark is an aleph of the world entire, the universal inhabiting the local. One must also take into consideration Roth's estimable work as cultural mediator in editing the Writers from the Other Europe series for Penguin and in publishing interviews with writers from a wide variety of countries. But the other side of the argument is true as well. He and his movie counterpart, Woody Allen, are actually kings of parochialism. Rome? It looks like Cinecittà. Barcelona? A vacation spa. In Roth's case, whenever he ventures out it is to places where another Philip Roth, a *doppelgänger*, is doing his tricks, as in the Israel portrayed in *Operation Shylock*. That is, he does go abroad—always to Europe—but the outcome remains the same: the world is there for him to become better. Hardly ever does the world exist on its own terms.

Examples showing the two sides of the debate are plentiful. Take John Updike, another icon: his *Rabbit* trilogy is as American as apple pie, and equally insular. Events in them always happen in the suburbs; the rest of the world is a rumor, an afterthought. Tim O'Brien and Robert Stone let themselves be puzzled in Vietnam, and occasionally in the Middle East or Latin America, but it always feels as if the whole journey is a variation on the theme of American Quixotism. In *The Poisonwood Bible* and *The Lacuna*, Barbara Kingsolver, another admirable novelist, sends her cast overseas; but they are missionaries of American values, struggling to inculcate them in others (even when they know the consequences) or to be tested by the political environment on which they stumble. Then there are more native cases, like the boy genius David Foster Wallace, whose focus is the American obsession right here and now. But the reverse is true too: Don DeLillo has cosmic aspirations; and Dave Eggers's books wander as they wonder (to use a Langston Hughes expression) from Somalia to San Francisco, distilling a genuine desire to look beyond, to explore what other realities are about. Adam Johnson's Pulitzer Prize–winning *The Orphan Master's Son* is about North Korea minus the American traveling abroad. The fact that it was a *New York Times* bestseller might be seen as proof of our antiparochialism.

It could be argued that foreignness in American literature is unique because this is a land of immigrants and foreignness is never outside our shores. Henry Roth, Toni Morrison, Louise Erdrich, and Chang-Rae Lee write about the shock of arriving, getting acclimated, and reinventing oneself here. The world entire is contained inside us. This view suggests that American literature is a microcosm. But this is a cheap excuse: precisely because we welcome the huddled masses yearning to breathe free do Americans have a responsibility to the rest of the world. That responsibility isn't about making others familiar with who we are but about acquainting ourselves—without subterfuges—to what life elsewhere is about and not doing so for our own benefit. American immigrant literature is as parochial, maybe more so. Take Junot Díaz, whose characters are mostly Dominican. In *The Brief Wondrous Life of Oscar Wao* he sets the plot in the Dominican Republic, as he occasionally does in his stories. But even then the material feels American-centric: a chubby American geek interacting with locals through the prism of American pop culture. That's what we all do: be in the world while never leaving home. Sandra Cisneros and Amy Tan seem to look at the globe through the rearview mirror.

Was American literature always impossibly local while envisaging ambitiously global dreams? There was a time—the Gilded Age—when writers needed to prove the United States was a worthy literary place. Hawthorne, Poe, and Emerson sought to claim a place for the U.S., to test its strength, to find its true worth. They positioned the nation's worldview as worthy of any European counterpart. Melville's *Moby-Dick* might well be the most cosmopolitan of American novels, or the most nearsighted, depending on how one sees it. (In my mind, it is the first encyclopedic *Latin* American novel ever written.) Arguably, the less parochial of these might also be seen as the most American. My reverence for Mark Twain is enormous. He recounts his travels abroad in front of American audiences, but that tourism felt authentic. Likewise, *Adventures of Huckleberry Finn*, which Ernest Hemingway saw as the source, the beginning of everything American, is a journey inside our national boundaries that forces us to confront our limitations: a child and a free slave live in limbo.

The writer that has best come to represent the fortunes of Americans abroad is Henry James. *The Portrait of a Lady* is about a spirited young American woman in European society, the clashes she encounters, the tension between the two cultures. In other works, James explores the vicissitudes of Americans outside their milieu. The bridge between the Old World and the New feels symmetrical in his oeuvre. At the end of the nineteenth century, America was still a young democracy, struggling to find its footing in the world. And during the first half of the twentieth century, the Lost Generation went to Europe to find itself. And therein the solipsism that defines us: exile was nothing more than an extension of home. Spain and France were the stage where Americans like Hemingway socialized, where they proved their true worth. The discovery of those cultures was important to their maturity, but it was a temporary stage, unlike trips by subsequent writers such as Paul Bowles, whose detachment from his home base is unequivocal.

All in all, it's a fact that the dominant culture of the United States is aliterate, often antithetical to serious literature, which doesn't mean American literature is inferior. During the modernist period, serious writers were fortified by the belief that they represented an adversary culture, that they were at odds with their time. American writers are not adversaries but symptoms of an ambient, complacent philistinism. Again, it is important to keep in mind that these traits aren't unique to the United States. How many people in Albania, Bolivia, and Kenya read Goethe? Americans possess an aversion to foreign languages, and foreign films are rarely shown on American screens. But when they are, they are invariably shown with subtitles, forcing audiences to acknowledge foreign sounds. By contrast, in Italy and many other countries *every* foreign film is dubbed, meaning that audiences are totally insulated from any contact with the language in which the film was made. That almost 45 percent of Italy's books are translations doesn't mean Italians are more cosmopolitan than we are.

For every writer sees the world from a provincial perspective. Franz Kafka's *Amerika* provides a look at Oklahoma from the vantage point of Prague. And to prove how cosmopolitan we are, how nonprovincial our view is, one might look at the nominees for the 2012 National Book Critics Circle Awards. Poetry finalist A. E. Stallings flew in from her home in Greece for the event. David Ferry was another poetry finalist, and much of his book consists of translations. Autobiography finalist Reyna Grande wrote about her immigration from Mexico. Other finalists in autobiography included Anthony Shadid writing about his family home in Lebanon and Ngũgĩ wa Thiong'o writing about his childhood in Kenya. In nonfiction, Katherine Boo provided a riveting account of life in a Mumbai slum. For fiction, as I mentioned, Adam Johnson set his novel *The Orphan Master's Son* convincingly inside North Korea. The winning fiction entry, Ben Fountain's *Billy Lynn's Long Halftime Walk*, is neoclassical in its focus on one day, Thanksgiving, and in one place, Dallas, yet it encompasses the world. In other words, our philistinism is the key to our sophistication.

I was once at a dinner party in Chile when a distinguished writer told me an invaluable truth: excitement in our time is rarely connected to literature anymore. It belongs to science. It is far more fun to have lunch with a scientist these days than with a writer. Scientists are at the cutting edge; the world belongs to them. Writers, instead, like to complain they don't get enough attention. And literary critics—like me—make a profession of these types of complaints. She added that Americans are prone to complain even more than everyone else. When something doesn't go their way, they let the world know about it. Since their ego is the size of their country, their complaints are louder. Her main argument was that in the twenty-first century, literature has lost its mojo but American writers haven't realized it. She concluded by saying—and this I remember as the apex of the evening—that to compensate for this, writers in the United States like to think of themselves as entertainers. They don't belong to the society of world literature because that society would parry that what American writers do isn't as entertaining as they think it is.

Another generation, for sure. Anyhow, the comment reverberates in my mind. American exceptionalism makes us believe we are extraordinary. Consequently, we trust our literature is outstanding as well. We are as narrow as everyone else, and our literature showcases it. What does it mean to be exceptional? The conviction that one is just like everyone else, except a little more so. Other nations don't believe they are exceptional, so their parochialism has fewer global consequences. But then again, perhaps we're just entertainers.

AMHERST COLLEGE

Ilan Stavans (b. 1961) is the Lewis-Sebring Professor in Latin American and Latino Culture at Amherst College, and publisher of Restless Books. His latest books are *I Love My Selfie* (with ADÁL) and *Quixote: The Novel and the World*. He has translated into English the poetry of Sor Juana Inés de la Cruz, Rubén Darío, Jorge Luis Borges, and Pablo Neruda, among others. He is also the editor of *The FSG Book of Twentieth-Century Latin American Poetry* (2011).

GOLDEN RICE SHEAVES   (2021)

ZHENG MIN

Translated from the Chinese by Ming Di

Golden rice stands in sheaves
in the freshly cut autumn field.
I think of many exhausted mothers and see
beautiful, wrinkled faces along the road at dusk.
This is the day of harvest, a full moon hangs
atop the towering trees
and in the twilight, distant mountains
circling my heart.
No statues can ever be more solemn.
Shouldering great weariness, you
lower your head in thought
in the far-reaching field of autumn.
Silence. Silence. History is but a small
stream flowing under your feet.
And you—you just stand there, your thought
becoming a thought of the human race.

Zheng Min (1920–2022) is one of China's most important contemporary poets. She taught poetry at Beijing Normal University, and her *Collected Poems* appeared in 2016. Also an accomplished translator and critic, she published *Contemporary American Poetry* (1987) and four books of critical essays on Western philosophy and comparative poetics.

The author of seven books of poetry in Chinese, a collaborative translation, and the editor/co-translator of several anthologies, Ming Di is a poet from China based in the US. She received the Lishan Poetry Award and the 2021 Best Ten Translator Award in China.

THE MODERN RENAISSANCE OF ARABIC LITERATURE   (1955)

TAHA HUSSEIN

Translated from the French by Ernst Erich Noth

TO APPRECIATE the true worth—and it is not at all negligible—of the renaissance of Arabic literature during the last quarter of a century, we must first make certain observations which bring themselves to our attention. They all go back to the many difficulties which for a long time prevented this literature from freely reaching its full scope. If we consider that it begins about 1925, we must state at once those obstacles which, for centuries, hindered the flowering of Arabic letters. They are of two kinds. The first are internal; they are concerned with an inherent difficulty of Arabic literature which, weighted down with a tradition more than a thousand years old, could not throw off the heavy burden of its complex heritage.

First, there was the pre-Islamic tradition: it imposed its imperious tyranny on every man of letters, be he prose writer or poet. Indeed, to be really literary an Arabic text had to have more or less the flavor of the desert, as much from the point of view of content as of form. Something of Bedouin nostalgia had to permeate every poem. A vague "something" had to be felt through everything written in prose. And the poetic forms which the Arabs learned toward the sixth century of the Christian era had to be respected. The slightest deviation was severely condemned. Not that several poets did not try sometimes to move away timidly from these desert forms; but they found that they always had to come back to them, take up the beaten path, and follow what the ancient critics called "the traditional column of poetry." Prose itself has developed only within a very rigid framework. It is known only through books of history, literary criticism, science, and philosophy; it lives also, thanks to certain translations from Hindu or Persian wisdom, thanks also to epistolary literature, thanks to what one might call official literature: decrees, proclamations, and discourses of the caliphs. But short stories, novelettes, even the saga novel, were considered as belonging to the domain of popular literature, which had nothing in common with genuine classical literature, the only kind worthy of interesting the intellectuals, that is to say, people of good taste.

The second difficulty, no less despotic, is, however, of an external character. I would like to call it the "Hellenistic difficulty." It was induced by the translation into Arabic, during the course of the eighth and ninth centuries, of the philosophy of Aristotle, but particularly by the translation of his *Rhetoric*. This work quickly familiarized the Arabs with the famous *fleurs*, artificial figures, and verbal ornamentation. That is, as time went on, poets and prose writers rivaled in the creation of a literature where the classicism of the desert and Greek rhetoric were more or less harmoniously wedded.

There remains a third and last difficulty, likewise of an external nature—the stagnation imposed upon the whole Arabic world by the Turkish-Ottoman domination. Indeed, for several centuries, all relations between the Arab world and the outside world were cut off. Iraqis, Syrians, Lebanese, and Egyptians were obliged to fall back upon themselves and be content with the heritage that they had received, without any hope of renewal. Their literature became formal and lost practically all its vigor. It was not until the nineteenth century that a contact was reinstated between this closed world and the Occident, and this communication was finally to bring a breath of fresh air into the too-long closed world of Arabic literature.

There is still one other obstacle to be pointed out which is really neither internal nor external. It is difficult to define. I mean the restraints caused by a religion badly understood by people long condemned to ignorance and withdrawn into gross conservatism. People believed, a little naïvely, that the Arabic language, since it was the language of the Qur'an, was a sacred language. Now, a sacred language controls those who speak it and leaves little liberty to those who make use of it. It becomes forbidden to invent. Therefore, the Arabs, instead of using their language, became its docile slaves. All innovation in expression was looked upon with a prejudiced eye and labeled near-heresy.

That, then, is the heritage left to the generation of the end of the last century and the beginning of this one. Indeed, an Arabic language existed, but it was paralyzed; there was still an Arabic literature, but it was enslaved. This generation had the gigantic task of liberating language and literature from their heavy chains. It was engaged in doing so during the first quarter of this century. Its work was not easy and the political circumstances made it still more arduous. It was not until the victory of the Allies in 1918 that Egypt first, then the other Arab nations, recovered a little of their personality. Ottoman Turkey had just been conquered: its domination over the Arabic world came definitively to a close. On their side, the Allies had made fine promises to the Arabic peoples; too many, really, for them ever to be able to keep them all. But at the time of the victory, the Arabs took these Western commitments very seriously, for they certainly did not intend to be freed from Ottoman slavery to fall under English rule in Iraq and Egypt, or French rule in Syria and Lebanon.

Also, we were going to witness a double struggle, begun in Egypt. From 1919 until today the Arabic nations have fought in the political arena to obtain their complete independence, and they are likewise engaged in an intellectual battle to shake off the stifling traditions and the old prejudices. The story of this spiritual freedom is, then, closely linked with that of physical liberation.

It was on the morrow of the Armistice of 1918 that Egypt began the struggle, and the other Arab countries followed. The Egyptian impetus was of importance: the breath of revolution animated the Egyptians, men and women, young and old. Everyone was proud to fight against the formidable British Empire which had just conquered Germany and Austria-Hungary in Europe, Turkey in Asia. The Egyptian people, in order to win their independence, agreed to enormous sacrifices and smilingly accepted English repression. However, in the wake of that revolt against foreign domination, another kind of reaction was born and developed rather rapidly to attain its first objective: I mean that revolution of the mind which soon secured liberty of thought and expression. In reality, parallel to the armed uprising against political oppression, a rebellion spread out against a long past laden with medieval traditions as irritating as military violence.

The first phase of this battle took place in 1920–21. A bitter argument began between young partisans of innovations in the domain of literature in particular and more generally in the things of the spirit, and the old conservatives, partisans of literary as well as religious tradition. The former maintained that the Arabic language should be considered like the other living languages, that is to say, as the servant of those who used it and not like a despotic mistress. Also, they assumed the prerogative of creating new words, ones that were not found in the dictionaries, and of adopting from the current dialect terms which were more suitable to their new manner of expression, of borrowing, even, from occidental languages a certain number of terms which had no equivalent in the traditional Arabic language. They declared, then, that, living in the twentieth century, it was right that they should express themselves and that they should think according to their period and no longer according to bygone times. The struggle in which they engaged was difficult; it was above all impassioned, and for several years the Arab world was absorbed in this great quarrel between the Ancients and the Moderns, which was reminiscent of that which stirred French intellectuals at the end of the seventeenth century and the beginning of the eighteenth.

Naturally, this quarrel soon crossed the borders of Egypt, where it had begun, and inflamed the whole Near East. Mustapha Al-Raf'l, Ahmad Al-Sakandari, and their disciples labored in vain to defend the Ancients. Victory belonged, according to the nature of things, to the spirited partisans of the Moderns; 'Abbas Al-'Akkad, Ibrahim Al-Mazni, Hussein Heikal, Salama Moussa, Taha Hussein won over to their cause not only all the youth of that day, but also some old poets who undertook, after the Revolution, a complete renovation of their technique. So it is that our great Ahmad Chawki, official court poet in his youth, completely renounced his first manner from then on. He became modern and, in company with Hafez Ibrahim and Khalil Mutran, became the precentor of the national movement in Egypt as well as in the other Arab nations. Chawki went even further; not content with celebrating in his verse the Egyptian Revolution and the Arab liberation, he wanted also to praise the Turkish Kemalist movement, and I do not think that the Turks themselves have praised their victory in Asia Minor more highly than the Egyptian poet did. Moreover, Chawki introduced into Arabic literature a genre that it did not know until then: the drama in verse. It was in the ancient history of his country that he first found his dramatic subjects. He chose

Cambyses, for example, because the invasion of the Persians permitted him to make the glorious resistance of Egypt to foreign armies live again. He also composed an "Anthony and Cleopatra," which sets forth Egyptian nationalism against a conquering Rome. But Chawki knew also how to draw from the ancient history of the Arabs: *Layla and Majnun* ("Layla and the Madman") evokes the Arab empire at the height of its glory, when it imposed its peace upon the ancient world, thus permitting citizens to devote themselves to a life of leisure and praise of the passionate mysticism of platonic love.

There was not only Chawki and poetry. An extraordinary renovation manifested itself in all branches of classic Arabic literature. To analyze that real "rebirth" of Arabic letters, which occurred almost suddenly in the years 1920–30, it would be necessary first to point out the principal causes. They are three in number. In the first place must be mentioned that reaction against what was foreign, a reaction which resulted in liberating minds and consciences. Then came the publication, thanks to the progress and amazing extension of printing, of classical works of the true Arab period. Finally, one must not underestimate the influence of the translation into Arabic of the great masterpieces of foreign literatures, notably French and English. Doubtless, it is only justice to remark that the printing of ancient books and the translation of Western works had begun and had been increasing since the middle of the nineteenth century. Nevertheless, it must be emphasized that they yielded their finest fruits only after the Arabs secured that requisite to the existence of all literature—physical and moral liberty.

In 1923 the first Egyptian constitution was promulgated. It guaranteed, among other things, liberty of thought, expression, and assembly. Thus it is that the history of Arabic literature from this moment, particularly in Egypt, exactly coincides with the history of Arab liberty. However, let it be mentioned at once that the king of Egypt, Fouad I, who promulgated this constitution, had done it in spite of himself; he cherished the mental reservation of seizing any opportunity that presented itself to violate its most important articles. But the majority of Egyptians, notably the intellectuals of this generation, decided to take this constitution seriously and firmly believed they had obtained in a definitive form the spiritual liberty to which they aspired, and they made use of it unreservedly.

That is why the conflict between them and royal power could not be long in coming.

In 1925 a man from the famous theological university Al-Azhar, then judge of the religious courts of personal laws, 'Ali 'Abdel Razek, brought out a book, *Islam and the Principles of Power*. The author broke with all established religious tradition and with all political tradition which sprang from it. He established, in reality, that the institution of the caliphate was not at all religious in nature, but that it was simply a political and human institution like any other; he concluded that since the caliphate was only a form of government similar to many different forms of government, the Muslims were not compelled, religiously speaking, to have a caliphate. They could then very well do without a caliphate and adopt any form of government which they pleased, monarchial or republican. Neither had the Turks failed in their religious duties by abolishing the caliphate at Constantinople. And 'Ali 'Abdel Razek concluded his study by affirming that no other Muslim country was obliged on account of religion to reestablish within it the caliphate so wisely rejected by the Turks.

The book upset completely, on one hand, solidly established traditions, and on the other, the secret aims of Egypt's sovereign, who was only waiting for an occasion to reestablish the caliphate in Cairo and proclaim himself caliph. So the royal power and the religious authorities combined to wage war on this dangerous thesis and punish its author. They mobilized some theologians and a certain number of lay conservatives in order to demolish the new doctrine, assuredly pernicious, and 'Ali 'Abdel Razek was brought before the tribunal of Al-Azhar University, which, after hearing him, declared him a "heretic" and struck his name from the role of the "Ulemas." If this sentence had as an immediate consequence making the courageous writer lose his position as judge, it resulted above all in provoking violent retorts from many intellectuals of Egypt and other Arabic countries. 'Abdel-'Aziz Fahrni, then minister of justice in Egypt, flatly refused to carry out this penalty of Al-Azhar, declaring it unconstitutional. He was dismissed from his position and a grave ministerial crisis was thus begun.

A year later, almost to the day, I published (I was then professor of Arabic literature at the lay University of Cairo) a volume titled *Pre-Islamic Poetry*. This objective study caused an even greater scandal than 'Ali 'Abdel

Razek's book. The institution of the caliphate was only concerned with politics and, naturally, indirectly with religion, while the problem of pre-Islamic poetry implicated both traditional literature, the exegesis of the Qur'an, and the very method of dealing with ancient things. I desired, however, in bringing out this work, only to approach ancient Arabic texts according to the philological and critical methods which Western scholars used when they wanted to study Greek and Latin literature. My work questioned the very authenticity of this poetry called "pre-Islamic" and established that the greater part of it had been invented at a much later time, that is, about a century after the great conquests of the Muslims; I then brought out the reasons why these poems had been invented after the event, the means which were used, and I gathered together a number of proofs difficult to refute.

But in so doing I demolished the whole system of the commentators on the Qur'an, who explained the sacred text by leaning, from the philological as well as from the grammatical point of view, upon this famous "pre-Islamic" poetry. Indeed, all the words of the Qur'an, all its grammatical forms, according to these commentators, should be found in this poetry, which was supposed to exist in Arabia since before the birth of the Prophet Mohammed. So then I completely reversed the roles, so to speak, and I maintained that far from proving the correctness of the Qur'an, this poetry required that the Qur'an on the contrary should prove its correctness, since the latter (related by an identical style of writing which leaves no doubt) came before the former, whereas this so-called "pre-Islamic" poetry was certainly composed afterward and recalled only by the memory of the bards exposed like everyone to a thousand weaknesses and to a hundred temptations which justify suspicion as to their sincerity and the authenticity of what they were able to transmit.

The reaction was vociferous. The king, the religious authorities, public opinion, and the majority of Parliament itself were in agreement in demanding that the government do away with the chair of Arabic literature which I occupied. 'Ali Al-Chamsi, then minister of public instruction, refused, however, in the name of freedom of thought. And the president of the Council, 'Adli Yeghen, went so far as to ask for a vote of confidence. They agreed on passing to the agenda and charging the prosecutor to open an inquiry against the author for "offending religion." After much questioning and several discussions between the representative of the religious university and the author, the prosecutor dismissed the charge and the affair was officially closed. But the polemics continued.

These two incidents, 'Ali 'Abdel Razek's book and mine, resulted in encouraging the Egyptian intellectuals, especially writers, to claim a greater liberty of thought as well as of expression. No censorship ought to be imposed upon them. They should not be exposed to annoying reactions from anyone. These Egyptian intellectuals knew, indeed, that liberty is not granted but won. That is why they undertook then to attack on all fronts, regardless of whether they were political, social, literary, moral. They finally won. Moreover, they now gained the support of the readers, who were at first most obstinate, and their public grew from day to day. So it happened that after a few years, the ideas of 'Ali 'Abdel Razek and myself, which were fought against so strongly, became classic, so to speak; they are generally accepted today. For no Egyptian of today—and I would go so far as to say no Arab—thinks seriously of the reestablishment of the caliphate; and wherever classical Arabic literature is taught, the authenticity of "pre-Islamic" poetry is considered questionable.

The twelve years that followed World War I were prolific years. Everybody seemed drunk with liberty, and each tried to prove to himself and to show to others that he was free.

So-called "vulgar" speech also experienced a new vigor and especially in Egypt was given such an impetus that a whole literature written in colloquial language became abundant. People who scarcely knew how to read and write began to compose verse in current speech; they told of the renter's hate, their enthusiasm for an independence finally within their grasp, their admiration for the leaders exiled by the British or even put in prison in Egypt. Or else they criticized the ministers who deserved it, and some of them had no fear of loosing satirical thrusts at the king and his court. Thus, a new genre found its place in popular literature: satire, the pamphlet, and the lampoon enjoyed more favor with the public at large than these same literary forms in the classical domain. And thanks to the satirical comedy, many spectators laughed every evening at the expense of the occupying English and the men in power. Later, when spirits were more calm, this theater evolved and was transformed into social satire, which rendered important services in stimulating a national conscience, sometimes a little numbed, and in pointing out certain vices and wretchedness; but its principal value was to dazzle the eyes of the Egyptians with a vast program of reforms and a whole ideal of social justice not yet dreamed of but never again forgotten. On one hand, consequently, the intellectuals who expressed themselves in a classical fashion moved the enlightened class of Arab society by their books, their poems, their novels, their articles; on the other hand, those of popular talent who made use of their dialects stirred the simplest hearts by their poems, their songs, and periodicals anyone could buy. There were not only the quasi-illiterates to be thus reached: the intellectuals themselves were interested to the point that about 1928–30 it was feared in the Arab world that there might be two literatures: the first, classical but renewed; the second, popular, more expressive, and more suitable for moving people.

Even a few classical writers almost went over to popular literature, and it is in this light that we see our great novelist and short-story writer Mahmoud Teymour begin to write stories in the common tongue. This was not all; after the Congress of Orientalists held at Oxford in 1928, we witnessed a scientific defense of popular speech. Fortunately, as soon as Egypt had made a start toward independence and was consequently engaged in problems of public instruction, she exerted praiseworthy efforts to extend education as much as possible. About this time she created thousands of primary schools and hundreds of secondary schools, and thanks to this double undertaking classical Arabic could predominate.

We have just seen that these twelve years were largely given over to two important quarrels: first, the one that can be called "The Quarrel of the Ancients and the Moderns"; later, the one which arose between the partisans of the popular language and the defenders of the classical language. Things could not remain in that state. Sometime later a third quarrel arose; it brought into conflict only the classical writers, one against the other. This dispute was of long duration, and fortunately it was finally recognized that it was vain and sterile. In it the champions of French literature opposed the supporters of Anglo-Saxon letters. Indeed, until then the Arabs in general and the Egyptians in particular cultivated only these two literatures for the good reason that only the English and French languages were then taught in the schools. And naturally those who knew one of these two literatures, often to the detriment of the other, gave that one the preference and did all they could to aid in its expansion. Neither side stopped with writing polemics; they tried to make the great master-pieces of these two important literatures known by means of translations or studies. However, there were Egyptians who went to Germany and Italy, and they introduced Goethe and Dante to the Orient. They even translated Tolstoy and Dostoevsky into Arabic, and it is then that we understood that a country which wanted to be really free must not give her spirit solely to one rather than to another of the numerous foreign literatures. Quite to the contrary, this country ought to welcome all forms of civilization and culture, lend itself to absorbing all literatures and all ideas, wherever they may come from. Just at this point these Egyptians began to demand the teaching of the principal foreign languages in the schools.

In addition, the creation in 1926 of the first large university in Cairo (there are two today) implied that the teaching of the two classical languages, Greek and Latin, was indispensable for all real culture. The student body was in that way put in contact with two essential literatures. It was not long before some translations of Greek words into Arabic were published, thus tying up again with the medieval Arabic tradition. I translated Sophocles, and *Antigone* and *Oedipus* were played in Cairo. Then the rising generation understood that not only living languages and literatures were worthy of interest, but that there were likewise among the Ancients, Greek or Roman, things which, just like the Arabic culture of antiquity, were worthy of attention and of being carefully cultivated.

The founding of the University of Cairo also brought the young people into contact with professors who came from almost all the nations of Europe. Egypt, in reality, in order to enrich the staffs of its new faculties, called upon French, English, Belgian, Swiss, German, and Italian scholars as well as Austrian, Russian, Spanish, Dutch, and Swedish. The result of this intelligent policy was that many Egyptian minds were broadened by contact with these exchanges from the West and that, finally emerging from its too-long solitude, our country could meet on its own territory intellectuals and scholars of the entire world. This imperative need for universalism did not stop there. Egypt sent her children to do or complete their higher studies first in Europe, then more and more students crossed the Atlantic to finish their work in America. By so doing, Egypt (and other countries of the Middle East followed her example) established solid cultural relations with Europe and the New World. They continue to grow stronger and to bear encouraging fruits. She did more; at the same time she opened her schools and her universities to the pupils and students of the Oriental world, from Morocco to China, and she sent her own teachers to teach in all the Arabic countries of the East. In this way, Egypt reestablished her historic mission: to serve as a bridge between the East and the West, a spiritual vocation which the Ottoman conquest first, then the British occupation, had tried to stifle. Thanks to Egypt, the whole Arab world, until then open to the politics and economy of the West, assimilated also its culture. The role assumed by Egypt deserves to be emphasized, for it has not ceased to have a considerable influence on the Arab literature of these last twenty-five years.

But to complete, in so far as is possible, this brief picture of foreign contributions to Arabic literature, one must mention a phenomenon which concerns Syria and Lebanon exclusively. It is the Syro-Lebanese immigration to America, notably South America. It goes back to a former period, it is true, before the time which concerns us; however, these Eastern immigrants who settled more or less permanently in that part of the New World certainly did not forget their mother tongue. On the contrary, they preserved it jealously, and some of them devoted themselves to literature. Doubtless they were strongly affected by the American physical and social influences; they made, in any case, an important contribution, in verse as well as in prose, very different from that which was written in the countries of their origin, both in form and content. In fact, these writers of the immigration attacked in their works metaphysical problems which the writers and poets of the Arabic Orient no longer hardly paid any attention to. When one reads Gibran Khalil Gibran, Amin Al-Rihani, Fawzi Al-Ma'louf, one feels a little expatriated, their thought seems so much fashioned in the mold of the American concepts which surround them. The form, also, which they use seems to have undergone a foreign imprint; so one frequently sees these writers and poets doing violence to the Arabic language and breaking more or less with the classic traditions; often also they set aside the rules of grammar. Nevertheless, thanks to the renaissance of literature in the East and to the shortening of distances, these émigré writers find themselves more and more in close communication with the country of their origin, with the literary works which are published there. So they cannot fail to return to the essentials of the general character of modern Oriental Arabic literature.

These permanent and close contacts of Egypt and the Arab world with the contemporary universe have had marvelous results. Arabic literature had to renew itself and harmonize itself, so to speak, with literature as such, and that is the real miracle which the generation of the last twenty-five years succeeded in accomplishing. It is enough, in fact, to compare the acquisitions of Arabic literature of today with the products of traditional Arabic literature (and I speak naturally of only the best, that which covers the first four centuries of Islam) in order to realize the truly extraordinary advance of our literature in just a quarter of a century. This notable progress can be seen in four well-defined quarters: prose, drama, novel, and criticism, whether it be literary, political, or social. [. . .] Thus, this generation, whose history I am trying to sketch broadly, will not only have given back to Arabic literature the splendor that belonged to it when it was at its apogee, but will have begun to make it a world literature. [. . .]

During the first four centuries of Islam the Arabs had translated and assimilated Greek, Persian, and Hindu cultures and had succeeded in building a civilization which was their own; however, the contemporary Arabs found themselves face to face with a task of a different complexity. They had before them an extraordinary diversity of cultures, and with courage and boldness they undertook to open the minds and hearts of their brothers to these multiple and varied heritages. Thanks to their persevering effort the Arabic language today draws on all the sources of civilization, Western or Eastern, ancient or modern. In our day it is a far cry from a modern Egyptian university to a medieval Arabic university, not to speak of a Western university of the Middle Ages. And this enormous work was accomplished in less than thirty years. That is a miracle. Obviously, one could indeed claim that the means which the contemporaries have at hand are more effective than those at the disposal of the Ancients who could not even imagine their existence. It is not less admirable that so-called "backward" peoples have been able to appropriate such methods so quickly and make use of them in so peremptory a fashion. This consideration acquires more weight still if one considers that the Arabic world has not yet entirely regained its freedom. It must do so. Many political, economic, and technical difficulties remain to be overcome, but it is no longer forbidden to dream of the incalculable importance of the contribution that the Arab world, once truly liberated, and using the means which independent nations have in their hands, will be able to offer to the great human work of civilization, culture, and spiritual progress, the attainment of the goal dear to every man who thinks: peace with liberty and justice.

Does this mean that contemporary Arabic literature has really attained its full maturity and surmounted all the obstacles which prevented its free unfolding? I do not think so. There are many paths yet to be trod, many problems to be solved before that literature may fulfill the dreams we hold for it. Let us take a quick glance at the shackles. First, Arabic poetry is very far from coming up to our expectations. It cannot be compared with ancient Arabic poetry, which played a preponderant role. In honesty it must be confessed that our poetry has shown an undeniable decadence in the twenty-five years. That is easily explained: to flourish, poetry doubtless needs a real equilibrium between men and life, an equilibrium of an inner nature, obviously. Now, the Arabic world of today has completely broken with its classical traditions of feeling and thinking and has not yet sufficiently assimilated new ways of living. For the moment it is lost between a heavy past of prejudices and traditions and a present which forces it to an adaptation not yet completed. That is why it is to be feared that so long as a modern way of life is not acclimated in the Arabic Orient, its poetry will remain without vigor.

Let us notice, besides, that prose accommodates itself much more easily than poetry to this unbalance between what one has been and what one hopes to be. It even becomes a valid solution for achieving that difficult balance and for making the transition from secular tradition to present reality less painful. Naturally, there was a fine flourishing of Arabic poetry so long as the Arabs sought their literary ideal in the classics of an earlier day; thus it flowered only in the restricted milieu of scholars. Therefore, in Iraq, Djamil Al-Zahawi (who died about thirty years ago) sought his inspiration in the Arab philosopher-poets of the tenth and eleventh centuries of the Christian era. Am'rul Al-Rassafi (who died about twenty years ago) turned toward the pure sources of archaic classicism of the seventh and eighth centuries of the Christian era. Let us not omit some poets,

Egyptian and Lebanese, who, without forgetting ancient classicism, cast a glance now and then toward the European and American West and more or less succeeded in effecting a certain harmony between these two modes of feeling and of expressing oneself; but they were not at ease in this genre and, moreover, they did not awaken profound or lasting response in the society which surrounded them.

It is only after World War I and the revolutionary movements to which I have referred that these poets succeeded in drawing closer to the masses and in moving them more. This generation of poets which attempted to compose verse by following two contradictory models, classic Arabic in form, classic European in content, disappeared with the death of the two great Egyptian poets Hafez and Chawki and with the recent passing of the very remarkable Lebanese-Egyptian poet Khalil Mutran. The young poets are today buffeted between an ancient classicism to which they do not sincerely belong and a Western modernism without roots. In conclusion, present-day Arabic poetry is groping its way, and I am confident that it will find itself someday, sooner or later.

These, then, are some of the many difficulties which contemporary Arabic literature has not yet surmounted. There are others, such as the question of illiteracy. That plague is still much too extensive in the Arab world, thanks to English colonial policy, on one hand, thanks to the despotic and feudal regime still in force in the majority of Arabic nations, on the other hand. It is a sad fact that 60 percent of the Arab world does not know how to read or write; that is to say, they remain complete strangers to literature. The primary result is that literature enormously loses its effectiveness, since at present it can reach only a minority—those who can read. In the second place, the Arab writers are deprived of essential liberties for, not being able to expect to be read by the majority, they find themselves constrained to seek other means of livelihood and consequently to earn their living outside of literature. And if it is true that in Europe, and elsewhere, literature does not "feed the man," it is still more true that an Arab writer who would expect his books to support him would be in grave danger of dying of hunger. Such a situation sometimes requires compromises, even surrender harmful to real intellectual liberty. It is only fair to mention that the governments of the Arab countries of the Orient are today expending greater and greater efforts to fight illiteracy and that it is reasonable to hope that in ten or fifteen years to come they will succeed.

However, although illiteracy should be checked and the number of Arab leaders considerably increased, a serious handicap would remain to be solved: our literature will remain ineffective for a long time, even if more people know how to read and write, so long as the knotty problem of the writing is not solved. A literature is first made by being easy of access; it is not so if it is not readable. That is a material condition of vital importance to the written book. Now, Arabic writing is difficult to decipher. It has remained, as it was in ancient times, a kind of shorthand which rebuffs the noninitiated. It is by nature destined for an elite, that is to say, a minority; it absolutely does not correspond to a democratic life which stipulates that instruction is a right of everyone and that the governments have the duty to dispense it to everyone. Arabic writing is not vocalized, and demands, to be read correctly, a sum of knowledge and culture sufficient to permit one to understand first and to read accordingly what one has previously understood. That ability cannot be required of every man. It is then imperative, if one desires that Arabic literature be read and appreciated by the greatest number, that our writing be reformed, democratized, and placed within the grasp of the masses who are in the process of overcoming illiteracy. They are now looking for a way to transform this writing without being forced to break with the past or to renounce the lofty Arab-Musulman heritage. The liberty and effectiveness of Arabic literature will not be assured until the day when the masses can read correctly and enjoy what they read.

There will remain, after all, a last difficulty. It is of a material sort and I do not think that it is peculiar to the Arab world. I am speaking of the standard of living of the average reader. It is difficult for men now to find the necessary leisure to cultivate their minds. In the state of the Oriental world today, the worker, the laborer, the artisan, or the farmer is obliged to live an existence which leaves him just enough time to earn sufficient for the bare necessities—when he can get them. He certainly does not have time to read. A tired man, whose daily concern is to assure his family a little bread, cares little for literature.

Finally, when all these obstacles have been conquered, Arabic literature will find itself, like all the other literatures, moreover, at grips with a last obstacle arising from the mechanical progress of the modern world: the difficulty which exists already and which is becoming intensified of coming to terms with radio, press, movies, television, and the future inventions of the human species. Naturally, Arabic literature suffers the consequences of these discoveries, which become more widespread every day. But I see in it a stimulating proof of its success. Henceforth, it is in a position to tackle the questions posed by the other great world literatures. The lag is largely caught up and our literature is testing now its young strength, its renascent virtues, and its new vigor.

CAIRO

A leading figure of the Arab Renaissance and the modernist movement in the Arab world, Taha Hussein (1889–1973) was one of the most influential Egyptian writers and intellectuals of the twentieth century. Known as "The Dean of Arabic Literature," Hussein was "influential in the introduction of a new secular university and a burgeoning press in Egypt—and prominent in public debates over nationalism and the roles of religion, women, and education in making a modern independent nation" (Stanford University Press).

Born in Berlin, Ernst Erich Noth (1909–1983) was the second editor of *Books Abroad*, from 1949 to 1958.

IN SPIRIT, IF NOT IN FACT (1940)

THOMAS MANN

65 STOCKTON STREET, PRINCETON, N.J., APRIL 20, 1940

DEAR DR. HOUSE,

I am greatly honored by the award which your jury has just bestowed on me, and which gives me great pride and pleasure. Had you been able to obtain the opinion of a larger number of critics and writers, the result of the vote might well have been very different, but I am none the less deeply affected by this recognition of my work, and am much beholden to you and your Committee.

My distinguished fellow-candidates for the award, Marcel Proust, James Joyce, Robert Frost, Jules Romains and Aldous Huxley, are writers with whom I am most happy to have been in company, and I regard the award to have included them, in spirit if not in fact.

With appreciation and gratitude,

Yours very sincerely,

Thomas Mann

Thomas Mann (1875–1955), Germany's 1929 Nobel laureate, sought refuge from the Nazi regime in Switzerland and the U.S. during the 1930s and '40s. In "*Books Abroad*'s Super-Nobel Election"—the results of which were published in the spring 1940 issue—various critics were asked to name "the most distinguished literary work of the entire post-1918 period." Thomas Mann, Marcel Proust, and James Joyce were voted first, second, and third place, respectively. Mann sent this reply to *Books Abroad*'s editor, Roy Temple House.

IN PRAISE OF THE REPUBLIC OF LETTERS (2009)

ALEŠ DEBELJAK

I'M A MODERN EVERYMAN. I make use of books to find for myself a dwelling place, if only a temporary one, within the pastiche of narratives and experiences, facts and fantasies. I leaf through the books, do not drink, and do not drive—I smoke and fly, through the tunnel under the city castle and over the main square, hovering for a second under the old plane tree before disappearing among the arcades of cajoling shop windows.

For me, the geography of towns, harbors, streets, and squares overlaps with literary topography. The poems and novels I read are chapters in a story about a *particular* place with which *any* place can identify. The tension between the fearful anxiety and the thrilling exploration that propels me on my wanderings around my imagined city delineates the modern mentality in which inescapable loyalty to a home place challenges one's need to freely choose identity.

I'm not an exception. I remain attached to my birth town, family house, and my reading-corner armchair. I lend an ear to poets and writers as I weave a literary cosmopolis and freely choose my home. I draw from many narrative stocks as I deny the authority of chronological time the better to respond to the melancholic gaze of a deer that flashes by through the morphine-laden verses of Georg Trakl; I trace the vestiges of a personal drama in the wet flowers on the façades of bourgeois palaces under the slopes of Kapuzinerberg; and I am unmistakably, although temporarily, at home in Salzburg!

The book flutters its pages and old-fashioned raincoats fan out in an effort to protect the dry loneliness of night strollers passing by the craft shops of Alfama, the heart of old Lisbon; the portrait of Fernando Pessoa emerges from under the jutting roofs of the past colonial glory written in sea salt and pigeon droppings; the portrait of a poet who produced an eternal homage to his Lisbon using the voices of imaginary authors who sing various songs but share one soul. His Lisbon is my Lisbon!

The book spreads its tattooed pages and I'm embraced by the smell of the sea-worn cliffs of the northern Adriatic; the tower of the *Thurn und Taxis* castle appears for a moment, a fleeting pulsation, and I slowly surrender to the recognition that I'm at home in Trieste; it is here that Rainer Maria Rilke wrote two of his dizzily inspiring *Duino Elegies*, and it is where I now find home, under the hills of the "gulf city" depicted in the books of Boris Pahor. I'm at home in the nostalgic *chiusa tristezza* from Umberto Saba's poem "Three Streets"; the steps of Nora Joyce rustle through the whiteness of the book while she paces around a rented apartment, one of a dozen she and her husband lived in, fleeing from creditors; I can hear the argument of farsighted Henrik Tuma, who as early as before World War I wanted to establish the first Slovenian university in cosmopolitan Trieste, the chief port of the Habsburg Empire, rather than in landlocked Ljubljana; although it is not visible to my eyes, I can nevertheless see Dragotin Kette's sad promontory of San Carlo in Trieste, where the poet went to soothe the wounded heart and the needs of the swollen body; I imagine that I can understand the dialect of Šavrinke, the peasant women traders from the Karst high plateau who together with the readers of Marjan Tomšič's novels head daily toward the vegetable market in the harbor as they did during the distant times of the Habsburg monarchy; the inscription on Italo Svevo's grave in St. Ana Cemetery tells me that he "smiles at evanescent life and glory which crowned his work late." Roberto Bobi Bazlen, a publisher and critic, despairingly reminds me from the desks of the Biblioteca Civica that there is no other way to write modern books but as footnotes.

I'm at home in Zagreb, too. Well, at least in the books about Zagreb that strive to confirm the ironic thought of the great Croatian bard Miroslav Krleža that central Europe begins on the terrace of the Esplanade Hotel; I'm at home in Belgrade, whose head resides in cosmopolitan heights thanks to the poets Vasko Popa and Miloš Crnjanski, and the writers Danilo Kiš and David Albahari, while its legs are entrenched under the swinging lamp of a brawly Balkan tavern!

And I'm at home, truly at home, in Sarajevo, defined by ineffable suffering but also with an ethical determination to continue to talk in many voices about the right to have many identities, through the supreme works of art such as can only be born out of extreme circumstances, finding expression in the quivering elegies of Izet Sarajlić, the noble sentiment of Abdulah Sidran, or the broad-minded critique of Dževad Karahasan.

The poems of Czesław Miłosz, Tomas Venclova, and Eugenijus Ališanka open for me the door to Wilna or Vilnius, the "city of ash" amid Lithuanian forests that lives a secret life of another reality, one that has been sifted through the sieves of my literary memory. I suck in the smoke, leaf through the books of poems and stories, and fastidiously sip the verses and passages in which the creative talent succeeded in conjuring up the shared destiny of immigrants and refugees, nomads and displaced people, roaming the streets and courtyards of the town whose walls demarcate the ultimate frontiers of freedom.

To be at home in a place where the sky meets the earth is to make the experience real! To be at home in a place that offers the elementary, emotionally laden and full-blooded experience! To be at home in a place in which every thing has a name! To breathe the metropolitan air that ever since the Middle Ages has been inviting all citizens of the urban republic to get rid of old communal ties! I myself would like to become a map of the city, a written page, a thin cobweb through which older and dimmer biographies and urban chronicles shine!

While I'm getting lost wandering along the boulevards of real megalopolises and among the covers of borrowed books, I actually search for my imaginary city. Wherever I discover it, a provincial village easily emulates the dwelling of gods and becomes the capital of the world! More precisely: it is the capital of my world that, along with many other and different worlds of other and different readers, travels the orbits of the "Gutenberg galaxy."

It is true that we readers are the citizens of various nation-states, each with our own home address and hometown. Yet the moment we open a book and yield, in our unique ways, to the adventurous challenge, we take part in the same ritual. We assert that our place of residence is in the same community, in the Republic of Letters. It cannot be found in any world atlas; its borders are unstable and are passionately negotiated time and again. With every story read, with every verse quietly recounted, we renew our citizenship in the Republic of Letters. Many opportunities arise and dissolve within it, faces distorted by horror offer a hand to fantastic patterns of paradise, and every page read turns a new chapter in a reader's biography.

We can all become citizens in this republic, without restrictions. The only condition required to obtain citizenship is a human capacity for empathy—that is, the capacity to put oneself in someone else's shoes. No one's human rights are curtailed in this republic, no one is discriminated against, sentenced, or erased from the register.

Moreover, no one in the republic of letters is forced to speak the language of the majority. The literary republic of letters speaks in one language. It is the language of translation. Literature is not what gets "lost in translation," as Robert Frost famously exclaimed in defense of poetic singularity. As for me, I prefer Turkish poet Nâzım Hikmet's definition, who said that the reading of poetry in translation resembles "a kiss through a veil." I could not care less for the ascetic chastity that, fearing loss, remains innocent, while with my lips parted in expectation I leaf through the pages of books written in languages I haven't learned. I take my hat off thankfully to translators, the exemplary citizens of the republic of letters, who continually make it possible for every reader, all of us, to be part of the story of a temporary community committed to the lost cause that represents our true home.

UNIVERSITY OF LJUBLJANA

Aleš Debeljak (1961–2016) was a Slovenian cultural critic, poet, and essayist. A former Roberta Buffett Professor of International Studies at Northwestern University, he was teaching at the University of Ljubljana at the time of his death.

"VOICES FROM THE DEBRIS FIELDS": A CONVERSATION WITH CAROLYN FORCHÉ (ABRIDGED) (2016)

CHARD DENIORD

CHARD DENIORD: You were a good friend of Daniel Berrigan (1921–2016), who recently died. You both come from a Catholic background and had intense discussions about witnessing and other matters. Could you talk a little about the nature of your friendship as well as some of the ongoing conversations you had with him? Do you think your religious background as a Catholic ended up having a strong influence on you as a poet who has followed in the prophetic tradition of witnessing, as Berrigan did?

CAROLYN FORCHÉ: I think the answer is yes, my poetry is influenced by the crucible of Catholic formation. My friendship with Daniel began upon my return from El Salvador, when I was involved with the anti-war, anti-intervention, sanctuary, and witness for peace movements. Daniel was also deeply committed to this work, and our paths sometimes crossed. We had long conversations and one recurring argument concerning the right of the oppressed to defend themselves and overthrow their oppressors by force after all peaceful means have been exhausted. Daniel, the radical pacifist, did not support the use of violence under any circumstances. In the immediate aftermath of my experience in El Salvador, I was persuaded of the right of the oppressed to armed revolution under certain conditions. Now, I no longer believe that change comes about through force of arms. I wish I hadn't wasted what time I had with Daniel on this particular argument. The rest of the time we talked about the theology of liberation, poetry, and other such worthy subjects. We taught a few workshops together, one in a monastery in upstate New York, presenting poetry of witness. He was an extraordinary human being, a dedicated and deeply spiritual priest. It is a great honor to have known him.

DeNiord: In your various interviews you show a familiarity with a large number of philosophers and critics like Emmanuel Levinas, Walter Benjamin, Jean-François Lyotard, Hannah Arendt, and Hans Magnus Enzensberger—to name just some of them. Are these authors ones you've largely read on your own? Leaving aside Benjamin, whose presence in *The Angel of History* is clear, how important are these writers for understanding your work?

Forché: As an undergraduate, I studied existential phenomenology, but since then I have read largely on my own, often guided by friends with scholarly expertise in continental philosophy and twentieth-century European thought. We've talked about some of them: Sandor Goodhart, Geoffrey Hartman, Tony Brinkley.

DeNiord: Near the end of your 2000 interview with David Wright, you comment: "Poetry is what maintains our capacity for contemplation and difficulty. Poetry is where that contemplation and difficulty converses with itself. Poetry is a very important endeavor. It's so important, it's so sacred a practice that the way in which it's been commodified is an angering problem for me. I don't want it to be that way. I'll continue to write it out of joy and longing to do so." How would you modify, augment, or intensify that comment *today*, some sixteen years later?

Forché: I still believe that writing and reading poetry and other forms of serious literary art preserve our capacity for meditative attention and contemplation; I still believe strongly in the necessity of poetry, of imaginative art. I would no longer say that poetry has been "commodified," and I'm not sure what I meant by that at the time. I have always considered poetry to be an artistic practice that most resisted commodification.

DeNiord: Besides people like Terence Diggory, are there any other critics whose work you value? Whether of your own poetry or of that of other poets you admire?

Forché: Calvin Bedient, Robert Boyers, James Longenbach, Dan Chiasson, Juliana Spahr, David Orr, Alicia Ostriker, and others.

DENIORD: Besides Ilya Kaminsky, what other living poets' work do you admire, find compelling, moving?

FORCHÉ: There are many, and may I be forgiven for omitting? I think I would like to mention some younger poets, if I may, such as Ishion Hutchinson, Tarfia Faizullah, Jericho Brown, Jamaal May, Natalie Diaz, Sherwin Bitsui, Don Mee Choi, Valzhyna Mort, Tracy K. Smith, Mai Der Vang, Nikola Madžirov—

DENIORD: You have written and said so many memorable things about the poetry of witness over the years, I would like to conclude by asking you to respond briefly to a few questions about some of your most incisive comments and insights with regard to your maturation from a lyrical poet at the start of your career to a poet of witness who has sacrificed her subjective muse for a more selfless voice that, in your own words, "lays open to the other [in] an unending address, a call to the other, which manifests that-which-happened." I'd like to start with this provocative quote you made several years ago: "One can say I'm political but not say I'm ethical? I remember the poet June Jordan once said to me, 'I don't know what my politics are, but I know what I want to help have happen.' I always liked that phrase." What's more appealing to you specifically about saying "I know what I want to help have happen" than talking about your politics?

FORCHÉ: I lean toward ethics rather than politics, toward intersubjective awareness, the practice and cultivation of imaginative empathy, a sense of interdependence within the biosphere.

DENIORD: You have often quoted this claim about language by Paul Celan: "One thing remained attainable, close and unlost amidst all the losses: language. Language was not lost, in spite of all that happened. But it had to go through its own responselessness, go through horrible silences, go through the thousand darknesses of death-bringing speech." Now that you have edited two large volumes of the poetry of witness, *Against Forgetting* and *The Poetry of Witness: The Tradition in English, 1500–2001*, could you talk a little about just what it is about "language" that survives extremity? Just how poetry finds the last word within the "horrible silences" and "thousand darknesses"? Are there any poets in particular in either of your anthologies that you feel address this mystery directly?

FORCHÉ: Czesław Miłosz acknowledges that in some poets, a peculiar fusion of the personal and historical appears, and in such poets, we may also observe a certain reticence; they are poets of silence as much as of the word; they have deeply assimilated personal and collective experience and have surrendered themselves to the work of poetic transmission. They are often perceived as hermetic and obscure while imagining themselves to be striving for utmost clarity. If I had to choose two poets who most exemplify this fusion, they would be Paul Celan and Ingeborg Bachmann.

DENIORD: You write this trenchant definition of the poetry of witness in your essay "Reading the Living Archives: The Witness of Literary Art":

> Witness, then, is neither martyrdom nor the saying of a juridical truth, but the owning of one's infinite responsibility for the *other one* (*l'autrui*). It is not to be mistaken for politicized confessionalism. The confessional is the mode of the subjective, and the representational that of the objective. . . . In the poetry of witness, the poem makes present to us the experience of the other, the poem *is* the experience, rather than a symbolic representation. When we read the poem as witness, we are marked by it and become ourselves witnesses to what it has made present before us. Language incises the page, wounding it with testimonial presence, and the reader is marked by encounter with that presence. Witness begets witness. The text we read becomes a living archive.

Your idea of the text becoming a "living archive" posits language with a sacred function, but not necessarily in the religious sense. William Blake wrote that the "most sublime act is to set another before you," which gets at your notion of "humans coming into being through relation." Where do you draw the line in your thinking, if you do draw a line, between the religious and human connotations of the poetry of witness as a "living archive" that wounds "with testimonial presence"?

FORCHÉ: There is a certain sacred radiance to the language of witness. After all, the term itself, witness, derives from the Greek μάρτυρας (*mártyras*). In my own apprehension, both sacred and secular connotations are available; the language suggests constellations of thought and awareness, human and divine.

DENIORD: Would you mind elaborating a bit more on this quote, especially what you mean by "poem as trace, poem as evidence"? It seems like a poem of witness in your description of it here takes on a metaphysical validity all of its own, one that must involve both the poet's sovereign imagination and the reader's faith in the poem. "By situating poetry in this social space, we can avoid some of our residual prejudices. A poem that calls us from the other side of a situation of extremity cannot be judged by simplistic notions of 'accuracy' or 'truth to life.' It will have to be judged, as Ludwig Wittgenstein said of confession, by its consequences, not by our ability to verify its truth. In fact, the poem might be our only evidence that an event has occurred: it exists for us as the sole trace of an occurrence. As such, there is nothing for us to base the poem on, no independent account that will tell us whether or not we can see a given text as being 'objectively' true. Poem as trace, poem as evidence."

FORCHÉ: Language here is regarded not as representational but as evidentiary; the word is indexical, pointing toward that which happened. One is moved or marked by the poem in the act of reading: by the vortices of the imagery, metaphorical resonances, metonymic play, by the music, the compression of utterance. Language written in the aftermath of extremity bears the imprint of that experience, regardless of its content; it is that which is written out of that which was endured. In many respects, this is ineffable. The words come not from recollection in tranquility but from wanderings in a debris field.

EDITORIAL NOTE:

THE FOLLOWING ADDENDUM WAS ADDED IN NOVEMBER 2016.

DEN IORD: The country is reeling in the wake of the recent election. What are your thoughts?

FORCHÉ: In times like these, and from what I know of the world, one must marshal inner strength, must be courageous and resolute, calm and vigilant, must connect with others of like mind, must not compromise with racism, bigotry, and hatred but must also be quietly prepared for the consequences of every confrontation (physical harm, imprisonment, death). Must do so, anyway. Must go to every length to protect others. Not many humans can do this. Many will live as many lived in Eastern Europe and in Russia under totalitarianism. They will mind their own business, get what they can to survive, and go about their daily lives. That's all right for them. We should not be judgmental of them. But there were dissidents too, and they worked together, and after decades of work, the system came down.

In this moment, because of environmental death, because the next five years so matter (are crucial to human survival), we do not have "decades." Harry [Mattison] and I have lived in countries under oppressive regimes, with governments supported by the U.S. We have not often been the good guys. Most people in the U.S. paid no attention to this. They lived their lives. While all this was going on, while the wars were going on, they had fun, studied, worked, had kids, took the boat out on weekends. But in those countries, people suffered greatly, disappeared by the tens of thousands, were tortured and mutilated, and still people fought back. They lived in clandestinity. I knew some of them. They saw the world clearly. They found a peace within themselves. A friend said to me once: "I don't fear death. When I made my commitment, I was already in the grave."

We are going, now, to wait. We're going to be courageous and resolute, stoic and clear-eyed. We're going to watch carefully and keep our intuition on high alert. We'll know what steps to take when the time comes. I believe that the president-elect will sit in the White House and everything will be done by others, most especially the legislators. They will change some laws, but he will not be able to deliver on his promises to the people who elected him. There will come a time when his supporters will realize that they have been betrayed. Then we'll see.

Born in Detroit, Carolyn Forché (b. 1950) is a poet, editor, professor, translator, and human rights advocate. She is perhaps best known for coining the term "poetry of witness." Her most recent book, *In the Hour of War: Poetry from Ukraine* (2023), was coedited by Ilya Kaminsky. In 2015–2016 Chard deNiord met with Forché on several occasions to discuss her multifaceted vocation as a poet, witness, and scholar. This extract concludes part 3 of their conversation.

Chard deNiord is the author of nine books of poetry, most recently *Westminster West* (2025), as well as two books of interviews with eminent American poets. Professor emeritus of English and creative writing at Providence College, he served as Poet Laureate of Vermont from 2015 to 2019.

SELECTIVE EMPATHY: STORIES AND THE POWER OF NARRATIVE (2017)

AMINATTA FORNA

HUMAN BEINGS TELL STORIES. This is a fact. Every society, however differently organized and structured, whether founded on the values of matriarchy or patriarchy, whether agricultural, seagoing, peaceful, or warmongering, tells stories. We know this because anthropologists tell us so. Anthropologists, historians (what are historians but storytellers themselves?), and archaeologists, who have traced the origin of stories as far back as human life. The first *written* story to have been found is the Epic of Gilgamesh, produced sometime between 2150 and 1400 BCE in cuneiform on fragments of tablets and unearthed in the sands of what is now Syria.

From epic legends like Gilgamesh to anecdotes, we tell each other stories every day: "Guess what happened?" Typically my seven-year-old son's first words when he dashes through the door at the day's end. A woman is late for lunch with a friend, she sits down, she says: "Just listen to the day I've had . . ." A man at a bar leans across to another man: "So I was driving down the freeway . . ." And so it goes. Storytelling is a symbiotic process, an exchange between teller and listener, between writer and reader. It is the way my son shares the highs and lows of his day, the way the woman who is late encourages her friend's sympathy rather than irritation, how the man at the bar extends the hand of friendship.

It is easy to revere stories for all that they do. Today I know how it might have felt to live under apartheid from Can Themba, how daily life unfolds during the civil war in Lebanon from Rabih Alameddine, sense the fear and courage of the enslaved from Colson Whitehead. Through books I can travel across distance, space, and time. I can imagine what it is like to be a man, or an elderly person, or recapture the experience of youth. It helps me understand the worlds of other people. Indeed, the link between reading fiction and empathy has been well established, most recently by researchers at the New School, who have found evidence that literary fiction improves a reader's capacity to understand what others are thinking and feeling. More than that, reading literary fiction—and interestingly the same doesn't go for nonfiction or genre fiction such as romances or thrillers—actually changes people's behavior.

Literary fiction focuses on the psychology of characters and their relationships. The characters in literary fiction are as real as a writer can make them, as full of the conflicts and flaws as any one of us. Literary fiction seeks to ask questions rather than provide answers. The outcome may not be predictable. The New School research shows that literary fiction prompts the reader to imagine the characters' introspective dialogues. This psychological awareness carries over into the real world, which is full of complicated individuals whose inner lives are usually difficult to fathom. Reading frees the reader from the constraints of the self, from our own prejudices and assumptions. Reading makes you a more highly functioning person. In other words—reading makes you a better person.

For all these reasons we cherish stories and we cherish those who write them. Societies venerate their storytellers almost as much as the stories. We talk about the wonders that stories can create, the ways they can change the world for the better. We do not talk about the pain stories can inflict and the damage they can do.

When I was six one of my children's books contained a poem about a little Black boy, a "blackamoor," who was being teased for the color of his skin by three white boys. A wizard who was also a giant heard them and picked up the horrid white boys and dipped them in black ink so that now they were black. I tried to figure it out, insofar as a six-year-old is capable. The giant wizard punished the cruel white boys. That seemed only right. But their punishment was to become Black. That made no sense to me.

I grew up between Sierra Leone in West Africa and Britain in the 1970s. In Sierra Leone, I borrowed books from the British Council Library. I read Jack London and I read Mark Twain's *Huckleberry Finn*. I didn't know London was apparently an enthusiastic eugenicist who thought that people of color, especially those of mixed blood, were biologically inferior. I liked dogs and I liked wolves and so I read *White Fang* and *Call of the Wild*. I did not critique his portrayals of Native American life; I would not have been able to. Even after making a documentary about him for the BBC, I'm not sure, as with so many writers, to what extent London's ideology penetrated his writing, but I can tell you this—that the human heroes portrayed in *White Fang* and *Call of the Wild* are all white men; it is *they* who conquer the wilderness, *they* who show compassion to mistreated beasts, *they* who put the world to rights. I read *Huckleberry Finn*. I loved his adventures. I was what was then called a tomboy and saw myself in Huck. The word "nigger," which appeared several times on each page, did not bother me, for I did not know that I was a nigger, for the reason that until then nobody had called me that name. I did not see myself as Black or white, not because I was of mixed heritage but because I simply did not see the world or myself in racial terms.

And then, when I was six, the political instabilities of Sierra Leone obliged my family to leave and go to live in London. And over the following years I learned the power of the word *nigger*, how it would be wielded against me, and all the damage it could do.

Frantz Fanon wrote of the comic books of the 1950s and their corrosive effect on the psyche. "In the magazines the Wolf, the Devil, the Evil Spirit, the Bad Man, the Savage are always symbolized by Negroes or Indians; since there is always identification with the victor, the little Negro, quite as often as the little white boy, becomes an explorer, an adventurer, a missionary 'who faces the danger of being eaten by wicked Negroes.' I shall be told that this is hardly important, but only because those who say it have not given much thought to the role of such magazines."

Toni Morrison has defined what she calls Africanism, both akin and different to Said's Orientalism, in her own words: "the denotative and connotative blackness that African people have come to signify, as well as the entire range of views, assumptions, readings and misreadings that accompany Eurocentric learning about these people."

Fanon thought the unending negative portrayals of people of color damaged the psyche of colonized people, producing a sense of their own inferiority. The legendary Nigerian writer Chinua Achebe took a more robust view of reading European depictions of Africa as a growing boy: "I don't think I ever believed those things were true, but I met a great many people who did. This is 'the black man's burden.' All Africans meeting a European who has never met an African before must first break through the preconceptions, reinforced by news reports and articles, of Africa as a place of unending misery."

Probably the truth lies somewhere in between, depending on the circumstances in which a person is raised. In West Africa we were colonized but never settled, unlike Algeria, where Fanon worked and wrote. How white people saw us had a lesser psychological impact, being at a distance. Did I ever think the portrayals I read of Africans and people of color were true? Certainly they didn't square with my own experience of growing up in West Africa. But perhaps as a child I accepted them as true in some other version of reality, unlived by me but somehow coexisting.

To see oneself only ever reflected through the eyes of another is to view the self through a distorting lens. This has to be true. In my teenage years the awareness grew that even if I did not see myself in the many depictions of Black people that surrounded me, a great many people did. And if you had told me that challenging, overturning one at a time, those false narratives would become my life's work, as it has become the life's work of every one of us not born at the center, persistently viewed as "other" to a presumed norm, either because of race or gender, sexuality or disability, I would certainly have disbelieved you.

As a writer I devote myself to the task, in part because to be a good writer makes it unavoidable, and because, as I have said, I believe profoundly that stories matter. "To poison a nation, poison its stories," says Ben Okri.

A demoralized nation tells demoralized stories to itself. Beware of the storytellers who are not fully conscious of the importance of their gifts, and who are irresponsible in the application of their art. . . . The true storyteller suffers the chaos and the madness, the nightmare, resolves it all, sees clearly, and guides you surely through the fragmentation and the shifting world. . . . Stories can change an age, turn an era round.

Or as James Baldwin said: "You write in order to change the world . . . if you alter, even by a millimeter, the way people look at reality, then you can change it."

TAKING THE CENTER

A few years back the promotional department of a publishing company sent me a book in the hope that I would review or endorse it. The writer was a psychologist who had been born in France in 1937, whose parents had been deported to the concentration camps and never returned. At the age of seven he joined the French Resistance as a runner, carrying messages back and forth across enemy lines. The book was called *Resilience*, the writer Boris Cyrulnik already a psychologist of great renown; this was my first introduction to him. I'd been sent the book because of my own work describing traumatic events and their impact in my memoir that describes the political upheavals of 1970s Sierra Leone, and in *The Memory of Love*, a novel set two decades later, during the civil war. I read *Resilience* from cover to cover, and it struck me that every word Boris Cyrulnik said was true.

Cyrulnik is a world-renowned expert in PTSD, post-traumatic stress disorder, one who has been critical of many in his own profession whom he accuses of subscribing to a kind of psychological determinism in their handling of people who have endured trauma, acting "like car mechanics," in his words, in their ideas of cause and effect. In his theories of resilience Cyrulnik has described how traumatic events can be framed by the narrative given to them, in ways that might exacerbate or mitigate those events. The narrative or context given for suffering is what determines survival; the feeling of selfhood is shaped by the gaze of others, namely the emotional reactions of people and of the culture around them. Cyrulnik found that, among children who survived the Nazi occupation of France, those who had, like him, joined the Resistance suffered the lowest levels of postwar depression. "Did these children join the resistance because they were already more resilient?" he writes. "Or did their narrative identity, or the stories they rehearsed in their heads after the war—'I am the boy who, at the age of eight, stood up to the German army'—give them a feeling of selfhood that had more in common with a hero than a victim?"

Cyrulnik thought it was the latter and argued that people's ability to frame their own narratives was vital to their own sense of self. In the war years, for example, he wrote, sacrifice and going without were seen positively. Today, when the measure of happiness is personal wealth, success, and fulfillment, we discuss sacrifice only in terms of victimhood. Cyrulnik devoted his career to freeing children who had experienced trauma from the narrative of damage, and thereby of inferiority, to which a wider society would have condemned them.

It's not hard to see the link between Cyrulnik's theories of resilience and storytelling in wider society. The power of the story lies in the hands of the storyteller. "The true storyteller suffers the chaos and the madness, the nightmare, resolves it all, sees clearly, and guides you surely through the fragmentation and the shifting world," said Okri. And to do so the storyteller must take control of the narrative. Writers from all minority groups, and women writers, and those from colonized nations—all of us who have been spoken for, instead of listened to, have had to seize our own narratives. In the case of African writers, to look back over the span of the last sixty years is to see the unbroken arc of a joint creative endeavor, one that has been in the main unspoken, a collective consciousness fueled by a collective outrage, one that would deny the Western gaze.

For the generation of African writers who came of age at the same time as their countries, this return to the center meant literally writing Africans into existence. For Chinua Achebe, writing *Things Fall Apart* meant challenging Conrad's portrayal of grunting, nonverbal Africans in *Heart of Darkness*, giving his characters the interior lives and relationships, conflicts and flaws that the New School research into reading insisted was the basis of the creation of empathy, the very agency and subjectivity that Conrad had denied to them. For Ngũgĩ wa Thiong'o it meant retrieving his Kikuyu language, the language he had been beaten for speaking as a child undergoing colonial instruction. To this day he writes his novels first in Kikuyu and only thereafter translates them himself into English.

"I began to write because I did not see myself in literature, and I wanted to see myself there," said Tsitsi Dangarembga, the Zimbabwean novelist. The same might have been said by Mariama Bâ, Buchi Emecheta, Ama Ata Aidoo, Miriam Tlali.

We have had to write ourselves into existence, to place ourselves at the center of the narrative. At the same time the willful amnesia of a dominant culture that would rather forget its historical transgressions must be challenged. Viet Thanh Nguyen, the Pulitzer Prize–winning author of *The Sympathizer*, has described the portrayal of the Vietnam War by the Hollywood movie machine and American writers as "the only time history has been written by the losers," and which has consistently portrayed Americans as the true victims of the war, overlooking the three million Vietnamese dead.

Lost narratives must be retrieved, those that have been omitted replaced. We must continually repeat ourselves: Binyavanga Wainaina's scorching satirical essay on the way in which some Western writers persist in portraying Africans: "How to Write about Africa," now a YouTube video featuring Djimon Hounsou; Chimamanda Ngozi Adichie's TED Talk, "The Danger of the Single Story," viewed two and a half million times.

Each generation of writers of African heritage builds on the foundations of the generation that went before. Not only have we taken back our stories and continue to do so, to place ourselves at the center of the narrative, but now we reverse the gaze. In *The Memory of Love*, my novel set in postwar Sierra Leone, a British psychologist arrives to help the war-afflicted. At first the reader sees the country through his eyes. I created Adrian Lockhart. And I also created Kai Mansaray, a young Sierra Leonian surgeon, who offers the reader a different way of seeing. Through Kai's eyes we see the country, its past and its secrets, the nuances to which Adrian is not privy, and we see Adrian, his assumptions, his preconceptions, and his mistakes.

We take back our stories, we take the center, we reverse the gaze, and we transgress boundaries, setting our narratives beyond the spaces we have been allocated. Teju Cole's *Open City* takes place in the streets of New York, Dinaw Mengestu's *Children of the Revolution* is set in a district of Washington undergoing gentrification, Chimamanda Ngozi Adichie's *Americanah*, Chris Abani's *The Secret History of Las Vegas*, Okey Ndibe's *Foreign Gods, Inc.* all feature African characters viewing the West through the prism of their own experience. My own *The Hired Man*, set in Croatia, written in the voice of a Croatian man and using the framework of an African war as a lens through which to view a Balkan one—imagining what it might be to be the "other."

In November 2016 I attended the National Book Awards in New York. Three out of the four winners were men of color. Congressman John Lewis, who won for his young-adult book *The March*, which tells of the 1963 civil rights march on Selma, spoke of growing up in rural Alabama, going to the library at the age of sixteen to get a library card, and being refused because the library was whites only. A note of triumph, accompanied that evening by a note of warning, from Cornelius Eady, one of the founders of Cave Canem, the collective of poets of color. One week on from the recent election he told the room of writers and publishers: "Right now, as we speak, uptown there are people in a building that are trying to write a narrative about who we are, and who we are supposed to be and what to do about us. When you lose that story or you . . . allow that narrative to be taken from you, bad things happen. It is our job and our duty to make sure we get to write our own story, the fullness of who we are . . . in our own language."

Who could have imagined Eady's words would be so prophetic? Months later and the phrases "alternative facts" and "fake news" have come to dominate media debates. What once was mainly relegated to academic and artistic discourse has entered the mainstream. If the rhetoric feels dangerous, it's because the stakes are high. The battle begins with control of the narrative. But resilience—the prerequisite to winning the battle—comes from the forging of an independent narrative identity. In other words, knowing your own story and telling it to yourself. And resilience wins the war.

GEORGETOWN UNIVERSITY

Born in Scotland, raised in Sierra Leone and Great Britain, and having spent periods of her childhood in Iran, Thailand, and Zambia, Aminatta Forna, OBE (b. 1965), is a prizewinning novelist, memoirist, and essayist. She is currently director of the Lannan Center at Georgetown University and professor of creative writing at Bath Spa University.

TOWARD A POETICS OF THE CARIBBEAN   (2002)

NANCY MOREJÓN

Translated from the Spanish by Alan West-Durán

HOW DOES ONE describe that indefinable substance that is poetry? Aristotle refers to "poetry being for the possessed, of being multiform, its plasticity, its potential for ecstasy." Lorca speaks of the essence of poetry as a kind of fire. Lezama Lima responded, "Poetry? It's a nocturnal shell in a rectangle of water." But poetry, more than being a form, is a state of being through which humanity has expressed ideals and sentiments of differing order.

How does race affect this poetics? Race has relevance for scientific thought and thinking done through images. Poets bring everything to their poetry, their culture, their language, their race. "Race in the Caribbean has been a fountain of events, a catalyst, an incentive, an act of faith, and more often than not a narcotic." But if closed in on itself, racial attitudes, such as Negritude, can become a dead end. Nicolás Guillén addressed this admirably when he wrote, "It's like trying to find a black cat in a dark room." Or Wole Soyinka, who, with a certain irony, speaks of tigers defending their "tigertude." But despite all this, many subaltern subjects of postliterature assume a discourse of identity that underlines their race, like Rigoberta Menchú or Carolina Maria de Jesus.

Poetry in the Caribbean has been sensitive to ethnic tension and made it a paramount concern. But given its burning urgency, it has not always been the only concern, nor has it always been dealt with fruitfully. Our poetic universe in the Caribbean goes from Walcott to Lezama, from Brathwaite to Eliseo Diego; it must deal with Césaire's *Cahier d'un retour au pays natal* and Virgilio Piñera's "La isla en peso" (*The Weight of the Island*).

Guillén and Césaire represent two emblematic positions. For Guillén, the issue of the nation is a ruling or governing concern; for Césaire, it is not. What predominates in his *Cahier*, despite its affirmation of Negritude, is an uprootedness and a search for nationhood in Africa, not his native Martinique. His vocation is for the whole American continent, particularly its African areas (like Brazil, the southern United States, the coasts of Central America, and so on). Guillén assumes that Cuba will achieve universal transcendence through the Cuban nation's vindication of its Black population. His optimism compared to Césaire's pessimism might be explained by the fact that in the 1930s Cuba was a republic (even if dependent on and exploited by the United States) and Martinique was still a colony.

Césaire has said, "I'm in the conjunction of two traditions: American by way of geography, African by way of history." While this implies cultural hybridity, it is not the kind of *mestizaje* that Guillén talks about. When we speak of America, we speak of Indigenous culture, which is not to be opposed to the ethnic *mestizaje* of our African heritages. Césaire's vision of Africa is mythical, Guillén's is not. There is nothing wrong with incorporating mythologies (of any kind, from Greek to Hindu) into your writing, so long as you know they are a literary device.

Myth, of course, is essential to the poetic aesthetic of the Caribbean. There is no culture that has been able to prosper without a rich mythological subsoil. It entails a reinvention of the imago and metaphor, organically nurtured by the nature of the region, and the arsenal of wisdom of popular culture. Caribbean poetry is a force that comes out from books and breathes in our plains, our jungles, our mountains in a unique fashion.

But I'd like to talk about myths in the plural. The vast scope of the myths derive from many places. From Europe—that is, Spain, France, Portugal, Great Britain, and Holland. From Africa. And from the remains of Indigenous cultures, wiped out by one of the most pathetic ethnocides in history. They are buttressed by the incredible telluric force of our nature and the constant collision of cultures and myths that are born of Galicians, Mayas, Catalans, Taínos, Andalusians, Bretons, Celts, Germans, Gauls, Iberians, Yorubas, Congas, Araras, Chinese, and Hindus.

Can we speak of transculturation in the Caribbean without mentioning Yoruba myths? Or of our new culture without music and dance forms from the coasts of Guinea? The Black presence is as obvious as the ocean in the Caribbean. When I say Black it is not to scare, blame, or victimize. I say it in the spirit of George Lamming's words: "When we say black, it is not meant in the biological sense, nor is it for racial applause. When I say black, it is the name of a profound and unique historical experience."

Linguistic concerns are of vital importance. They form part of the transculturation experience, and Creole, both in the anglophone and francophone Caribbean, forms part of that mythic zone of which I've spoken. Myths elaborated by women writers have opened up previously unexplored zones in our literature. Much of this is close to Glissant's cross-cultural poetics (*poétique de la relation*).

The mountains, the sea, become an integral part of mythic poetry. In the Caribbean, there is always a voyage, there is always a boat. Our poetry has been sensitive to that, without forgetting that the sea is the scenario of the Middle Passage. Ecology and history merge in our myths.

Caribbean popular poetry is based on an infinite oral tradition, which is rich in myths, of characters like Mackandal in Haiti, Anancy in Jamaica, the *taitas* of the Cuban countryside, or Juan Bobo in Puerto Rico. They wind up in different cultural expressions: painting, music, literature. Mythology in the Caribbean is a poetics transplanted from one genre to another. The poetry of the Caribbean or, better yet, its poetics, multilingual and plural, multiple and one, challenges us by being faithful to the origins that created it.

HAVANA

A widely published poet, critic, translator, and past director of the Academia Cubana de la Lengua, Havana-born Nancy Morejón (b. 1944) has collaborated with prominent musicians, playwrights, and actors throughout the Caribbean. Currently, she is director of *Unión*, the journal of the Unión de Escritores y Artistas de Cuba (UNEAC). The recipient of Cuba's National Prize for Literature, she has been called "the best known and most widely translated woman poet of postrevolutionary Cuba."

Alan West-Durán is professor of cultures, societies, and global studies at Northeastern University, Boston. Born in Cuba and raised in Puerto Rico, he is a poet, translator, essayist, and critic.

ANCIENT WORDS, MODERN WORDS:
A CONVERSATION WITH ANNE CARSON　　　　(2014)

PETER CONSTANTINE

PETER CONSTANTINE: As a translator of Ancient Greek myself, I'd like to begin by asking about the extent to which you feel that the ancient texts have affected your own writing.

ANNE CARSON: the ancient texts are a source of constant refreshment to me

because a constant source of problems. problems revive engagement. easy to become anesthetized to the problems of one's own language, which are no less real but slip below the surface of habit. the effort of translation can jolt all this awake.

and problems come in many different forms. e.g. the artist Jenny Holzer is currently carving bits of Sappho (translated into English) onto rocks in a park in Oslo. she is using my translation so has been asking me questions about choice and placement of texts on boulders and cliffs, which has given me new angles of thinking on the texts themselves and the reader's experience of them. when i wrote a book about Simonides of Keos some years ago i tried to make the point that as a poet he had to think ahead to the constraints of the stone on which a poem would be carved, had to think about space and surface and economics in a particular way. it was all rather theoretical to me at the time, but now it comes alive in Oslo!

it is also true that i like constraints in general,

there being no better freedom.

CONSTANTINE: Some of your works, particularly *NOX*, have a powerfully visual, spatial placement on the page. Would you say the ancient poetry that has come down to us both as poem and object has also been a starting point for you?

CARSON: the starting point for me from the beginning was drawing/ painting. i had little interest in writing as a child but did drawings all the time and still seem to approach writing as a very complicated, rule-bound form of drawing.

when i discovered Sappho at age fifteen, the physicality of ancient poetry (transmitted via the mystique of the fragment) fitted easily into this aesthetic. and Greek letters themselves, the first time i saw them, seemed to me fantastic drawings.

CONSTANTINE: One of the aspects that fascinates me in your book *The Economy of the Unlost*, where you counterpoise Paul Celan and Simonides of Keos, is your approach to my two mother tongues, German and Greek, taking their words and reaching down into their layers of meaning. Do you find yourself approaching English words in the same way?

CARSON: yes, when possible.

[Robert] Currie gave me the *OED* in its full (and going out of print this year) twenty-volume form, and i have been doing a drawing project that allows me to scamper about from entry to entry. despite the *OED*'s sixteenth-century bias, i am finding lots of useful layers!

CONSTANTINE: The drawing project sounds fascinating. Can you describe it?

CARSON: i can describe the rules of the project, although they will seem abstruse.

it started when i decided i was too frustrated and bored with my own writing to keep on being a writer, so Currie (two weeks ago) bought me a small drawing book. not sure what to draw, i looked up the word "void" in my *OED* and found a sentence i liked among the examples of usage, *viz.*

"the small corn lyeth in the hollowe and voyde places of the great beans"

then i looked around my yard for something related to this sentence that i could draw (i'm not very good) and found three green beans growing. so i picked them and drew a picture of three beans in the small book and added the sentence as caption. then went back to the *OED* and looked up "beans." found a sentence i liked, etc.—the whole procedure repeats with each page and leads me from drawing to drawing and sentence/word to sentence/word.

CONSTANTINE: In Greece we tend to see our language as a continuum, Greek having been spoken in its various forms through the millennia, which seems to make us particularly sensitive to the etymologies of our words. What are some of the ways in which word histories have affected your work as a poet and translator?

CARSON: etymology is the place where i begin any research.

the story of how a word began to mean what it means is a point of entry to everything else about it.

CONSTANTINE: You have been extensively translated into Modern Greek, and Greek seems to be a language that works particularly well with your poetry. When you first traveled to Greece, did you feel a particular response or connection?

CARSON: just ghosts now.

A prizewinning Canadian poet, essayist, and translator, Anne Carson (b. 1950) has taught classics, comparative literature, and creative writing at various universities in the U.S. and Canada. She is the author of more than twenty books of poetry, essays, and translations.

Professor of translation studies at the University of Connecticut and publisher of World Poetry Books, Peter Constantine's translations include works by Augustine, Solzhenitsyn, Rousseau, Machiavelli, Gogol, and Tolstoy. A Guggenheim Fellow, he has been awarded a PEN Translation Prize and a National Translation Award.

MISUSED BOOKS

ROBERT MUSIL

Translated from the German by Roy Temple House

VIENNA, AUGUST 12, 1938

IT IS MORE DIFFICULT than one might think to reply to your friendly question. I'm afraid that I wrote with more conviction from my fifth to my seventeenth year than I have done since and that I am no longer able to conjure up what it was that made a writer of me then. From age seventeen to twenty—this was the period of "modernity" in Germany—I was encouraged more by the literary atmosphere than by specific books; moreover, even at that time I already felt the formation of my style and my views to be almost more attributable to science than to belles lettres.

Nonetheless, I would like to name several books from the literary sphere which I misused during my youth in order to gain some understanding of myself: namely, Maeterlinck's *Wisdom and Destiny*, Emerson's *Intentions*, Nietzsche's *Beyond Good and Evil* and *Genealogy of Morals*, a selection of Novalis's aphorisms, D'Annunzio's *The Child of Pleasure*, [Jens Peter] Jacobsen's *Niels Lyhne* and *Marie Grubbe*, Dostoevsky's *Crime and Punishment*, and Tolstoy's *Resurrection*. (I must add that *The Child of Pleasure*, for all the beauty that it contains, influenced me more through its mistakes.) I might also list [Peter] Altenberg's "As I See It" and perhaps several of Schnitzler's earliest works.

I feel that this information is very insufficient, and I am gladly at your disposal if you should wish to elaborate on your questions.

Robert Musil (1880–1942) was an Austrian-German novelist, journalist, and playwright. The first section of his unfinished modernist novel, *The Man Without Qualities* (1930–43), was awarded the Goethe Prize. In 1942 Musil died in Switzerland in exile from the Nazis, leaving the final section of his most famous work unfinished.

Roy Temple House (1878–1963) was the founding editor of *Books Abroad* from 1927 to 1948.

ELIE WIESEL

Translated from the French by Joan Grimbert with the author

IN EVOKING apocalyptic messianism, a famous Hasidic Master said, "At that time, summer will be without heat, winter without frost, the wise will have forgotten their wisdom, and the elect their fervor." Another Master expressed the same idea, but in a different way: "At that time, one will no longer distinguish light from what negates light, twilight from dawn, silence from speech and speech from its content; there will no longer be any relation between man and his face, desire and its object, metaphor and its meaning."

Orwellian premonitions and predictions before their time. The enemy resides not in the triumph of evil but in chaos. The confusion of values is worse than their disappearance. Satan will be punished not for having tempted man to sin, but rather for having pretended it was in the name of Good. As long as day and night are separate, everything is possible; should their realms intermingle, both will be cursed.

Such is the stirring lesson of the Jewish tradition. It is in discernment that truth becomes manifest. For creation to be revealed, God must recede within His secret. "Blessed be the Lord for having given the rooster the ability to distinguish between darkness and light," says the Jewish man every morning. And after the seventh day, as twilight falls, what does he say? "Blessed be the Lord for having set apart the Sabbath from the rest of the week, the sacred from the profane." Let the separations be abolished, and it will be Apocalypse.

As a child I dreaded the messianic times, and yet I prayed they would come. I was not the only one to have such conflicting feelings. Already in the Talmud we find a Sage exclaiming, "I wish for the coming of the Messiah, but I do not want to be around to welcome Him." Too many torments will usher Him in. Too many wars. Too many massacres. Kafka was right in saying that the Messiah will not arrive on the last day, but on the day after—too late for too many people.

However, unlike the Talmudic Sage, I was ready to accept the event in its totality. I lived in expectation of it. It told myself and I was told: to be Jewish is to wait. What sets my people apart from others? We have not gone beyond waiting; we are going beyond ourselves while waiting.

You see, for us the Apocalypse was not in the distant future but in the immediate present. Some days we needed only to go into the street to perceive it. Danger was everywhere. For us, there was no solid ground anywhere. Always in exile, always in flight. The world of men, human happiness, eluded us. Often we had the feeling that we were living out the curses of the Scriptures: at night we waited for day to dawn; in the morning we waited for night to fall.

Driven out of every place, pursued everywhere, accused of every misdeed, blamed for every evil, we did not understand what was happening around us. We seemed to live in a separate universe, to speak a separate language. When they looked at us, people seemed to glimpse an ancient vision of terror. We, on the other hand, had nowhere to look: expelled from geography, we sought refuge in books.

Therein we discovered the glory and suffering of another time, and we used it for guidance and support. We recounted the suffering of our ancestors in Egypt, and suddenly our own seemed more tolerable. We spoke of the destruction of the Temple of Jerusalem, the murderous persecutions at the time of the Crusades from Mayence to Blois to Jerusalem, the victims of the Inquisition, the burning of the synagogues during the pogroms. We felt strangely reassured, even encouraged. Times were tough? Well, hadn't they always been? Yet we were still around, unchanged. The Apocalypse? We knew how to survive it. Through endless dying we had learned the art of survival.

We considered the future—I mean the immediate future—with apprehension. Any change is for the worse: that was our conviction. Even our friends treated us differently when they came to power. "Whoever persecutes Jews establishes himself as a leader," according to the Talmud. And conversely, "Whoever attains a position of power takes to persecuting Jews." So it was better to endure the known, familiar punishments of those already in power. In our prayers we spoke of the days that passed, not of those to come. Rooted in the past, we responded to the present. To look beyond was to sense the imminence of the final age, that of the Apocalypse.

Now, that is something one must not do. The Apocalypse does not have good press in Jewish tradition. We admire Ezekiel and we like Isaiah because, like Jeremiah, they do not let their vision and their discourse sink into melancholy. They offer consolation and hope. Certain works of merit, both from an ethical and literary standpoint, have not been included in the sacred canon because they are imbued with too much despair. Ben Sira and Baruch Dalet, for example, inspire too much pessimism, which is why they are found in the Apocrypha. Even Job nearly had the same fate. Numerous scholars discussed his case for generations before deciding in his favor. Undoubtedly, that was because of the optimistic conclusion of the drama. After the catastrophe, Job becomes happy again, at peace with heaven and obedient to His will.

For us, today, it is not so easy to close the parentheses. More than ever, the future, a source of terror, reflects our past, a cemetery of illusions. To the extent that my contemporaries believe in the Apocalypse, they refer to the one they lived through. They speak of memory more than of vision. They are afraid. They are afraid because they remember. The tragic imagination does not attain the limit of pain; the tragic memory goes further. When the two meet, there is no way out of the nightmare.

Now, that is the case of the survivor: his memories, linked to an Event of an absolute character, weigh on the future as much as on the past. What was in the realm of fantasy or premonition for Orwell is for the survivor of Auschwitz a life experience. For Orwell, it was before the event; for us, it is after—and before. In other words, for us, time stopped between Auschwitz and Hiroshima.

But please, no comparisons. In the realm of the concentration camps, analogies can only be false—and blasphemous. Despite, or because of, its universal implications and applications, the Holocaust remains unique: its universality lies in its very singularity. And yet, negating History, Auschwitz represents a kind of aberration and culmination of History. Everything brings us back to it. Illuminated by its flames, the present appears more understandable, if only at the existential level. Today's commitments can be explained by the indifference of the past, which they strive to challenge and condemn. Dehumanized and dehumanizing, the

Nazi system showed the way for many other systems. If our language is corrupt, it is because at that time language itself was perverted. Fine and innocent words were used to designate the most abject crimes. Night and fog, selection or evacuation or special treatment—we know now that these terms meant torture and torment by starvation, isolation, and terror. The first crime committed by the Nazis was against language. It excluded from the experience all those who were not directly involved. Only the executioners and their victims understood each other. The others listened and read without understanding.

Do people understand now? I am not sure. I would be more certain of the contrary. The concentration camp experience will forever defy any possibility of understanding. In that respect, it differs from the Orwellian vision of society, where, in spite of everything, things are held together by a rigorous and implacable logic. For Orwell, the antinomian principle asserts itself as an immutable law. When the roles are reversed, the relations between the actors remain constant. Changing signs would be inconceivable in the Realm of Night: there, it is not a question of pure metamorphosis per se, or just of metamorphosis. Auschwitz and Treblinka are something else entirely—and they will forever remain something else—*other*. To say that Good was replaced by Evil, truth by lie, life by death, would not suffice to grasp the profound significance of it. As a permanent questioning of the human condition, the concentration camp phenomenon wounds and challenges us, but it never offers an answer. That is what we learned from Auschwitz: it is possible to live and die exclusively in a climate of questioning—that is, deprived of solutions. Just as there is no reasoning to explain Majdanek to us, so there is none to tell us how we managed to live after Majdanek.

Perhaps we should evoke Noah here rather than Job. After the Flood, Noah makes a new home. How does he manage to forget? He has forgotten nothing. It is because he forgets nothing that he decides to begin everything anew, to confer meaning on his survival and to justify the work of God by refuting death. Is he happy? If he were, he would not seek refuge in drunkenness. How could he be happy? All those dead haunting him, calling out to him, accusing and repudiating him. Worse still, he knows what will happen next. Already the horizon is clouding over: a new storm approaches. Driven by immense, unreasoned pride, men are rushing to erect a Tower that would touch the heavens. But don't they know that human salvation is defined in relation to one's fellow human beings? Haven't they learned anything? Drawn by space, they betray the earth and its inhabitants. Therein lies the tragedy of Noah. He, the survivor, realizes that history continues as if nothing happened, that it repeats itself. For Noah, the Apocalypse is at the same time a reminder and a warning. It is his task to make of it a revelation—and a lesson.

But such is the nature of men. They refuse to listen. Eager for diversion, they shun the testimony of witnesses. How have the survivors not gone mad? They spoke, yet nothing changed. Their works, dealing with the common destiny of men, are not received. Hence their despair. If Auschwitz has not forced society to come to its senses, what hope is there? The tragedy of the Apocalypse is this: instead of confronting it, men turn away from it. They act as if they had not discovered the ways to the abyss.

Hence the anguish that permeates my generation, or at least its thinkers, writers, and artists. Will they succeed in saving from oblivion everything that could save humanity? In order to manage this, they would have to believe in their mission. But they no longer do. All the heritage gained from philosophers and creative individuals over centuries and centuries, from various cultures and collective quests, could not prevent the civilization of self-repudiation. The triumphs of the mind, inscribed in the history of diverse peoples with a variety of titles, could not keep away defeat. Socrates and Spinoza, Dante and Dostoevsky, Bach and Michelangelo bear their share of responsibility for what has been done in Christian countries, proud of their progress, to serve Death. The murderers of Treblinka had all read Goethe and admired Schiller. There were scientists and doctors, psychiatrists and opera singers among the officers of the *Sonderkommandos*.

Imagine them at work, and you have a glimpse of true Apocalypse. Mad, savage killers cutting the throats of children and old people while screaming their hatred are less terrifying than cultivated individuals massacring their victims with absolute calm, their actions not in the least evident in their faces. The Apocalypse is well-dressed barons slaughtering ten thousand Jews a day at Babi Yar; it is doctors welcoming the crowds at Birkenau and sending the weak and the children straight to the gas chambers while their sleep goes undisturbed; it is doctors of letters and doctors of law drawing up, in Wannsee, the Final Solution. The Apocalypse is a spacious and well-lighted office, well-bred technocrats, efficient secretaries. It is government employees working together with or without passion, with or without conviction, first to imagine, then to bring about, Auschwitz.

The Apocalypse, then, is no longer great beasts spewing forth flames, or horsemen ushering in destruction, or homes ransacked and collapsing in an earthquake imparting to History a hallucinatory, fiery end. The Apocalypse is individuals who appear gentle, generous, and intelligent, for whom the disappearance of a person, a family, or a community seems to have no real significance. It is individuals for whom abstraction alone counts.

Originally a virtue, abstraction, or the power of abstraction, now reveals itself as a source of calamity. It is abstraction, which, pushed to its ultimate, insane consequence, has ended by condemning our century, one in which all the ideals have failed because they turned against the very men whom they had intended to save.

Marx and Lenin led to the Gulag, and National Socialism to scientific massacres. In both cases, the human being was stripped of his identity, his right to individuality.

I think about what I myself saw, felt, and experienced. The Enemy forbade us to live first in our family home, then on our street, then in our neighborhood, eventually in our town and in our country. He took away from us first our house, then our belongings, next our clothes, our hair, and finally our identity: we had become numbers, objects, functions. An abstraction. An invisible sign in the vast scheme of the mute, mysterious Apocalypse.

Can we transpose this into the future? Yes and no. I do not believe the Jewish people are threatened as they were in my time. I do not believe a system, a legal government, could conceive of appropriating for its own use the methods tested by Hitler's Germany. Ghettos and gas chambers? Impossible. We will be shielded by memory.

But I do fear something else. I fear a different kind of transfer. I fear that what happened to us will now happen to all peoples. Born of indifference, the Holocaust has proved the malevolent power of indifference. Humanity need only be sufficiently apathetic for a few individuals to usurp the right to trigger, from their air-conditioned offices, the nuclear

Apocalypse. And then—no, I can't go on. I am incapable of imagining what would follow.

To imagine it would be, somehow, to accept it, hence to suppose it possible—that is, somehow, to make it possible. Although unreal in its initial phase, the vision of the Apocalypse carries the risk of becoming reality. Would it be better not to speak of it? Not at all. A contradiction? So be it. I am ready to assume it. Since the war, since the liberation of the camps, I have learned not to evade paradoxes but to accept them. Otherwise, where would I have found the strength to sanctify life and to trust in man?

To speak of the Apocalypse that was is as difficult as—and no less dangerous than—to articulate the one to come. The solution? It is imperative for creative individuals to keep the vision in mind, but without putting it into words. They must be able to speak of children who are happy—or still happy—even as they imagine the planet in flames. They must be able to describe the poor daily ambitions of their poor selves, even as they see in their mind's eye the heavens being covered by that mortal cloud which the prophets of science have portrayed so well for us.

Yet, by looking, we risk losing our taste for, if not our knowledge of, discourse. How can we use words while knowing, while recognizing their futility?

Perhaps it would be useful to speak no longer of the vision of Apocalypse, but rather of the voice: the voice of the witness rendered mute by his inability to say what he might to help men live. And hope.

BOSTON UNIVERSITY

Born in Romania, Elie Wiesel (1928–2016) survived the Auschwitz and Buchenwald concentration camps during World War II. A writer, professor, and political activist, he authored more than fifty books, including *La nuit* (1958; Eng. *Night*, 1960). As a juror for the 1984 Neustadt Prize, he nominated Manès Sperber for the award. Wiesel was awarded the Nobel Peace Prize in 1986.

Joan Grimbert is professor emerita of French and medieval studies at Catholic University of America. She received her PhD in Romance philology from the University of Chicago.

JAMES E. GUNN

TO CONSIDER science fiction in countries other than the United States, one must start from these shores. American science fiction is the baseline against which all the other fantastic literatures in languages other than English must be measured. That is because science fiction, as informed readers recognize it today, began in New York City in 1926.

That isn't to say that authors didn't write science fiction earlier or that people didn't read and appreciate it, but that it wasn't considered a literature apart—a genre. Certainly E. T. A. Hoffmann and Edgar Allan Poe wrote works about robots and strange events rationalized as being possible through science or technology or the passage of time (in the case of Poe's "Mellonta Tauta") in the first half of the nineteenth century, or that, earlier than either, Mary Shelley wrote about a creature put together from human parts and revivified through electricity. Nathaniel Hawthorne included scientific speculations among his stories of Puritan guilt, and, as H. Bruce Franklin illustrated in his book *Future Perfect*, many American writers of the nineteenth century wrote stories and novels identifiable today as science fiction. But before 1926, such works were considered literary adventures, interesting uses of nonrealistic materials—rather like the works of contemporary mainstream literary figures such as Margaret Atwood, Joyce Carol Oates, Philip Roth, or Doris Lessing.

What happened in 1926 is that Luxembourg expatriate Hugo Gernsback created the first science-fiction magazine, *Amazing Stories*, and gave science fiction an identity and a characteristic flavor. The flavor would change as new magazines came along and new editors recruited writers with different ideas and different talents, but the groundwork was laid by *Amazing Stories*, and science fiction would assume an American identity it retains to this day. As Borges once observed, every writer creates his own predecessors. The same is true of genres. Historians can look back and identify science-fiction stories, but only after the genre had been created.

The American character of science fiction occurred in spite of the fact that its major influences were European, first Jules Verne, who may have been the greatest force toward an acceptance of this new kind of literature, with his *voyages extraordinaires*, because he focused his writings almost entirely on the way technology would change humanity's exploration of the earth and the solar system; and then H. G. Wells, the "English Jules Verne," who pioneered, in his "scientific romances," the science-fiction novel of ideas and social concerns, the way technology and science would change humanity. And, at the turn of the twentieth century, the German author Kurd Lasswitz created the novel of space exploration.

But it took a magazine devoted to these kinds of stories (reprinting in its first issues stories by Poe, Wells, and Verne, "those charming romances of science" by which Gernsback described what he was trying to publish) to create a genre, establish a readership, and attract new writers. After World War II, the genre got exported to western Europe and then, more slowly, to eastern Europe and the Far East, generally following the progress of industrialization. The immediate predecessors of science fiction got started when writers noticed the social change created by the Industrial Revolution and the habit of mind derived from the Scientific Enlightenment, and those have been the criteria for developing science fiction in other countries. Where the agricultural past has been strong and social change has been limited (and often resisted), science fiction has had difficulty finding an audience.

As a final contribution to the genre, Darwin provided a new way of looking at the natural world—and even humanity itself—and science fiction, beginning with Wells and continuing to this day, has been Darwinian—that is, regarding humanity as adaptable and concerning itself with the fate of humanity rather than the fate of any individual. C. P. Snow, in his 1959 "Two Cultures" lecture, summed up the distinction between the literary culture and the scientific culture (with which science fiction writers generally—with some exceptions—identified) as the howl of protest at industrialization by the literary culture while the scientists "have the future in their bones."

World War II created a promising environment for science fiction, seeming to validate the persistent themes with which it had been ridiculed before the war: the rocket ship and the atom bomb (as well as atomic power). World War II was won in the laboratory and promised a new and maybe more dangerous world. Some twenty years later, with the first manned landing on the moon, Isaac Asimov would say, "we live in a science-fiction world," but publishers and many readers believed that it had happened at the conclusion of the war. Science fiction had an explosion of publishing, mostly in magazines but also in books. Ten years later the magazines would implode, but book publication continued to grow from about seventy-five titles in 1952 to more than two thousand by the 1980s.

American stories and novels flowed into foreign countries, and particularly into Europe, and their translations made the American brand seem like the only true SF. In Germany, authors even adopted American pseudonyms or signed their work with Americanized spellings to make it seem more legitimate. Gradually, though, the role of American SF began to fade (though it and British SF translations continued to be published), and local cultures began to exert their influences.

In Germany, that took the form of psychological and philosophic stories and novels, typified by the work of Herbert W. Franke and Wolfgang Jeschke (who also served a vital function as science-fiction editor at the leading publisher of German SF, Wilhelm Heyne Verlag). That compares with the popularity of the pulp hero Perry Rhodan, whose adventures went through nearly two thousand volumes. The situation in Germany was complicated by its postwar division into West and East Germany, with SF selling far better in the GDR and authors, such as Erik Simon, able to sustain a full-time career. All that changed with reunification, and in recent years SF in Germany has become subordinated to fantasy.

France, the birthplace of Jules Verne, had a different experience. Although American and British SF were common, the French resistance to outside literary influences made France less susceptible to American traditions. French publishers (and presumably readers) seemed fondest of such distinctive voices as A. E. van Vogt (translated by Boris Vian) and Philip K. Dick. The most characteristic French SF questioned reality to the point of absurdism, as in the case of Vian's own fiction, and the mock "pataphysics" of Alfred Jarry. French SF also got politicized by the New Wave and the student uprising of 1968, which also contributed to its decline in recent years. Alex Jakubowski summarized French experience is this way: "French SF had no grimy pulp heritage to mar its credibility.

In fact, modern French SF is often a demanding cocktail of Verne, misunderstood American and British genre influences, French pragmatism, and popular romance, with a zest of structuralism, political commentary, and absurdist preoccupations."

The experience of eastern Europe was influenced by a background of folktales and a foreground of postwar Soviet influence that encouraged "social realism" or sometimes subtle protests that required sophisticated reading between the lines. Individual writers emerged, Stanisław Lem in Poland, with his character-focused, literate novels and stories; Josef Nesvadba in the Czech Republic (home of Karel Čapek); Mircea Eliade and Ovid S. Crohmălniceanu in Romania, and others in the former Yugoslavia and Hungary. And in the Soviet Union, with its political control of publishing through the Writers Union, there was, nevertheless, a thriving science-fiction community in which the Strugatsky brothers, Arkady and Boris, bestrode the landscape as Lem did in Poland, and published their imaginative fictions with intimations of antigovernmental positions.

Italy resembled France rather than Germany in its approach to science fiction. The gulf between the mainstream and science fiction was even wider and deeper than the rest of Europe, perhaps because the mainstream tradition extended virtually unbroken back to the Roman Empire, and even with the coming of the Dark Ages, the Church and its monasteries kept classical learning and the past alive. As Carlo Pagetti wrote, "To trace an Italian [SF] tradition is not easy, because of the well-established split between scientific language and 'literary culture.'" The best-known writers have been more in the mainstream tradition, even when using SF tropes: Italo Calvino, Tommaso Landolfi, Dino Buzzati, and Umberto Eco. But American-style SF and works in translation still have an audience.

While Spain came to science fiction late, Latin America made significant contributions, though primarily from the mainstream, like Italy. Mauricio-José Schwarz and Braulio Tavares wrote, "Although deeply influenced by US-UK [SF], modern [SF] in Latin America is also affected by the fantastic tradition of Indian and colonial times, and in some instances by a conscious decision to depart from English-speaking traditions. Latin America's major contribution to science fiction and fantasy (and literature itself) has been 'magic realism,' as practiced by Jorge Luis Borges, Gabriel García Márquez, and Carlos Fuentes."

In the Far East, China and Japan represent different responses to science fiction and its potential. Japan, with its industrial development, accelerated after World War II, took readily to American-style SF and even fandom, developing SF publishing houses and significant SF authors such as Sakyo Komatsu, Yano Tetsu (a major translator as well), Ryu Mitsuse, and Shin'ichi Hoshi. At the same time, fantasists from the mainstream, such as Kōbō Abe, have contributed significantly to the Japanese tradition. John L. Apostolou describes the Japanese preoccupation as follows: "The future holds no great fascination for most of Japan's SF writers; instead they use the genre to examine the past and the present, attempting to understand their rapidly changing society." Both Japan and China experienced science fiction early in translations of Verne and Wells, but China's development was retarded by the government's identification of SF (particularly after the Communist takeover) as children's literature and valuing it for its contribution to scientific interests and education, with periodic rises and falls due to changes in the political climate, such as the Great Cultural Revolution of the 1960s and the outcry against "spiritual pollution" in 1983. That changed a few years later with the founding of SF World in Chengdu (now the largest-circulation SF magazine in the world) and the opening up of Chinese publishing to foreign SF (particularly U.S. and British) in translation. Major SF writers, with their own Chinese perspective on SF issues, have been Zheng Wenguang and Ye Yonglie.

All this is changing, just like science fiction itself. New authors are emerging, some of whom are making themselves heard in English-language translations as well as in their native languages. One of the persistent concerns of non-English SF writers has been the difficulty of getting published, and recognized, outside their own countries. Part of that has been due to the cost of translation and the marginal nature of SF mass-market publishing in the United States; part has been the difficulty in translating attitudes to an American readership. Even Stanisław Lem and the Strugatskys have a readership limited to readers and critics capable of appreciating science fiction that does not seem aware of the Gernsback/Campbell/Boucher/Gold traditions of American science fiction; much of their work, and periodically that of other foreign authors, has been translated into English with critical acclaim but limited commercial success. And yet America, with its thousands of titles published every year and a readership willing to buy most of them, represents the Promised Land of science-fiction publication, and foreign authors yearn for it—both for its financial rewards and for its imprimatur of having been recognized where SF was born.

What will emerge from this melting pot of tradition and speculation and imagination remains for the future to determine. In the United States, the American brand is shifting as more writers from the mainstream pick up science-fiction tropes and as more writers from science fiction venture into the mainstream, often to considerable acclaim. The magazine influence is dwindling along with circulation; book publishers are becoming more conservative as the major businesses continue to merge and the mid-list book, where much of SF emerged, is abandoned. The future of science fiction may lie with the small publishers that have taken over the mid-list—and just when foreign SF is beginning to assume a more significant role.

But that's what keeps SF interesting.

LAWRENCE, KANSAS

The founding director of the Center for the Study of Science Fiction at the University of Kansas, James E. Gunn (1923–2020) was a renowned science fiction writer, editor, scholar, and anthologist. Among his many honors, he was the recipient of a Hugo Award as well as a Science Fiction and Fantasy Hall of Fame inductee. The Science Fiction and Fantasy Writers of America made him a Grand Master in 2007.

ANDRÉS NEUMAN

Translated from the Spanish by George Henson

I RECALL, I translate my beloved Larkin: "La noche no ha dejado nada más que mostrar: / ni la vela ni el vino que dejamos a medias, / ni el placer de tocarse; / solamente este signo de tu vida / caminando por dentro de la mía" (Night has left no more to show, / Not the candle, half-drunk wine, / Or touching joy; only this sign / Of your life walking into mine).

Love and translation look alike in their grammar. To love someone implies transforming their words into ours. Making an effort to understand the other person and, inevitably, to misinterpret them. To construct a precarious language together. In order to translate a text satisfactorily, you have to desire it. Covet its meaning. Have a certain need to possess its voice. In that dialogue which alternates between routine and fascination—prior knowledge and learning in progress—both parts end up modified.

The lover sees himself in the beloved, looking for similarities in their differences. Every small discovery is incorporated into their shared vocabulary. Still, no matter how much he tries to capture the other's language, what he ultimately receives is a lesson about his own language. Their coexistence is that seductive and stubborn. The person who translates approaches a strange presence in which, in some way, he recognizes himself. The text offers him a partially indecipherable mystery and, at the same time, a kind of essential familiarity. As if translator and text had already spoken before meeting.

Translators and lovers develop an almost manic sensitivity. They doubt every word, every gesture, every insinuation that confronts them. They jealously suspect everything they hear: I wonder what they really wanted to say to me? By loving and translating, the other person's intention runs into the limit of my existence. I read myself reading you. I hear you to the extent that you know how to talk to me. But if I say something, it's because you have spoken to me. I depend on your word, and your word needs me. It's saved in my correct answers, it survives my mistakes. In order for this to work, we have to admit the obstacles: we're not going to be able to read each other literally. I'm going to manipulate you with my best intentions. What isn't negotiable is emotion.

BARCELONA

Andrés Neuman (b. 1977) is an Argentine writer and a poet. He has been awarded the Alfaguara Prize and Spain's National Critics' Award, longlisted for the International Dublin Literary Award, included in the Bogotá39 list, and named one of *Granta*'s Best of Young Spanish-Language Novelists. His books have been translated into over twenty languages.

Oklahoma native George Henson is the author of eleven book-length translations, including works by Cervantes laureates Sergio Pitol and Elena Poniatowska. A frequent contributor to *World Literature Today*, he currently teaches Spanish translation at the Middlebury Institute of International Studies at Monterey.

A REPUBLIC OF THE IMAGINATION:
IN CONVERSATION WITH AZAR NAFISI (2023)

DANIEL SIMON

DANIEL SIMON: The theme of our May issue is "The Future of the Book," and it's an opportune moment to speak with you about your own passion for reading, writing, books, and how they've played such a large part in your life. In the epistolary genre consisting of letters to "Baba," your late father, you write beautifully in *Read Dangerously* about the intergenerational thread that connects teachers and readers, such as your parents, Nezhat and Ahmad, to your own children and now your grandchildren; Professor James Yoch here at the University of Oklahoma and your student Razieh in Tehran; even your own reading of writers from Plato to James Baldwin, Toni Morrison, and Margaret Atwood during the 1970s and then again more recently as you were composing these letters. If a student in Norman or Tehran were to ask you what it means to read dangerously in 2023, what would you tell them?

AZAR NAFISI: Well, this book is partly a response to the trend I had noticed, especially in the U.S., where we use books as comfort food. We read them not in order to be disturbed or find something new, but we read them in order for them to confirm what we already know, at times to confirm our prejudices: "Why don't they speak what I want them to?" So, there's no challenge—we're uncomfortable with challenge. We want to eliminate rather than create an exchange. And so, for me, reading dangerously means that we take that risk to read in order to be disturbed. As James Baldwin says, artists are here to disturb the peace. Writers are not here to warm the cockles of your heart.

For me, the best example of a good reader or a reader who takes risks is Alice in Wonderland. Out of millions of little girls, there's this one little girl who is bored with the routine of her life, and she's after something different. What makes Alice so exceptional is the fact that she has what Nabokov calls the third eye of the imagination. She sees not just reality in terms of appearances, but she also sees beyond reality, the magic of reality. And she sees not only a white rabbit but a white rabbit who talks and wears a waistcoat and a watch. She runs after that white rabbit, not saying, like some of our readers, that this is not how rabbits act. She risks going into the world of the white rabbit. And when she jumps into that hole, she doesn't say, *Am I going to survive this? What's going to happen to me next?* And her reward, of course, is the world—everything, every creature in that world, has a sign of being in her real life, but she's now seeing them in a new light. Her vision of reality is changing as she goes from one person to another.

The last thing that I want to say about Alice, which I think is really important, is that, like all good stories, it challenges and questions not just the world outside but the reader as well. Alice has a lot of questions from these creatures, but every time she asks them about who they are or why they are like this, they ask the question of her, *Who are you? Why do you look like this? You look strange.* She tells the caterpillar, *Who are you?* And the caterpillar throws the question back to her, saying, *Who are you?* So, that is my concept of risking when we read. Writers take a risk when they write; the reader should also take a risk when they read.

SIMON: You write so beautifully about your father, his example of reading and writing dangerously, even when he was imprisoned. As an example for you, it sounds like that was quite an inspiration to create your own imaginations of alternate realities, and to encourage your students to do so as well.

NAFISI: Yes. My father, when he was in jail and he was in the prison library, he told me that he was not alone because he was surrounded by these books. And every time he opened a book, even a book that he disagreed with, he discovered something new.

SIMON: That makes me think of what you say about David Grossman in the book as well: recognizing the enemy in the mirror. And in this time of great inhumanity, recognizing the humanity of someone who may be threatening your very survival. I think that's so valuable to remember in these times.

I was also thinking about a conversation with Moniro Ravanipour that appeared in an issue of *WLT* called "Writing Beyond Iran" in 2015. She remarks, "[The extremists] don't want any change, and the writer, by virtue of her craft, tries to change things, change minds and perceptions." In the conclusion to *Read Dangerously*, you also write that "where lies masquerade as truth, we need the clear eyes of imagination to see the reality behind and beyond the show." Is there a writer you've read recently who expresses this imagination most compellingly for you?

NAFISI: Well, there are so many writers, it's very difficult to choose. I always say that I'm promiscuous when it comes to books. Recently, I have been trying to organize and rearrange my bookshelves because every time I write a book, every room becomes filled with books and with notes. And then I have to go and find a place for them.

As I was doing that, I came across a book in Persian, actually, but it's been translated into English, *The 1,001 Nights* stories. I'd like to talk about that frame story because I think it is the mother of all stories. When we talk about imagination and the healing role that imagination plays in our lives, we can go back to Scheherazade and *The 1,001 Nights*. If you remember the story, there's this king who actually is a just king, but he discovers his queen making love to a slave and goes nuts. And without hearing the queen and the slave's side of the story, he kills them. From then on, he decides because she was unfaithful, all women are unfaithful. So, every night he marries a virgin, and at dawn he kills her before she can betray him.

Then comes Scheherazade. Of course, all these heroines are beautiful, but Scheherazade is known not for her beauty but for her wisdom. And that makes a difference—wisdom as an attraction. She decides that she is going to save the virgins and herself. Now, the first thing that comes to one's mind is taking a weapon to bed and killing him. What have you got to lose if he's going to kill you? You kill him. But that is the whole idea behind imagination: you don't do what your enemy does, you don't go into their domain. You're probably not good in their domain anyway. So, every night she tells a story to her sister as the king is listening, and she leaves it unfinished so that the next morning, the king wants to know more. And that's another thing about imagination: it arouses our curiosity. We want to know, we want to go to places we have not been, meet people we have not seen.

Anyway, to make a long story short, she tells him stories for 1,001 nights. During this time, he changes because two things happen to him. One is the curiosity, wanting to know about others and discovering that not all queens are betrayers and not all kings are just. The second thing that happens to him is that he finds empathy. And fiction, storytelling, is the bearer, the carrier of empathy. We all talk about difference, but the shock of recognition that we all share a common humanity is very important. Scheherazade heals the king rather than killing the king. I think that this is a great description of what imagination does to us or should do to us.

SIMON: Thank you so much for that lovely response, which makes me think of the oral tradition of storytelling—you write that where there are stories, there is hope and, ultimately, love. In a world where Rumi and Shakespeare exist, there must be hope, right?

NAFISI: Yes.

SIMON: My next question is more about contemporary events in Iran related to the recent protests. As you know, of course, Iranian security forces brutally cracked down on the protests that erupted after the death of Mahsa Amini in September 2022. What news have you heard from your friend whom you call Shirin in the book? How is she doing?

NAFISI: You know, the first few weeks of the uprising, I was desperately trying to get in touch with her, and I couldn't—the government had blocked all communication, and I was going crazy because I couldn't get in touch with anyone. Finally, through WhatsApp, we connected. And right now, we connect mainly through WhatsApp; she sends me videos and documents and tells me what is happening. But the first time I talked to her, I noticed that both of us—I, living in Washington, DC, and she, living in Tehran—had the same reaction toward the uprising. On one hand, it was a feeling of anger and outrage and, she told me, frustration, that she could not prevent this violence: shooting into their peaceful demonstrations, targeting people's eyes, making them go blind. But the difference between this one, Shirin said, and the feelings she had during protests in other years before this, was that in those other protests, it all ended in people going home, finally. But, she said, now the Iranian people are done with reform. They don't think that this regime is capable of change, and they don't see any future. So they are fighting for their lives. There is nowhere else to go but to fight, to challenge.

She said something, which I actually mention in *Read Dangerously*, where every time we talked, she would complain about the Western media and how they give so much space to the regime and its apologists, and they don't show the people of Iran. She said, with a sort of glee in her voice, "We did it! Now they are listening to our songs, giving prizes to our songs." This uprising, she told me, did something that felt akin to a miracle: connecting us to the world, allowing the world to come into that part of Iran which was forbidden before. So I have a lot of fear for her and for those who are in Iran—I almost feel that fear runs in my veins, like blood. But each time I talk to her, I also have a lot of hope. I agree with her, that we're not going to go back.

SIMON: It really does sound like there has been a sea change in the aspirations of everyday Iranian people that this may end, this must end. So that's hopeful.

NAFISI: Iranian people, especially the women, have discovered their power. They're not afraid anymore. You see, the roles have changed: it's the regime that is afraid. And this violence doesn't come out of strength; it comes out of weakness, because they have nothing else in their arsenal except violence, which doesn't work, which makes people more resolute.

SIMON: In a recent interview with Mary Louise Kelly that aired on NPR, the Iranian foreign minister, Hossein Amir-Abdollahian, blamed the recent protesters for committing acts of violence, supported by arms from the U.S. and Israel (February 9, 2023). Such hypocrisy seems to be one of the oldest tactics in the regime's playbook. When thinking about the future of Iran, however, what else gives you hope? Are there other things that you find hopeful, despite this entrenched mentality?

NAFISI: I'm glad you brought up this person's interview with NPR, because totalitarianism feeds on lies. I mean, it doesn't only feed on lies, it lives on lies, it can't survive without lies. And that is why we need imagination even more, because imagination is in search of truth. And truth, once you know it, you cannot remain silent. If you remain silent, you would become complicit in the crimes that are being committed, even against you.

Let me first clarify the way I define hope. Václav Havel says that hope is definitely not optimism, it is not the conviction that something good will come out, that there will be a reward for what we do. It is the certainty that what we do makes sense, has meaning, no matter what the reward. I believe *that* is the kind of hope that the Iranian people have reached. They are fighting for their existence. And that is why the slogan "Woman, Life, Liberty" is so different from any political slogan. The reason for this is that for Iranian women and Iranian people as a whole, this struggle is not political or is not only political, it is existential. I remember the way I felt when I was first expelled from the University of Tehran for refusing to wear the veil. I didn't wear my veil properly, not because I wanted to stand up to them politically but because my existence was in danger. If you do as they tell you, you are changed; for all practical purposes, it is sort of like a death.

So you're fighting for your life. Life becomes synonymous with liberty, and that is why we fight. For women, it became a matter of pride, a matter of dignity. If I, as a woman, as a writer, as a reader, as a teacher, as just a person, cannot be or feel or express who I am and how I am, then there's something wrong. Then there is an assault on my integrity as a human being. So we are fighting for our humanity. And that is why I have hope, because we are fighting for life. And there is a great deal of hope, not just for your own, but for the world.

SIMON: That's so beautifully said. As you say in the book, freedom is not just a Western construct. You write that it's a universal human right as well as an aspiration, not something the West has a special privilege to in terms of being able to express. The example of Iranian women and young women protesting about the hijab means so much more, as you say, in terms of dignity and survival.

NAFISI: Could I just say something? What you were saying reminded me of when at the very beginning of the 1979 revolution, Khomeini gave a fatwa for women to wear the compulsory hijab, and tens of thousands of Iranian women came into the streets, challenging him, and he had to take it back. At that time, they were attacked with scissors, and acid was thrown into their faces, but their main slogan speaks to what you were just saying. Their main slogan was freedom is neither Western nor Eastern, freedom is global. When you were talking about it, I kept thinking about that slogan and how true that is.

SIMON: That's a wonderful perspective, historically, as well as on the most recent protests. I have a final question about the future readers that you talk about in your book. You quote Margaret Atwood, who writes that "every recorded story implies a future reader," and "readers become keepers of memory, keepers of truth." In the context of this issue's focus on "The Future of the Book," what memories and what truths do you hope future readers will take away from your body of work?

NAFISI: I think there are three points that I would like to make. One is the fact that the imagination transcends all the limitations that reality puts in front of us or imposes on us. Imagination transcends the limitations of nationality, language, race, gender, ethnicity, religion. And it creates what I call a republic of imagination in which all of us live. Because we're passionate about life and we're passionate about imagination.

The second thing relates to Atwood and readers as keepers of memory. That reminds me of Tzvetan Todorov, the eastern European thinker. He said, "Only total oblivion calls for total despair." Imagination goes far beyond just totalitarianism and democracy. It addresses our humanity, against any kind of absolutism, including the absolutism of death. We have our memory, we have what Nabokov calls conclusive evidence that we have lived. That is how we stand up to whatever is transient, to whatever appears to us as absolute. That is why memory is so important, because it addresses our humanity.

The last thing I want to say is that Saul Bellow, in talking about totalitarian regimes and democratic ones, writes that totalitarian regimes like the Soviet Union are very obvious. I mean, Stalin pours on death, and we know about this naked violence. But in democracies, we don't kill our opponents or put them in jail—or just ban their books, as we're doing right now—what threatens us is our sleeping consciousness and our atrophy of feeling. That is what worries me today. What imagination does, it awakens our senses, it awakens our consciousness. What fiction does, it celebrates life, with all its pain and joy, and makes us alive, simply alive.

So, I want to involve the reader. I want to tell the reader that you're not just a passive observer. Once you read the book, you are responsible. I want to end with a quotation from Nabokov, which I use in *Read Dangerously*. He says, "Readers are born free, and they ought to remain free." What we should remember is that you fight for that freedom. Otherwise, they come and burn your books or ban your books. Even in a democracy.

SIMON: Which goes back to Plato and the noble lie versus the subversive truth of the poet, who sees beyond the shadows on the wall of the cave and claims that freedom and life.

NAFISI: That is very true, very true.

Iranian American writer Azar Nafisi (b. 1948) is the critically acclaimed author of *Reading Lolita in Tehran*, a number one *New York Times* bestseller published in thirty-two languages, and *Things I've Been Silent About*, also a *New York Times* bestseller. In this exchange, Nafisi discusses her 2022 book of essays, *Read Dangerously: The Subversive Power of Literature in Troubled Times*, including the power of storytelling embodied by Scheherazade and Lewis Carroll's Alice; the intergenerational threads that connect readers; and the role of writers and readers in preserving memory and defending truth.

PART IV

FIRST TAKES ON MODERN CLASSICS

1976–2025

JÁNOS PILINSZKY

János Pilinszky is a poet whose work belies Adorno's dictum that there can be "no poetry after Auschwitz." In fact, the world of extermination camps and prison camps was one of Pilinszky's fundamental poetic experiences, and after World War II, when his first important poems were produced in Hungary, he did indeed "speak from the disaster-center of the modern world." Yet he could not have grasped the enormity of crime against man to the point of equating the dehumanized camp inmate with Christ without an already existing guilt complex of his own; there is an "extreme" Christian conscience functioning in his poetry. The world that it projects is a barren, bleak, and cruel one, full of mute suffering and continuous deprivations which are only rarely alleviated by flashes of ecstatic happiness or moments of inner peace. Though seen against the backdrop of recent history, this poetry is very meaningful. It encapsulates the agonies of our age; nonetheless, without the totalitarian experience one might find it disturbing with its air of helpless suffering and impending annihilation. God's grace and human love may help one to endure this world, but Pilinszky's philosophy or attitude toward life is summed up best in these lines: "Creation no matter how vast / is more cramped than a roost."

Ted Hughes, author of *Wodwo* and *Crow*, is an outstanding English poet. This collection reveals a hitherto unknown quality of his: the capacity to identify with another poet's traumas and inflections. He knows no Hungarian and had to rely on his co-translator's understanding of the original text (János Csokits, by the way, is a London-based Hungarian poet), and it is all the more surprising that he has managed to resist the obvious temptation to paraphrase Pilinszky. The translation is "as close as I could make it," claims Hughes in his illuminating introductory essay, and this tendency to stick close to the original has produced mostly good results. Poems like "Harbach 1944," "World Grown Cold," "Impromptu," "The Desert of Love," and "Under a Portrait" are powerful and moving in Hughes's renderings; also, the short unrhymed poems from Pilinszky's latest (post-1971) period come through rather well. Hughes is perhaps less successful with some of Pilinszky's longer poems (unrhyming in the English version), where the rhyme scheme of the original is more intricate and where the rhymes play a special organizing function in the structure of the poem. On close inspection it is possible to find some inadequacies and minor mistranslations, but these can easily be forgotten in view of the overall achievement.

Pilinszky's strangely hypnotic tone, the "simple, helpless accuracy" of his verse, is captured by Hughes in most pieces of this slim but impressive collection—the poet whose voice is "more homeless than the word" gains new life in English thanks to this successful transfusion of energy, inspiration, of poetic blood.

GEORGE GÖMÖRI, SPRING 1977

Selected Poems was translated from the Hungarian by Ted Hughes and János Csokits.

SELECTED POEMS   (1976)

LEAH GOLDBERG

With Anna Akhmatova, Else Lasker-Schüler, Edith Sitwell, H.D., or Nelly Sachs, Leah Goldberg ranks among the major women poets of our century. Born in Lithuania, she completed her studies in Russian before obtaining her doctoral degree in Semitic languages at a German university. Meanwhile she had learned Hebrew and adopted it as the language for her writing. In addition to writing her own poems in Hebrew, she translated into Hebrew Shakespeare's *As You Like It* and Petrarch's *Sonnets* as well as selected works of Akhmatova, Baudelaire, Verlaine, Rilke, Hofmannsthal, Chekhov, and Thomas Mann, among others. Her critical writings include an important essay, "The Art of Fiction," and a study on Dostoevsky. She settled in Palestine in 1935 and from 1952 until her death in 1970 was professor of comparative literature at the Hebrew University. In Israel her poems are already considered to be classics of modern Hebrew literature.

Her intense scholarly, linguistic, critical, and literary activity might well lead one to expect her poetry to be complex, perhaps even cryptic, certainly rich in allusions to her extensive readings. On the contrary, most of her lyrics are disarmingly simple, with a sensitivity to nature that might almost remind one of some classical Japanese poets:

> Sometimes from my nightly grave,
> lying in my bed, I see
> a tree in starlight looming black,
> and once again I must remind my heart
> that dawn will bring my green tree back.

In her sonnets, however, she achieves a greater complexity:

> In what a careless calm I lived
> before you came, and how secure
> in wisdom, wearing my ripe years
>
> with dignity, and free at night of fear.
> Yet dear are the moments when we sit together,
> or when I wait for you in shy confusion here.

Often, too, her poems, however simple, reveal a sense of paradox. In her last poems, written and published when she knew that she would soon die of cancer, she expresses a calm and dignified awareness of destiny:

> As I approached that night
> that has no end,
> suddenly it was morning.
> The sun lit up
> the faces of the living
> who envied the dead.

ÉDOUARD RODITI, AUTUMN 1977

Selected Poems was translated from the Hebrew by Robert Friend.

WAITING FOR THE BARBARIANS   (1980)

J. M. COETZEE

Coetzee's is a remarkably rich and mature talent. In this his third novel he continues to explore the psychosis accompanying the forced contact between primitive and advanced societies. His first book, *Dusklands* (1974), contained a remarkable novella dealing with an early journey of exploration beyond the frontier of the Cape Colony. The second, *From the Heart of the Country* (1977), showed the dominant white society teetering toward collapse.

In his new book the frontiers are succumbing to onslaughts of the "barbarians," and the "empire" is caving in. Although time and place are kept vague and the location is somewhere in an inhospitable corner of the northern hemisphere, the application to South Africa, Coetzee's country of birth and residence, is hard to ignore. For this—like his previous books—is an allegory of sorts. Books on the demise of white South Africa by other South Africans come to mind: Karel Schoeman's *Promised Land* and Nadine Gordimer's recent *July's People*, to name a few.

The title is probably taken from Cavafy's poem which concluded that the barbarians were "a kind of solution": that their threat had served to justify stern measures by the central government. The book makes for compelling reading, largely due to the successful use of the present tense throughout and the vivid presentation of unfolding events. The story is told in the first person by a minor official, a magistrate on the distant frontier whose tolerant administration had become suspect by the government, bent on suppressing any indication of restiveness. The magistrate, weak, ineffective, but a decent human being, shoulders the guilt of the atrocities committed by his government and is destroyed in the process. The tightly controlled writing as well as the theme brings to mind Graham Greene's *The Power and the Glory* with its "whiskey priest." The book won the James Tait Black Memorial Prize, the Geoffrey Faber Award, as well as the South African CNA Literary Award for 1980.

BAREND J. TOERIEN, AUTUMN 1981

THE COMPLETE STORIES OF LU XUN   (1982)

LU XUN

Certainly the most highly acclaimed of modern China's writers is Zhou Shuren (Chou Shu-jen, 1881–1936), better known by his pen name Lu Xun (Lu Hsun). Scholar of classical Chinese fiction, college professor, collector of woodblock prints, virulent essayist, and political refugee—these roles took the bulk of his energies; his stories number only twenty-five, written between 1918 and 1925. However, the two collections presented here, *Nahan* (*Call to Arms*) and *Panghuang* (*Wandering*), do not include his very first story, written in 1913 in the classical literary language instead of the vernacular style for which he is famous, nor the updated fables and legends he published in 1935 under the title *Gushi xinbian* (*Old Tales Retold*).

The complexity of Lu Xun's genius shines in each of these stories: his satiric attacks on the hypocrisy and inhumanity in the dregs of traditional Chinese values, his sense of the crushing helplessness and isolation of the individual in his time, his arresting use of disturbing images, recurring refrains that build his gloomy picture of a blighted and disintegrating society. Despite his official reputation as "standard-bearer" of revolution in the People's Republic, Lu Xun reveals precious little hope for social change in these stories. Instead, he is a writer for all ages, excoriating his own culture while revealing perhaps more than is comfortable of mankind's common cruelty and ignorance.

All these stories have been translated into English before; most appeared in volume one of the four-volume *Selected Works of Lu Hsun* (1956) and in the two editions of *Selected Stories of Lu Hsun* (1954; 1972). Even though later translations have improved on these versions, they are scattered across a variety of publications. Until now there has been no single-volume edition of all Lu Xun' s fictional works; Indiana's volume has made a substantial contribution in this regard. Moreover, here the Yangs have chosen their best translation of each story and revised them all still further: e.g., "The True Story of Ah Q" from Gladys Yang, *Silent China: Selected Writings of Lu Xun* (1973), and "Kong Yiji" and "The New-Year Sacrifice" from W. J. F. Jenner, ed., *Modern Chinese Stories* (1970). They have also added new versions of stories they had previously neglected and have expanded their notes to assist foreign readers.

Here at last Lu Xun's creative writing is faithfully and fully presented in English; this volume should be on the reading list for any course on Chinese or world literature of the twentieth century.

ROBERT E . HEGEL, WINTER 1983

The Complete Stories of Lu Xun was translated from the Chinese by Yang Xianyi and Gladys Yang.

THE LOVER   (1984)

MARGUERITE DURAS

"What I have most in common with Proust," wrote François Mauriac, is that "I do not observe, I do not describe, I rediscover, and what I rediscover is the . . . world of my childhood." Similarly, Marguerite Duras rediscovers in *L'amant* the world of her childhood in French Indochina and reveals to the reader a part of her life that she has kept hidden for almost fifty years. Although she did write about her mother and brothers before, she did so when they were still alive, and she merely hinted at the truth. Now she hides nothing; in this extraordinary, erotic confession, she provides the key to the themes and images that run throughout her work.

In a series of paragraphs of unequal length in which the chronology follows the order of memory, the author presents an album of pictures of her childhood. The pauses between the paragraphs function as fade-outs between the scenes of a film. The verbal images here, more vivid than any photographs, also evoke the sounds and smells of colonial outposts in the bush, "lost in the quadrilateral expanses of rice, of fear, of madness, of fever, and of forgetfulness."

In *L'amant* Duras reveals that the stifling, almost unbearable family situation that exists in her early novels, as well as the desperate desire of her protagonists to escape from unbearable poverty, an unstable mother, and a despicable older brother, was based on her own experience. She reveals too that she effected her escape from her family at the age of fifteen and a half, when she became the mistress of a Chinese multimillionaire whom she met on the ferryboat crossing the Mekong River. It was this crossing of the river between adolescence and adulthood and between the races which the author considers to be the decisive event in her life and which constitutes the leitmotiv of *L'amant*.

LUCILLE F. BECKER, SUMMER 1985

Reviewed in the French; *L'amant* was translated into English by Barbara Bray in 1985.

DICTIONARY OF THE KHAZARS   (1985)

MILORAD PAVIĆ

I have always maintained that tradition is bound to produce selected inclinations and superior achievements. The case in point is illustrated in Milorad Pavić's latest book, "The Khazar's Bibliography." Pavić is a professor at the University of Belgrade whose ancestors have been linked with Serbian literature for the past two hundred years. (As for me, who often struggles with words, I realize that the military tradition of some of my predecessors, along with the notable Serb, Baron Mihaila Mikašinović, born 1657, would have perhaps made it easier for me to be a soldier rather than a writer.) In Pavić's case, I have a distinct feeling that two centuries of literary tradition have crystallized him into a great novelist.

"The Khazar's Bibliography" has been hailed as the greatest book of this generation, "the ultimate in literature . . . the book of the future. . . . The book is one of the rare awards which the author bestows upon his literature" (Raša Livada); "Pavić's writings are perhaps the best creations in our contemporary fantastic literature" (Igor Mandić). It also received NIN's literary award for 1985. What is "The Khazar's Bibliography"? The book is not a bibliography, although it is written in dictionary format; it contains three smaller "books" or sections: the Red book (Christian sources on the Khazars), the Green book (Islamic sources), and the Yellow book (Judaic sources), as well as two appendices and a final note by the author. The work can be opened and read at any point. It is a novelbibliography, and although prose, it reads like poetry. One can read only a segment, some segments, or the whole book at random or in sequence, creating new texts and meanings, various interpretations and impressions. It is based mainly on folklore, myths, and imagination and fantasy. Most of all, the underlying tone of the book is that of irony and tragedy.

The subject of the book is the Khazars, a nation that existed long ago and disappeared without a trace. Their story is therefore a timely warning to all small nations, including the Serbs, about their vulnerability and precarious situation. The truth about the Khazars probably will never be found in the sea of stories, myths, allegations, and contradictions. Along with the author, we can only search for that truth in the hope of its resurrection.

BRANKO MIKASINOVICH, WINTER 1986

Reviewed in the Serbian; *Hazarski rečnik* was translated into English by Christina Pribićević-Zorić in 1988.

DECOLONISING THE MIND:
THE POLITICS OF LANGUAGE IN AFRICAN LITERATURE   (1986)

NGŪGĪ WA THIONG'O

Ngūgī wa Thiong'o makes a strong argument for the adoption of African languages in the development and writing of African literature by African writers. In his own case he indicates that the present book is the last he will have written in English. Henceforth he will write either in Gīkūyū or in Kiswahili, the first language being his mother tongue and the second the lingua franca of East Africa. He does state, however, that his works will continue to be translated into other languages.

Throughout *Decolonising the Mind*, Ngũgĩ argues persuasively that language is political and is a very important part of a people's culture: it mirrors a culture and is itself molded by it. Therefore a literature produced in a foreign language can never truly mirror the complexities and richness of a people's culture. He further argues that African literature in English is no more than an African variant of English literature, although it is an important contribution to literature in general. He contends that such literature is incapable of uncovering the many nuances of African culture; nor is it capable of reaching the African masses, most of whom do not speak or write European languages. Moreover, the author argues that the languages of colonialism produced literatures which denigrated the Africans and their cultures. Thus, continued use of these European languages by African writers has promoted neocolonialism. Instead, Ngũgĩ strongly advocates that the African writer join the African peasantry and the working classes—who constitute the majority of the African population—producing a literature which appeals to them and which mirrors their cultures and struggles against neocolonialism. To do less is to betray the African masses and to collaborate with neocolonialism, he argues.

Although *Decolonising the Mind* is likely to stir scholarly controversy especially among African writers in European languages, it is an important contribution to literary criticism and offers further evidence of the author's growing identification with the political struggles of the peasant and working classes in Kenya, Africa, and elsewhere. For an understanding of the author, one of Africa's leading writers, the book is indispensable.

JIDLAPH G. KAMOCHE, SPRING 1987

BELOVED   (1987)

TONI MORRISON

Toni Morrison writes eccentric novels: novels about characters who appear not to be "normal" human beings, who appear to be away from the center of their society and their history, and novels in which she says things we the readers may consider to be strange. She did this in her first four novels—*The Bluest Eye, Sula, Song of Solomon* (which won the 1978 National Book Critics Circle Award for fiction), and *Tar Baby*—and she has done so again in her fifth, *Beloved*, which received the Pulitzer Prize for fiction in 1988.

The story focuses on Sethe, an escaped slave in post–Civil War Ohio who had tried to kill all her children when she was about to be recaptured but had succeeded only in killing her baby, whose gravestone read "Beloved." The spirit of the dead child is haunting the house, for we learn from Sethe and her daughter Denver that "nothing ever dies." The two sons have left because of the haunting, but Paul D turns up to love Sethe and drives the spirit away. Not quite, for the spirit comes out of the water as a human being, Beloved, and builds up a relationship with Denver and later Sethe, driving Paul D away, until the end, when he returns: "There was something blessed in his manner. Women saw him and wanted to weep."

Such a summary does *Beloved* an injustice because it mistranslates the characters, actions, and language. The novel is about memory, history, and language from the perspective of Black Americans while simultaneously taking in the whole world, not forgetting white people (including vicious slaveholders, kind slaveholders, abolitionists) and American "Indians." Here is the language question for Black Americans, presented in the actions of a chain gang: "They sang it out and beat it up, garbling the words so they could not be understood; tricking the words so their syllables yielded up other meanings." As for the written language, the Black Americans did not want to learn reading, "since nothing important to them could be put down on paper." It is a question not of culture but of power: an answer by a slave named Sixo is "clever, but schoolteacher beat him anyway to show him that definitions belonged to the definers—not the defined." Worst of all is the Black/white relationship.

> The more colored people spent their strength trying to convince them how gentle they were, how clever and loving, how human, the more they used themselves up to persuade whites of something Negroes believed could not be questioned, the deeper and more tangled the jungle grew inside. But it wasn't the jungle blacks brought with them to this place from the other (livable) place. It was

the jungle whitefolks planted in them. And it grew. It spread. In, through and after life, it spread, until it invaded the whites who had made it. Touched them every one. Changed and altered them. Made them bloody, silly, worse than even they wanted to be, so scared were they of the jungle they had made. The screaming baboon lived under their own white skin; the red gums were their own.

If nothing is lost, if everyone is wounded emotionally since nobody can permit himself or herself to feel too much for children who will soon be gone, if nothing is lost through time, if *rememories* are there waiting for us, and if language is suspect, what forgiveness? How can the Black American novelist write at all? To paraphrase a line from the novel, Morrison circles the subject. She gives voice to the voiceless. She lets us know the true feelings and perceptions of her characters as though that were what language was made for. The word is made flesh, and flesh is made the word. Through language, Morrison is seeking to redeem the people and their history, to love the people and the land. Hence the epigraph from Romans 9:25: "I will call them my people, / which were not my people; / and her beloved, / which was not beloved." The "strangeness" in the writing is the result of Morrison's undermining our fixed perceptions and making us see history, reality, and ourselves afresh.

PETER NAZARETH, AUTUMN 1988

THE RETURN OF THE CARAVELS   (1988)

ANTÓNIO LOBO ANTUNES

"O Retorno das Naus" would have been a fitting title, for the subject matter, rarely dealt with since António Pires published two verist novels, is the exodus of hundreds of thousands of Portuguese colonists from Africa, flooding their homeland within a few months in 1974–75. António Lobo Antunes has chosen seven cases, recounting the hardships faced, first in war-torn Africa, then in Lisbon and its environs. He makes the stories even grimmer by telling them from the self-pitying, embittered, and defeatist viewpoint of the *retornados* or "returners" (a term he avoids). Forced to start all over again, they feel despoiled, exploited, shipwrecked.

The seven cases are barely connected, however. Antunes places them in the worst possible scenario: a decadent Lisbon beset by poverty, prostitution, extortion, disease, and other evils, thus dramatizing the transitional postwar and postrevolutionary period. He heightens the turmoil by submerging the comings and goings of the returners in a chaotic mass of details of Lisbon street life, observed with a remarkable sarcastic acuity. Adopting a fashionable mannerism, he makes it all the harder to piece the action together by constantly shifting from the "I" of whoever is the protagonist of the current section (there are eighteen sections in all) to third-person narration. Further confusion is created by such grotesque anachronisms as naming the returners after celebrated Portuguese discoverers and *conquistadores* and having them act at one moment plausibly as ordinary Portuguese of the twentieth century and the next implausibly as those heroes of yore who had safely come home from their dangerous overseas exploits.

The very first *retornado* we meet, a poor fellow back from Angola with a mulatto family, is given the name of Pedro Álvares Cabral, the discoverer of Brazil. The second, "a one-eyed man named Luís" who has returned with his father's corpse in a coffin, is identified as the poet who—in twentieth-century Lisbon!—is in the process of writing *The Lusiads*. And so forth. Actually, the modern-day colonials have nothing in common with their famous countrymen. The satiric, incongruous masquerade amuses at first, but the joke wears thin with constant repetition. It extends to the very title, *As Naus*, a term designating the largest oceangoing sailing ships of the sixteenth century but now applied by Antunes to the modern ships and airplanes that carried the colonists back to Portugal.

Antunes must have a large readership in Portugal for his mock-serious treatment of national history. His six previous novels have gone through as many as fourteen editions since 1979. *As Naus*, however, is hardly the novel which the theme of the Great Colonial Runaway deserves.

GERALD M. MOSER, WINTER 1990

Reviewed in the Portuguese; *As Naus* was translated into English by Gregory Rabassa in 1988.

OMEROS   (1990)

DEREK WALCOTT

Derek Walcott writes in at least four authorial guises in his latest book-length poem, *Omeros*: as novelist, autobiographer, playwright, and lyrical epic poet. The reports of all four storytellers cohere and compose a grand, meditational whole. "Omeros" is the Greek Anglicization of "Homer," who, throughout the seven books of the poem, is evoked as a St. Lucian fisherman or an East Indian shaman or a layabout in the streets of London or some of the many mythical personae in African, African-American, and Afro-Caribbean folk cultures.

The modern contemporary present and the ancient classical past, two historical strands ostensibly at variance but which when construed in hindsight prove not all that dissimilar in contexts of cause and effect and social and psychological consequences, are here woven together into a dazzling unity throughout the richly layered and echoic storylines. Certainly, too, the Caribbean fishermen Achille and Philoctete, protagonist and subsidiary character, respectively, do assume a loosely parallel resemblance to their prototypes in Greek myth.

Exile, spiritual alienation, the dispossession of Native Americans from their centuries-old continental heritage, slavery and its continuing after-effects of racism and class antagonism, the aftermath of empire and the contradictions of neocolonialism, and the magnificent unpredictability of nature are some of the preoccupations of the poet in what is his finest work thus far. But of course, Walcott's evergreen preoccupation is with his ever-renewable poetic diction, ever representable and emotionally satisfying: a waterfall personified as "garrulous"; mountains being "tacit"; the suppurating wound on Philoctete's shin "like a radiant anemone"; sunrise and the heated ring on the horizon, where "clouds were rising like loaves"; and superannuated Major Plunkett's Guinness-drinking habit of "freckling his pensioned moustache / with a surf-curling tongue." Walcott's wit and wordplay (he is one of the few poets writing today who excite their readers by their elegant and serious use of humorous phrasing) show through inventively in the following four-and-a-half lines:

I said, 'Omeros',
and *O* was the conch-shell's invocation, *mer* was
both mother and sea in our Antillean patois,
os, a grey bone, and the white surf as it crashes
and spreads its sibilant collar on a lace shore.

ANDREW SALKEY, SPRING 1991

PEOPLE ON A BRIDGE   (1990)

WISŁAWA SZYMBORSKA

Long recognized in Poland as a leading voice in contemporary Polish poetry, Wisława Szymborska has not achieved the same popularity in the English-speaking world as other poets of her generation such as Zbigniew Herbert and Tadeusz Różewicz. Still, *People on a Bridge* is not the first introduction of Szymborska's verse to English readers. Czesław Miłosz included poems by her in his seminal anthology *Postwar Polish Poetry* (1965), and in 1981 Princeton University Press published a selection of her poems translated by Magnus Kryński and Robert Maguire. Let us hope that the present volume, a welcome addition to those earlier translations, will help bring Szymborska the recognition that she deserves.

The poems selected by Adam Czerniawski come from four different collections and span a period of twenty years. Rather than adhere to chronology, Czerniawski has grouped the poems according to recurring themes, most prominently the problem of art's relationship to time, death, and reality. Thematic unity is further emphasized by a ring composition. The poems opening and closing the book (the only two given both in English translation and in the Polish original) deal with the precariousness of human life, symbolized both times by the age of a bridge, and the inability of art—despite its futile attempt to resist the flow of time—to penetrate the mystery of death and existence.

At the center of Szymborska's attention is the disparity between the limitations of the poetic imagination and the unlimited vastness of reality:

"Four billion people on this earth, / but my imagination is as it was" ("Big Numbers"). The mathematical value of π comes closer to expressing the infinite richness of the universe than does the poetic imagination: "It cannot be grasped *six five three five* at a glance, / *eight nine* in a calculus / *seven nine* in imagination, / or even *three two three eight* in a conceit, that is, a comparison." Art catches only individual facts and existences, a fraction of reality. Poetry, marked by insufficiency and imperfection, is a selection, a renunciation, a passing over in silence, and a "sigh" rather than a "full breath." The poet, like anyone else, is unable to transgress his or her own "I," his own particular existence. Being himself, he cannot be what he is not.

In the opposition between reality and art, life and intellect, Szymborska declares herself on the side of reality and life. Ideas are most often pretexts to kill, a deadly weapon, whether under the guise of an artistic experiment ("Experiment"), a political Utopia ("Utopia"), or ideological fanaticism ("The Terrorist, He Watches"). Szymborska sides with reality against art and ideology, and this choice situates her in the mainstream of postwar Polish poetry alongside Miłosz, Herbert, and Białaszewski.

Like Białaszewski, although in a different idiom, Szymborska extols the everyday and the ordinary. Her "miracle mart" is made of barking dogs, trees reflected in a pond, gentle breezes and gusty storms, the world "ever-present." Even in dreams she appreciates most of all their ability to create the illusion of reality. In the theater she is moved by a glimpse of actors caught beneath the curtain more than by tragic tirades. Her poetry reverses the accepted view of what is important and what is unimportant; it puts forward common and humble reality at the expense of history and politics: "Pebbles by-passed on the beach can be as rounded / as the anniversaries of insurrections" ("May Be Left Untitled").

Pervaded by the spirit of contestation, Wisława Szymborska's poetry thrives on paradox. A mixture of "loftiness and common speech" ("Unwritten Poem Review"), it is subtle, witty, and ironic.

BOGDANA CARPENTER, WINTER 1992

People on a Bridge was translated from the Polish by Adam Czerniawski.

TINÍSIMA (1992)

ELENA PONIATOWSKA

A common element in the work of the Mexican writer Elena Poniatowska is the commitment to portray her country, its society and culture, and to interpret Mexico's social and political history, most notably since the Mexican Revolution of 1910. Oftentimes this portrayal and this interpretation take place through the voices of women and minorities, for Poniatowska has always shown in her writing a deep concern for those who have been silenced and marginalized by the dominant social order. Another characteristic of her work is the merging of the nonfictional and the fictional, and many of her books bring together the work of the journalist and that of the writer of fiction. These two elements—the social concern for Mexico and for the marginalized voices of its people, and the blending of fiction and journalism—are present in Poniatowska's latest novel. The book started out as a simple movie script, but during ten years of work, and after much research and innumerable interviews, the initial project developed into a novel of some 663 pages.

Tinísima is the story of the life and trajectory of Tina Modotti, an Italian woman who lived in Mexico in the 1920s and who participated actively in the cultural, intellectual, and political life of the country. Modotti was a photographer, social militant, and member of the Communist Party in Mexico, who later worked as an agent of the Soviet government and as a "María" (a Mexican term for a nurse in Spain) during the Spanish Civil War. The narrative completes a full circle, following Tina from her first years in Mexico, through her imprisonment and expulsion by the Mexican government in 1930, her life in Europe and in the Soviet Union, and the Spanish war, to her return to Mexico and her death there in 1942 at the age of forty-four.

During her first period of residence in Mexico, Modotti had relationships with the North American photographer Edward Weston (with whom she lived for many years), with the Mexican painters Diego Rivera and Xavier Guerrero, and with the Cuban revolutionary Julio Antonio Mella. The novel also narrates her friendship and contacts with other people whose names are well known among the Mexican intelligentsia of that day, such as Alejandro Gómez Arias and Miguel Covarrubias, and with foreigners who were in Mexico at one time or another, like the Nicaraguan revolutionaries Augusto César Sandino and Farabundo Martí. Thus Poniatowska composes a vivid portrait of Mexico at the time: the culture, the ideals, the political fights, the revolutionary struggle, the hopes and disillusionments. The novel is also a declaration of the author's love for her country expressed through the characters' voices, as when the narrator quotes what Weston writes in his diary: "Oh, México, lo tocas a uno desgarradoramente" (oh, Mexico, you touch one heartbreakingly).

Mexico is an important presence in the narrative, achieving in a certain way the status of a protagonist. Tina's story follows the story/history of the country, or vice versa, and the fact that Mexican history is told through the perspective of a woman and a foreigner is highly meaningful. Poniatowska offers the reader a vision of Mexico that is seldom exposed, just as the story of Tina herself has been all but forgotten, hidden behind a male-dominated "official" history. Another element that plays a significant part in the novel, not only for its impact on Tina's development but also for its historical consequences, is the Spanish Civil War, its hopes and its horrors. Poniatowska is careful in depicting in detail the participation of women in that conflict from the two fighting sides, but especially from the Republicans, again bringing to the fore a marginalized group often ignored by the dominant perspective.

In her portrayal of Mexico and of Spain, following Tina around Europe and the former Soviet Union in the years leading up to World War II, Poniatowska invites the reader to reflect on social and historical events that certainly have had a great impact upon the shaping of today's Mexico and the world. Likewise, Poniatowska's portrayal of Tina as a woman grappling with problems of identity, love, social acceptance, aging, et cetera, invites the reader to reflect on the condition of women within the dominant patriarchal order. *Tinísima* shares a common theme with many contemporary novels by women in that Tina is a woman in search of her true self, trying to define an identity: "No quisiera morir en el papel equivocado. . . . Quisiera morir con mi rostro verdadero habiendo encontrado lo que me toca hacer sobre la tierra" (I wouldn't want to die in the wrong role. . . . I would like to die with my true face having found what I have to do on earth). It is quite troubling, however, to see how she repeatedly seeks to define herself through the men with whom she has relationships. In this respect, we may not say that Tina is a feminist, although she is indeed an avant-garde woman, in her work, in her social commitment, in her behavior, in the way she lives her sexuality without guilt.

A feminist awareness comes somewhat late for Tina. It happens as an epiphany when, after she has returned to Mexico, her friend Concha Michel gives her a little book entitled *Dos antagonismos fundamentales*, the antagonism between men and women. Reading the book, Tina realizes the position of subordination to men in which she and so many other women lived, a subordination that not even communism, to which Tina gave so much of her life, addressed adequately. Michel's book also allows Tina the awareness that, as a human being, she is constantly changing. Her struggle to find her role in society, her search for an identity, is, then, a never-ending process.

In the more than six hundred pages of the novel there are few occasions when the reader comes across passages that seem unnecessary or irrelevant to the narrative. A few passages, especially in the first part of the book, are somewhat long: for example, the dialogue between Diego Rivera and the Mexican journalist Pérez Moreno. Rivera as a character here borders on the stereotypical, and the whole passage has a slightly comic effect, diluting the dramatic nature of the situation. Nevertheless, *Tinísima* is a novel that certainly involves the reader. It stimulates much reflection, and the issues it addresses, through its portrayal of a woman, a country, and a time, are disturbingly contemporary.

CRISTINA FERREIRA-PINTO, WINTER 1994

Reviewed in the Spanish; *Tinísima* was translated into English by Katherine Silver in 1996.

RED SORGHUM: A NOVEL OF CHINA   (1993)

MO YAN

Red Sorghum may be the best—surely it is the most startling—twentieth-century Chinese novel yet to appear in English translation. Belatedly, it fulfills the promise that seemed to loom in Chinese literature's future when it first "thawed out" in the late 1970s but somehow got lost in the decade after. The story told here, already well known to many Americans through the film of the same name, also quells another, more recent anxiety among some critics: that famous film versions of Chinese novels by Zhang Yimou and other visually sophisticated Fifth Generation directors actually are better than the literary works on which they are based. *Red Sorghum*, in this inspired translation by Howard Goldblatt, is incomparably more interesting than the conspicuously patriotic film that followed it (as is Michael Duke's superb translation of *Raise the Red Lantern* by Su Tong, another author well served by Zhang).

Mo Yan is a young, defiantly experimental writer, and his story takes a modernist track, interweaving past and present fragments of a main plot and several subplots in a slightly mystifying yet cinematic and classically suspenseful grand narrative—cinematic because of his mesmerizing red symbolism: red sorghum (the original color of the crop; modern hybrids are colorless), red blood, red sunsets, red bridal veils, red wine. The story tells how one Yu Zhan'ao's ragtag village militia suicidally but memorably ambushed occupying Japanese troops during World War II (they felled an enemy general). This is interwoven with an even more fantastic tale of how Yu rescued, then raped (in an open sorghum field), and finally married a heroic woman destined ultimately to fall from enemy gunfire during his ambush. A second mininovel, originally a sequel to the first but now part 2 of one long *roman fleuve* (if the term may be applied to a modernist novel), tells how the couple took over a red-sorghum winery in the days before the war. The third part shows a band of orphaned children fighting for their lives against a pack of hundreds of wild dogs eager to devour the corpses with which the Japanese "refertilized" the red-sorghum fields during their My Lai–style massacre after the great ambush. (The piece evokes *Lord of the Flies*, with the dogs regressing into fiendishly human cleverness.)

These narratives are familiar yet eerie, for the text refers to Yu Zhan'ao as "my grandfather" and his heroic mistress as "my grandmother"; the narrator, in his flights of surrealistic and gory description, relates nearly ecstatic states of mind in his forebears that he could never have known himself or learned of from others. The novel winds up with evermore incredible and gory epiphanies in the final chapters, when "my grandmother's funeral" ends in a bloodbath, only to be outdone by the gang rape and murder of "my second grandma" (Yu Zhan'ao's second "wife").

Red Sorghum is unique among modern Chinese novels in elevating its tale to mythic proportions—though the two standard national myths engaged, filiality and patriotism, are turned on their heads, through exaggeration whose very beauty attenuates its irony, and a change in tone in the last two parts that recasts the narrator's heroic forebears as demons. Still, his unconditional love for them is never in doubt. The novel will be remembered for its inventiveness, its mythmaking, its heroism and antiheroism, its violence ("The fluids of his brain had oozed into his ears from the shattered scalp, and one of his eyeballs hung from the socket like a huge grape on his cheek"), its absurdity ("Grandma" would go on bound feet to the local dumping ground for infanticides to find lucky lottery numbers by weighing infant corpses). The "magic realism" that informs Mo Yan's work is evident not only in his plot—the first Chinese tale to demonstrate that even familiar heroic motifs can turn fantastic in the hands of one whose imagination is equal to the task—but also in the rapture of his imagery: of "crushed and broken sorghum," "sorghum corpses," "sorghum everywhere . . . crying bitterly."

JEFFREY C. KINKLEY, SPRING 1994

Red Sorghum was translated from the Chinese by Howard Goldblatt.

BLINDNESS   (1995)

JOSÉ SARAMAGO

In a recent interview José Saramago refers to a temporary loss of vision in 1991 to explain in part the genesis of his latest novel, an "essay on blindness." However, such an experience, no matter how unsettling, could hardly account for this story of an entire society swept by a mysterious epidemic that leaves its victims helpless when their vision is suddenly blocked by a curtain of white. The first case of such blindness concerns a motorist stricken on the novel's first page as he stops at a traffic light. A passing pedestrian helps him return to his nearby apartment, only to drive off with the man's car. But the thief is himself stricken shortly afterward as he parks the stolen vehicle. The first victim, taken by his frantic wife to the nearest ophthalmologist, leaves the doctor baffled. After alerting health officials, the doctor himself becomes sightless while researching the possible causes of the mysterious malady. At this point the alarmed authorities order the immediate internment of the afflicted, who now include the first man's wife and the doctor's regular patients, who had been exposed in his waiting room. Only the doctor's wife remains immune, but she feigns blindness to accompany her husband to an abandoned insane asylum where the epidemic is to be contained. Its first victims constitute the novel's main characters.

Guarded by terrified soldiers, the growing numbers of sightless people transform the former asylum into a scene of horror as rudimentary plumbing fails and food supplies become sporadic. When panicked soldiers shoot some inmates who venture too close in collecting their rations, the patio becomes a makeshift cemetery: there can be no contact with an outside world desperate to control the plague. A faulty transistor radio, however, tells of internment centers established throughout the country, until all programming ceases when hysterical announcers suddenly declare themselves blind.

At times Saramago's pitiless account of developing apocalypse becomes expressionistic in its excess. In the midst of a nightmare even the doctor's wife longs for blindness as she strives to keep her little group united in an institution where three hundred sightless people of all ages and conditions struggle among themselves for decaying supplies. Extortion, enforced prostitution, and, worst of all, general selfishness culminate in chaos when fire breaks out and the compound is destroyed. Only then do the survivors realize that the soldiers have disappeared, "among the last to lose their sight." They emerge into a ruined city where sightless people roam silent streets littered with abandoned vehicles as they grope for food and water amid the stench of death and decay.

Clearly, *Ensaio Sobre a Cegueira* is not easy reading in any sense, and the squeamish are especially forewarned. It is equally the case, however, that the reader is struck by an air of compassion that pervades what would otherwise be unrelieved horror. Central to such compassion is the doctor's wife, who reminds her companions that "if we can't act quite like human beings, let us at least try not to live like animals," a plea that she will consider somewhat unjust when a large dog appears to lick away her tears shed in a moment of despair. After the group takes refuge in the doctor's apartment, a torrential downpour provides a welcome moment of purifying solidarity as the survivors bathe one another on the terrace above the reeking city.

The novel ends as abruptly as it begins when the first blind man regains his sight, followed by the doctor and his patients, while on the streets below there are happy cries as the epidemic recedes. The plague passes, but it is by now clear that the blindness Saramago studies in his "essay" has been less physical than ethical. The devastation that swept away social stability and all civility resulted less from a loss of vision than from the absence of respect for communal interests based on reason. As the doctor's wife points out, "To organize is in a way to begin to see," and only the truly "blind" find hope in squares where demagogues rally their followers with appeals to "salvation through penance . . . or through a mystic vision . . . or through the power of sacred signs" and similar departures from reason. She reminds her friends that even sighted people would perish in the absence of a social order founded on rational behavior, the only guarantee of a community's survival.

The reader familiar with Saramago's earlier novels will once again find an opulent narrative where dialogue, scene, and narration are interwoven in such a way that one is tempted to read aloud, as in passages where the doctor's wife reads to her sightless little band. We are reminded specifically of *O Memorial do Convento* (1982) and *A Jangada de Pedra* (1986) as we encounter the familiar figure of the strong woman and the sympathetic dog. Also, the narrator's self-deprecation and ironic humor once again deflate any suggestion of melodrama, truly a feat in a novel like this one. Unlike Saramago's earlier fiction, though, *Ensaio Sobre a Cegueira* is profoundly allegorical in structure and intent. No character is given a proper name; instead, the figures are referred to as "the first blind man," "the doctor," "the little cross-eyed boy," "the girl in dark glasses," et cetera. Equally vague are chronology (an unspecified time in the contemporary period) and place (anywhere in the industrialized world). Thus, the reader is witness to the consequences of irrational behavior that may occur anywhere and at any moment when communal interests and reason are subverted by panic and egoism. In the novel the fragile tissue of civil society is rent by the absence of understanding and a sense of shared responsibility. For the reader, the experience proves to be as harrowing as it is (one is tempted to say) insightful.

RICHARD A. PRETO-RODAS, SPRING 1996

Reviewed in the Portuguese; *Ensaio sobre a Cegueira* was translated into English by Giovanni Pontiero in 1997.

THE GOD OF SMALL THINGS   (1997)

ARUNDHATI ROY

How does one write a novel that can fetch a $1 million advance? Arundhati Roy shows the way, as did Vikram Seth earlier. Roy's *God of Small Things* is a story of a large, sprawling Syrian Christian family living in a small village called Ayemenem in Kerala, the members of which are tossed from Ayemenem to England, then to America, Shillong, and Delhi and back to Ayemenem, badly battered, badly bruised. It is also a story of profane love between an untouchable and a respectable lady, as it is a story of painful childhood and broken marriages.

Benaan John Ipe, an entomologist in government service, retires as director in the Department of Entomology and returns to his village, where his wife makes pickles. Baby Kochamma, his sister, is sent to a convent school, where she has a crush on a priest called Father Mulligan and returns to the family with unrequited love. Chacko, Ipe's son, a Rhodes scholar at Oxford, fails the exams, takes to dishwashing, marries a maid-servant called Margaret, is divorced by his pregnant wife, and returns to Ayemenem to turn his mother's fondness for pickles commercially profitable. His sister Ammu marries a Shillong-based laborer and gives birth to twins. Her husband hits the bottle, and she leaves him and returns to Ayemenem with her twins Estha and Rahel; there she soon feels drawn toward an untouchable worker called Velutha, who lives across the river.

Ammu makes nightly visits to his house, whereas Estha and Rahel visit it during the day, because they love the man in their own way. Margaret visits Ayemenem with her daughter Sophie Mol (from her first marriage) for a change after her second husband, Joe, dies in an accident. On one occasion Ammu loses her temper and calls her children a millstone round her neck. The children decide to protest and leave the house. Sophie Mol also insists on accompanying them as a mark of her solidarity with her cousins. As they are crossing the river, their boat overturns. Estha and Rahel reach the shore safely, but Sophie drowns. In the meantime, Velutha's father tells Mamachi and Baby Kochamma of his son's affair with Ammu, and all hell is let loose.

Complications arise when Baby Kochamma implicates Velutha with a charge of abduction and murder. The police, all touchables, close in on Velutha and lock him up. The children testify to the charge to save their mother. The story ends with Velutha dying in custody, leaving Ammu to fantasize the details of their lovemaking in the forsaken hut. Estha is returned to his father in Calcutta, only to be rereturned to Ayemenem after twenty-three years. Rahel wins admission into a mediocre college of architecture in Delhi. She remains there for eight years without finishing the undergraduate course. But she does get married to Larry McCaslin, an American in India completing a doctoral thesis, and follows him to Boston. The marriage falls apart. Rahel works as a waitress for some time, then returns home to Ayemenem.

The failures and misfortunes of the Ipe family touch the heart, but the most remarkable aspect of the novel is that it eschews sentimentality or romanticizing altogether. On the contrary, the narrative is splashed with humor and irony and is reminiscent of Rushdie's felicity and freedom in using English. Roy's depiction of the cross-cultural encounter between Chacko and Margaret reminds one of Jhabvala's exquisite stories in this genre. She is at her best when she describes the sky-blue Plymouth with chrome tail fins surrounded by slogan-shouting communist procession-ists, the family's fondness for the film *The Sound of Music*, a vendor forcing Estha to hold a bottle of Coca-Cola in one hand and his penis in the other, and Mr. Pillai's mix of communist jargon with caste. Roy, like Rushdie, Vikram Seth, Vikram Chandra, and a host of other Indian writers in recent times, confirms the fact that English is no longer a straitjacket for Indians and that they are no longer required to be staid and proper while using it. Yes, all this deserves praise, unqualified praise, no doubt.

RAMLAL AGARWAL, WINTER 1998

INTERPRETER OF MALADIES   (1999)

JHUMPA LAHIRI

Born in England of Indian parents and raised in America, Jhumpa Lahiri has evidently benefited from all three cultures. Their aroma drifts from the pages of her first collection of short fiction, titled *Interpreter of Maladies*, where she has woven their idiosyncrasies into well-crafted stories with a keen eye for observation and an admirable gift for details. Eight of the nine stories have been previously published, in slightly different form, in various literary and nonliterary journals across the nation. They not only study the experiences of immigrants but also deal with perennial universal issues.

The title story, "Interpreter of Maladies," is about a young couple named Mr. and Mrs. Das, by birth American, who go to India with their three children to visit the land of their ancestors. While viewing monastic dwellings on the hills of Udayagiri, Mrs. Das confides in the car driver, a translator for a doctor, that her husband has not sired their eight-year-old boy. He is the product of an encounter with a guest in the house. This is the secret, the malady if you will, which she hides from her husband, just the way Dev hides his extramarital affair from his wife in "Sexy." Shoba is not so lucky in "A Temporary Matter." She thinks that her husband did not see the stillborn baby she had delivered while he was away at a conference. But when Shukumar tells her that he returned early from the conference to hold his son in his arms before the boy was cremated, the secret is out, adding more pain to their already miserable marriage.

Lahiri's stories are not just about this malady of secrets between spouses, but also concern broader social issues. In "A Real Durwan" the residents of a Calcutta tenement unjustly cast out an old sweeper because of a theft in the building while she was away in town. They show no sympathy for the innocent victim despite her pleading. Such lack of understanding forces BiBi to lead a desolate life in "The Treatment of BiBi Haldar," and pushes a professor's wife into an embarrassing car accident in "Mrs. Sen's." Compassion, on the other hand, goes a long way toward resolving differences in "This Blessed House," "When Mr. Pirzada Came to Dine," and "The Third and Final Continent." The last story, hitherto unpublished, is a first-person narrative of a man who has journeyed from India to America via England in search of a livelihood. He marries a traditional Indian woman who seems to be steeped in her native customs, which he, as a modern man, finds hard to accept. But when they visit his former landlady, an ancient who once found happiness in his sympathy, the old woman thinks his wife is "a perfect lady," a compliment that makes the couple smile at each other, lessening the distance between them. Thus, with sympathy, understanding, and a smile, one can narrow the gap not only between spouses but also between continents. E. M. Forster expressed it best with his "only connect" precept.

The value of these stories—although some of them are loosely constructed—lies in the fact they transcend the confined borders of immigrant experience to embrace larger human issues, age-old issues that are, in the words of Ralph Waldo Emerson, "cast into the mold of these new times" redefining America. So it is not surprising that the title story of Jhumpa Lahiri's laudable collection has been selected for both *The Best American Short Stories* and the year 1999's O. Henry Award.

RONNY NOOR, SPRING 2000

MOTHER'S BELOVED: STORIES FROM LAOS   (1999)

OUTHINE BOUNYAVONG

If you are looking for a Chekhovian or Joycean epiphany in stories, then *Mother's Beloved* is not the book for you. Nonetheless, the scope of the fourteen stories included in this first-ever collection of contemporary Lao fiction in English in the United States is universal. Effectively translated by Bounheng Inversin and others, and put side by side on facing pages with the originals, these stories by the Vientiane journalist, editor, translator, and fiction writer Outhine Bounyavong are about compassion for fellow humans, effects of modernization, war, and politics.

The most interesting story in the collection is "Wrapped-Ash Delight," which brilliantly celebrates traditional customs that show compassion for fellow humans. A village girl steals a silver belt a bather has left on a riverbank. She feels guilty about her action but, afraid of being branded a thief, does not come forward when the village headman, at a meeting in his house, orders that the culprit return the belt to its owner. So the headman asks everyone to wrap ashes in a package of banana leaf, hoping that the culprit will reconsider his or her mistake. Nang Piew returns the belt anonymously in her package. Unrestrained joy breaks loose when it is found, symbolizing "love, solidarity, sincerity, and brotherhood" that is shared by all villagers. Similar themes of compassion also appear in "Longing," "Sacrifice," "Contribution," "Fifty Kip," and the title story, "Mother's Beloved."

A writer who celebrates such traditional wisdom as mentioned above understandably condemns the destruction of nature brought about by the rapid pace of modernization and industrialization. In "Frangipani," trees are chopped down to make way for power lines. And in "The Eternal Pair of Birds," not only are forests wiped out for lumber, but also birds are shot dead by tradesmen. Bounyavong's protest against war is evident in "A Voice from the Plain of Jars," in which a Lao refugee writes to an American formerly with the International Voluntary Services in Laos about how ancient stone jars, which were "among the world's wonders," have been destroyed by B-52 bombers. The rest of the stories deal with political and social issues. Their real significance can be properly understood only in the context of Laos's turbulent history, which Peter Koret provides in his excellent introduction.

These stories from Laos are not elaborately structured. Some of them are mere anecdotes in the realistic mode, devoid of such detail, the texts stripped to the bare bones à la minimalist writing. Bounyavong approaches reality in a linear fashion, with simple, declarative sentences like Hemingway. However, the point he makes is not implied but explicit, as in the fiction of the famous Yugoslav writer Ivo Andrić. The settings are exotic, as are the names of the characters, but these stories convey powerful messages of universal interest.

RONNY NOOR, AUTUMN 2000

Mother's Beloved was translated from the Lao by Bounheng Inversin and Daniel Duffy.

ÉMIGRÉ JOURNEYS   (2000)

ABDULLAH HUSSEIN

Amir Koreshi purchases illegal passage to England with family gold to buy more farmland back home on English wages and to better all their lives. This is the only way he sees out of his hard life as a village blacksmith. In the Punjab, he lives with his parents, a wife, and two children, emotionally secure, protected from fear by the local religion. Like most people around, he is also superstitious and vulnerable, has little education, and no other means of advancement or comfort. His father works "a few acres of no-rain land," but can only do so much, having lost a leg fighting for the British in Burma in World War II. Now he thinks each generation must fight its own wars. The decision to leave his family (particularly his wife Salma, daughter Parvin, and son Hasan) behind is painful for Amir, and he can't help remembering them and his life back in the village, while in England he is packed in a hovel in Birmingham with another sixteen men, all illegal, often working night shifts at factories and living their "half-lives in the daylight hours," hiding from the world.

All these men, daring in a way yet afraid of this world around which excludes them, have made and are making journeys similar to Amir's, from various countries, ex-colonies of the late British Empire. They all came here to improve their lives and the well-being of their families by sending money home, but right in the middle of the 1960s labor boom they all (Roshan, Ghulam, Ram, et cetera) find their lives ever more thwarted at the destination; they gain little acceptance in the new country and lose touch with their families, in England or back home, and even with their own lives. Of course, this is just one part of the story, which suggests several other dimensions.

Therefore, unlike the usual first-person narrative, which posits an omniscient interlocutor, the book here divides the narrative "I" and its point of view between the father and his daughter in alternate chapters. Thus each has an equal, competitive, and complementary claim to a share of personal truth or objective reality according to his and her experience—not to mention memory or perception. Of necessity and natural time sequence, it appears, the father, Amir Koreshi, must have the first chapter, the daughter Parvin the last, which is not to put too fine a point on *intention* above generational sequence. The many characters here all have different backgrounds, but their lives are nearly at the same point of "progress" in England as they seek a new existence in the new country. As the first narrator says, "Anybody can think, but to remember is to face one's existence." And remember they do, their lives or parts thereof left elsewhere.

This is also the point of intersection where many journeys overlap. Their life or "half-life" together, described so vividly, also turns them into a compulsive, tight community; they work as cheap labor in factories, cook and eat at home, keep their hard-earned savings in mattresses, and never go out except for a weekend Indian/Pakistani film in the ghetto. Any leisure time is spent either on the prayer mat or in bed with local call girls—"Sex and prayers and deaths are occasions of the same likeness." All partake of these rituals of custom and nature. The Hafizabadis, the Mirpuris, the Pathans, and the Bengalis are all quite peculiar; Roshan, Ghulam, Sher Baz, Irshad, and Hussain Shah rise barely above types. The *namazis* (those who are very particular about five-times prayers), if somewhat ludic, are portrayed humanely. They are seen by at least one white British character (Mary) as normal. This is qualified by the fact that she comes from a broken home and in her twenty years has not known a greater happiness than carrying a certain Jamaican's child in her womb or later becoming Hussain Shah's live-in mistress. Life within the house changes with her arrival, and the residents begin to have some reasonable view of the outside world.

For one thing, the young man Sakib, who, unlike the others, "was drawn to this country . . . and its 'beautiful language' . . . to become a writer," falls in love with Mary and ends up in jail as a murderer on account of an investigation error, while Hussain Shah and his nephew Irshad actually commit the crime of passion, each stabbing the other to death over Mary. For another, this incident brings the community to insidious light, destroying the dark that sustained it and making the members disperse. Amir finds refuge with a kind old lady in Glasgow, but then has to leave that city on a false charge of molesting a young woman in a market. However, with help from Mrs. McTaggart (the kind Glaswegian) and a solicitor, Mr. Kelley (an Irishman), he is acquitted and later legalized when the government passes a new law concerning illegals. The occasion prompts Amir to call his family over to England to live with him.

Each alternate chapter in the novel finds its basis in the family's life in England, as Amir's daughter Parvin sees it from her English toilet-training days onward. Gradually, it is her narrative that appears to take over, as it must in the narrative, natural, and social scheme. More is learned about the family, its individual members, and its friends from her than from the other narrator. When Amir's wife, son, and daughter arrive, the longing for them is eventually replaced by a lack of communication among them. The children adapt to the new life as well as they can, adjusting to the English life outside, to the Punjabi home, to a solicitous and religious Punjabi-speaking mother, and to an industrious if demanding father who tries to instill in them the British postulates of law, progress, and prosperity. Salma, the wife, cooperates but remains bewildered and distant. Hasan, the son, never makes it to public (meaning private) school "to rise to a position." Parvin is the opposite of what her father thinks a daughter should be like. All his family turn away from Amir Koreshi as the children grow up: Salma has nothing to say to him; Hasan wants to be with his English girlfriend Janet; Parvin wants to marry her friend Martin. And Amir is left moping and complaining as the son leaves the house in anger and the mother and the daughter move away to stay with Auntie Shirin. Now all he can do is query himself: "What I have done wrong? Give me an answer, Salma."

The original objectives of the journeys each character has made are forgotten in the face of life's new conditions. There is no returning for these émigrés, who are merely a vestige of lost languages and cultures which some would like to keep alive for a generation or two as personal consolation or identity anchor. Abdullah Hussein has known the challenge of displacements, cultural adaptations and discrimination, and appropriations of place and language since at least 1963, when his Urdu novel *Udas*

Naslein (translated by him as *The Weary Generations* [1999]) was published to much praise. Then the scene was early and mid-twentieth century in the Indian subcontinent. Now he takes on Everyman's Pakistan (or the Other Britain) of the late twentieth century and John Bull's Own Island, and comes off with flying colors. The language of multicultural Britain is English. Hussein, who has lived in Britain since 1967, knows it as well as Amir Koreshi, and takes to this language "of utmost importance" (Amir's pet words) with native gusto.

ALAMGIR HASHMI, WINTER 2002

NO ONE WILL SEE ME CRY   (2003)

CRISTINA RIVERA GARZA

How does a woman go crazy and how does a man become a photographer of crazy people are only two of many crucial questions that Cristina Rivera Garza has answered brilliantly in her recent novel *No One Will See Me Cry*. Through the characterization of its main protagonists, Matilda Burgos and Joaquín Buitrago, Rivera Garza portrays a kaleidoscopic vision of Mexican history between 1885 and 1958. Some of its phases include: an indigenous family devoted to the harvest of vanilla pods in Papantla who lost their mental sanity and life after losing their land; a fifteen-year-old who arrived to the city to be treated as the experimental object of her uncle, a positivist bourgeois who firmly believed that education would crush "a woman's innate sense of abnegation and self-sacrifice, the best of the feminine virtues" and who lived obsessed with hygiene and strenuous work as the most important civilizing agents to reduce the effects of a deplorable genetic inheritance; liberals who were killed dreaming to free their country from a cruel dictatorship; a population unable to earn a decent living without entering the realms of corruption and prostitution; husbands and politicians willing to confine their wives and opponents in an insane asylum instead of listening to their claims; and artists who struggle to find a niche in modern times.

In spite of the pessimist tone of the novel, however, there is a glimpse of hope in those magical moments in which various characters are sincere with each other and to themselves. Friendship takes place between Joaquín and the psychiatrist who keeps the records of the patients in the hospital where both work, a "place so remote from history yet so filled with it." They also wonder about their love stories, their pain, and the boredom of the future. On the other hand, Matilda learns that although there's nothing safer for a woman than self-sufficiency, no one can escape an embrace. Matilda and Joaquín manage to transcend their gender differences and their self-absorption to open, however slightly, their souls to each other.

Joaquín might never have freed himself from his addiction to morphine, but he stands out for his perseverance in the examination of Matilda's pain with the discretion and the patience required to observe the movement of a sunflower. There might not be any other way to read the sadness of those who choose not to show their tears and whose lives must be changed if we are going to believe in the progress of the nation.

LUCRECIA ARTALEJO, SEPT. 2004

No One Will See Me Cry was translated from the Spanish by Andrew Hurley.

PURPLE HIBISCUS   (2003)

CHIMAMANDA NGOZI ADICHIE

Chimamanda Ngozi Adichie's voice in her debut novel, *Purple Hibiscus*, is a quiet one. She tells her story with something akin to the psychological disinterest of a deeply traumatized person who has cultivated the skill to seem calm as a way of holding back the emotional collapse that appears on the verge of consuming her. This, of course, is no accident. The narrator, Kambili, is a teenage Nigerian girl whose father, a devout and tyrannical Catholic patriarch, has managed to abuse emotionally and physically his middle-class family in his attempt to wrestle with his own cultural, emotional, and ideological demons. His Catholicism amounts to a devotion to a Western colonial order that he has concluded to be far superior to the traditional belief system of his family. He is determined that his wife and children will adhere to Catholic ideas and teachings, even as he uses his notable wealth and power to repress those in his family who hold onto traditional values. On the surface, the novel could easily read as another salvo against colonialism and attendant patriarchy that has marked much West African fiction. Indeed, Adichie offers a hint that she is beginning, at least, with Achebe's monumental narrative of "a clash of cultures" in the first sentence of the novel: "Things started to fall apart at home when my brother, Jaja, did not go to communion and Papa flung his heavy missal across the room and broke the figurines on the étagère."

Indeed, things fall apart, but the edifice that falls is the rigid Catholicism of the father, which becomes a metaphor for abuse, hypocrisy, deep pathology, and something imposed and alien to the heart and spirit of the people. The son rebels against his father's tyranny; the father's sister, a beautifully drawn character—struggling university professor and practical mother figure—abets the rebellion; and Kambili falls in love with a young priest— an act that forces her to recognize her own maturation and need to break from her father's hold. Things fall apart on this personal level even though it is quite clear that what is being eroded is the edifice of colonialism and its attendant horrors. All this could make for a much too easy polemic of anticolonial angst, but Adichie proves too intelligent and honest an author for that. Her narrator/protagonist cannot bring herself to hate her father. Indeed, her pathology is as consuming and disturbing as that of her father, who brutally beats his wife, tortures his children with crude acts that are supposed to make them penitent, and completely alienates himself from his own father. Kambili wants to please her father and her maturation is a subtle narrative of deeply painful conflicts with loyalty and fear. It is her quiet voice, always teetering on the edge of emotional collapse, that haunts this work, allowing us to actually feel pity and some empathy for a monstrous father while drawing from us a certain outrage at the complete vulnerability of the narrator herself.

The family will rebel against the father. Eventually, he will die at their hands, and they will embrace this with quiet acceptance—the shell-shocked quality of people who know that their own means of survival is to become as coldly violent as their oppressor. Nevertheless, as dark as the story seems, it is filled with humor, intimations of love, affection, and a sometimes nostalgic sense of modern Nigeria, especially the Nigeria of university campuses, ambitious middle-class people, and folks who live in that liminal space between modern life and traditional life. Adichie's prose is confident and charged with a certain emotional intelligence that draws us so fully into her story that we barely notice the craft: the literary sophistication of her use of symbols and metaphors, of her engagement with deeply political and ideological issues. In other words, we are never allowed to think that her work is anything but a fascinating story about how a family deals with its own demons. We would be mistaken, however, not to recognize in this work the larger ideological issues that remain central to the best writing from Africa.

After Tsitsi Dangarembga convinced us with her brilliant *Nervous Conditions* that there is an urbane and complex woman's narrative to be told about contemporary Africa, we were left hungry for more. Dangarembga went silent and has remained so for too long. It is a wonderful relief to discover Chimamanda Ngozi Adichie's fresh and compelling voice. *Purple Hibiscus* is a remarkable debut by a writer whom I hope will not fall into the long silences that have haunted a few other notable brilliant first-book novelists: Dangarembga and Arundhati Roy. We want to read more from this writer; she is good—very, very good.

KWAME DAWES, JAN. 2005

THE INHERITANCE OF LOSS (2006)

KIRAN DESAI

Kiran Desai, the thirty-four-year-old daughter of well-known novelist Anita Desai, is rapidly becoming well-known in her own right. Her first novel, *Hullabaloo in the Guava Orchard*, won her a great deal of praise. Her second novel, *The Inheritance of Loss*, has recently appeared. One major narrative strand in this musically composed novel follows the New York City adventures of Biju, an immigrant worker from northern India. As well as Desai knows New York, she seems to know Biju's home territory even better: the district of Kalimpong, where his father works as a cook for a retired British-educated Indian magistrate and the judge's inquisitive granddaughter, Sai. The judge is a bit of a prissy old fellow, immersed in his love for his pet dog. Granddaughter Sai is a glorious teenager, in love with the world around her and in love with reading, reading faster and faster until, as Desai tells us, "she was inside the narrative and the narrative inside her, the pages going by so fast, her heart in her chest, she couldn't stop."

While Sai immerses herself in her books, we get a look at the world around her where indigenous Nepalese exiles, the cheap labor of the region, rise up to call for an independent state within a state. One of these young rebels is a handsome fellow named Gyan, who happens to be the science tutor of young Sai—and the first great love of her life—though he abandons her rather rudely for the burgeoning political movement.

Fortunately for us, Kiran Desai is wildly in love with the vital landscape and all the characters who inhabit it. Even when Biju calls home from New York City, we can smell the humid air over the telephone line, we can picture the green-black lushness, "the plumage of banana, the stark spear of the cactus, the delicate gestures of ferns; he could hear the *croak trrrr whonk, wee wee butt ock butt ock* of frogs in the spinach, the rising note welding imperceptibly with the evening." This is a story of exiles at home and abroad, of families broken and fixed, of love both bitter and bittersweet. You can read it almost as Sai read her Brontë, with your heart in your chest, inside the narrative, and the narrative inside you.

ALAN CHEUSE, JULY 2006

THE SAVAGE DETECTIVES   (2007)

ROBERTO BOLAÑO

In terms of every aspect of its consistent brilliance, *The Savage Detectives* immediately makes one rethink *Hopscotch* and *One Hundred Years of Solitude*. A work of genius, superior in scope and conception to the masterpieces of magical realism and the varieties of postmodern novels that followed them, Roberto Bolaño's bittersweet epic is the result of combining Borgesian long narratives with Musil's essayistic and fragmentary style. Add to that mix the counsel of a humorous John Le Carré abetted by Camusian ideas. Bolaño also easily anticipates Kundera's injunctions in *The Curtain* against kitschy or ideological dogmas in novel making.

A calculatedly autobiographical tour de force, this encyclopedic novel runs rings around novelistic conventions and traditions, forcing us to find patterns in the chaos of the nomadic cosmos its characters cannot escape. Structured around a quest of heroic proportions as related by scores of restless narrators drunken with literature and the need to testify—in Natasha Wimmer's persuasive and painstakingly careful translation of the 1998 original—*The Savage Detectives* engages any desire for endlessly satisfying prose.

In a pilgrimage that takes the poet-protagonists Arturo Belano (Bolaño's well-known alter ego) and Ulises Lima across four continents during two decades, history serves as a moving landscape in which young idealists are mere pawns; perhaps the reason why Belano and Lima never speak, or why we don't read their poetry. The long 1976–96 period narrated by various voices in fugue is framed by events set in 1975 and 1976, as told by seventeen-year-old poet-in-training Juan García Madero, who joins the protagonists' quest for Cesárea Tinajero (with Lupe, a hooker, along for the ride). Tinajero was the founder of "visceral realism," a fictionalized Mexican avant-garde movement, mirrored by the "infrarealists" group that Bolaño and his fellow poet Mario Santiago (Lima in the novel) had started.

Glowing reviews repeat ad nauseam that literature is the real protagonist of *The Savage Detectives*, but it is self-begotten literature, because Bolaño preferred to play with his own allusive creations, even underdeveloped ones, who keep appearing in his earlier and new prose and poetry. Thus, the third part of the novel is set in Mexico's Sonora desert, in the fictional Santa Teresa in which a considerable part of *2666* takes place. Bolaño could not write a boring sentence, in keeping with the wisecracking hippies, pseudophilosophers, drifters, pot dealers, street performers, student radicals, hookers, literary workshop groupies, and other alternative types (the untamed detectives) who shared the vocabulary of ranting against the system that eventually swallowed them whole.

The Savage Detectives is a radical generational and paradigmatic turn in Latin American letters, and its publication in English is a momentous occasion, a necessary awakening from the slumber of continental exoticism and bestsellers. Just as the great "boom" novels of forty years ago mapped out how readers made sense of words and things at that time, Bolaño's aesthetics of astonishment allows us to decipher the full nature of the purported disarray in which we found ourselves between centuries. It is illuminating to watch his, well, bewitched, bothered, and bewildered detectives (the narrators) with the irreverence and iconoclasm that characterized their maker's boundless talent. Everything is new in and about *The Savage Detectives*, as Roberto Bolaño, our newly minted Joyce, has already shown to legions of Latin American readers.

WILL H. CORRAL, NOV. 2007

The Savage Detectives was translated from the Spanish by Natasha Wimmer.

THE SONG OF EVERLASTING SORROW: A NOVEL OF SHANGHAI   (2008)

WANG ANYI

Certain to take a preeminent place in China's literary canon, Wang Anyi's *The Song of Everlasting Sorrow* is at last available in a masterful English translation by Michael Berry and Susan Chan Egan. First published in 1995, this major work has, like many of Wang's books, waited too long for an English version despite winning China's most prestigious literary award, the Mao Dun Prize, and having been adapted for the stage, television, and film.

A direct reference to a Tang Dynasty poem by Bai Juyi, the title may be seen as an allusion to the travails of the putative main character, Wang Qiyao, but it is the subtitle, "A Novel of Shanghai," that names the tale's true center—the city itself. On the surface the novel reads as the story of "Miss Third Place" in the Shanghai Beauty Pageant—an apparent window of opportunity for a beautiful young woman living in a traditional Shanghai *longtang* (slum), dreaming of becoming a movie star—but it is the city's modern history that forms the backbone of the tale, creating the subtlety and "sorrow" necessary to spin out a simple story to more than four hundred pages.

Like Qiyao, modern Shanghai has never controlled its fate, bowing in turn to the forces of Western colonization, communist "liberation," and contemporary capitalism. Through forty years of political and social upheaval, Qiyao serves as an unwitting guide as we observe Shanghai groaning under the weight of overwhelming forces. Both the city and Qiyao are beauties determined "to meet all challenges . . . to follow . . . fate through to the bitter end." Unfortunately, the more beautiful the woman, or the city, the less she controls her own existence. As Qiyao ages through relationships with five men, becoming a symbol of the "old Shanghai," the city likewise declines from its colonial splendor of the 1940s to the crumbling *longtang* and polluted rivers of the industrial 1980s. Qiyao's violent death while guarding a gift of gold from her first lover seems to prophesy an end to any vestige of what once made Shanghai the "Paris of the East."

Readers seeking a fast-paced story of romance and intrigue will be disappointed, but Wang's intricate art makes vivid the mundane trivialities of city life and "liberated" young women who seek love where it cannot be found. Tempting as it may be to compare Wang Anyi's descriptions of physical objects and psychological states to those of realist-naturalist writers such as Zola, James, or Wharton, to do so would be to miss much of what makes her writing unique: subtly shifting views of the *longtang*, discursive meditations on the day-to-day details of living not merely to survive but to live well. Those willing to read as reflectively as this novel demands will find it more than worth the time and effort. (*Editorial note:* Wang Anyi went on to win the 2017 Newman Prize for Chinese Literature.)

BAOCHAI CHIANG AND J. B. ROLLINS, MAY 2009

The Song of Everlasting Sorrow was translated from the Chinese by Michael Berry and Susan Chan Egan.

OPEN CITY   (2011)

TEJU COLE

Julius, the narrator of Teju Cole's first novel, is a solitary man who frequently ruminates on solitude itself. A dedicated walker, Julius uses his walks around New York and Brussels to reflect on history and contemporary politics and culture, generally espousing a postcolonial sensibility, but trying as well not to be "claimed" by simplistic, superficial affinities, as when Black men presume that they have something in common simply because Julius comes from Nigeria. In a novel of few events, Julius is beaten by three Black teenagers while he walks in New York, an event that confirms his suspicion of identity and underscores his commitment to the city. Preoccupied more with ideas than actions, Julius at times expresses poignant insight, as when he recalls childhood visits to the tailor, the barber, or the doctor. "These were the rare cases in which you gave permission to a stranger to enter your personal space. You trusted the expertise proffered, and enjoyed the promise that the opaque maneuvers of this stranger's hands would yield a result."

A student of art history, Cole can transmute the virtues of landscape and portraiture into delicately observant prose. Viewing the work of a deaf painter, Julius remarks, "How great is the peace palpable in those great artists of stillness. . . . I lost all track of time before these images." He leaves the museum "with the feeling of someone who had returned to the earth from a great distance." Sometimes, however, this quasi-still life of a novel exasperates with its randomness and lack of connection among Julius's observations. A character in the novel claims to be an autodidact, and the novel can seem like a grab bag of eclectic references, from 9/11 to Rwanda to Mahler to Cannonball Adderley to Paracelsus to Ota Benga to Mohamed Choukri to Primo Levi. While it is exciting to encounter a wide-ranging intellect, sometimes the novel's learnedness is like a clumsy book report. After noting the resurgence of bedbugs in New York, Julius intones that "AIDS remained a devastating problem, especially for the poor, and for people who lived in the poorer countries."

Indeed, but such awkward reporting doesn't develop Julius's character or our interest in him. The limitations of obscure historical facts become apparent when Julius, charged with wrongdoing, remains silent, able only to recall a journal entry by Camus. While quirky details can be profound, this novel could shed some of its detachment and engage more directly with the lives being lived all around Julius.

JIM HANNAN, JULY 2011

THE VEGETARIAN   (2016)

HAN KANG

Han Kang's *The Vegetarian* is a taut novel that tells the story of two sisters—Yeong-hye and In-hye—and their marriages. Told in three parts, each a novella in its own right, the complete work focuses on survival in a world that demands conformity.

The novel's painful conflicts begin when Yeong-hye unexpectedly breaks cultural mores and declares herself a vegetarian, leading to her husband's consternation, confusion, and anger over his wife's seemingly small subversion. She lectures no one, proselytizes not in the least: she wants to stop eating meat after a vicious dream repels her from it. Her husband cannot abide this small desire of his wife's. After "embarrassing" him at an important work dinner, he wonders, "What shadowy recesses lurked in her mind, what secrets I'd never suspected? In that moment, she was utterly unknowable." The section ends with a haunting family scene that escalates into an act of abuse that permeates the following two sections.

Section 2, "Mongolian Mark," gives voice to Yeong-hye's brother-in-law. A video artist who has not produced any work due to his obsession with the idea of his sister-in-law's birthmark, he creates a work that destroys the rest of his life so he can find out what tableau his and Yeong-hye's body would create: "Would they seem like one body, a hybrid of plant, animal, and human?" When he is caught by his wife, he sees how his desire subsumes both of the sisters.

"Flaming Trees" brings the sisters together to come to terms with their violent upbringings. Yeong-hye now refuses to eat and is hospitalized on the edge of death. Diagnosed with anorexia nervosa, she remains misunderstood: catatonic for hours and then animal-like in her resistance to a feeding tube. Her sister sits by her bed, trying one last time to coax her sister to eat by bringing childhood favorites to her younger sister's lips. In-hye, also separated from her husband, works to understand her sister's motives and desires, though they remain inscrutable.

The individual remains incomprehensible in this stunning novel. Kang's structure of three stand-alone novellas strung together to tell one larger story illustrates the loneliness of the individual who is forced to try to connect with others.

Such a separation between the individual and a community—shown through cultural mores surrounding food, illicit desires upending sexual taboos, and familial responsibilities rendering the sisters mute—is reflected by the novel's structure and sparse prose that distances the reader from the text itself. *The Vegetarian* models the gulf between its characters with a reliance on disparate narratives and terse dialogue.

COLLEEN LUTZ CLEMENS, MAY 2016

The Vegetarian was translated from the Korean by Deborah Smith.

EXIT WEST   (2017)

MOHSIN HAMID

Mohsin Hamid's latest novel explores the tender and tenuous relationship between Nadia and Saeed, young adults coming of age during a time of strife in their unnamed home country. Their stories begin before they were born as the reader learns about what the world looked like for Saeed's parents—and how he came to be. By the time Saeed and Nadia meet, both are comfortable in their stations in life. Nadia is a fully covered woman who surprises Saeed when he learns she rides a motorcycle and lives on her own, bucking the norms he assumes she follows based on her dress.

Their tentative relationship is both strengthened and weakened by the civil unrest that begins to permeate their formerly quiet city. When bombs disconnect them from their phones, the budding couple cannot speak to each other. Meanwhile, their desire for each other grows exponentially due to their forced separation. When terror strikes Saeed's family, the young couple decide they must take advantage of the "doors" that pop up around town and that lead people into another country.

When Saeed and Nadia walk through the first of many mystical doors, they arrive in Greece, where they are introduced to the life of a migrant. They choose to treat this first stop as a tourism trip, during which they sightsee and make a few friends. But when Greece begins to pressure the migrants, the couple enter another "door." They realize they are in London. The story continues as the couple move more and more west until their story ends in Marin, California.

An extended meditation on the challenges and dangers of migration, *Exit West* allegorizes migration through its picaresque love story. The novel works to show the microcomplications of migration while nations argue on macro terms. Hamid humanizes a migration crisis that has become background noise to those not living it. How else can one describe the lack of worldwide outrage and compassion such a migration should cause? Hamid summarizes the nature of migration when musing on Saeed's decision to leave his father in the war zone when the latter refuses to depart from the land where his wife is buried: "For when we migrate, we murder from our lives those we leave behind." In the end, Saeed and Nadia learn more about themselves and their relationship, and much is left behind upon their arrival in the West.

COLLEEN LUTZ CLEMENS, MAY 2017

MINOR DETAIL   (2020)

ADANIA SHIBLI

Adania Shibli's third novel, *Minor Detail*, cements her position among the top ranks of Palestinian novelists working today. In her latest book—a short but powerful novel—Shibli interrogates a world of unstable and shifting boundaries and borders, from the Negev Desert a year after the 1948 war to a contemporary version of the tightly controlled lands of Palestine and Israel.

Written in two discrete sections, Shibli centers the first on an encampment of Israeli soldiers in the Negev Desert during the late summer of 1949. The buildup of dreamlike, haunting prose, which describes the soldiers' lives in the desert and their patrols in the intoxicating heat, finally builds to the rape and murder of a Palestinian teenage girl, who is then buried in the sand.

The book's second half is set decades later and follows a woman office worker in Ramallah. The unnamed narrator offers the reader unfettered access to her interior philosophical ruminations. Early on, she muses, "Borders grant a person a sense of serenity, despite everything else." Yet the woman is restless and unsatisfied. At work, she reads an article about the death of a girl in 1949. The woman discovers the girl was killed on the same day as her own birthday, but twenty-five years before she was born. The woman surmises, "One cannot rule out the possibility of a link between the two events, or the existence of a hidden connection." The terrible nature of the girl's death, a minor detail in the history of the region, becomes a catalyst for the woman to investigate the case further.

Shibli artfully plays out the rest of the novel as a quest narrative. The woman leaves the West Bank to search for the girl's burial location and soon contends with security checkpoints and hostile soldiers and informational dead ends. On her journey deep into the interior of Israel, we feel the paranoia and claustrophobia, the assaults on the idea of Palestinian autonomy. Parallels between the woman and the girl now reverberate emphatically between the novel's two sections.

Shibli's use of stylistically different timelines marks her boldness as a novelist. Indeed, the novel's shocking conclusion amplifies Shibli's artistic version of aligning the lives of the women, reminding the reader that the region is still an area fraught with oppression and needless death.

CHRISTOPHER LINFORTH, SUMMER 2020

Minor Detail was translated from the Arabic by Elisabeth Jaquette.

THE BOOKS OF JACOB   (2022)

OLGA TOKARCZUK

The year is 1752 (the page, 900 or so), and a carriage is barreling through misty Podolia, a historic region that now sits on Ukraine's eastern border. Rumors of a young and charismatic Jew, said by some to be the Messiah, reach the region's townspeople through long chains of scholars and merchants along the trade routes from Smyrna (Izmir) on the Mediterranean coast to the settlements on the North Sea. Whether Jakub Lejbowicz Frank is a true mystic or a fraud is not clear, neither in Nobel laureate Olga Tokarczuk's long-anticipated *The Books of Jacob* nor in the history books. Jacob Frank, as he would come to be known, was a real man who inspired legions of followers into "Frankism," a Sabbatean Jewish movement that held, at its core, the belief that people should transgress every moral boundary they know. The movement espoused "redemption through sin": fast days became feasts, and rules on modesty, purity, and even incest were overturned.

Tokarczuk never gets too close to the character of Jacob, instead presenting him through the eyes of his contemporaries, both ardent believers and staunch skeptics. She is particularly attentive to the perspectives of women and outsiders, who bore the brunt of the Enlightenment's growing pains yet are conspicuously missing from official histories. This polyphonic approach is never deliberately obscure: each character has a deep, sincere, and (because it is in Tokarczuk's nature) often humorous "psychological portrait." We get glimpses of the supposed Messiah as a child, saying goodnight to every soul in the world, like Adam naming the creatures of Eden. Yente, an elderly woman on her deathbed at a wedding, is given a Kabbalist amulet to postpone her death and, with a conspiratorial smile, swallows it. She floats into a state of permanent omniscience, "a witness, an eye that travels through space and time."

In addition to Jacob and the not-quite-dead Yente, we meet a broad cast of supporting characters: Jacob's wife and daughter, Asher the world-weary doctor, the Kabbalist Shor family, the literary Rabbi Nahman, and Father Benedykt Chmielowski, who maintains a long and entertaining correspondence with Baroque poet Elżbieta Drużbacka on his encyclo-pedic works. The title of the real Chmielowski's encyclopedia—the first in Poland—mirrors Tokarczuk's own extended title for the novel ("*New Athens or the Academy full of all science, divided into subjects and classes, for the wise ones to record, for the idiots to learn, for the politicians to practice, for the melancholics to entertain . . .*") and contains such amusing entries and annotations as "Horse: Everyone can see what a horse is" and "Dragons existed for sure." Drużbacka, less whimsical and more resolute, urged Chmielowski to stop writing in Latin and make his text accessible to women and the lower classes. As a lyricist, she wrote mostly on beauty in nature but also composed poems like "Complaints from a bunch of ladies, because they do not want to live with their husbands" (my inelegant translation). Whether the two ever met in real life, we will never know.

Tokarczuk covers all the calamities of the era—pogroms, war, abject poverty—but pays mind-bogglingly detailed attention to everyday spec-tacles: kitchens and courtyards, fairy tales told to small children, dances, Turkish tobacco, embroidered tablecloths, the arrangement of the mer-chants' caravans snaking their way through Europe—all evidence of years of research. *The Books of Jacob* contains an entire overflowing, sensual world to get lost in. Hopelessly lost, in fact, for everything in it has a disorient-ing aim—from its obfuscating weather ("great grey fustian clouds") and temporal shifts, to the migratory catalog of characters with many names. Even the pagination runs in reverse, like a Hebrew book, perhaps remind-ing us that every familiar order only exists out of habit.

Of course, all heresies and heretics call the existing order into ques-tion. With three major religions at play (and countless minor ones), the pent-up historical energies bubbling under the surface of Europe are ripe for release. The Enlightenment was a time of great contamination and diversity—of ideas, people, religions (not to mention a host of nefarious viruses). Tokarczuk captures this corner of society at the moment it is held open in suspense; its failure to be whole, together, or complete creates that vital opening for the coming of something new—a self-proclaimed Messiah. Jacob's pragmatism (converting to new religions when they became convenient) and spiritual hedonism may have been heretical, but they also laid foundations for a distinctly modern disregard for dogma and tradition.

In her translator's note, Jennifer Croft calls the book a polyglot. Like all encyclopedias, histories, and sacred texts, it exists in conversation with many others, and not only its contemporaries. It references scores of figures and fables, each mysterious enough to warrant a history of their own. Croft's translation is energetic and inventive; she's proven to be a brilliant collaborator with Tokarczuk, having previously translated the award-winning experimental novel *Flights*. Her work is attuned to Tokarczuk's polysemy, the delicate ambiguity built into the Polish language—an ambiguity Tokarczuk has previously lauded not only for its use in poetic language but also in political critique.

Tokarczuk writes that "history is simply a never-ending interpretation of real and imagined events from the past that allows us to perceive formerly invisible meanings in it." Whatever meaning we find in his story, Jacob Frank himself remains beyond our grasp—as a shape-shifter, an enigma, a sage, a revolutionary, a quack, who nevertheless sparked an entire movement around his ideas. It is our job to answer how—or why. Perhaps it seems like an odd time to study the forgotten history of a Jewish mystic and the cult he inspired, but at its heart, *The Books of Jacob* is about the desire for emancipation amidst a fractured and multifaceted reality—one that looks a lot like ours. And a Messiah, even an ambiguous one, only ever arrives in the darkest moments of human scourge, war, persecution, and rot.

This colossal book is a truly bewitching account of untold fissures in history, minor religions, little lives, and splinterings-off. It is rich, strange, astonishing in scope, and delightfully enigmatic—whether the reader plunges deep into its metaphysics or simply obtains "some slight enjoyment" is up to them. Tokarczuk's magnum opus shows us a world on the precipice of a great change, one hand clinging to certainty while the other reaches for transcendence. Of course, history shows us that certainty doesn't exist, and we will have to live with that—or wait for our Messiah.

HANNAH WEBER, JAN. 2022

The Books of Jacob was translated from the Polish by Jennifer Croft.

KAIROS   (2023)

JENNY ERPENBECK

Is the bond between a government and its citizens comparable to the relationship between lovers? I couldn't help but ask myself this question again and again while reading Jenny Erpenbeck's *Kairos*. The novel starts with Katharina receiving a box of papers and mementos from Hans, her recently deceased former lover. As she sorts through the letters and cassettes, she not only delves into her youth but also revisits a state that no longer exists.

Kairos is a Greek word meaning the opportune time. A fitting title for the tale of nineteen-year-old Katharina and her doomed affair with Hans, a married writer in his mid-fifties, against the backdrop of the collapsing East German state in the late 1980s. Or is their first meeting—by chance as they get off the tram on a rainy afternoon—the eponymous Kairos?

During their first encounter and subsequent night together, Erpenbeck's narration artfully alternates between the perspectives of Katharina and Hans, inviting us to read the mirrored thoughts of this couple, unequal both in terms of age and power. As we progress through the novel, Katharina, who is initially perceived as weaker, becomes the dominant voice.

The lovers enjoy taking in the cultural establishments of East Berlin in the first weeks of their relationship. They are happy in each other's company while Hans's wife is absent, and they resolve to reaffirm their love with monthly anniversaries of the day they met as well as invented traditions such as rewalking the route they took from the tram. But when do the cracks in their relationship appear, exactly? Is it when, just a few weeks after meeting, Katharina is granted an exit visa to the West to visit her grandma in Cologne? Or when on her return east, she takes a trip to the Baltic coast to surprise Hans while he vacations with his family?

It becomes another tradition they repeat year after year. Are there hints of something more sinister? In the first flush of love, a friend of Katharina tells her she has lost her radiance since meeting Hans; and when Katharina goes to his flat, he is not there at the arranged time because, seemingly besotted, he wants to watch her walk to his door. Yet, as the relationship becomes more controlling, Katharina stays, the claustrophobia seeping through in Hofmann's translation.

The age difference between the two protagonists means that while Katharina changes apprenticeships, briefly moving to the town of Frankfurt/Oder and later starting university, Hans remains stationary in Berlin, writing a novel and freelancing as a radio writer. Yet it also roots them in different periods of Germany's turbulent twentieth century: Hans thriving in the Hitler Youth in the former German Eastern Territories and Katharina being entirely the product of a communist state, apparently content with the opportunities it allows her. Hans's family were sent as refugees to West Germany, meaning he consciously chose to become a citizen of East Germany, but could his past play into his role as the aggressor in their relationship while Katharina's socialist upbringing leaves her accepting of his increasing endeavors to control her? Are they both simply products of their times?

Only occasionally mentioned by name, the Stasi and the secret police are still omnipresent. Katharina moves to Frankfurt/Oder and sleeps with one of her colleagues. She writes about the event on a sheet of paper instead of the diary she keeps to show Hans. He discovers her betrayal and embarks on years of investigation into Katharina's personality. His questions, tricks, and accusations delivered in person or in the form of cassettes are nothing short of the methods used by the Stasi. But still Katharina does not leave him and loyally listens to the cassettes and answers his questions, believing this reeducation is penance for her transgression. The couple travel to Moscow, where their relationship briefly improves as they visit all the sights. Notably, the only metro station they don't stop at is Lubyanka, the KGB headquarters.

Over time, Katharina begins to refute Hans's narrative of the events in Frankfurt/Oder. She initially just thinks it but later voices it. This rejection is reflected in the events in Germany in the slow buildup to the fall of the Berlin Wall. As Katharina begins to question Hans's authority, it is noticeable that Soviet newspapers are no longer available in Germany due to their depiction of glasnost and perestroika.

Katharina's confidence grows; she refuses sex with Hans and is emboldened as a citizen of a new country, although she seeks the illusion of power through petty theft. It was Hans who convinced her to go to West

Berlin, but she adapts with the changing times and takes advantage of the new opportunities to travel. Simultaneously, Hans's field of influence shrinks—his book is not released, and he is made redundant along with many other former employees of the East German state radio. In the epilogue, Katharina accesses Hans's Stasi files, discovering that he was once an informer and later became the subject of an investigation himself—another instance of how relationships change.

Nobel Prize–tipped Erpenbeck admits that this book is in part autofiction, referring to Katharina's visit to Cologne, where she sees homeless people for the first time, and a Berlin night in October 1989, where the stage for the GDR fortieth-anniversary parade is being built while just a few streets further away dissidents are meeting in the Gethsemane Church. Having lived through the period herself—she would have been the same age as Katharina when the wall fell—her eagle-eyed observations are both poignant and accurate (e.g., she describes the communist leaders who built the foundations of the GDR as *"looking for their reflection in a void generation"*).

On the face of it, *Kairos* can be read as the downfall of a controlling relationship, but due to its setting it becomes much more: an analysis of the power balance between a state and its subjects. A compulsive read that leaves you wondering where/when the relationship deteriorated so badly and why Katharina stays, yet at the same time providing some insight into her motives.

CATHERINE VENNER, NOV. 2023

Kairos was translated from the German by Michael Hofmann.

OTRARSE: LADINO POEMS   (2024)

JUAN GELMAN

Ilan Stavans's selections from seven of Juan Gelman's collections, originally published between 1982 and 2001, showcase Gelman's ephemeral and situated voice. This ambivalence is grounded in Gelman's exile from his native Argentina, his dialogues with medieval and early modern Jewish and *converso* poets, and his commitment to learning Ladino, a precarious form of Old Spanish spoken by Sephardic Jews.

Originally published in 1994, *Dibaxu* (Underneath) is the resulting bilingual collection of poems in Ladino and Spanish. Exile, Jewish literary tradition, and a nearly extinct language combine in Gelman's poetry to trace a certain idea of home; one that recognizes home's essential importance, its frequent elusiveness, and the dangers of fixing it to a given place or way of being. The lines in Ladino that conclude the seventh poem in *Dibaxu* give readers a sense of the beautiful musicality and delicate approach to the poetic voice's home that graces *Otrarse*: "si dispartara la yuvia / di un páxaru / qui aspira al mar / nil mar /" (the rain woke up / from a bird / awaiting the sea / in the sea /). Flowing and flight coincide in this image with the slight disjuncture of place expressed by the fact that the site of waiting is the same as that which is awaited.

A disjuncture between poet and voice also structures *Otrarse*, as indicated by the title's challenge "to other oneself." The idiosyncratic use of slashes at the end of a poem, as in the lines cited above and in almost all of the poems in Stavans's edited collection, is an example of how Gelman communicates the slightly imperfect overlap between one voice and another. The final slash suggests incompleteness and a distinction between the last word of an utterance and what still may be to come. What comes next does not have to be written by the same poet who wrote the slash. It could be an invitation to read one of Gelman's historical interlocutors, like Saint Teresa of Ávila or Yehuda Halevi, from, respectively, *Quotes*, originally published in 1982, and *Com/positions*, from 1986, or Gelman's heteronym, Eliezer ben Jonon, who also appears in *Com/positions*. What comes next could also be from Gelman's mother, with whom his poetic voice forms an inextricable edifice in *Letter to My Mother*, from 1989.

In many of his poems, Gelman's voice is light, fragile, and fleeting but also rooted, this apparent contradiction an analogy of his oeuvre's incursions into the multiple poetic and linguistic traditions and trajectories that span the volumes represented in *Otrarse*. Gelman's rhythm intensifies the occasional uncertainty of the voice's movements, as in the stuttering cadence in these lines from *Com/positions*: "en el mundo sólo tengo esta hora

// este ahora que soy /" (in the world this hour alone is mine // this now that I am /). "Esta hora" and "este ahora" echo each other while shifting from a possession to a subject position. The image in the poem cited above of awaiting the sea from inside the sea is here like the subject conditioned by the hour he owns. Likewise conditioned is the voice, at once possessed and grounded in a concrete experience as well as belonging to something else, but never only one or the other.

Otrarse invites its readers to follow its title's instruction and reassures them that they will do so within the embrace of Gelman's call to speak beyond the illusory conclusions of poetry and life.

RYAN LONG, JANUARY 2025

Otrarse was translated from the Ladino, Spanish, and Hebrew by Ilan Stavans.

LA NUIT S'AJOUTE À LA NUIT   (2024)

ANANDA DEVI

Who would have thought that Alina Gurdiel's idea to put a Japanese tradition on its head would have such editorial success? Her "Ma nuit au musée" series, offered by Stock since 2018, counts twenty-one volumes and has been extremely well received in France and around the world. Everything in the series, however, is the opposite of the art practices on Naoshima Island, where art is installed outdoors or exhibited close to large bay windows and skylights and is open 24/7 to the public. Gurdiel asks one author to lock themselves in an indoor museum's finite space for one night to explore solitude through an introspective conversation. Does the resulting book reveal the author's inner structure and culture to the world? Does it provide a broad cultural Baedeker for the museum's collections? Does it create virtual, vicarious cultural knowledge, saving its readers the trouble of discovering and interpreting?

Ananda Devi initially considered the Château de Ferney for a lively debate between Jean-Jacques Rousseau and Voltaire ending in a party *à trois* worthy of the Marquis de Sade. Yet, being an author who, in the words of her translator Jeffrey Zuckerman, doles out "darkness and beauty in equal measure," she chose a place of incarceration for humans: the Montluc prison in Lyon. From the very start, her stay in this crucible of darkness is inseparable from the beacons of light of her beloved Western cathedrals and from the relentless search for the triumph of soul over body. She keeps using doubt, her favorite *modus operandi*, and peppers her narrative with interrogations about what and how to write this new book—something she has quite adeptly explored throughout her long writing career of twenty-three novels, countless short stories, and five volumes of poetry.

Devi's stay in Montluc prison during one dark, rainy, and cold night awakened a slew of "violent memories" that made her toggle back and forth from the "absolute deafness" of the act of writing back to "the din of reality." In the darkest hour of the night, at 4 a.m., when fate decides between life and death, she receives the gift of clarity. She is ready to witness, to relate emotions and feelings; although her narrative will contain a slew of historical events and citations, she will not write a metanarrative. This choice makes her feel "perfectly gathered" and "inside myself." It takes her six hours to shed her nagging impostor syndrome, which casts doubts about her project and herself. Six hours to shed a multigenerational feeling of shame that originated with her forebears' exile from the southern state of Andhra Pradesh on India's east coast in the nineteenth century, followed by their descendants' peregrinations in South Africa and Mauritius Island. Six hours to relate numerous stories of social, linguistic, and national degradation, exclusion, and resistance and rebirth to finally be able to make the Montluc prisoners' experience hers.

Devi's entire experience with *La nuit s'ajoute à la nuit* (Night upon night) is presented in a chiastic structure. Progressing from prewriting, previsit stages (chapters 1 and 2), her narrative plunges into a detailed explanation of her approach to her writing assignment. This is mirrored by her postvisit writing and her disclosure of "The Sixth Life," a previsit fictitious short story about the reopening of the prison to migrants whom she considers to be today's "genocide of the poor" (chapters 13 and 14). Chapter 3 recounts her arrival at the prison and settling for the night, while chapter 11 sums up her last walk through the cells at dawn. Chapters 4 through 10 recount her visits to the prisoners' cells and read like stations of the cross.

Devi's first stop is at the cell of the Izieu children of World War II and adolescent female resisters; her last stop will be for the infants and mothers of the common-law female prisoners as late as 2009. Her second visit is for the World War II male resisters, and her next-to-last visit is for the Algerian prisoners of war, Jean Moulin, and Marc Bloch. At the center of these visits are the cells of two men, André Devigny, a World War II resister famous for his daring escape, and Klaus Barbie, "the butcher of Lyon."

The descriptions of the cell visits are interrupted by rhizomes—short vignettes triggered by a detail that prolongs the central story with true stories—be it the phenomenology of the body's degradation and pain under confinement and torture, the evocation of cathedrals, her own upbringing on l'Ile Maurice, slavery, violence toward women, or Bobby Sands's hunger strike. These rhizomes function like throbbing cries of anguish and reality checks, avoidance mechanisms, deep introspection, and sober assessment. Citations from former prisoners' memoirs also provide perspective, like Michaël Ferrier's memoir, *Scrabble*, where she found the title for the book. Devi also cites Zionist writer André Spire's phrase that survivors have acquired "an infinite sort of knowledge that cannot be transmitted." This is where suffering separates the soul from its dross.

The deepest lesson from *La nuit s'ajoute à la nuit* is Devi's interrogations about the "infinite chain of pain," the coexistence of good and evil in each of us, and human responsibility. Did Devigny, the intrepid resistant of World War II, torture Algerian prisoners during the Algerian War where he served? How about Barbie, who rendered countless services to the CIA during the Cold War? Devi's long night's journey through the contrapuntal phases of herself leaves her and us with a painfully clear question: what choices would she have made? Her question about how to balance living in a happy cocoon and letting the tragedy of the world devour us has an urgency that makes *La nuit s'ajoute à la nuit* a must-read book for our troubled times.

ALICE-CATHERINE CARLS, MARCH 2025

Reviewed in the French; *La nuit s'ajoute à la nuit* has not yet been translated into English.

THE CITY AND ITS UNCERTAIN WALLS   (2024)

HARUKI MURAKAMI

After six years of eager anticipation, Haruki Murakami has finally delivered *The City and Its Uncertain Walls*. Picking up where *Killing Commendatore* left off, this new, surrealist novel immerses readers in his signature blend of mythical plots and stark realities, unfolding a coming-of-age tale that focuses on the overwhelming clash between ego and the external world.

The seventeen-year-old protagonist encounters a nameless girl who introduces him to a strange city. The chosen ones can enter the town, but their shadows must remain outside. The girl confesses that she is a shadow and pleads with him to find her in the town library. Though initially dismissing this as a joke, the boy soon finds that the girl has vanished without a trace. Life continues until one night, at the age of forty-five, the character falls into a pit in his dream. Upon waking, he is already outside the walls of the city. A clock tower without hands, unicorns under a golden sunset, shape-shifting walls out of nowhere, and philosophical riddles exchanged with his own shadow—all these dazzling elements, set to a jazzlike rhythm, are reminders that readers are on a journey into Murakami's wonderland.

Divided into three parts, the novel sees the disoriented protagonist entering the mysterious city toward the end of the first section. In part 2, the character's shadow manages to escape and return to the real world, where it encounters a ghost librarian. The story then proceeds to focus on the protagonist's true self also attempting to quit his duty as a dream-reader. The city, without a doubt, serves as a refuge for lost souls, a place where characters like the middle-aged protagonist and the "Yellow Submarine boy" find solace from modern loneliness that never seems to dissipate.

Unlike the menacing atmosphere of *Killing Commendatore* or the mystery-driven tension in *1Q84*, this novel presents a more serene meditation on the loss of love. Even without the rare statement in the afterword, any reader with some knowledge about Murakami's previous work would immediately recognize the thematic and structural similarities to his 1980 novella under the same title and the 1985 novel *Hard-Boiled Wonderland and the End of the World*—the latter often considered one of the author's most outstanding masterpieces. If *Hard-Boiled Wonderland* was an ambitious response to a theme that fascinated the thirty-six-year-old Murakami, then choosing to rewrite it at seventy-one during the pandemic lockdown suggests that this is more than just an ordinary addition to Murakami's literary universe.

Evaluating the literary merits of this novel, or deciding whether it should be recommended without hesitation, is not an easy task. From the outset, the gesture of rewriting implies a division among potential readers: whether or not one has read the 1980s prototype largely determines how one approaches this novel and the response it may elicit. If defined as "fan fiction," the riddlelike dialogues, the smooth crossover between the real and the imagined, and the exploration of philosophical themes can easily evoke the same excitement one experienced while reading *Hard-Boiled Wonderland*.

But the problem is, what made Murakami's 1980s narrative so exhilarating was the wild imagination—like an untethered horse dashing on the grassland. The unpredictable twists in the stories often gave the impression that even the author himself was unsure where his creativity would lead. Given that *The City and Its Uncertain Walls* is designed to be a revision and extension of the ideas presented in *Hard-Boiled Wonderland*, the driving force for loyal readers to finish the reading is less about deciphering "old" metaphors and more about locating intertextuality and speculating what "new" messages Murakami aims to convey through this rewrite.

On the other hand, for those unfamiliar with his earlier works, the masterful narrative skills and captivating magical images transcend cultural boundaries, making it an outstanding story that should not be skipped—even though, like many of his recent releases, it is quite lengthy. Like the confused protagonist, readers will have to take the challenge to unravel myriads of literary puzzles to grasp the meaning of the "uncertain walls."

In contrast to the cold, closed ending of *Hard-Boiled Wonderland*, *The City and Its Uncertain Walls* offers a more open and warm response to its central themes. The town's walls, designed to keep out all forms of plague—including what the inhabitants see as the "plague of the soul"—are constantly reconstructed to form a self-contained system. This metaphor carries special weight in the postpandemic era. The isolation of the town faithfully reflects the author's state of writing during the harsh lockdown. However, the belief that extreme solitude and warm feelings of empathy can coexist seems to be the most crucial message Murakami attempts to pass on to his readers.

During an interview, the author confessed that this was the only work he had ever considered rewriting, and if possible, he would still feel the urge to revisit it forty years from now. Inspired by this statement, readers may as well consider this act of rewriting from a different perspective. Regardless of what paths we have taken and how confident we are in our choices, these paths inevitably resurface with the passage of time, leading to endless regrets. On one end, this self-doubt points to the uncertainty of past decisions; on the other, it stresses the need to summon new courage to face the future. Lost in the labyrinth of hopelessness, yet still holding on to an innocent anticipation for tomorrow's sunrise. This is the most enduring and fascinating merit of Murakami's work, and this new novel is no exception. In this sense, *The City and Its Uncertain Walls* is not a nostalgic revisit to Murakami's previous narrative but a book of catharsis that readers in the postpandemic world should not miss.

SIYU CAO, JULY 2025

The City and Its Uncertain Walls was translated from the Japanese by Philip Gabriel.

PART V

BOOKS AS LIGHTHOUSES

WHAT USE IS POETRY? (2013)

MEENA ALEXANDER

1

A WHILE BACK, I was in Colorado in a hall with huge windows that gave out onto the Rockies. I was stunned by the rugged, slashed beauty of the mountains I could see if I turned my head just slightly. As often happens, after a reading came voices from the floor. A woman in a red sweatshirt stood up. She was near the back of the packed hall, and I had to strain to see her—but her voice was loud and clear.

The question ricocheted off the walls: "What use is poetry?" I caught my breath. She might have been Plato's daughter asking me. I remember the hall as deathly silent. I thought: nothing, there is nothing I can say. Out of my mouth shot a few words, words that, a whole year later, I turned into the unshriven heart of a poem. The poem has a simple enough title— "Question Time"—and it will appear in my book *Birthplace with Buried Stones*, to be published in October 2013.

QUESTION TIME

I remember the scarred spine
Of mountains the moon slips through,

Fox fire in a stump, bushes red with blisters,
Her question, a woman in a sweatshirt,

Hand raised in a crowded room—
What use is poetry?

Above us, lights flickered,
Something wrong with the wiring.

I turned and saw the moon whirl in water,
The Rockies struck with a mauve light,

Sea creatures cut into sky foliage.
In the shadow of a shrub once you and I

Brushed lips and thighs,
Dreamt of a past that frees its prisoners.

Standing apart I looked at her and said—
We have poetry

So we do not die of history.
I had no idea what I meant.

2

We might think of history as what is rendered up of the past in recorded memory, recorded by those who are in a position to do so, having access to the power of public inscription. But there is an important underground stream of history I have learned to recognize: secret letters, journals, inscriptions, scribblings on bits of paper smuggled out of prisons. Poetry is closer in intent, it seems to me, to this buried stream that takes as its purview what is deeply felt, "felt in the blood and felt along the heart," as Wordsworth once wrote in lines that lie at the core of a meditation on the past and its impossible nature—impossible, that is, for a consciousness that would seek to return.

3

Poetry takes as its purview what is deeply felt and is essentially unsayable; that is the paradox on which the poem necessarily turns. A poet uses language as a painter uses color, a primary material out of which to make art. But language that is used all the time and all around us—in sound bites, advertisements, political rhetoric, newsprint—needs to be rinsed free so that it can be used as the stuff of art.

The poem in its act of meaning-making turns away from the literal, its truth bound to what can be evoked. And evocation is sparked by memory. Abhinavagupta (ca. 950–1020 CE) realized this clearly. In his reflections, he writes of how poetry—far from dealing with the literal—reaches into what lies in memory, in memory fragments. It is in this way that *rasa*, the quick of aesthetic pleasure, is reached:

> On the other hand *rasa* is something that one cannot dream of expressing by the literal sense. It does not fall within workday expression. It is rather of a form that must be tasted by an act of blissful relishing on the part of a delicate mind through the stimulation of previously deposited memory elements . . . beautiful because of their appeal to the heart. . . . The suggesting of such a sense is called *rasadhvani* and is found to operate only in poetry. This in a strict sense is the soul of poetry. (*The Dhvanyāloka of Ānandavardhana with the Locana of Abhinavagupta*)

4

While poetry is bound to the sensorium, to the sensual powers of bodily being, to memory that draws its power from feelings heightened by the senses, it is also bound to place. It is in place that we locate ourselves, mark ourselves in relation with others; it is in place that we survive. But what becomes of the past when place is torn away, when the sensorium is radically displaced, and when exile or dislocation marks out the limits of existence?

5

Why do we have poetry in a time like this? For me that question folds into another: What does it mean to belong in a violent world?

I think of the invisible archive that each of us bears within, a deeply personal ingathering of sights and sounds and scents and bits of the sometimes ruined materiality that memory allots—and perhaps this is another way of thinking about the coruscating flow of the inner life that gives meaning to our existence, all that comes up when we dare to say "I." And surely this is the province of poetry.

6

Embedded at the heart of Percy Shelley's "A Defence of Poetry" (1821) are lines in which he evokes the unbidden power of the poem: "It creates for us a being within our being. It makes us inhabitants of a world to which the familiar world is a chaos. It reproduces the common universe of which we are portions and percipients, and it purges from our inward sight the film of familiarity which obscures from us the wonder of our being."

What is this counterworld, this being within our being, this zone of desire that poetry evokes? Surely there is a great and buried truth here, something to do with our ecstatic being, the piercings of sense that mere rationality cannot afford, a way of making sense, lacking which we would all be hostages in our own skins.

7

There have been moments in our shared human history in particular parts of the world where poets and also singers have been banned. But why? What is there to fear? Precisely this: the force of the quicksilver self that poetry sets free—desire that can never be bound by laws and legislation. This is the force of the human, the spirit level of our lives.

8

The poem is an invention that exists in spite of history. Most of the forces in our ordinary lives as we live them now conspire against the making of a poem. There might be some space for the published poem, but not for its creation: no ritualized space is given where one is allowed to sit and brood, although universities can give you a modicum of that.

In a time of violence, the task of poetry is in some way to reconcile us to our world and to allow us a measure of tenderness and grace with which to exist. I believe this very deeply, and I see it as an effort to enter into the complications of the moment, even if they are violent; but through that, in some measure, poetry's task is to reconcile us to the world—not to accept it at face value or to assent to things that are wrong, but to reconcile one in a larger sense, to return us in love, the province of the imagination, to the scope of our mortal lives.

9

Poetry is a forsaken art not for those who write or practice it, but for many others. Yet there is a kind of grace that poetry offers, something that paradoxically is hard to catch with words, an elemental rush that Shelley tries to evoke in his "A Defence of Poetry," that extraordinary chronicle of the exalted, impossible task of the poet from which we have taken the line for today's resolution.

Toward the start of his essay, Shelley speaks of beauty and the way by which the intuition of what he calls "this indestructible order" is something granted to the maker of art. Then comes a leap of faith. He argues that artists are "the institutors of law, and the founders of civil society"—in short, legislators: what they were called in earlier times.

Now this seems to me to be a leap that could not sustain the body that sought to land, from its free fall, into some possible space of survival. Surely we need to unhook the idea of the intense apprehension of beauty and "this invisible world" from ordinary legislation, our notion of congresses and parliaments, of procedures and plenipotentiary powers.

10

I hear little hooks popping.
A bodice unbuttoning.
A heart pounding, breathing.

But should we? Surely the affective life—and, I would argue, poetry in the broadest possible sense that Shelley meant—is crucial even in the life of legislators and the decisions that are made. The nature of gun laws and the issues of immigration are just two examples that we might make, drawn from our recent debates.

But perhaps for Shelley the shadow of prophecy is what allows for the poet as legislator—in his words, poets as "hierophants of an unapprehended inspiration; the mirrors of the gigantic shadows which futurity casts upon the present."

My mind turns to the poet George Oppen's response to Shelley. In a poem called "Disasters," Oppen writes:

> of wars o western
> wind and storm
> of politics I am sick with a poet's
> vanity   legislators
> of the unacknowledged
> world . . .

What is this unacknowledged world? All too often it is a world that lies too deep for tears.

11

I was in New York City on 9/11. Poetry was a way to survive. I wrote on tiny bits of paper I carried around with me. People read out poems to each other, on the radio, in Union Square and other public places. There was something about the poem that could allow one the intense expression of emotion so necessary to a time of crisis. I wrote a cycle of elegies for the dead. Here is one of them. All these poems found their way into my book *Raw Silk*.

The lyric poem is a form of extreme silence, which is protected from the world. To make a lyric poem I have to enter into a dream state. But at the same time, almost by virtue of that disconnect, it becomes a very intense location to reflect on the world.

AFTERMATH

There is an uncommon light in the sky
Pale petals are scored into stone.
I want to write of the linden tree
That stoops at the edge of the river
But its leaves are filled with insects
With wings the color of dry blood.
At the far side of the river Hudson
By the southern tip of our island
A mountain soars, a torrent of sentences
Syllables of flame stitch the rubble
An eye, a lip, a cut hand blooms
Sweet and bitter smoke stains the sky.

New York City, September 13–18, 2001

I made a cycle of poems that I called "Late There Was an Island"; the poem I just read, "Aftermath," is the first of those. While making my poems, I kept walking down to Ground Zero, as close as I could get, making returns, a pilgrimage, the site a graveyard for thousands, the stench of burning flesh and wires. Once, as I walked past Liberty Street, I was struck by the extreme youth of the soldier guarding the perimeter, a young lad freckled, fresh-faced. Behind him was the shell of the south tower, against which an ancient patriarch was getting photographed; small children screaming in delight at pigeons; a rescue worker, hands on his own throat, face sunk with tiredness, his gas mask at his hip.

12

The following month there was a meeting of a newly established Asian/Asian-American Research Institute. I had been asked to serve on the governing board; the meeting was at the Graduate Center where I teach. It was the sort of occasion to which I would wear a sari without thinking twice—but now something nagged at me.

Two of my South Asian students had encountered trouble wearing non-Western dress: men yelling, one throwing a paper bag at her. A friend of mine who had gone out one evening in Boston told me on the phone how a man had yelled and spat at her.

There was a zone of suspicion that was extending over Asians, South Asians, brown people who looked like they could be Arabs. I wanted to pick my battles. I wanted some control over the small things of life. If it could be dangerous to look different, it made no sense to stick out deliberately. I needed to save my energies for writing, and I was writing a great deal of poetry.

I rolled up my sari in a manner that would not crease it, set it carefully in a plastic bag that I lodged in the center of my book bag. In the fourth-floor ladies room I slipped out of my slacks and put on my sari. I watched the silk on the tiled floor and stared at my face in the mirror.

How dark I looked, unmistakably Indian. I needed to think through my fear. Later as I made my poem, I heard Kabir, the medieval poet saint, singing to me, giving me the courage to live my life. This is the poem I made.

KABIR SINGS IN A CITY OF BURNING TOWERS

What a shame
they scared you so
you plucked your sari off,
crushed it into a ball
then spread it
on the toilet floor.
Sparks from the towers
fled through the weave of silk.

With your black hair
and sun dark skin
you're just a child of earth.
Kabir the weaver sings:

O men and dogs
in times of grief
our rolling earth
grows small.

13

Art in a time of trauma, a necessary translation. "Fragments of a vessel," writes Walter Benjamin, "to be glued together."

But what if the paste shows, the seams, the fractures?

In a time of violence the work of art must use the frame of the real, translating a script almost illegible, a code of traumatic recovery.

It seems to me that in its rhythms the poem, the artwork, can incorporate scansion of the actual, the broken steps, the pauses, the blunt silences, the brutal explosions. So that what is pieced together is a work that exists as an object in the world but also, in its fearful consonance and its shimmering stretch, allows the world entry.

I think of it as a recasting that permits our lives to be given back to us, fragile, precarious.

14

A few words to conclude.

I think of the poet in the twenty-first century as a woman standing in a dark doorway.

She is a homemaker, but an odd one.

She hovers in a dark doorway. She needs to be there at the threshold to find a balance, to maintain a home at the edge of the world.

She puts out both her hands. They will help her hold on, help her find her way.

She has to invent a language marked by many tongues.

As for the script in which she writes, it binds her into visibility, fronting public space, marking danger, marking desire.

Behind her in the darkness of her home and through her pour languages no one she knows will ever read or write.

They etch a *corps perdu*.[*] Subtle, vital, un-seizable body.
Source of all translations.

NEW YORK CITY

Meena Alexander (1951–2018), described in *The Statesman* (India) as "undoubt-edly one of the finest poets in contemporary times," was an Indian American poet, scholar, and writer. Born in Allahabad, she was distinguished professor of English at the City University of New York. This is the revised version of an address she delivered to the Yale Political Union on April 23, 2013.

---

*   A reference to Aimé Césaire's cycle of poems *Corps perdu* (Éditions Fragrance, 1950), with etchings by Pablo Picasso.

BURIED ALIVE IN AN INSTANT   (2022)

SERGEI GLAVATSKII

Translated from the Ukrainian by Ilya Kaminsky & Katie Farris

A PERSON—like a rat—acclimates to everything. While he's alive. While not yet at the boiling point.

It's possible to get acclimated to everything: to the fact that there's no good news, to separation from those I love, to destroyed cities, to an unthinkable tsunami of hate, which for a poet—whether the hate is internal or external—is the end. It's possible to get used to hearing—but not listening to—the endless air-raid sirens.

A completely new feeling for me is missing my son. He is still young, we haven't yet been able to have a heart-to-heart conversation, and then—and now he's escaped to Europe, while I am in Ukraine.

An all-consuming feeling: How is my child doing? Is everything okay? I must convince myself constantly that he's okay. Will we see each other again? A person in Ukraine is especially and suddenly mortal.

Poetry? Books? Truly, it's funny. Everything good, created by humankind, can be buried alive in an instant.

And anyone can come and show you who you really are: a powerless child, whose life is worth less than a single bullet.

ODESA

Sergei Glavatskii is a poet and writer from Odesa whose work has appeared in numerous journals in Ukraine.

Born in Odesa, Ukraine, in 1977, award-winning poet, translator, and editor Ilya Kaminsky was nominated for the Neustadt Prize in 2014.

A finalist for the T. S. Eliot Prize, Katie Farris is a poet, translator, and associate professor of poetry at Princeton University. They guest-edited the 2022 Ukraine issue of *WLT*.

ANZHELINA POLONSKAYA

Translated from the Russian by Andrew Wachtel

I FELT A STRANGE and troubling attraction to her from the moment her form, her face, out of the myriad faces and forms, caught my attention. She was thirty-two, I was sixteen. And she was my teacher. In the atmosphere of spiritual poverty that characterized my school, in the absence of liberty, optimism, or anything remotely individualized, the only thing I learned was to look through the windows at the landscape that stretched back to my childhood, ignoring the screams and the voices, the scrape of chalk on the blackboard. In any part of my homeland, that depressing land-scape—with its damp tree or hopeless streetcar with frosted-over windows or lonely figure carrying his burden of everyday slavery—immediately became a canvas, a painting of frozen nuances. I examined it carefully, and whenever an image would unexpectedly appear, my tongue felt the taste associations of words. Yes, words carried a taste, like food, and the most important thing was to roll them around in your mouth so as not to lose the aftertaste and to be able to continue to examine their forms. That is how the material for poetry came into being. My school could give me nothing more. But I thank that yellow, low-slung building for my meeting with her, she who for many years would be my secret, my incredible inner turmoil from which, as from a spring, I drew inspiration.

My only school friend had left at the beginning of the academic year, abandoning me to loneliness, and I had to quickly turn that loneliness into something funny—only the jester is allowed to kick the king—to prevent my classmates from smelling blood. Despite what many people believe, the most flagrant of human vices are concentrated in children, although those vices have still not fully developed, thanks to a lack of experience. But their innate ability to persecute is perfection itself. I started to drop out of reality, in the way people go into a faint or a lethargic trance, separating myself from the world more and more thoroughly, not wanting to have anything to do with the space that surrounded me. And slowly, my world narrowed down to two things—contemplation and books, stolen from my father's library when he was away from home. His library was a sacred place and therefore locked away from mere mortals, who could desecrate its holiness by, for example, leaving a book open and face down on the polished library table. But still, I am grateful to my late father for his upbringing. He was ill, and slowly and in ways dangerous for us, he was collapsing. He staked and lost his life as if on a card, or as if he had arrived late for the last train. And he remained standing forever in the emptiness of the station, empty hands hanging by his sides, in his worn-out gray suit jacket, a man with an exceptional mind, broken by fate. He was torn from the world into endless space, like a character from a Chagall painting, and he took with him a piece of our narrow world. That same winter my dog died. We'd bought her as a puppy from a drunken stranger one New Year's. She died, having lived a long but unhappy life, on a frozen December night, quietly, while I was sleeping. We wrapped her in a plastic bag and carried her body to the garbage bins by the infectious disease hospital—the ground was too cold to dig a grave. And so my childhood came to an end, though I never really had one—I was never a child.

It's hard to recall when a flood began. Who can pinpoint what love is? All my life the only answer I have been able to give is "yearning for the impossible." For love you can die or not die, you can sacrifice yourself or sink into your own ego, but in any case it will remain irrational, like a flower or a cloud, indebted to no one.

My history teacher. Between us a strange relationship arose. Long and unbearable, like a sound, yearning and strangled. Frequently falling flat, like a cut stalk of morning glory. I couldn't stand her gaze and would lower my eyes because everything was so blindingly clear and impossible simultaneously that a cold sweat would go running down my back, and my pulse would beat wildly in my neck. I would ask for any job at all—put up wallpaper or paint the door. I didn't care about the work, just about being there. Sleep interfered with my disease, stealing precious moments, so I cursed sleep. The closer we got to the end of the school year, the more despotic my love became. I was jealous of anyone who asked her anything, her equals or not; I was jealous of older people, of disgusting infants who, other than the simple fact of their appearance on earth, were totally unworthy of being fawned over, of others, of my own absence, of every passing day. She forgave my tantrums, my clowning, with demonstrative silence. From nonexistent but nevertheless obvious messages I heard, "You are not they." Not they.

But . . . this country is the Soviet Union. This school is a Soviet school. Where a same-sex relationship can land you in prison for many years. And where a girl who wears earrings deemed to dangle too far can be kicked out of class. Just imagine what would happen in a country like this if there were even a hint of someone's being different, dissimilar to everyone else? And the worst of the nightmare was that I was completely incapable of understanding or accepting what it was I wanted from this relationship—if the omnipresent physicality had even touched me, I would have broken down and run out of the room in horror. My desire was meager, only faintly touched by Eros. What could be done with this closeness, with the possibility of such closeness?

Much later, when I had grown up and was living in another city, foreign and bitter, this same yearning, this youthful pain, would hit me again with incredible power, like an attack of fever. One November evening, just a few steps away from my dorm room, amid a forest of skyscrapers, I stopped among the gray, multistory towers and, lifting my head up to the skies, I did not whisper but screamed your name.

Later, all sorts of things happened—life: relationships that gave and took, momentary flashes, passion in all its wildness and impatience, humiliation. And what humiliation—lapidary! Hard to believe. Over the years nothing heals over and passes away. That "something" turns into a straight line, a constant hum, which the human ear has to put up with. In my dreams, during various accidental meetings, in all sorts of places, as I rise up from the depths to take a gulp of air, I see your face and I don't have the courage to lean toward it.

Once we were sitting together in a group of empty shades—that is how little they meant to our fates—who were nevertheless connected to us through shared links to the past, and not one of them could guess our secret. That nature in its monumental control is like a concentration camp ruled by a single law—the law of impossibility. It is dull and simple, like any prescription repeated an endless number of times. It prevents chaos from taking over. Oh life, we are your slaves and your creation and we need to pay for our own tranquility, for the ancient order of things, with our obedience, and therefore we are always unhappy and deprived. "But what if we were to run away?" "Flight as the end of the beautiful illusion?" And everything becomes so blindingly clear that I can't stand your gaze and lower my eyes.

Anzhelina Polonskaya (b. 1969) is a writer and artist from Malakhovka, Russia. She is the author of four poetry collections, including *A Voice*, *To the Ashes*, and *Paul Klee's Boat*, all of which were translated into English by Andrew Wachtel.

Andrew Wachtel (b. 1959) is a translator from multiple Slavic languages. His translation of Polonskaya's *Paul Klee's Boat* (2014) was shortlisted for the PEN Poetry Translation Prize.

WHY LIVE? A QUESTION FOR 21ST CENTURY THEATRE   (2016)

JORDAN TANNAHILL

EIGHT PERFORMERS wearing cheap red cloaks and yellow cardboard crowns sit in a row of eight wooden chairs along the edge of the stage. Plainly visible below their cloaks are the performers' everyday street clothes. Footlights illuminate their faces, recalling both vaudeville and the flashlight held below one's chin while telling a ghost story. In the upstage darkness there is a table with a pitcher of water, bottles of beer, and snacks—the kind of table one might set out at a party.

A king begins to tell a story. He recounts it as one might to a friend over a pint, casually and without affect: "Once upon a time, a lonely night watchman noticed a pixelated spot in the footage from a security camera installed in a corridor. The footage was otherwise clear except for this one little spot of pixelation. Intrigued by this anomaly, the night watchman went to investigate, only to discover that the pixelation existed in the fabric of reality itself . . ."

"Stop," says one of the queens, who revises the story: "Once upon a time, a lonely night watchman watched the footage from a security camera installed in a corridor and saw his mother . . ." She continues telling the story until another queen stops her and begins telling a story about a sex-crazed plumber. Then, another king stops her and returns to the story of the night watchman, until he too is interrupted, this time by a king telling a story about a talking dog. Over the course of the night, during these stories, a sprawling cast of characters multiplies, as do sub-plots involving gay soldiers, wizards in forests, murderous children, and philosophical robots.

Each story—or is it simply one long, endlessly mutating story?—is dragged up from the memories and imaginations of the eight performers on the spot. Over the course of the six hours we are gathered together, this prismatic narrative seems to contain every story ever told, though no story is ever completed. As in life, we are perpetually in the process of experiencing the narrative, grasping but never truly able to apprehend its conclusion. Moving from the extraordinary to the banal, we encounter stories of religious ecstasy, fables, ghost tales, love stories, domestic tragedies, and a few raunchy sexcapades.

It is clearly a game, and the audience becomes giddy watching the kings and queens play it, competing with one another to hold our attention, interrupting one another and commandeering the narrative, exaggerating certain details or removing key points altogether. The storytelling is at times weary, at other times hysterical, obscene, absurd, tender. At times, some of the kings and queens leave their chairs and wander over to the snack table and take a swig of beer, or lie down for a rest in the darkness beyond the chairs while the others carry on.

At one point in the night, perhaps around ten or eleven, there are only two kings left speaking, and then, twenty minutes later, two queens return, a king leaves, and a half hour later, without my even noticing it, all eight are back in their chairs. This ebbing and flowing of performers mirrors the ebbing and flowing of the audience in the theatre; we are given permission to come and go as needed, to take a break, grab a bite, empty our bladders. The show is six hours long after all. And there is no pretense of what "should" happen in the theatre. I feel total permission to laugh out loud, to groan, to rest my eyes when I am bored. It feels as if the audience and the performers are truly in this together.

The show is *And on the Thousandth Night . . .* by the seminal Sheffield, UK–based performance company Forced Entertainment. I caught it during its 2010 run at the Hebbel am Ufer performance center in Berlin. The company describes its work as exploring what theatre can mean in contemporary life and that this exploration is "always a kind of conversation or negotiation, something that needs to be live."

Something that needs to be live. This feels like the most crucial component to my experience of *And on the Thousandth Night . . .* This was a piece that could not exist in any other context but as a live performance for an assembled group of people. It was an event, a one-time experience that could never be re-created in quite the same way again, and one that could not exist without our collective presence feeding into it. It was an event insofar as there was a palpable sense of excitement for the performers and audience alike in simply being there and being together, doing this slightly impossible, insane thing with a group of strangers.

In an era where the screen reigns supreme, why live?

The dual reading of this question is intentional. What keeps us alive? And in a moment when our lives are becoming increasingly virtual, why bother telling stories the old-fashioned way, with a bunch of bodies gathered in a room? I think both interpretations of this question have a shared answer.

Theatre artists of any age and experience set out to make plays because they're attempting to access what theatre does best: a live engagement that forces us to confront the humanity of others. It's likely that at some point in their lives these artists experienced a transformative work of theatre and decided to dedicate themselves to creating similar experiences for others. A play, even a boring one, is rooted in an empathic desire to commune with others, which is more than you can say about mowing a lawn, waxing your car, trading stocks, or any of the millions of other ways that we spend our brief moments on Earth. Plays sit outside our daily routines. They require more of us. And, in their best moments, they can provide us with even more in return.

In his essay "Why Theatre?", Canadian theatre director Brendan Healy reflects on theatre's ability to cultivate empathy: "One of the most powerful pieces of theatre that I have seen was a show entitled *Rwanda 94*, created by a group of survivors from the Rwandan genocide. Over six hours, these survivors, witnesses, musicians, and actors told the horrific story of that nation's encounter with mass murder. The physical presence of these people who had faced unspeakable darkness prevented me from dissociating myself from the experience; I could not hide behind the protective veil of television or film. I left the theatre transformed. This show truly taught me that the proximity, 'liveness,' and immediacy of the theatre allow us to directly experience the world of another person and to learn—intellectually and emotionally—about others. The theatre taps and develops our capacity for empathy."

Australian playwright Alison Croggon proposes that theatre, with its emphasis on the here and now, is a profoundly local and humanizing force in our increasingly depersonalized global economy: "In an era of globalization the intensely local and unique context of a theatre performance should be something treasured." Unlike mass media, plays are performed for a specific community, for an audience who must be physically present in order to participate. Often, they are performed for the community in which the actors belong, an audience comprising one's peers, neighbors, acquaintances, fellow citizens. Healy amplifies this further: "From the rehearsal process to the experience of live performance, the theatre presents the world with a working model of cooperation, collectivity, and community. This makes the theatre essential to a world where the pursuit of individual wealth and consumerism is leading us to economic, environmental, and cultural collapse. The theatre provides citizens with a space to experience the joy of togetherness."

Of course, people also make and attend theatre simply to have a good time, to be transported and invigorated. In my first year of high school in 2003, I saw a production of Peter Froehlich's play *Simpl*, about Weimar Republic beer-hall comedians Karl Valentin and Liesl Karlstadt, at the National Arts Centre in Ottawa. I vividly remember a scene in which the Nazis killed the power to the beer hall. The lights in the theatre abruptly cut out, and five minutes of the play were performed in total darkness. There was a palpable sense of excitement in the adolescent matinee audience; to be plunged into pitch-black with a hundred other people while the play continued all around you (and most remarkably, within your head). I remember thinking at the time: I didn't know you could do this. In a theatre, a cinema, or anywhere. It was a simple and electric moment that felt unlike any other I'd ever experienced.

Ironically, we have cinema to thank for providing us with the notion of liveness. In his book *Liveness: Performance in a Mediatized Culture*, Philip Auslander suggests the very concept of liveness only came into existence once recording technology was invented. We could only truly comprehend the characteristics and value of a live engagement once its mediated equivalents were created. Something live occurs only once; like that which is living, that which is live is temporal. But this ephemeral and dynamic aspect of liveness is something that theatre still struggles to reconcile within the age of mechanical reproduction. We continue to rehearse and perform shows with the aim of reproducing the same event—the same text, the same ebbs and flows of laughter and pathos, the same moments of revelation—night after night. In other words, we often aim to create an inert, knowable, and replicable entity.

Montreal-based performance creator Jacob Wren suggests theatre still largely operates in a precinema production model: "To do something many times was the only way. Now, to do something many times, you can have a film. It opens up the space for theatre to be something different." Wren maintains that there are many theatre artists who realize this, but that there is a general resistance within the community to fundamentally reevaluate the model. "Those artists who realize this will do a few things and the rest of theatre gets scared because it means rethinking everything in a way. It's the same reason revolution doesn't happen."

Lumi Tan, associate curator of The Kitchen, the seminal New York City performance space, argues that theatre needs to embrace the power of its liveness and the uniquely communal aspect of its audience engagement: "Plays need to offer a reason to be experienced live, to accept the flaws that liveness brings, and to leave room for ambiguity as to what and how I am seeing or perceiving. I hate walking away from a play and wondering why it wasn't a video, why my body needed to share space with others in order to understand it, why it needs to be experienced in 'real time.' . . . Even when I'm acting as 'just' an audience member and not as a curator, I hope to feel responsible for being there as much as the performers, and I want to be surrounded by others who feel the same way."

At one extreme, this means productions that just can't, or won't, be the same night after night, like Forced Entertainment's *And on the Thousandth Night* . . . But a piece doesn't have to offer quite such radical instances of audience engagement to possess a sense of liveness. Liveness can exist just as readily in Shakespearean comedy or Chekhovian naturalism as it can in a textless, postdramatic performance piece. Ultimately, liveness is an embodied awareness of time, space, audience, and the potentiality of any given moment.

There's an unforgettable sequence in Brooklyn-based playwright and theatre director Young Jean Lee's *The Shipment*, for instance, in which three Black actors in impeccable formal evening wear stand silently and still at the apron of the stage, looking out over the audience (which, sadly, is usually a sea of white faces). It is a moment that exists alongside scenes of top-drawer American naturalism, and it is unexpected and charged. It's sustained far longer than you'd expect, and longer than feels comfortable.

But discomfort is precisely the point. As is the exquisite vulnerability of witnessing and being witnessed. Slowly, the eyes of the three actors seem to make contact with every audience member in the theatre. Then, in a moment to restart a dead man's heart, they suddenly begin to sing an a cappella rendition of "Dark Center of the Universe" by the American indie rock band Modest Mouse. "I might disintegrate into the thin air, if you'd like," sings the actress in a green evening gown. "I'm not the dark center of the universe like you thought," sing the two men in tuxedos standing either side of her.

Whenever I look out over an audience I think: How miraculous it is, all of us gathered together like this. We could literally be anywhere else in the world right now, and we have all chosen to be here. We've paid for a babysitter, put on a clean shirt, wrestled with traffic, searched for parking, spent our hard-earned money to buy a ticket—and now we're here! *Theatre artists: make use of us!* Speak to us! Why are we here? And why are you there onstage? Why are you not on Netflix? The vital theatre of the twenty-first century will be the theatre that innately understands why it's a live event and reminds us why we, as humans, continue to live.

TORONTO

Jordan Tannahill (b. 1988) is a novelist, playwright, and director of film and theatre whose work has been translated into twelve languages. His plays, performance texts, and productions have been presented at venues in London, New York City, Berlin, Vienna, Toronto, and Montreal. He has twice won Canada's Governor General's Literary Award for Drama, and his second novel, *The Listeners*, was shortlisted for the 2021 Giller Prize and adapted into a series for the BBC.

THORNTON WILDER

PETERBORO, N.H., JULY 12, 1940

I THINK THAT the lapse of time is the best critical activity in the world, and that the verdicts of posterity are right.

I am afraid that your inquiry will encourage a lot of needless young iconoclasts to disparage Virgil, Cervantes, Molière, and Milton.

I beg you not to give publicity to any such deprecations unless you have (1) the critic's assurance that he can read the despised classic in its original language, (2) some evidence that he has read the work carefully, (3) that he has some knowledge of literature and its history.

American writer Thornton Wilder (1895–1975) won three Pulitzer Prizes for his novel, *The Bridge of San Luis Rey* (1927), and two plays, *Our Town* (1938) and *The Skin of Our Teeth* (1948). To date, he is the only writer to win Pulitzers for both fiction and drama. In 1940 Roy Temple House wrote to a number of writers, including Wilder, to gauge their opinions about "The World's Worst Book." The results were published in the Winter 1941 issue of *Books Abroad*. About Wilder's letter, House wrote: "Wilder is severe, but reasonable. We accept his terms, and have tried to observe them."

LITERATURES OF THE NEAR EAST: A GENERATION OF RENEWAL (1972)

TALÂT SAIT HALMAN

THE CONVENTIONAL EPITHET for the Near East is the cradle. In it, numerous major civilizations grew, countless states came into being and died, and three of the world's major religions—Judaism, Christianity, and Islam—emerged. In modern times the region's political and cultural life is marked by upheaval. There is rebirth in the cradle.

Literature in the Near East is in search of a new identity. In the past half-century the area itself has witnessed vast changes as well as violent strife: the Ottoman Empire collapsed and gave way to the progressive Turkish Republic in 1923. European colonialism held Arab lands under its yoke. Most Arab nations went through monarchic rule, witnessed the fall of dynasties, and finally became republics. After long years of bitter conflict, the state of Israel was created. For a quarter-century, the Arab–Israeli clashes, culminating in tragic battles, in destruction and refugee camps, have been playing havoc with peace and progress in much of the region, which has also witnessed internecine strife—Muslim against Muslim, Arab against Arab.

No region of the world has ever had a wider variety of regimes in so short a period: Near Eastern countries in modern times have been ruled by emperors, kings, sheikhs, benevolent dictators, petty tyrants, small juntas and crowded juntas, one-party dictatorship, constitutional monarchy, military-civilian administration, and parliamentary democracy. The range in governmental organization has included American-style democratic institutions, sharia (Muslim holy law), Israeli socialism, Arab socialism, fascism, et cetera. The Near East has seen tooth-and-nail combat for independence, bloody coups d'état, bloodless takeovers, minority revolts, and assassination or execution of kings, presidents, prime ministers.

Today the Near East is torn within itself between those who control its major resources (particularly oil) and those—the vast multitudes—who live in abject poverty, between dominant traditions and the progress that westernization seems to promise, between the Soviet Union and the United States, both of which are vying for the region's oil and geopolitics. Arabs, Iranians, Turks, and Israelis are living under strong external pressures, but the clashes, which form their vital reality, are internal. The Near East is experiencing a double convulsion—"crisis culture" and "culture crisis." Western civilization exerted its impact on Arab lands during many decades of colonial rule. In Israel, Western influences became established almost organically, thanks to the emigration from Europe and America. Turkey and Iran consciously and systematically embraced the West. Although disillusionment with and resentment against the West have been increasing, Near Eastern cultural elites still look to Europe and America, to former colonial rulers, teachers, allies, clients, and suppliers from the West for the urgently needed technological methods, materials, and tools. The exposure to Western civilization has meant the end of the indigenous political systems, of theocratic rule, of religious law. It has also meant the weakening of Islam's hold over daily life, national culture, and education in Arab countries, Turkey, and Iran. The quest for Western culture has accelerated the loss of traditions.

Near Eastern literatures have a long and impressive legacy, the youngest going back more than twelve centuries. By the nineteenth century, Arabic, Persian, Hebrew, and Turkish were suffering from their own ancient and tired traditions, from lack of self-renewal. Cultural contact with the West placed at the disposal of Near Eastern authors a whole spectrum of literary forms and values. Most Arab, Turkish, and Persian writers, perhaps grudgingly, but certainly with conviction, started to imitate and emulate Western literatures. As in such fields as technology, medicine, political and social institutions, they felt there was no other creative alternative. "There is only one civilization in the world," a prominent Turkish intellectual wrote sixty years ago, "and that is Western civilization."

For decades Near Eastern countries have willingly, sometimes voraciously, absorbed the patterns of Western cultures. This assimilation has not always been without evaluation, criticism, or comparison. The prominent Egyptian writer Tawfiq al-Hakim has observed: "Europe's strength lies in its mind; Egypt's strength lies in its head." The famous Turkish poet Mehmet Akif Ersoy disparaged Western civilization as "the dragon which has only one tooth left." Most Near Eastern authors who resent having to bow to Western military and technological superiority salvage their cultural self-esteem by stressing with pride the long literary heritage and the humanistic values of their nations. Now, following decades of anxious and envious imitation, a strong reaction against the West has emerged. Perhaps the most fruitful approach is "syncretism." Eminent writers like the Egyptian Taha Hussein, for example, have emphasized the importance of bringing about a confluence or synthesis of cultures rather than exclusive reliance on the West or remaining within the confines of indigenous traditional culture. Particularly in Arabic writing, there has been extensive debate about East versus West in such broad categories as soul versus intellect, spirit versus materialism, humanism versus modern technology, et cetera. Most Western-oriented Near Eastern writers realize at long last that trying to meet the West on its own terms can at best lead to a pyrrhic victory—the production of excellent imitations or copies which are as good as the originals and are thereby failures in terms of creative achievement. Nationalism in the Near East has fluctuated between "revival of native culture" and "assimilation of Western norms and values." In the entire region, there is fierce pride in "our glorious history," "our dazzling culture," et cetera. The mystique of the past nurtures national solidarity as the foundation of political ideology, but also for purposes of national survival. Literature has often conveyed the hyperboles of chauvinism. The Egyptian-born Syrian author Rashid Rida flatly states that Arabs are "in truth the best nation born into the world." The Israelis continue to regard themselves as "the chosen people." Iran lavishly boasts of her grandeur while the Turks take pride in quoting a line by the patriotic poet Mehmet Emin Yurdakul: "I am a Turk, my faith and my nation are supreme."

In seeking progress and prosperity, nationalism has embraced westernization even at the expense of acculturation. While traditionalists uphold neoclassicism or folklore for the creation of a viable and valuable "national" literature, the majority of Near Eastern authors have looked to—and still look to—Europe and America for modes of modernization.

To what extent is the past useful or necessary for a literature seeking a new identity, striving to modernize itself, to join the mainstream of an alien—at times hostile—civilization? Egyptian novelist Naguib Mahfouz has stated this dilemma: "The truth is that my mind is sometimes convinced of the revolution, but my heart is always with the past. And the problem is whether there could be a reconciliation between my heart and my mind." In a much-quoted line, the neoclassical Turkish poet Yahya Kemal Beyatlı tried to resolve the problem: "I am the future with roots in the past." There is indeed the tendency in Near Eastern literatures to borrow from yesterday for tomorrow.

Tradition and the past are utilized in a whole variety of ways: neoclassical poetry perpetuates lyrico-philosophical values, including the ethics and the aesthetics, of classical verse as well as the popular traditional stanzaic forms like the "ghazal," "rubai," et cetera. History—usually as a corollary of romantic nationalism—is presented in sweeping panoramas. Arab writers like Farid Abu Hadid use history and legends for symbolic depictions. Israeli authors utilize biblical themes and stories, Hebraic myths and symbols, as can be observed in the works of Agnon, Shamir, Raab, et al. Egyptian Al-Hakim consciously seeks inspiration in the past, as in *Avdat al-Ruh* (Return of the Spirit) and treats a Greek legend—the seven sleepers of Ephesus. Numerous Turkish poets and playwrights—Gungor Oilmen, Melih Cevdet Anday, Selahattin Batu, Refik Erduran, Orhan Asena—have produced major works utilizing Greek and other non-Turkish legends. Near East literatures still have much "recollection of the past in tranquility," as in the Egyptian Shawki's poetry, which experiments with meters and forms, but retains the classical spirit, or the Iranian Rashid Yasimi's reflective lyric poems which remain faithful to conventions. Many Israeli authors utilize their long cultural legacy with a sense of confidence. Yitzhak Orpaz, for instance, endeavors to arrive at a Jewish and European cultural synthesis.

In Near Eastern literatures innovation is inspired by the West; it does not emanate from new valuations of tradition. The old literatures in Arabic, Persian, Hebrew, and Turkish have gone West. A vast majority of their ideas and ideologies, norms and values, genres and aesthetic views are borrowed from European and American literatures. Poetry of course is the oldest and the proudest achievement of Near Eastern cultures. But fiction (distinct from the antiquated narratives, i.e., *mathnavis* written in verse) is an "import." The novel made its appearance in Turkey a hundred years ago, in Iran at the end of the nineteenth century, and only fifty-five years ago in Arabic, while Hebrew novellas date back to the 1820s and the first Hebrew novels to the 1850s. European-style legitimate theater is barely a century old in the Near East. Today Israel is quite active in the dramatic arts and Turkey can boast of the richness and the superior quality of its theater, but Iran and the Arab countries are still at the incipient stages of theatrical activity and dramatic writing.

The influences on Near Eastern writers read like "Who's Who in European and Anglo-American Literatures": Sartre, Eliot, Mallarmé, Verlaine, Camus, Brecht, Faulkner, Beckett, Mayakovsky, Kafka, Éluard, Prévert, Joyce, Wallace Stevens, Albee, Pound, exponents of the nouveau roman, German Romantics, and Russian symbolists. All Western philosophical movements, literary schools, aesthetic fashions, ranging from existentialism to epic theater, from socialist realism to concrete poetry, from stream of consciousness to the theater of the absurd, have found disciples in the Near East.

Social and political concerns are paramount in Near Eastern literatures. A vast number of authors place their arts and crafts in the service of their nations, ideologies, and communities. This is to be expected in countries which are new political entities, or caught in strife, and in communities beset by economic ills and evils. The traditional "art for art's sake" attitude lingers in some literary circles, but it is often overshadowed by the literature of engagement. Ibn Khaldun's once influential idea that the art of poetry is concerned only with words and not with thoughts finds few followers. Patriotic poetry and topical verse, fashionable in the region since the mid-nineteenth century, are still in practice although looked down upon by the literati for their rhetoric and bombast.

Among the leading literary figures of the Near East are progressive militants, firebrand Marxists, European-style socialists, passionate reformers, vehement critics of the establishment, relentless satirists. Turkey has produced the internationally famous Marxist poet Nâzım Hikmet Ran, far-left novelists like Yaşar Kemal, Orhan Kemal, and Kemal Tahir, and leftist satirist Aziz Nesin. Iran's A. Q. Lahuti, Bozorg Alavi, Ali Dashti, Ali Jalali, et al. have vigorously protested social injustice. In Egypt, King Farouk had banned some of Hussein's novels as subversive propaganda. Many Syrian writers have gone underground. In many Near Eastern countries, during oppressive regimes, dozens of men of letters, who depict conditions of deprivation and who protest inequities, have been jailed. Hebrew literature has also served the function of communication and propaganda of Zionist ideals.

Socially committed authors are not mere publicists but accomplished men of letters who use the best resources of their languages. Arabic poetry about Palestine, for instance, rises from the level of invective to poignant beauty and tragic impact in the hands of a poet like the Syrian Nizar Qabbani. Women's rights, a recurrent theme in Arabic and Persian fiction, can be treated without rancor but with effective subtleness by masterful storytellers like Layla Baalbaki, Colette Suhayl, Muhammad Hijazi, and Abdel Quddous. The Arab–Israeli conflict has produced, in addition to much drivel, a number of excellent novels, i.e., Halim Barakat's *Six Days*, Abdel Quddous's *Far from Earth*, Haim Hazaz's chronicle of the Israelis' fight for independence, Shimoni's stories of the pioneers in their new state.

The socialist-realism movement is widespread in Near Eastern literatures. The output of short stories in this vein has been particularly impressive and deservedly popular. In Arabic, Mahmoud Taymur has excelled in the genre. In Iran, Ali Jamalzadeh has been notably effective in exposing social malady through his fiction. In Turkey, a whole generation of writers, beginning with Sabahattin Ali, has created awareness of rural poverty in "Village Fiction," a genre devoted to exploring the economic and psychic plight of peasants. The Egyptian Abdal Rahman Sharqawi, who wrote after the 1952 revolution, "A writer in this age cannot be just a writer. He must adopt a message. His message should be to defend life, the future of mankind, and the spiritual heritage of civilization," produced *Al Ard* (The Earth), which won accolades as a paragon of revolutionary literature for depicting village realities and affirming faith in the peasant as the folk hero. Village fiction, as represented by Yaşar Kemal, Fakir Baykurt, Necati Cumalı, et al., commands wide popularity in Turkey and perhaps constitutes the best achievement of modern Turkish fiction. As the Iranian Bahar puts it, literature in the Near East assigns itself the duty of serving social causes: "The aims of poetry can be attained if one writes for the sake of the people, in the interest of the people, according to the demands of the people, and in the language of the people." So, the war against the "ivory tower" litterateurs goes on: in Iran, Aḥmad Gulchīn

Ma'ānī berates the neoclassical "nightingale and roses" school, and Dihati, like Zola, delineates grim social conditions while some extremists use literature to wave the banners of revolution. In Turkey, satirists Aziz Nesin, Haldun Taner, and Rifat Ilgaz expose bureaucracy, political hypocrisy, and bourgeois morality.

Religious faith in Near Eastern literatures is a swiftly changing element and concern. Arab fiction and poetry retain a broad interest in Islam. In Israeli literature religious identification serves as part of national identification and as sociocultural context. Turkish and Iranian literatures are essentially free of religious allegiance. Islam's traditional fatalism looms large in fiction (least of all in Turkish). Unlike Israeli literature, which utilizes biblical material, Islamic literatures have a very flimsy Qur'anic content. In Turkey, where Atatürk's reforms have succeeded in secularizing high culture and the educational system, Islam is seldom a theme or motif in literature, except for attacks on religious reactionaries. Most Israeli writers are confident and comfortable about religion. However, as in the Islamic countries, Israeli literature reflects the antagonisms between progressive forces and regressive orthodoxy. The language of piety and a quasi-religious tone prevail in Agnon's work, which sometimes sermonizes and moralizes. Occasionally religious themes are used to depict man's degradation by means of biblical symbols and references, as in T. Carmi's work which emphasizes the importance of God or His absence. In Islamic countries some leading authors have spoken in favor of reconciling religion and progressive socialism: Egypt's Mahfouz is one author who has articulated the need for such a synthesis. But Islam, which vies for total control of man's soul and society, has not blended effectively with any ideology. Muslim men of letters, by the same token, have not succeeded in positing the principles of "Islamic socialism."

Some of the most impressive accomplishments of Near Eastern literature are in that vast nonsocial and apolitical domain which ranges from individualistic pure poetry to cosmic consciousness. Here the clash of old and new values, in social and aesthetic terms, has been resolved or removed. Lyrical hermeticism, bereft of all social concern, is the hallmark of David Rokeah and Amir Gilboa in Israel, Behcet Necatigil and İlhan Berk in Turkey, Forugh Farrokhzad in Iran, Abdel Sabour in Egypt. Israeli poets Avraham Shlonsky and Avigdor Hameiri are expressionists who have turned out escapist unconventional verse with bold metaphors and distorted imagery. Turkish neosurrealism, which proudly called itself "meaningless poetry" at the outset, the psychic exile and stark revulsions of the Syrian-born Lebanese poet Adonis, the struggle with man's spiritual anguish and salvation in Iranian Hossein Ghods Nakhai's work, exploration of reality through insanity in Benjamin Tammuz's fiction, the phantasmagoria of dejection and alienation expressed in Kafkaesque terms by the Persian Sadegh Hedayat, Israeli Aharon Megged, and Turkish Oktay Akbal are all moving documents of man's malaise in a hostile world. Israeli authors Yehoshua Bar-Joseph and Shloshah Sheazvu depict the terror of death in a godless universe, and Natan Alterman gives a chilling portrayal of violence and despondency in human existence.

The hero in Near Eastern literatures emerges either as true to life, in realistic proportions, or as a tragic being embattled by forces he cannot control let alone vanquish. Orhan Veli Kanık in Turkey and Zalman Shneour have delineated an idealized common man—Everyman is hero. Few heroes in Near Eastern fiction project the vision of larger life, of the power to transcend their human limits, but nonheroes and antiheroes abound. Most protagonists in recent novels are gripped by despair, alienated, gloomy. They are often presented by means of internal monologue, stream-of-consciousness, expressionistic devices, and appear as exiles from reality. But there are characters in fiction and drama who accentuate man's affirmative aspects. Not all themes and personae are vehicles for pessimism. Iran's Bihadhin and Turkey's "abstractionists," like Melih Cevdet Anday and Oktay Rifat, refuse to submit to despair although they, too, acknowledge man's absurdities. Satirists, although they criticize man's foibles and fallacies, renew the readers' faith in man's essential goodness, as shown by the comic characters of Hijazi in Iran, Kishon in Israel, and Nesin in Turkey.

Near Eastern literatures are witnessing the emergence of a new humanism, which is even softening the harsh misanthropy and the abysmal despair of the "literature of alienation." Socialist realists have feverishly endeavored to create a human and social ideal. Even in works divorced from social concerns there is deep compassion. Israeli poetry has followed the lead of Saul Tchernichovsky, "the poet of revolt": "I the dreamer say to you / That I believe in man / Because I still believe in you." Yehiel De-Nur has depicted the love of a one-time Auschwitz inmate and an Israeli girl who dedicate themselves to the idea of coalescence between Arabs and Jews. Yizhar has written a poignant story about an Israeli soldier who, for simply human reasons, feels like freeing an innocent and suffering Arab prisoner.

The language crisis is a crucial fact of Near Eastern literatures. Hebrew is in a process of rejuvenation. Turkish has gone through cataclysmic changes—alphabet, vocabulary, syntax—since the late 1920s. Arabic varies from country to country, and Arabic literature remains in the grip of the clash between literary versus colloquial language, unable to forge a middle language. Only Persian has had relative continuity, but, like the other languages of the region, it has been forced to change in order to accommodate the new norms and devices adopted from Western literatures during the process of modernization.

In most of the Near East there is a publication explosion (fifty thousand titles published in Turkey alone in the past ten years), and an abundance of translations. Israel and Turkey are surfeited with translations. No important Western author or poet goes unnoticed, it seems. By contrast there is remarkably and regrettably little cross-fertilization within the region, even between Iran and Turkey, which are close friends and allies.

Israeli literature finds broad exposure in Europe and America, but there is precious little translation from Arabic, Turkish, and Persian into the major Western languages. Perhaps as a result of this neglect, some Near Eastern authors write in foreign languages themselves—Andrée Chedid, Fereydoun Hoveyda, Sadeq Hedayat, Vahé Katcha in French; Halide Edib Adıvar, Edward Atiyah, and E. M. Esfandiary in English.

Critical evaluation is steadily gaining ground and provides significant perspectives for creative activity. Criticism, although considerably behind its Western counterparts, has become influential in Israel, Egypt, and Turkey in the past two decades.

The best literary output of the Near East seems to be the work of individualist writers who have steeped themselves in the best resources of their languages, who have a profound appreciation of their respective cultures and literatures, and who avoid slavish imitation of the West and create a synthesis of legacies. Among them are Agnon and Orpaz in Israel, Al-Hakim and Abdel Quddous in Egypt, Nâzım Hikmet

Ran, Fazıl Hüsnü Dağlarca, and Kemal Tahir in Turkey, and Hedayat in Iran. These and many other prominent Near Eastern authors have created out of their culture and concerns—crisis of faith, rural poverty, the Holocaust, private nightmares, love and death, squalor in cities, injustice, hope and salvation—literary works which constitute their real and ideal world.

PRINCETON UNIVERSITY

Talât Sait Halman (1931–2014) was a Turkish poet, translator, cultural historian, and Turkey's first minister of culture. He wrote or translated over eighty books; published some three thousand articles, essays, newspaper columns, and reviews; and translated thousands of poems, including the poetry of Shakespeare, Langston Hughes, and Wallace Stevens. This essay introduced a selection of eight articles on Near Eastern literature that appeared in the Spring 1972 issue of *Books Abroad*, which Professor Halman guest-edited.

READING LATE AT CAMPAGNATICO   (2000)

DAVID MALOUF

A lighted room high up
among others at this hour
dark. My neighbours sleep,

so many windows
in a sky fogged with breath.
The traveller sees

from far off a light
hung low among clouds,
so close, another planet.

It is the book
I'm lost in, as mind
swings loose on a fresher track

and green as ever was
on this star, into fields all
folk, all creatures,

a concordance of such
breathy quick
ghosts sharing my watch.

David Malouf (b. 1934) is a poet, novelist, and laureate of the 2000 Neustadt International Prize for Literature. Born to Lebanese and British parents in Brisbane, Malouf has published numerous novels as well as collections of poetry and short stories. He was made an Officer in the Order of Australia in 1987 and an Australian National Living Treasure in 1997.

HEAVY LIES THE WORLD ON THE PEN (2024)

ANANDA DEVI

The enemy resides not in the triumph of evil but in chaos.
The confusion of values is worse than their disappearance.

—Elie Wiesel, "A Vision of the Apocalypse"

HOW HEAVY the world lies, today, on the pen. . . . How fraught and weighted each word, each sentence, each piece of writing that we set on the page. And yet, how easy it is to spout lies and leave poisonous trails crisscrossing the earth in a few seconds, just as fighter jets leave their contrails in the blue sky long after they have gone to some unknown war. A soul-destroying mendacity, which has become the easiest solution for those who wish to rule, to dominate, to destroy, to grow the seeds of hate. How can different voices be heard, we ask, the voices of those who choose to bear witness, to delve into each subject in order to sift truth from fabrication, to try to understand the origins of conflicts rather than pass judgment without thought and inflict retribution without compassion?

How can one not feel powerless against this tsunami of hate? How do we even begin to fight?

The answer is closer than we think: I only have to look at my bookshelves, with all the books collected over the years—some falling to pieces from having so often been read, others waiting to be rediscovered—to feel a sense of hope, of brightness, of elation: here, set out black on white, here is a universe so powerful it breaks open all cages and soars over all boundaries, here is the world that we know and wish for, and it has been here all the time . . .

Indeed, it came into existence as soon as humans acquired language and began to weave their lives into a tapestry of fiction and imagination. It has existed as long as *we* have existed, and will continue to do so, despite all attempts to silence it. This tapestry of hope and dreams and resistance, this story of human greatness and history of human transcendence, are here for us to see, to hold in our hands, and to drink in their glorious, intoxicating, and vulnerary absinthe.

To name but a few that face my writing table: Woolf, Eliot, Morrison, Albert Cohen, Plath, Céline, Molière, Aragon, Coetzee, Rimbaud, Dante, Calvino, Soyinka, Darwish, Arundhati Roy, Le Clézio, Césaire, Rushdie, Achebe, and, and, and—these are but a few of those I have read an untold number of times, and who still resonate as magnificently and tragically today as they did upon the first reading. These are some of the suns I gravitated toward and orbited as I grew up, both as a person and as a writer.

Just below them (not out of any sense of pretentiousness but because I need them to be easily accessible) are the thirty-odd books I have written over my own lifetime. The very first is a short story entitled "La Cite Attlee" that I wrote when I was fifteen, which was published in a French anthology. The very last is a nonfiction book entitled *La nuit s'ajoute à la nuit* (Night prolongs the night), published in 2024. It is about a World War II memorial in Lyon, France, a military prison built in 1921, where French Resistance fighters were incarcerated and where thousands of Jews (including forty-four children) were held before being shot or sent to the concentration camps. After the war, Nazis, German soldiers, and French collaborators were held there before their trials. Later on, French communists were imprisoned for protesting against the Indochina War (1946–54). During the Algerian war of independence, Algerian resistance fighters condemned to death were imprisoned in Montluc. Eleven of them were guillotined in this very prison. It subsequently became a common-law prison before closing for good in 2009. In a single place, in the very center of Lyon, almost a century of history has passed through, leaving its marks, its wounds, its tragic memories in the seeping walls; proof, if need be, of the criminal forgetfulness of humankind.

It made me realize that, from that first short story, published in 1973, to this last, very personal book, published in 2024, I haven't changed much as a writer. My preoccupations, my obsessions, the way I always wanted to inhabit other people and even sometimes animals, have been there from the start. I have always felt the need to listen to those whom the world rarely listened to. To become a kind of translator of bodies, minds, hearts, in order to fight against their erasure. I learned the craft of writing, of course, over these five decades, but I can recognize myself in that first collection of short stories, published when I was a teenager. How odd to think that something in me had been shaped since my childhood and would never change!

There were, I believe, three reasons for this: one was the themes I felt compelled to write about. I belong to the first generation of women of my family who had been given this extraordinary opportunity to be heard and read. As a Mauritian whose history bears the double wounds of colonial slavery and the transport of Indian laborers from India (not equal by any means, for the dehumanization of slavery is a unique crime), writing was, to my mind, a responsibility that I could never take lightly. I often say that several generations of my kinswomen seem to be reading over my shoulder—none more so than my maternal grandmother, whom I have never known, and who died mysteriously at twenty-two, and my mother, who bore the grief of loss. As far as I can remember, my mother railed against her powerlessness as a woman, despite the fact that she was an extremely intelligent, self-taught woman who read avidly and could hold conversations with the most learned of professors. This feeling of responsibility has never left me and is even more urgent today.

The second reason was my love of language. How I reveled in books, as soon as I learned to read on my father's knee when I was four years old! My father used to bring back to our village a boxful of books from the capital, Port-Louis, every Saturday. My sisters and I waited to pounce on them like lion cubs pouncing on their feed. Reading, indeed, fed us, nurtured us, made us grow up perhaps before our age, but there were no limits, our parents allowed us to read voraciously, and the eclectic nature of the books bought by my father helped widen our outlook in a way that would perhaps not be possible today. What I derived from this is an absolute passion for languages, not just words and meaning but the sonority of it, the sheer music of it. I didn't realize it at the time, but when I wrote, it was as much with my ears as with my mind, and not only that: with all my senses. So, when I am told I write poetically, it is true but not the whole story: I also write with my entire body.

The third reason brings me back to my starting point: I wasn't afraid. From that early age, and perhaps because I read many books intended for adults, I wasn't afraid of what I wrote. Of course, at the beginning, I didn't show any of it to my family. But once that first short story was published, they did read it and my other books. But I never allowed myself to fear either their reactions or those of my compatriots, especially as the image I gave of Mauritius was miles away from the tropical paradise that tourist brochures described. I didn't fear writing about the female body, or tragedy, or death. Once, when I was very young, my mother asked me if I was unhappy. I told her I wasn't, indeed, because as the youngest of three siblings, and my father's pet, I had been pampered since my birth. However, I had subconsciously absorbed my mother's sadness, and she herself hadn't realized how much she told me of her unhappy childhood. And thus, it has always been through her own prism that I saw the world. But again, there was no fear of what I wrote, even from that early age.

I am lucky to have been born at that time. It was a time when I started writing by hand, then typed on a small Olivetti typewriter, then on an electric golf-ball typewriter on which I also wrote my PhD thesis, and finally on a computer. But whichever medium I used, I have always felt free to write what I wanted, from whichever viewpoint I wanted. This is, after all, the point of being a writer: to be able to inhabit others and to do so with so much honesty and feeling that readers are able to feel inhabited by them in the same way. Even if the characters are as repulsive and monstrous as my narrator is in *Le sari vert*.

Dostoevsky said that, "while nothing is easier than to denounce the evildoer, nothing is more difficult than to understand him." Here we find the key to how writers are able to shed light on the world and illuminate it. By delving into the darkest recesses of the human mind and heart, they help us, readers, to find a way out through understanding. When the road is at its darkest, literature brings forth its own light to guide us through, not with answers but with questions that we often fail or fear to ask ourselves.

And thus it is that, while we follow these Virgils into the deepest levels of hell, the language itself, the poetry and the humanity of their thoughts and creations, make the unbearable bearable and help us navigate these troubled paths. All art, in this sense, opens a door into truths we dare not face. Where modern communications show us in real time every tragic event happening in the world behind the comfort and protection of our screens, writers and artists make us step out of this comfort and protection to become and inhabit their protagonists' fate. In what other context can we become so acutely, so obsessively, so painfully someone else? And

I will not say *the Other*, because this is precisely the point: it is no longer the Other but ourselves that we meet in stories, as their magic works upon us. After all, myths are the great common denominator of all cultures, going back to early human societies, to the fabulous paintings of Lascaux. Myths have always been our way of resolving the enigma of our selves, our presence, our existence, our reality. As opposed to religion, whose dogma (as seen by men) prevents deep questioning or changes, myths adapt themselves endlessly to our thought processes and our emotions. They are ever renewable, reinterpretable, elastic, organic.

Jean Cocteau, for example, reworked the Oedipus myth in *La machine infernale*, using modern language and yet conveying viscerally the horror of Oedipus's and Jocasta's fate. Anouilh did the same with *Antigone*, following the next generation of the story. Not only did they keep these myths alive, they also made them as urgent and relevant to us today as they were during Sophocles' times. "Le temps des hommes est de l'éternité pliée," writes Cocteau: human time is folded eternity. Fate (or history), says Cocteau, is the pin that pierces the folded cloth of time. When it is unfolded, nobody would guess that each of these pinholes was made by a single pin. Today, too, we must remember that every historical event, every tragedy, every atrocity is linked by a long chain of human cruelty and barbarity. Nothing happens in a vacuum. The responsibility is ours, all of us.

I was recently asked to write a foreword to a translation of *La machine infernale* in Mauritian Creole. The title of the play in Creole is *Kales kase*, the broken chariot. While referring to Cocteau's infernal machine, a broken *deus ex machina* that might have saved Oedipus but didn't do so, or else one that appeared only to strike him down, the Creole title also referred (consciously or subconsciously on the part of the translator) to a story from the Ramayana, which dates back to 700 BCE: the king and queen of Ayodhya, in Northern India, are traveling in a flying chariot when the queen realizes that one of the wheels is coming lose because of a missing screw. Without saying anything to the king, she inserts her little finger into the hole and prevents the wheel from falling. When they land, the king realizes that she has irreparably damaged her finger while saving their life. Filled with sorrow and gratitude, he tells her that she can ask anything of him, and he swears on his life to fulfill her request. She replies that she will do so when she has something important to ask.

Many years later, she will ask him to disinherit his firstborn son, Rama, who was destined to be king, and to send him into exile for fifteen years, while naming her own son as his heir and king. And thus, that broken chariot, the *kales kase*, sets up a sequence of events that will lead to the great war between India and Sri Lanka, and the entire story of the Ramayana.

It was wonderful to find this unexpected link between the Greek myth of Oedipus, via Cocteau's unsettling French play, and the Indian myth of the Ramayana, via a translation into Mauritian Creole. It amazed me once again how my own birth in Mauritius, from a family of Indian origin, together with the Creole language, my Western-based education, and my cultural proximity to the African continent and especially to African writers, have made of me a hybrid creature and allowed me to fully appreciate the complex connections and exquisite interlacing of all these different cultures. Proof, if need be, that works of art are endlessly malleable and able to transcend all kinds of frontiers, which is precisely why great art is universal.

This is why *The Odyssey*, the Mahabharata, *Don Quixote*, Shakespeare's plays, and so many texts have kept on living over centuries and millennia. Contemporary ones will do so too, as far as they open up worlds, unfurl an immensity of wonders, constellations both close to us and infinitely far: burning suns and the birth of a single bud at our feet are all miracles at which to marvel. They also lead us to rethink our own place amidst these miracles: are we part of them or have we decided that, as the dominant species, we are free to destroy them through our actions and through a distorted form of language?

The language of social media tends to imprison people in a bubble where their beliefs are set in stone and reinforced by a self-sustaining phenomenon that leaves out any ambiguity, complexity of thought, balanced outlook, or questioning of oneself. This is the opposite of what writers try to do. The language of social media is not that of the world: it is the *narrowest* expression of the world, one person's beliefs, to the detriment of any constructive thinking, of any enlightenment, and especially of any creative undertaking. Writers, on the contrary, bring us the world in its myriad expressions, shapes, forms, beauty. And in this, the translators who work alongside them are to be honored far more than they have been, because without them, we would not have had access to this treasure trove.

But a word of warning is needed at this juncture: when Oskar Maria Graf wrote about how the burning of books in 1933 by the government of Adolf Hitler was at the time ignored and derided but was in fact a foreshadowing of the horrors to come, it is as if he is writing for us too, right now. In the U.S., in Russia, in China, in Nigeria (where a jihadist group is actually called Boko Haram, i.e., education, or books, are forbidden), books are being banned, admittedly for different reasons. But are they really that different? If a book that does not conform with the dominant viewpoint is banned, is this not an early warning of a dictatorship? Democracy has shown its limits in many countries. We are teetering on a brink. Make no mistake about it: prohibiting books from being read is not an anodyne measure. It is the silencing of voices that leads to the silencing of reason, of compassion, of hope. Of humanity.

So, yes, the world today lies heavy on my pen. Heavy because I don't know if what I write has any weight by itself. Of course we writers cannot change the world. We have always known this. But the saying that the pen is mightier than the sword is being proven true in a disquieting way: increasingly, people are being pushed toward hate and violence by social media—namely, words that become swords, rather than leading toward compassion and justice. Can writers change this trend?

Can I? Can you? Can we?

Not alone, I'm afraid. Not alone. We need one another, and most of all we need these books, these writers who have been our guides, our cicerones, our sources of understanding and reason, to win back the power of our pen.

FERNEY-VOLTAIRE, FRANCE

One of the major literary voices of the francophone world, Mauritian writer Ananda Devi (b. 1957) is the author of thirty books, including novels, collections of poetry, short stories, and essays. She was awarded the Neustadt International Prize for Literature for the body of her work. She read this acceptance speech at the University of Oklahoma in October 2024.

CONCEIÇÃO LIMA

Translated from the Portuguese by Shook

> The enigma is some other thing—no gods live here
> Just men and the sea, immovable inheritance.

Conceição Lima (b. 1961) is a poet from the island nation of São Tomé and Príncipe. *No Gods Live Here*, a collection of her poetry translated by Shook, was published in 2024.

Raised in Mexico City, poet, translator, and filmmaker Shook founded the nonprofit publishing house Phoneme Media in 2013 and was a 2017 NEA Translation Fellow.

A GIRL IN LITLAND (2016)

DUBRAVKA UGREŠIĆ

Translated from the Croatian by Ellen Elias-Bursać

THE FIRST TWO BOOKS I wrote were for children. When I published my first book I was twenty-one. I soon gave up on writing children's literature when I realized that I didn't have the very particular god-given talent that only the exceptional writers for children possess. I still believe that the career of the children's author—with the gift of a Lewis Carroll—is the most joyous career a writer could wish for, and it is, at the same time, a "natural" choice: writing for children means living in an extended childhood. I say this because adults work at jobs that are useful, while children work at tasks that have no practical application. Literature, too, is a nonuseful task. It has no price tag, there can be no compensation for it—just as a child's drawing has no price tag—nor can it be manipulated, though many people are hard at work at precisely that, "manipulating" literature. Even writers, after all, do not hesitate to manipulate.

At a historical turning point for the cultural community it was decided that literature, this useless task, should be granted a more serious standing. The status of modern literature began at the moment when it became a subject of study at universities, and this happened only several hundred years ago. Any standing is vulnerable to change. In other words, a vast amount of time is needed to build a pyramid, even more to maintain it, but only a few short moments to tear it down. In this sense literature, as a system of knowledge devised and built by hardworking people over the centuries, is a fragile creation. Those who work at literature should keep this in mind. Perhaps it would be apt here to think back to Ray Bradbury's cult novel *Fahrenheit 451* as well as to the many postapocalyptic science-fiction movies. There are no books to be seen in the latter. At least I haven't seen one. And besides, when the time comes for everybody to start writing books—and that moment, thanks to technology, is upon us—there will no longer be literature. This is because literature is a system that requires arbitration. The arbiters used to be "people of good literary taste": theoreticians, critics, literature professors, translators, editors, and, don't forget, the attendant mediocrities: the censors, the salespeople, the "Salieris," the ideologues of various stripes—from religious to political. Today the market has anointed itself as arbiter, as have the readers. The market is allied with the "majority reader." Authors are no freer as a result—along with politicians and entrepreneurs, today authors are expected to *please* the consumer, to *lobby, blog, vlog, post, tweet,* to be *liked,* to spread with diligence to their digital fan base who will support them and buy their books.

I was born into a world in which the first technological wonder was the radio. I remember waking up at night and turning the big dial to move the red line across to the stations inscribed on the display while I listened to languages I didn't understand. Our radio was called a Nikola Tesla, and it had a green eye that glowed in the dark. I was born a few years after the close of World War II in a small country, poor and ravaged by war, where there was a pressing need to manufacture goods that were more utilitarian than those from a toy factory. That's why I got my first "real" doll when I was already too big to play with dolls. In my early childhood, what I found sensational had nothing to do with toys but with books, the radio, and Hollywood movies for grown-ups: the text, sound, and image gave me the illusion of flight from my provincial little town into the grand, thrilling world. I envisioned the world with the help of books, and the role played by interactivity—to use contemporary jargon—was huge. The field of the imagination is more circumscribed today; the cultural industry has satisfied every need we could only have dreamed of before. Here are our "prechewed" products (*Anna Karenina for Beginners*), or streamlined, readapted, and commercialized versions of original works (*Anna Karenina and the Zombies*), or experiments such as the use of hologram books. The new media today are filling the space of the imagination to its last inch: they are taking the soul, time, and money of their "consumers" and leaving nothing behind.

In my childhood and even in my student days, publishing was not yet referred to as an *industry*, nor was there a literary marketplace, and the borders between children's literature and writing for adults were not so sharply drawn. There were no psychologists hovering over the process of consumption; with passion we read whatever we could get our hands on. Thanks to the media and the marketplace, our taste today is standardized. The powerful industry nourishes every consumer capillary of the world. In the very poorest quarters of Kolkata, where people inhabit space the size of a matchbox, they may be impoverished, but miniature screens (television and otherwise) glow day and night from their makeshift abodes.

In the bygone days of Yugoslav publishing there used to be an unpopular penalty known as *the pulp tax*. Those who chose to satisfy the more "pedestrian" tastes of the readership had to pay a special tax for the pulp fiction they published. If the tax for pulp were to be levied at a global level, this would amass a vast store of money, which could be used for publishing both high-quality and inexpensive books for a free and fine education, for teachers, for artists, for the creative folk. All this can be imagined, of course, but the only thing that defies the imagination is the decision of who would evaluate what fiction is pulp and what isn't. And it bears mentioning that the terms *pulp fiction* and *kitsch* have faded from the parlance. Some thirty years ago kitsch was still a subject for discussion and a focus of research among theoreticians of art and literature. Then the powerful global market elbowed the concept of *kitsch* out of its vocabulary. Anything that separates the "wheat from the chaff" is undesirable in a global marketplace that works to sell everything, and sell as much of it as possible.

There are key tags to be found in the vocabulary of the brilliant sociologist Zygmunt Bauman that have relevance not only for our age but for the culture industry, including that of literature right now. One of them is *waste*. Our industrially hyperactive civilization generates, among other things, waste. With the most popular commands of *copy and paste* there appears the need for a command to *save*. Our digital age is shaping the mindset and physicality of the digital human. Our fingers are growing thinner, longer, and more adept, but we're keeping ophthalmologists busy as we constantly adjust the lenses in our eyeglasses. Our language, too, is changing. Now, not just children but adults rely on abbreviations and emoticons. Our emotions, too, have changed, as have our sensors for reception, our codes, our ways of communicating, and, foremost, our sense of time. We feel we're immersed in an all-accessible, domineering NOW. In this sense a feeling of cultural discontinuity has crept into older specimens of the human race, such as myself, despite the all-accessible search engines that can connect us, in seconds, to bygone times. In parallel to the emancipating and powerful sense of control through digital devices such as the smartphone, a *liquid fear*, as Bauman would put it, has come to dwell in people, a neurosis of insecurity (perhaps this being our need to leave millions of selfies in cyberspace to confirm that we lived).

The story "Who Am I?" was born out of a sense not only of security but of literary plenty thirty-three years ago, at a time when I was as happy as a mouse nesting in a wheel of cheese. My wheel of cheese was the library, a university job, the certainty that literature was autonomous and that the only thing worth dedicating myself to was literature. The short story that has been staged by the students from the OU Helmerich School of Drama, directed by Judith Pender, came about out of a powerful feeling of literary well-being, of continuity. I was intrigued by the idea of a defamiliarized reading within a profound familiarization with world literature.

Internet literature, the fan fiction I explored while writing my essay "Karaoke Culture," is today guided by a similar principle, but the canon is different. These are not classic works of the literary canon but belong to a new, contemporary canon of millions of readers and viewers: *Harry Potter*, *Twilight Saga*, *Hunger Games*, and others like them.

Because of all this, and perhaps because of my unjustified feeling that the system of literature as we know it is on the way out—what with digital civilization taking over Gutenberg civilization—we should invest all our energies in supporting people who are prepared to invest in literature, not in literature as a way to sustain literacy but as a vital, essential creative activity, people who will preserve the intellectual, the artistic, the spiritual capital. I couldn't have dreamed that one day a student theater in Norman, Oklahoma, would be putting on the first-ever staging of my story, written thirty-three years ago. Literary continuity, therefore, does exist, and the fact that it describes an unexpected geographical trajectory only heightens the excitement.

The literary landscape that has greeted me in Norman has touched me so deeply that I, briefly, forgot the ruling political constellations. I forgot the processes underway in all the nooks and crannies of Europe, I forgot the people who are stubbornly taking us back to some distant century, the people who ban books or burn them, the moral and intellectual censors, the brutal rewriters of history, the latter-day inquisitors; I forgot for a moment the landscapes in which the infamous swastika has been cropping up with increasing frequency—as it does in the opening scenes of Bob Fosse's classic film *Cabaret*—and the rivers of refugees whose number, they say, is even greater than that of World War II.

A continuity of literary evaluation does, nevertheless, exist. The knowledge of what is good literature has not been lost for good. This is a moment to recall Vladimir Nabokov and his words, which belong to the realm of sorely needed literary evaluation:

> There are three points of view from which a writer can be considered: he may be considered as a storyteller, as a teacher, and as an enchanter. A major writer combines all three—storyteller, teacher, enchanter—but it is the enchanter in him that predominates and makes him a major writer. . . . To the storyteller we turn for entertainment, for mental excitement of the simplest kind, for emotional participation, for the pleasure of traveling in some remote region in space or time. A slightly different though not necessarily higher mind looks for the teacher in the writer. Propagandist, moralist, prophet—this is the rising sequence. We may go to the teacher not only for moral education but also for direct knowledge, for simple facts. . . . Finally, and above all, a great writer is always a great enchanter, and it is here that we come to the really exciting part when we try to grasp the individual magic of his genius and to study the style, the imagery, the pattern of his novels or poems.

We are met here at the Neustadt Festival, a literary festival for celebrating the enchanter, whoever he or she may be. We have gathered to celebrate all those who have been, who are, and who will be our past, present, and future—enchanters . . .

AMSTERDAM

Born in the former Yugoslavia, Dubravka Ugrešić (1949–2023) established herself as one of Europe's most distinctive writers, with multiple novels, short-story and essay collections, and children's books to her credit. In 1991, when war broke out in her homeland, Ugrešić took a firm antiwar stance and became a target for nationalist journalists, politicians, and fellow writers; she left Croatia in 1993 and eventually settled in Amsterdam. As the 2016 Neustadt Prize laureate, she delivered this acceptance speech at the University of Oklahoma.

Ellen Elias-Bursać is an American scholar and literary translator of numerous works from Bosnian, Croatian, and Serbian, including three books by Dubravka Ugrešić. She is a past president of the American Literary Translators Association.

BOUBACAR BORIS DIOP

Translated from the French by Bojana Coulibaly

1

IN THIS PARTICULAR STORY, the orphan, who was coming of age, was named Youmané. I loved her name so much that I am not quite sure if I hadn't invented it myself. In fact, I was never passively listening to my mother-storyteller; my lively reactions were an integral part of the unfolding of her story. So, I am going to tell you the story of a young girl named Youmané.

Her mother had forbidden her from going to the nocturnal tam-tam sessions. But the tam-tam's calling made her lose her mind. Every night, she would secretly go there, "when the sand under her feet had turned cold," as my mother-storyteller would beautifully utter. Yet Youmané wasn't aware that she was the only human being in an assembly of supernatural creatures, the Jinne. There she fell in love with a young man, devilishly handsome of course. And what everybody dreaded the most ended up happening: she became pregnant. At this point, the storyteller had a serious problem: How to talk about the torrid sexual relationship between two lovers to children who were only eight or nine years old? I can still remember with an amused smile the narrative creativity of the storyteller; "every night," she would say, "a strong wind lifted Youmané's dress on her way back home." That was it. But after the wind swirled around her several times, which in fact were breezes of another kind, Youmané was pregnant!

What happened next? Whether Youmané was punished by her mother or whether her child became a great king, I had no idea at all. And to tell you the truth, it was because I wasn't really interested in finding out. I can only remember the dread with which my heart was beating when I imagined Youmané in the midst of the Jinne, with distorted or, worse, triangular faces, ready to drink her blood at any moment. The fact is that out of the hundreds of stories I had heard in my early childhood, only vague impressions have remained, images of dark-blue or gray colors, as in a painting, and in the abyss of twisted forms, vulnerable beings face-to-face with elements running wild. In fact, those frightened beings were often young women, like in the tale "Niantanta," which impressed me so much that I believe I have included it in every one of my novels in one form or another. What I quickly learned with these stories is the extent to which *what happens in a story*—its content, in sum—remains almost always accessory. One can very well stop reading a novel before even reaching its final page, after a good portion of the narrative dazzles. That's why every time someone asks me to sum up *Anna Karenina*—or other great fiction—I do my best but can't stop thinking that they don't know what writing is actually about.

Indeed—shouldn't we consider this to be universally true?—tales should only be narrated at night. It made more truthful and worrisome the supernatural realm that I became familiar with, even before my reading of Ahmadou Kourouma or Amos Tutuola, and later Latin American authors from Juan Rulfo to Julio Cortázar, Gabriel García Márquez or the Argentine Ernesto Sábato, one of my favorite novelists. In other words, I wasn't really impressed by "magical realism" since, in Macondo, I was on familiar ground.

I know it may sound paradoxical, but those oral tales have been my best writing workshop, even before French school initiated me to the mystery of the alphabet. The aura of those beautiful stories was primarily the result of a sort of impenetrability. The whole of their meaning resided in a sort of orgy of sound and a power of suggestion that gave them a rare intensity. I strongly believe, had I not got lost in the imaginary maze of my mother-storyteller, that I wouldn't later have experienced such a great pleasure in reading, again and again, fully esoteric tales. I never felt dismayed for not being able to access "the message"—the most terrible word of all—of an author. The truth is, most texts have been and still are a delight to me by their sole vibration and because they scattered, so to speak, in all directions. It is not surprising that I chose to make Khadidja, the heroine of my third novel, *The Knight and His Shadow*, a peerless storyteller.

2

A few years before hearing those tales, the town of Thiès, Médina—the district in Dakar where I was born—had been my school of life, or rather my street school, as we lived in it by lack of choice. It is only now in retrospect that I realize what a filthy, poor slum it was, as we see today in certain outer zones of Dakar. As a teenager, I didn't see the misery of Médina but instead the glorious modernity of a place that was, at that time, the source of all new trends. In Médina, called Niarela in my novel *Doomi Golo*, the most brilliant minds would meet: doctors and lawyers, artists and athletes, particularly those who are still remembered as Senegalese soccer and basketball legends.

Médina was adjacent to the European district of Plateau, against which it constantly measured itself, although this was during the colonial era. In between they built in Rebeuss the biggest prison of the country—which is still there—and which was frequently visited by some of our elders adept at defying the law, especially the laws of the *toubab*, the white man. One of them was Yadikone, a kind of Robin Hood, immortalized by the great filmmaker Djibril Diop Mambéty. Médina was also, naturally, the stage of epic political confrontations between the "red party" of Lamine Guèye's Senegalese Socialist Party (SFIO/PSS) and the "green party" of the poet Léopold Sédar Senghor, who was more progressive—or maybe less reactionary—than his "socialist" rival (who, anecdotally, was my maternal great-uncle). Senghor ultimately became the father of independent Senegal and its first president. The country could have found someone better, but that is another story . . .

Médina is also where a few friends and I created the "Culture and Leisure Club." Its main members were the Bèye twins, Assane and Ousseynou; Ben Diogaye Bèye, who became a renowned filmmaker; the late Assane Preira; and finally Babacar MBow, the Master of Ndem (aka "Chacun"), who today is a respected figure of Muridiyya spirituality. Near the area of the Corniche we had a "ciné-club" where we discussed for hours and hours the very first African films, all short features, as well as Momar Thiam's *Sarzan* and *Black Girl*, by Ousmane Sembène, the father of African cinema, whose *Borom Sarret* was frequently at the center of our debates. There was also *Afrique-sur-Seine*, by Paulin Soumanou Vieyra, and one of our favorites, *Et la neige n'était plus*, by Ababacar Samb-Makharam. However, our most common activities revolved around books. While I discovered there Malick Fall's *La plaie*, Sembène's *God's Bits of Wood*, Cheikh Hamidou Kane's *Ambiguous Adventure*, and Aké Loba's *Kocoumbo, l'étudiant noir*, our choice of reading went far beyond Africa's borders.

In our sometimes-stormy reading sessions we read Camus's *L'étranger* or another French classic. And Gregor Samsa's name, the main character of Kafka's *The Metamorphosis*, would often come up in our jokes. I remember also that one of us, Ousseynou Bèye—to this day one of my best friends—loved to repeat, "Thank God, at least we can act," like Chen in *Man's Fate*, by André Malraux. We would also organize discussions about economics and politics. I found out later that our early taste for politics had attracted the attention of an underground Communist movement that would regularly send us their recruiters. To top it all off, we created a journal—mimeographed, of course—titled *Le bourgeon*. I had myself found the title in an article by the poet David Mandessi Diop, who died in a plane crash off the coast of Dakar at the age of thirty-three, in which he wrote the following: "Literature is the expression of reality in movement. It begins where reality starts, captures it, seizes it while it is just a bud [*bourgeon*], and helps it bloom." Thinking back, I am stunned that we were able to do so much at such a young age. . . .

Even so, it is not surprising that I wrote my first novel, entitled *La cloison*, when I was about sixteen. It was handwritten, of course, with the seriousness of a shy teenager who had a severe stutter. The novel was about the friendship between Kader Cissé, a Senegalese adolescent, and his French classmate Lucien Gercet. They were both of modest circumstances and met at Van Vollenhoven, a high school with mostly white students and teachers. I was attending it too and felt discriminated against by the teachers, especially by Monsieur Nègre, which was indeed an unexpected name for a racist. *La cloison* therefore "courageously" denounced racism, and, in a candid, happy ending, the partition, symbolic of the division between the two races, spectacularly caught fire, allowing Kader and Lucien to be reconciled forever.

I didn't write a novel of more than two hundred pages just like that for no reason and without knowing what I wanted to do with it. I would pretend that I was published like all the great authors I had such pleasure reading and rereading. The manuscript was sent from Dakar to the

Parisian publisher Présence Africaine, which was everyone's lodestar at the time. In response, I received a standard rejection letter signed by a certain Jacques Howlett. That name is the only thing I remember from this failed initial publishing experience.

Very quickly afterward came the time when, in the Faculté des Lettres of Cheikh Anta Diop University (UCAD), we had to read the Marxist classics and make a clear choice between Mao, Tito, Stalin, Trotsky, or Enver Hoxha. It luckily didn't prevent us from also reading Cheikh Anta Diop, Frantz Fanon, Mongo Beti, Amílcar Cabral, and Aimé Césaire. In fact, all those authors well complemented one another. Much could be said about that period, including with regard to the "Club Frantz Fanon," founded in a neighborhood in Dakar to which my mother had moved.

I soon became an even more avid and solitary reader. The American Cultural Center gave me the opportunity to read all of Steinbeck but also some less well-known novelists like Erskine Caldwell. I read Faulkner's *Light in August* and Richard Wright's *Native Son*. At the French Cultural Center, I discovered and read all the books by Jean-Paul Sartre, except his monumental and cryptic philosophical treatises. I ended up declaring myself an existentialist when everybody around me was wild about Marxism. I admired so much Boris Serguine, a character from Sartre's trilogy *The Roads to Freedom*, that it gave me my pen name. Like everybody else I was very fond of Latin American literature to the point of writing in my first novel, *Le temps de Tamango*, that "*One Hundred Years of Solitude* is the absolute masterpiece of universal literature." This was a naïve enthusiasm of my youth, but it also showed the emotional shock triggered by García Márquez's novel. My opinion about his book would be much more measured today!

These eclectic reading experiences and all the activities I was engaged in, often at a very early age, coincided well with the typical journey of a francophone writer.

3

There was, however, a sudden halt for me after 1998. It was the year I went to Rwanda for the first time with a group of writers from different

African countries to assess the extent of damage caused by the 1994 genocide against the Tutsi. The organizers of the project asked us to provide a fictional testimony of our experience, but only if we wanted to. This exceptional initiative, involving ten African authors going to investigate at ground zero of an enormous contemporary tragedy, was called "Rwanda: Writing as a Duty of Memory." This experience gradually led me to put the genocide against the Tutsi at the center of my reflection and to give a greater importance to my mother tongue in my creative writing. In sum, it ultimately led me to convey in Wolof a genocide that had completely turned my mental sphere upside down.

The Knight and His Shadow is the first book I wrote that mentions the genocide in Rwanda. It had devastated the country four years earlier, and having never been interested in it, I saw in the genocide, with the typical contempt of the writers of my generation, yet another African disaster. I was so ignorant about the real facts that had occurred between April and July 1994 in Rwanda that my narrative lightheartedly blurred the line between the perpetrators and their victims. The leaders of refugee camps in the former Zaire, whom I depicted as heroes, were in fact the masterminds of the genocide who had fled Rwanda after having committed the worst atrocities. The episode indeed only takes up a small amount of space in *The Knight and His Shadow*, but it was nonetheless embarrassing, given the historical importance of the event.

The genocide in 1994, when at least ten thousand people were killed every day for one hundred days and without a single day of reprieve, involved Tutsis being butchered with machetes, burned alive, thrown alive in cesspools, or deliberately infected with HIV. A gigantic disaster had befallen a small African country, and, four years later, I was still reading it upside down. By digging a little bit, I realized that if African tragedies repeat themselves with such a sinister regularity, it is because either we don't know how to prevent them or we simply accept not to *see* them at the very moment they are destroying entire countries.

How not to question oneself after such a realization? I didn't want to let myself be trapped by the old stereotypes, which perceive Africa as a bloodthirsty place where tribes massacre one another, almost for no reason, since time immemorial. That is why *Murambi: The Book of Bones* is by far my most documentary novel. To write it, I read many books and articles and watched every movie on this topic I could find. I talked to survivors and to killers in prison. A harvest of facts, which I insisted on using with great caution, had emerged. For example, I made sure that the realistic description of certain barbaric acts did not incite the reader to see the entire novel as pure invention and thus remain in their comfort zone. In fact, the old question whether we can write fiction or not about genocide was tormenting me: Who would indeed believe that something like *this* actually happened?

That's exactly why any novel about genocide never stops denying being a novel. I wrote *Murambi: The Book of Bones* while making sure that I always remained one tone *below*, and it is therefore not a coincidence that it's the most accessible of my books, from *Les tambours de la mémoire* to *Les traces de la meute*. Writing amidst the stench of so many dead bodies quickly eliminates the urge for complicated literariness. Those "signatures" of avant-garde aesthetics, which I was so keen on before Rwanda, suddenly seemed frivolous in the face of such human suffering. It's because of similar writing pirouettes that I ended up praising the assassins who fled to the DRC. I decided that it would never happen to me again. This experience can make anyone lose their innocence since, beyond literature—I know that I don't write the same way since *Murambi* was published—I wanted to understand what had really happened in Rwanda.

In particular, I discovered that it was to promote its language that the French state under François Mitterrand, actively and with boundless determination, got involved in the genocide alongside mass murderers of the elderly and newborn babies. Having been denied with indignation for a long time by Parisian intellectuals, this complicity is now widely documented and recognized by everybody, including by the French public.

As for me, until my stay in Rwanda I had criticized imperialism and neocolonialism in the vein of classical Marxist theorists, and thinkers such as Frantz Fanon, Kwame Nkrumah, and Cheikh Anta Diop had taught me how to despise these notions. It all remained quite abstract in my mind, however. The dead of Rwanda brought to this reflection the weight of their blood. In fact, it pushed me to analyze the domination that former French colonies are *still* the victims of sixty years after independence, which is well conveyed in the neologism *Françafrique* coined by François-Xavier Verschave. Beyond the book *Négrophobie*, which I co-authored in 2005 with Verschave and Odile Tobner, I have never stopped denouncing this system of mafia-type economics and the archaic pillage of Africa.

All that allowed me to better understand why France was investing so much money and energy on the African continent for the defense of its language. And yet I had chosen to write fiction in French. I therefore realized my involvement in an extroverted African literature, written in colonial languages and "historically condemned," to borrow a phrase from David Mandessi Diop. Apart from Ngũgĩ wa Thiong'o and Cheikh Anta Diop, "The Novel in Africa," by J. M. Coetzee, had triggered my interest in the subject. In it, Elizabeth Costello says to the Nigerian novelist Emmanuel Egudu:

> The English novel . . . is written in the first place by English people for English people. The Russian novel is written by Russians for Russians. But the African novel is not written by Africans for Africans. African novelists may write about Africa, about African experience, but they are glancing over their shoulder all the time as they write at the foreigners who will read them. Whether they like it or not, they have assumed the role of interpreter, interpreting Africa to the world. Yet how can you explore a world in all its depth if at the same time you are having to explain it to outsiders?

4

My desire to write in Wolof has always been there. Although it was somewhat scattered and uncontrolled, it was part of my cycle of reflection, triggered by a wish to better understand the genocide against the Tutsi, which ultimately pushed me to take action.

Here I want to bring back my mother-storyteller. She had never set foot in a French public school, so it was in Wolof that she described the love story of Youmané and "the storm." Without even knowing it, she was preparing me for literary creation in my mother tongue. It would take too much time to explain how I switched from one language to another, but I can simply say that I owe an immense joy to my three novels *Doomi Golo*, *Bàmmeelu Kocc Barma*, and *Malaanum Lëndëm*, as well as the translation of Césaire's *A Season in the Congo*, which I had never experienced when I was writing in French. This process of self-reconnection, eminently political, is not limited to creative writing. My friends and I have created a publishing house in African languages. And it is not by coincidence that we chose to call it "EJO," which is a word in Kinyarwanda. We also teach Wolof and have created *Lu defu waxu*, which to this day is the only online Senegalese newspaper in Wolof.

Being born in Dakar and coming back several years later from Thiès, my mother-storyteller's town—as much as my father's library, which I have often talked about—has had an enormous impact on my intellectual growth. I was able, without much effort, to get rid of my destiny as a *francograph* writer and to start expressing in my mother tongue the dreams and suffering of the Rwandan people, of the Senegalese people, but also of all humanity.

DAKAR, SENEGAL

Award-winning Senegalese author and 2022 Neustadt Prize laureate Boubacar Boris Diop (b. 1946) is one of Africa's most prominent novelists, playwrights, and essayists. Diop delivered this keynote talk at the University of Oklahoma, which was also livestreamed to participants from more than forty countries, from Albania to Uzbekistan.

Bojana Coulibaly is the African Language Program Manager at Harvard University and managing editor of EJO Editions, a publishing house specializing in literature written in Wolof and other African languages, founded by Boubacar Boris Diop.

ANNA BADKHEN

I OFTEN FEEL a sense of discomfort that resembles lostness—a feeling of displacement, of not-quite-being there. Like drinking from a water fountain: the stream hits somewhere inside your mouth but most of the water falls back out, never reaches the throat, does not quite quench. It can come sudden and ravenous and also feels somehow slightly shameful, the way it rises as a deep blush, a gasp: what have I done? My mother once described hot flashes this way.

What is this sense of dislocation? Do others have it? The writer J. M. Ledgard describes "a feeling of discordance that is like arriving at a terminal identical to the one I have just left . . . and the effect on me is that I feel trammeled and shoved away from the important living things." My own lostness, too, feels as if I am overlooking something important yet ineffable, missing something I cannot quite identify.

A philosopher friend tells me: "I think that our modern illness is our sense of homesickness, our sense of being lost in the world, our sense of alienation. We moderns have no home. . . . We had one on the savanna in small, largely self-sufficient groups, but we abandoned it of necessity: overpopulation and climate change. We've been searching for home ever since. The story of the Garden of Eden is our collective unconscious at work." Maybe this odd yearning is a nag for a sense of a kind of completion, completeness, a home that is now gone: a forever chase, an asymptote.

Once—for most of our existence on Earth—our extended family, our tribe, our cluster of villages were our world entire. (*To lose touch:* to no longer be able to feel with your fingertips.) Only the self-exiled or the banished moved away. Those were the Cains, the suspicious ones. (*To fall out of touch:* to fall, like Azazel.) Now, one in seven people on the planet is displaced, their Eden lost to war, epidemics, totalitarian regimes, hunger. A billion souls are on the move, searching for home, a place of safety, of dignity. And still the sedentary world treats their rootlessness as a failure—worse, a crime. It militarizes borders, builds fences, tears apart families, incarcerates children. It misplaces children: in 2016, ten thousand unaccompanied minor migrants went missing in Europe. The seekers of home become lost in the settled world's callous indifference. Is it because their search is a more urgent version of our own, an unwelcome reminder of our own primeval loss?

I board a flight from Barcelona to Dakar, and there, in the back row, a young African man thrashes and screams between two grandfatherly white men in eyeglasses and gray beards. I think: an epileptic seizure, how lucky these two doctors happened to be onboard. But something is awry. The doctors are holding the man by the shoulders to keep him in his seat, but they are not restraining him from bashing his head backward against the wall of the plane, over and over and over and over. And surely they need to put something in his mouth so he won't bite his tongue, isn't that what you are supposed to do when a person is having a seizure?—and then the screaming man rises out of his chair high enough that I see the handcuffs on his wrists, and one of the doctors, the one in the window seat, silently laces his hand through the man's hair and squeezes, and the glove on his hand is not a medical glove, it's a black leather glove, and I know: they are not doctors, they are torturers. Many of us passengers on the plane have risen too now and are screaming, too, in Spanish and in Wolof, stop this, stop, and we film the torture in the back row with our useless cell phones. I yell too, *arrêtez*, I don't know why it comes out in French, my language oddly misplaced. A white man in a white uniform, I assume he is a pilot, rushes from the cockpit down the aisle, slaps our phones down. He also says stop stop stop. No filming.

Eventually the fake doctors disembark with their failed deportee. Where do they take him? To brutalize him some more in the dungeons of some detention center, away from the public eye? To sedate him and put him on another plane to Senegal? What place on Earth does he call home? Does he have children, and if he does, where are they? We, the passengers, take our seats and fasten our seat belts and take off in silence, lost in our inadequacy.

Maybe that sense of lostness *is* an expression of inadequacy, our power-lessness before the world's wretchedness. "Since once again, O Lord, in the steppes of Asia, I have no bread, no wine, no altar, I will raise myself above those symbols to the pure majesty of reality, and I will offer to you, I, your priest, upon the altar of the entire earth, the labor and the suffering of the world," prayed the Jesuit priest and paleontologist Pierre Teilhard de Chardin on Easter Sunday 1923 in the Ordos Desert of Inner Mongolia.

Haplessly we try to patch up this uselessness, this disjointedness of ours. We gather against it. Like the time my parents, sister, son, and I meet on the Canary island of Tenerife. We hike a lot. We hike down barrancas to coves; we hike up mountains to summits. We carefully plot our routes and drive our rental car to particularly alluring trailheads and walk hard and with determination, and we celebrate reaching each destination with a high five, an exhilarated chuckle of disbelief. We made it, we have arrived!

But then, a thousand feet or so below the summit of El Teide, the island's main dormant volcano, we pull over by an absolutely pathless plane of beige volcanic foam. A tract of lava flow so smooth it feels spherical. Outcrops of darker lava liberally and with no order grow out of this pallor. Splotches of icy snow, disorienting in their bright white randomness. There is a parking lot: evidently the park rangers intend for us to be here. But there are no trails to guide us on the flow, no instructions, no specific terminus, nowhere obvious to proceed. Nothing to look forward to. The plateau ends in an abyss. Beyond, El Teide's dark outer caldera banners out and out, and behind us, across the road from the parking lot, the only tangible landmark, the only point of possible direction, the volcano itself looms unassailable, unreachable.

It is so indifferently beautiful! So surreally uncharted! What to do with it? We walk in circles. We stand dumbstruck. A child picks up a handful of snow, tosses a snowball at a friend. The ball disintegrates in mid-flight into melting crystals that patter to the surface and evaporate in no time. The child's arms fall slack: now what? And it washes over me again, so familiar, this sense of displacement.

My philosopher friend writes: "The self is a process, a flow like time or a river. The best one can do is guide oneself by some project, what Sartre calls our fundamental project, that is, if we can find one." On the lava plateau I find a temporary project: I scamper up an outcrop, turn on my iPhone video camera, and document our lostness.

Against the ashen surface each person on the plateau is highlighted in his or her particular separateness. Like humans in outer space—all that untrodden, gravity-free expanse up there!—except in hiking clothes. Not a lot of conversation among us: the disorientation hushes. I wonder if anyone would hear me if I screamed, if a scream would penetrate the immense absence that cottonwools us. I don't scream. I film. There is Dad. He is walking a few paces behind Mom. Their footsteps uncertain, slow: such an oddly disconnected space. Dad stops, wheels around, lifts his camera and aims it at my son. Dad, too, has found a project, a raison d'être on the white lava flow.

At 12,198 feet, El Teide's summit is the highest point in Spain. The Guanches, a Berber-speaking people who fished and raised sheep and gathered fruit here until the Europeans colonized them and exterminated their culture through slave trade, war, and forced assimilation, believed that, once, the devil Guayota had kidnapped the god of light and sun, Magec, and imprisoned him inside the volcano. The world plunged into darkness. The people were instantly lost. A liberation of Magec by the supreme god followed; Guayota was jabbed down the crater; light was restored—and with it, humans' ability to tell where they were going. It was Eden again, for a while. The islanders could not, of course, predict the cultural annihilation that lay ahead. Pedro de Vera y Mendoza, who helped conquer Tenerife in the late 1490s, slaughtered most of the Guanche men and sold the Guanche women as chattel. Now the Guanches are lost forever.

I have read somewhere that "Teide" comes from the Guanche word for "hell." How thoughtfully compact: heaven and hell on the same 785-square-mile island.

One bewildering thing about that lava flow is the complete absence of paths. I think of Machado—"Traveler, there is no road, the road is made by walking"—but truly we do prefer there to be a road of some kind, a sense of purpose. What is a road? An escape, the shoah, an exodus. A *hejira*, a pilgrimage, a hope. Muslims pray: "Show us the straight Path." What is a person without hope? A person lost. But for all we know, the point of arrival may well be a trackless lava flow.

Or we may never arrive at all.

The most trafficked migration route in the world today lies across the Mediterranean Sea. Hundreds of thousands of people have taken it in pursuit of imagined lands of plenty, in pursuit of hope. This may have been how the screaming man on the plane wound up in Barcelona. This route is also the deadliest. Since 2015, more than fifteen thousand people have perished in the crossing. "Great mother of life, the sea," wrote Rachel Carson. "The beginning and the end." Its tidal pull the aching call of the primary womb, insatiable. The perished migrants' road across it a journey that leads nowhere, heaven and hell in one.

For four centuries the route of the world's most immoral migrations, too, lay across the sea. Back then Europeans shackled Africans not to return them to Africa but to traffic them out. That route was perilous too. Tens of thousands of people stolen from Africa during the transatlantic slave trade carpet the ocean floor with their bones.

For a time, the Canary Islands served as a naval base for that slave trade. From the slopes of El Teide I look for traces in the ocean. It is blue blue blue.

The reason my family meets in Tenerife is because some of us are dislocated, *déplacés*. My parents and my sister arrive from St. Petersburg, Russia, where they live and where all of us were born—to be semantically precise, all of us but my son were born in Leningrad, USSR. But my son and I left Russia years ago, when he was seven and I was twenty-eight, and we moved to the United States. We are migrants. My son flies to Tenerife from Ohio, where he attends college. I fly in from Senegal, where I am researching a book about boundaries. In a way, our disjointed family outing on the white lava flow is a visual metaphor for our apartness.

I am an immigrant, and I am also on the road a lot. I was a war correspondent for many years; later, I researched books in Central Asia, in West Africa. It is as if, for me, the road has become a destination in and of itself, a place from which I can begin, a starting point, a state of commencement, of setting out, something maybe as simple as a stanza from a Bei Dao poem:

> Let's go—
> The road, the road
> Is covered with a drift of scarlet poppies.

(Machado, you trickster: the decision to do the walking is a road in and of itself.)

The question I am asked most frequently is this: You are not from here, where are you from? Everyone wants to know. My hosts in Afghanistan or Iraq or Senegal, defenders of their ancestral homes from foreign armies, from their own abusive governments, from cataclysms and man-made devastations. My settled neighbors in the United States, who are trying to pin down my accent, my background, my ethical allegiances. I am perpetually working on my response. If I trust the questioner and we have some time, I explain that I grew up an outcast in a country that no longer exists, an underweight and sickly specimen of a despised minority, a Soviet Jew. That I moved away, and keep moving, transient, in transit: the Wandering Jew. Ahasuerus. The defender of no claimed geography. It makes for relatively effortless travel. It makes for uncomfortable silences, odd hesitations.

If I feel like being flippant, I offer a response I learned from my nomadic Fulani friends in the Malian Sahel, with whom I spent several seasons herding cattle, researching a book, and hoping to walk away from grief. (To sum up: the book came out; the grief remained; my feet grew some good callus.) The Fulani say: We are here now.

But I don't know what my Eden is, if it even exists. That is the point. I stand on an empty plateau. It is a privilege. In another version, I am in handcuffs, screaming in the back of a plane.

If, as my philosopher friend says, the self is a flow, then it desires movement. "Solvitur ambulando," promises Diogenes; my Fulani friends have been walking, generationally, for ten thousand years—but it seems their path may be ending. Chasing clouds in the time of climate change has had them struggling over vanishing resources for decades, and now the war over Mali's northern desert has spilled southward into the bush. In some areas, local governments have forbidden Fulani nomads from camping in the bush, in others, from riding motorcycles, in both cases depriving those on the move of freedom of movement. Last summer, settled people marched into one village, separated Fulani residents, and massacred them. Two months later, outside another village, militiamen killed eleven Fulani people walking to a weekly market. Ethnic cleansing is an outlet for an ancient and visceral mistrust of the rootless, the dehumanizing hatred of the nonsettled. Here is Toni Morrison in *The Bluest Eye:* "Cholly Breedlove . . . having put his family outdoors, had catapulted himself beyond the reaches of human consideration. He had joined the animals."

President Trump has said of some migrants: "These aren't people. These are animals." The massacres of Fulani people in the heart of Mali have the same origin as concentration camps for migrant children on the U.S. border with Mexico.

Of course—this is how I comfort myself against my own homelessness—Western civilization (from the Latin *civis*, a townsperson, who is settled: a *bürger*) doesn't mind and even loves a migratory artist: Roberto Bolaño, say ("The homeland of a writer is his tongue"), or Georges Perec, who wrote: "We should long ago have got into the habit of moving about, of moving about freely, without it being too much trouble," or an artist who romanticizes nomadism, for instance, Bruce Chatwin. But that's because in the eye of most townsfolk an artist is already necessarily deranged, wild, rootless, one whose mind wanders—a griot who for her otherness will be buried not in a proper cemetery but inside a tree.

Like an animal.

Incidentally, it was a trilingual Fulani poet and religious leader who, two hundred years ago, delivered Sufi Islam to rural West Africa on the tip of a spear: a nomad jihadi who converted sedentary animists. All the great monotheisms were founded by nomads: in the absence of physical walls we must create boundaries of the soul. The Prophet Mohammed himself was a nomad, raised by Bedouin. Two poets were assassinated at his behest.

It is late spring, and I am driving on Interstate 10 through the northern Chihuahuan Desert in West Texas, en route from Senegal to a casita on a small ranch where I will write my book. Humans first came to the region thirteen thousand years ago, maybe earlier. Then, in the 1530s, came Álvar Núñez Cabeza de Vaca, a grandson of de Vera y Mendoza, the murderer of Tenerife's Guanches, and paved the way for the genocide of local civilizations—first by the Spanish Catholic conquistadors, later by the Anglos with their mythology of homesteader supremacy. The land to either side of the highway maps a history of pain. Splotching lavender and gold and green, with horse pastures and wildflower leas, the land is also exquisitely beautiful, if you believe that natural beauty can be indifferent to our joys and sufferings, if you can appreciate El Teide rising majestic over its despoiled island. Seeing beauty amidst iniquity seems a tall order, but I insist we must—otherwise we will not survive our own history of violence, we will stop falling in love and die off as a species. To resolve his feeling of discordance, Ledgard endeavors to "find a still point in a wilderness that was free of any human thought or memory" in a national park in the war-wracked South Sudan, one militarized border away from the origin of humankind.

Two hours from my destination, I drive head-on into a massive storm. Lightning stabs everywhere, white, purple, curlicued, jagged. The creosote wind of wet desert fills the car and then rain slams onto the highway. Distant horses that muzzle grass are no more, wildflower meadows become smears until everything just becomes white. Ashes of a bombed city look this way when they flake down to earth. Volcanic ash, too.

I slow to a crawl, but it doesn't really matter how fast or how slow I am going: I am lost in the wet whiteout, and there is really nothing to do but be lost, embrace the lostness. This is probably cheating, since the embracing, the choice of it, is a kind of direction. But this storm is just so crazy beautiful, and I pull over and cut the engine, and it will have to do for now.

TULSA, OKLAHOMA

Anna Badkhen (b. 1975) is the author of seven books, most recently *Bright Unbearable Reality*, longlisted for the 2022 National Book Award and for the 2023 Jan Michalski Prize for Literature, and *To See Beyond* (2026). Her awards include the Guggenheim Fellowship, the Barry Lopez Visiting Writer in Ethics and Community Fellowship, and the Joel R. Seldin Award from Psychologists for Social Responsibility. A former war correspondent, Badkhen was born in the Soviet Union and is a U.S. citizen.

THE WANDERER'S TALE

ÁLVARO MUTIS

Translated from the Spanish by Alastair Reid

FOR ALASTAIR REID

I come from the North,
where they forge iron,
where they make locks and grills,
iron gates and inexhaustible arms,
where great bearskins cover walls and litters,
where the milk waits for a signal from the stars;
from the North, where every voice speaks an order,
where the sledges draw their breath under a sky
with no shadow of storm.
I am going eastward, toward the warmest channels
of mud and clay,
and the patient, vegetal sleeplessness
fed by the immeasurable waters.
It's to the estuaries I'm finally going,
to the delta where the light rests, brooding on
the magnolias of death,
and the heat spreads across vast regions
in a dense siesta
lulled by the wings
of restless insects.
Even so, I would still yearn for
the leather workshops, the sparse sand,
the cold slithering through the dunes
where the glass sings
and the wind scourges
the ground and the grave-mounds,
blurring the tracks of the caravans.

I came from the North.
Ice annulled the labyrinths
where the sword obeys
the summons to its destiny.
I speak of traveling, not of resting places.
In the East, the moon broods over the region
that my hurt self reaches out to for relief
from a clutching fear, a fear that has no cure.

Born in Bogotá, Colombia, poet, novelist, and essayist Álvaro Mutis (1923–2013) was best known for his seven-part novel *The Adventures and Misadventures of Maqroll*. His many awards included the Prix Medicis and the 2002 Neustadt International Prize for Literature.

Alastair Reid (1926–2014) was a Scottish poet, prolific translator of South American literature, and longtime *New Yorker* contributor. He helped fête Mutis during the 2002 Neustadt Lit Fest.

JOÃO CABRAL DE MELO NETO

Translated from the Portuguese by Djelal Kadir

ON THE OCCASION of being the recipient of so prestigious a prize, conferred upon a writer of the Portuguese language for the first time, I ought to explain one thing before all else: you have rewarded a Brazilian writer who, practically, has only written poetry—that is, a poet.

I do not know how it is in your northerly country, but in mine, in its colloquial usage, the word *poet* has a certain connotation between bohemian and irresponsible, contemplative and inspired, all things that have nothing to do with my way of conceiving poetry and with what I have managed to accomplish.

I regret that Miss Marianne Moore, who died, unfortunately, before receiving the laurels of your prize, cannot, like Francis Ponge and Elizabeth Bishop, laureates both of the Neustadt Prize, comfort me with her poet's counsel today upon receiving this prize as a poet. In truth, these were poets whose vision of poetry has nothing to do with that confessional lyricism that nowadays, since Romanticism, passes for everything that is considered poetry. In a way (and upon saying so I cannot help the feeling of a certain *mauvaise conscience*), what I have written until today has nothing to do with the "lyricism" that has come to be not only the quality of certain poets, but synonymous with what is expected of all poets.

In reality, starting with Romanticism, and in the name of individual expression, poets have left by the wayside the greater part of the kinds of material that previously could be treated in poetry. Historical poetry, didactic poetry, epic poetry, dramatic poetry, narrative poetry, confrontational poetry, all abandoned in favor of poetry of personal expression of states of mind. Everything has been sacrificed to lyricism, and this has been generalized and called poetry. Now, lyricism was merely one of the aspects in which poetry manifested itself. Thus, I do not know why today's critics and historians, though they find it strange, admit that poetry is a literary genre that survives in small circles. Meanwhile, those same critics and historians of today's literature do not keep from dedicating to that genre that is so minoritarian the best of their studies, even while they systematically begin with this genre their manuals and histories of literature, and this not just here but in any country. We know that lyricism was originally a genre to be sung, and thus it is not surprising that the current lyricism, postromantic, not sung, should be restricted to a small circle. The question is, wouldn't the true lyricism of our time be in what is called the popular song, produced and consumed all over the world, beyond geographic borders and language differences, in incomparably greater quantities than any other literary genre, however popular? Might not this natural necessity for lyricism that human beings feel be tended to today by that incalculable volume of works at which the very refined turn up their noses and which the erudite exclude from their studies? That is, might not that needed lyricism be today in the lyrics of popular songs? In those songs that, by virtue of the new technologies of communication, are produced and consumed in our time in quantities enormously larger than those of literatures ever reached in all countries and in all epochs?

Ladies and gentlemen, it is not because of simple aversion that I refuse to inscribe myself into that exclusive club of "lyrics" that today constitutes almost entirely the poetry written in our world. Nor is there any disdain on my part for that lyricism manifested in popular music—I think, on the contrary, that those new techniques have given lyricism a possibility of expression and communication never known before. I am merely offering a possible topic of meditation to the theoreticians of literature, and appealing to them not to seek in not-sung (or unsingable) poetry written today a quality, that of lyricism, that was never the intention of the authors to achieve or even to explore.

Poetry seems to me something much broader: it is the exploration of the materiality of words and of the possibilities of organization of verbal structures, things that have nothing to do with what is romantically called inspiration, or even intuition. In this respect, I believe that lyricism, upon finding in popular music the element that fulfills it and gives it its prestige, has liberated written and not-sung poetry and has allowed it to return to operate in territory that once belonged to it. It has made possible too the exercise of poetry as emotive exploration of the world of things and as rigorous construction of lucid formal structures, lucid objects of language.

RIO DE JANEIRO

Born in Recife, Brazil, poet and diplomat João Cabral de Melo Neto (1920–1999) was elected to the Brazilian Academy of Letters in 1968 and awarded the 1990 Camões Prize. He delivered the 1992 Neustadt Prize lecture in Rio de Janeiro.

Djelal Kadir, born in Cyprus in 1946, is the Edwin Erle Sparks Professor of Comparative Literature at Pennsylvania State University. He was the editor of *WLT* from 1991 to 1996.

MOZART: ROMANCE $\qquad$ (1958)

ODYSSEUS ELYTIS

Translated from the Greek by Kimon Friar

FROM THE CONCERTO FOR PIANO, P. 20, K. 466

Lovely saddening life
Piano distant and subterranean
My head leans on the Pole
And grass holds me in its dominion

Secret Ganges of the night where are you taking me?
I see roe-deer emerging from black smoke
Running in silver running
And I do not live and I have not died

Neither love not even glory
Nor was it even ever a dream
As on my side I am sleeping sleeping
I hear the machinery of the earth traveling.

Odysseus Elytis (1911–1996) was a Greek poet, essayist, and translator. He was awarded the Nobel Prize in Literature in 1979.

Kimon Friar (1911–1993) was a Greek American poet, scholar, and translator of modern Greek literature.

HEADLIGHTS (2006)

PATRICIA GRACE

MONICA COOKED UP a pot of pasta and watched the whitish water spurt out of the holes of the colander as she strained it, the water flooding into the sink and down the drain where everything goes.

She shook the colander. Shook and shook. The remaining drops gathered, combined and trickled down the plughole until the liquid was all gone and it was no use doing that any longer. In a moment she would have to turn round.

Taking a bowl from the cupboard she let the flat, grub-colored ribbons slither into it, and opening a jar of sauce slugged the mixture over the pasta, scraping it all out with a spoon. She mixed and stirred until she couldn't do that any longer either. Now she would have to turn round and see her daughter Yvette creeping about, setting the table as though afraid to make a noise in case a bomb went off or something leapt out of a cupboard and swallowed her.

Knives and forks, spoons for the twins, salt and pepper, a plate of bread, the container of margarine.

Without a sound.

The table-setting completed, Yvette stood back against the kitchen wall, hands at her sides, her feet pointing towards each other. Monica saw one foot twitch. Was her daughter about to take a step, two steps, three steps, and get out of the kitchen altogether?

No.

Yvette hooked a big toe under the instep of her other foot and jigged her heel. High insteps, muscular calves, shoulders half-lifted, half a smile.

Swallowing. As if a whole egg.

Silent, like a spider who could pounce on me, entangle me in all its legs, squeeze the life out of me.

Monica put three plates on the table and one on the bench.

Another shift. Yvette was drawing one leg up and placing a bare foot on the wall behind her. One-legged.

Shorts too short, T-shirt tight.

Begging eyes.

Not moving. Locked, as though she felt someone or something was holding her, preventing her from being a gymnast or a ballet dancer.

"Get your slippers on, and some decent clothes," Monica said, turning back to the bench as she spoke. "And tell your brothers to hurry up. Make them wash their hands."

She began dishing the pasta onto the plates, deciding that she would eat her own food later when they all got out of the kitchen.

Yvette came back, urging her twin brothers ahead of her. She was wearing jeans now, but they were short in the legs too. Slippers with toes bunched up inside. The boys had wet, dripping hands and were scrambling up on chairs to sit at the table where they would stuff food into their mouths and their eyes would water. Their noses would run because they had colds, or because the food was too peppery, too spicy, or too something.

Everything about them dripped and dribbled. They oozed and exuded from eyes, noses, ears and backsides. They threw up. They spurted and sprayed all round the bathroom, for ever liquefying without ever becoming smaller or disappearing. They had come out of her bloody, taking all of her entrails with them, turning her inside out, two heads screaming.

Monica left her plate of food on the bench, went into the lounge and turned on the television where she watched two men in an office drinking whisky from large crystal glasses. One was presenting all options to the other and advising him to remain silent on a certain matter.

"Which would put all the blame on Kath," the other said.

"Then maybe you should plead guilty," his adviser told him.

To what?

Murder, theft, kidnapping, infidelity, fraud? Monica couldn't be bothered waiting to find out so skipped around the channels using the remote.

There was a woman packing a bag because she was leaving.

Leaving who? Leaving what? Why? Going where?

Who cared?

She turned the television off and went back into the kitchen where Yvette was whispering something to the twins, wiping their messes with paper towels, wiping their faces, buttering their pieces of bread.

Telling them to ask me for something because she doesn't want to be the one to do it.

Peas.

They were asking for peas, which wasn't even worth whispering about. She took a packet of peas from the freezer, poured them into a bowl, and put them in the microwave to cook. When they were ready she served a spoonful onto her own plate and put the bowl and spoon on the table.

"Thank you, Mum," they said. "Thank you, Mum. Thank you Mum, Mum. You. Thank you, you, Mum, Mum, Mum. You, you, Mum."

That's enough thanking, she wanted to shout. Enough. Enough shouting. It's peas. Peas. Not a present or lollies. Not a gold medal or some great fortune.

"Eat up," she said. "You haven't got all night. You have to have your baths and get to bed."

She stood at the bench forking pasta into her mouth, jabbing peas. Once they were in bed and out of the way there was junk she had to get rid of, something she'd been meaning to do.

After she'd sent Yvette off to run the bath she stacked the dishes in the sink, put the plug in, squirted in a bit of green soap, and turned the hot tap on. She washed the plates and cutlery, the pot and jar and bowls, taking her time. As she dried the dishes and put them away she could hear the boys splashing and laughing in the bath and Yvette was trying to shush them.

So that I won't blow my top.

Monica pulled out the plug, wiping round the sink as the gray, soapy water coiled itself down into the outlet. She wiped the bench, rinsed and squeezed the cloth, but then threw it into the bin because it felt slimy.

All rubbish.

She had to clean out the wardrobe, something she'd been meaning to do, get rid of rubbish. The sooner the better.

But first she went into the bathroom, cleaned the bath, collected up the dirty clothes for washing and set the washing machine going. The boys were calling out to her from the bedroom but she knew if she ignored them they would go to sleep.

In her own bedroom she pulled a box and a suitcase out of the wardrobe. These contained the left-behind traces of her husband who had made a quick getaway. There wasn't much—a carton of sports trophies and a suitcase of old clothes, which she began emptying into a rubbish bag. When she'd finished she looked about in case there was anything else that needed discarding.

On the dressing table was a photograph of the five of them, taken four years earlier when Yvette was four and the twins were a year old. All dressed up.

Smiling.

Framed.

She put it in on top of the trophies and clothes and took the bag to the outside bin. The washing machine was singing its way into the spin cycle, the rinse water spilling down into the outside drain and laughing its way off to somewhere.

Back in the bedroom she turned her back on the now-empty box and the gaping suitcase, and standing in front of the mirror, looking into her own eyes, saw that the pupils had become segmented, sectored into sixes, like the crisscross grids covering plugholes which prevented scraps from going down. She could see that light was cutting into her, showing all the tubes and pipes of herself. Not that it mattered.

What would it matter if I drained away from myself?

In the meantime it made her feel sick seeing the carton and suitcase yawning empty behind her. She knew she had to do something about them.

So Monica began taking her own clothes from the drawers and wardrobe and filling first the box and then the suitcase. But when she had done that she saw that the drawers and wardrobe were now gaping at her, so she turned her back on them. Taking the luggage with her she shut the bedroom door, going out to the garage where she put the box and bag into the boot of the car. She got into the car, started the motor, and backed down the drive.

Round town the petrol stations and takeaway bars were open, the pub lights were on, and there were people sitting at darkened tables in the restaurants. But she didn't want anything from any of those places or any of those people, or anything from any part of the town. Not from shops, road, lit-up houses or houses of darkness; not from houses on the flat or on the hillsides; not from school, college, footpaths, cars on the road or turning into driveways; not from cyclists with fluorescent strips on their backs and flashing heels.

Nothing.

Nothing from any of them.

Through lights and roundabouts she came to the exit road curving up past the clock-garden which was the way out of everything. The road broke into two arms, one dipping to come out onto the northbound lane of the motorway, and one rising to come out onto the southbound lane.

Hers was the only car on the north off-ramp, but once on the motorway she joined other traffic, her lights drawing into them the road markings, the railings and the signs. On the left of her were the lights of the town, on the right the lights of vehicles going south.

All of us going somewhere.

The road pulling us all along it.

The town was soon left behind, giving way to dark paddocks where she knew sheep and cows would be sheltering among the hummocks. Now the motorway had ended and most of the cars had exited as she continued on through the night.

There were times, especially finding her way through towns and cities, when signs were confusing, but it didn't matter which road she chose to take because all roads led somewhere.

All I have to do is keep going.

After filling her car with petrol on the outskirts of one of the cities the road ahead became long and straight, the countryside wide and flat under a vast black sky. From time to time there were other vehicles on the road, sometimes up ahead, sometimes coming in the opposite direction, occasionally coming from behind and passing.

Eventually the road began to rise and wind. She seemed to be nosing towards the sky, on and on up to a sweeping curve at the top. Once around the curve, she began winding down again. And as she descended, the night-traveling trucks pulled their way up towards her, flat-faced, large-eyed, grinding and wheezing, squeezing the road until there was only just enough room for her to get by. She decided that once the road levelled out she would find an off-road rest area, pull in, make herself comfortable in the back seat, and sleep until daylight.

It wasn't long before she came to the final section of the winding road, where once down past the last bend it flattened out and straightened and was joined by other entering roads to form a wide thoroughfare. On this new sweep of road rows of unbroken white lines and reflectors defined four lanes, while two strips of broken lines and reflectors marked out the mid-sections.

Her headlights picked up the white markings and reflectors and made them all glow. She was the only one on the road now, the only one making all that light and all that shine ahead of her. She was the only one causing all light and reflection to disappear behind her too—lighting up the road then making it disappear, lighting it and disappearing it, lighting it and disappearing it.

And looking back through the rear-vision mirror into that long funnel of darkness, she could see now that there was nothing behind her. There was nothing back there at all.

HONGOEKA BAY, NEW ZEALAND

Born in Wellington, New Zealand, in 1937, Patricia Grace's first novel, *Mutuwhenua* (1978), was the first novel ever published by a Māori woman writer. A writer of novels, short stories, and children's books, she was awarded the Neustadt International Prize for Literature in 2006, nominated by Joy Harjo.

GUADALUPE NETTEL

Translated from the Spanish by Rosalind Harvey

"I WAS BORN with a white beauty mark, or what others call a birthmark, covering the cornea of my right eye. That spot would have been nothing had it not stretched across my iris and over the pupil through which light must pass to reach the back of the brain. They didn't perform corneal transplants on newborns in those days; the spot was doomed to remain for several years. And in the same way an unventilated tunnel slowly fills with mold, the pupillary blockage led to the growth of a cataract. The only advice the doctors could give my parents was to wait: by the time their daughter finished growing, medicine would surely have advanced enough to offer the solution they now lacked.

In the meantime, they advised subjecting me to a series of annoying exercises to develop, as much as possible, the defective eye. This was done with ocular movements . . . but also—and this I remember most—with a patch that covered my left eye for half the day. It was a piece of flesh-colored cloth . . . covering my upper eyelid down to the top of my cheekbone. . . . Wearing the patch felt unfair and oppressive. It was hard to let them put it on me every morning and to accept that no hiding place and no amount of crying could save me from that torture. . . . With the patch, I had to go to school, identify my teacher and the shapes of my school supplies, come home, eat, and play for part of the afternoon.

At around five o'clock, someone would come to say it was time to take it off, and with these words I would return to the world of clarity and precise shapes. The people and things around me suddenly changed. I could see far into the distance and would become mesmerized by the treetops and infinite leaves that composed them, the contours of the clouds in the sky, the tint of the flowers, the intricate pattern of my fingertips. My life was divided between two worlds: that of morning, built mostly out of sounds and smells, but also of hazy colors; and that of evening, always freeing, yet at the same time, overwhelmingly precise."

This is the opening to *The Body Where I Was Born*, the novel that tells of my childhood, a childhood defined by certain profound events: in the personal realm, my struggle to see with both eyes, and in the political, the exile of so many Latin American peoples who were fleeing the dictatorships of the 1970s.

Moving back and forth between these two worlds, that of light and that of shadows, taught me to marvel, as I relate in the book, at the most quotidian objects and occurrences, to seek out different, unsuspected angles to them, to know that silhouettes and shapes are just as important as details, to never, ever trust first impressions, nor to take anything for granted. Every writer has a particular way of seeing the world, and in mine, these chiaroscuros, this play of light and shadow, hold a very important place. Since I have never been able to take much in with my sight, I must take great care when deciding which things I wish to focus my gaze on.

Wearing a patch over my left eye and being practically blind in the right one turned me, psychologically at least, into a child who, if not openly marginalized, was at least different. The attitude of my classmates as well as my parents' constant battle to try and *put me back together* made me feel, from a very early age, that I had come into the world with something broken, something defective, something it was necessary to fix at all costs. *The Body Where I Was Born* speaks of the superhuman effort my parents made to integrate me into what they considered the group of "normal people." In fact, from my first novel, *El huésped*, right through to the most recent, *Still Born*, I have tried to question the ideas people tend to have about what is "normal" and what is "abnormal"—concepts I do not believe in—and to invite my readers to do the same.

"No one is normal close-up," as the Brazilian saying goes, and this is why in almost all my books I have tried, on one hand, to enact a kind of close-up of these supposed abnormalities, which to me seem beautiful, and, on the other, to turn a spotlight on those subjects that people tend to keep in the shadows, if not in utter darkness—the uncomfortable subjects, those that many people feel it is better not even to glance at.

For instance, when I began my career at the start of this century, the prevailing idea of beauty was far more uniform and conventional than it is today. The bodies that we now call nonconformist were considered obscene, and the concept of body positivity did not exist yet. Back then, it was rare to talk about this, and still less common to celebrate unconventional beauty as I did in *El huésped* or *Bezoar*, whose characters are individuals with peculiarities, whether they be physical or psychological, that at times lead them to be marginalized. For me, these characters were not only interesting but also beautiful in their uniqueness. *Still Born*, my most recent novel, also explores the subject of divergent bodies, in particular the body of Inés, affected by a severe neurological disability, and her parents' wish to discover who their daughter really is, beyond any medical diagnosis or the ideas that others have about her. It also explores the experience of women who chose not to be mothers—a group that, in my view, are still underrepresented in literature—and the prejudices that hang over them.

El huésped has, as an epigraph, some lines by Jean Paulhan that could perfectly well describe any one of my books:

Know that it is about saving oneself whole with one's deficiencies, with one's calluses, with all the inconsistencies, contradictions, and absurdities that a man may have. All this is what we must bring out into the light: the madman that we are.

In this first novel, which has not yet been translated into English, blindness is one of the central themes. Ana, the young female protagonist, knows from an early age that when she grows up she will go blind. The story takes place in Mexico City and is a kind of ode to the city and its residents, especially those who live in poverty, who camp out next to ATMs, in the stations of the metro or under bridges, and who are constantly apprehending us yet without our ever stopping to talk to them, all these "invisible" people over whom many of us cast another type of shadow: indifference and disdain. *El huésped*, *Bezoar*, *After the Winter*, and *Still Born* emerge from this endeavor to look at what hurts us, at what makes us uncomfortable.

Let's return to my childhood. The decade I was born in, the 1970s, was also an interesting one from a historical perspective. Latin America was being ravaged by military dictatorships such as those of Augusto Pinochet in Chile, Jorge Videla in Argentina, and Juan María Bordaberry in Uruguay, fascist regimes that repressed dissidents with torture and clandestine assassinations. Most artists and intellectuals were opposed to these governments, and many were forced into exile to save their lives. Mexico opened its doors to all these refugee families, and I had the good fortune to be born in and spend my childhood in the neighborhood where they all ended up living. I grew up hearing different accents in Spanish. I found out, for instance, that *calabacitas*, or courgettes, can also be called *zapallitos* or *calabacines*, zucchini or little squash; I learned customs that were not precisely my own, such as drinking maté or a glass of milk at four in the afternoon. Living among migrants led me to develop a sense of curiosity toward different cultures, something that has stayed with me, as has as a deep respect for people who are forced to leave their countries and start from zero.

Human beings, like many other animal species, are migratory. According to historians, Homo sapiens has spent more time being nomadic than sedentary. Movement and the ability to adapt to a highly diverse range of environments are ingrained in our DNA. In recent years, however, migration has been seen solely as a problem to tackle. We have forgotten all about its complexity and the beneficial effects it can also have. In my most recent collection of short stories, *The Accidentals*, I use the albatross, those beautiful austral birds, to represent the South American exiles who had to cross long distances in order to survive, but also all those who, without being migrants, have been blown off course by the speed with which the world is changing, what with the global health crisis we went through in 2020 (the psychological aftereffects of which we are still seeing today), all the dizzying political events, but also the uncertainty and anxiety the climate crisis stirs up in us. I think we can all agree that we are witnessing a difficult moment for humanity. In the last few years, the world seems to have moved closer to obscurantism, authoritarian politics, nationalist prejudices, racism, and other attitudes that in the past have led to catastrophes such as World War II.

Although I have always thought than neither art nor literature is obliged to serve any political cause, no matter how important or urgent it might be—that is, that its only real purpose is *to be art and to be literature*—I also believe they are both particularly effective when it comes to describing extreme situations, such as persecution, deportation, hunger, exile, immigration, and to putting those of us who have not lived through these things personally in the position of those who have. More so than the great majority of journalistic texts, literature is a powerful vehicle for empathy. I am thinking of such books as *If This Is a Man*, by Primo Levi; *A Bag of Marbles*, by Joseph Joffo; *The Phone Call*, by Leila Guerriero; *Hurricane Season*, by Fernanda Melchor; and *Small Country*, by Gaël Faye, in which the experience of being uprooted, especially the anguish of being persecuted, are superbly dealt with.

Although I do not believe that literature should have a political cause, I do believe in its capacity to allow us to imagine and to see our neighbors. The capacity to imagine the other, to put ourselves in their shoes, is an incredibly powerful spell against fanaticism. Literature has the power to allow us to connect with one another, to see ourselves beyond ideologies and prejudices, to enter into a zone of intimacy, into the everyday lives of other people, other nations, and to share their stories, their fears, their hopes, and their life experiences—in other words, to shed light on the other, permitting us to truly see them.

Difference and migration, the acceptance of humans by other humans, are, in short, the subjects I have tried to tackle in my fiction. But there is another aspect of my work that I would like to share with you. For this, let's return one last time to my childhood. When I was in primary school, that Montessori school I described in *El cuerpo en que nací*, some friends and I put together a news bulletin called *La Hormiga* (*The Ant*) that was pinned up on a board each week, and later a photocopied magazine called *The Voice*. Ever since then I have been a keen follower of literary and cultural magazines. Years later, when I was a student at university, I edited along with a different group of friends a magazine of Latin American youth literature called *Semestral*, and then one called *Número Cero*. Back then, as incredible as it might seem now, there was no internet yet, and magazines were an essential public platform for youth to be able to read about one other and keep up-to-date with what our contemporaries were doing in other countries around the world. In the pages of these magazines, the endeavors of people with different stories, different points of view, all converge. They constitute an exceptional space for dialogue that it is crucial to defend. While some went on to find institutional support, at first these magazines were published with our own money and that of our friends.

Between 2017 and 2024 I was lucky enough to edit the *Revista de la universidad de México*, published by the National Autonomous University of Mexico (UNAM). It was a thrilling project because it involved taking a historic publication and transforming it in such a way that it appealed to young people while still honoring its tradition. The magazine was published online as well as in print form and ended up having 300,000 readers around the world. We produced around eighty special interdisciplinary issues in which the sciences, literature, and the humanities all converged, covering topics as important as identity, the climate emergency, racism, water, families, extinction, decolonization, feminism, violence, and school.

I think every writer should edit at some point in their career. For someone accustomed to the silence and serenity of their study, to the rhythms their own work (often self-referential) suggests to them, editing constitutes a genuine challenge, an opportunity to escape from solipsism and take an interest in the work others are engaging in, not selfishly, as happens when we read to fortify our own creations, but with the joyous, generous attitude of someone planning a party. As I edited, I realized that both tasks had more in common than I first believed. In order to put together each issue of the magazine, it is also necessary to find a tone, a rhythm, an order, a focus. As with writing, editing forces us to go through moments of ecstasy and of despair.

Editing a cultural magazine allowed me to cover political subjects that I would never have been able to talk about on my own; it allowed me, in short, to shine a powerful spotlight on those who, because of where they come from or their social class, or simply because they lack the necessary language, cannot always find a space where they will be listened to as they deserve to be—to help their light be reflected in its pages.

In Mexico we have a saying that goes, *de la vista nace el amor*—something like "love begins in the eyes." It means that in order to love something or someone, first we need to see them. This applies very well to food and to attraction between people, but also to another kind of love, which is that of compassion, in its etymological sense, "to feel with the other," precisely what our society and our planet need most these days.

To conclude, I would like to say that I do not believe there is a great deal that we as individuals can do to change the incredibly dark direction the world has taken over the last few years, which is putting so many human lives in danger. What we can do—and what I would like to exhort you to do—is to care for our own light, just as one cares for the flame of a candle, and to keep it burning brightly, so that, when the occasion arises, we can offer it to whoever is near us and might need it, and also so that, when the time comes, we can add it to the light of so many others: the light of the collectives and communities that still believe in the possibility of a better world and are prepared to build it.

PARIS

The author of award-winning novels and collections of short stories translated into more than twenty languages, Mexican writer Guadalupe Nettel (b. 1973) is writer in residence at Columbia University's Center for Ideas and Imagination in Paris. Her work has been adapted for theater and film, and *Still Born* was a finalist for the 2023 International Booker Prize. Nettel visited the University of Oklahoma as the 2025 Puterbaugh Fellow. She delivered this keynote, "Escribir con luz," in Spanish, alternating with the English read by her translator Rosalind Harvey.

British literary translator and writer Rosalind Harvey is a Fellow of the Royal Society of Literature, an Arts Foundation Fellow, and a founding member of the Emerging Translators Network. She teaches for the MA in Literary Translation program at the University of Warwick.

WRITING AND PLACE   (2004)

ABDULRAZAK GURNAH

IT WAS IN THE FIRST few years of living in England, when I was about twenty-one or so, that I began to write. In a sense it was something I stumbled into rather than the fulfillment of a plan. I had written before that, while still a schoolboy in Zanzibar, but those efforts were playful, unserious tasks, to amuse friends and perform at school revues, done on a whim, or to fill idle hours or to show off. I never thought of them as preparatory to anything, or thought of myself as someone aspiring to be a writer.

My first language is Kiswahili, and unlike many African languages, it was a written language before European colonialism, although this is not to say that the literate mode was predominant. The earliest examples of discursive writing date back to the late seventeenth century, and when I was an adolescent, this writing still had meaning and use as both writing as well as part of the oral currency of the language. The only contemporary writing in Kiswahili that I was aware of, however, were short poems published in newspapers, or popular story-programs on the radio, or the very occasional book of stories. Many of these productions had a moralizing or farcical dimension intended for populist consumption. The people who wrote them also did other things: they were teachers or civil servants perhaps. It was not something that occurred to me that I could do, or should do. Since then, there have been new developments in Kiswahili writing, but I am talking about my perceptions then. I could only think of writing as this occasional and vaguely sterile activity, and it never occurred to me to try my hand at it except in the frivolous way I described.

In any case, at the time I left home, my ambitions were simple. It was a time of hardship and anxiety, of state terror and calculated humiliations, and at eighteen all I wanted was to leave and find safety and fulfillment somewhere else. I could not have been more remote from the idea of writing. Starting to think differently about writing in England a few years later had to do with being older, thinking and worrying about things that had seemed uncomplicated before, but in a larger part had to do with the overwhelming feeling of strangeness and difference I felt there. There was something hesitant and groping about this process. It was not that I was aware of what was happening to me and decided to write about it. I began to write casually, in some anguish, without any sense of plan but pressed by the desire to say more. In time, I began to wonder what the thing was that I was doing, so I had to pause and deliberate and think about what I was doing as writing. Then I realized that I was writing from memory, and how vivid and overwhelming that memory was, how far from the strangely weightless existence of my first years in England. That strangeness intensified the sense of a life left behind, of people I casually and thoughtlessly abandoned, a place and a way of being lost to me forever, as it seemed at the time. When I began to write, it was that lost life that I wrote about, the lost place and what I remembered of it. In a way, I was also writing about being in England, or at least about being somewhere so unlike the place in my memory and in my being, a place safe enough and far enough away from what I had left to fill me with guilt and incomprehensible regrets. And as I wrote, I found myself overcome for the first time by the bitterness and futility of the recent times we had lived through, by all that we had done to bring those times upon ourselves, and by what then seemed a strangely unreal life in England.

There is a familiar logic in this turn of events. Traveling away from home provides distance and perspective, and a degree of amplitude and liberation. It intensifies recollection, which is the writer's hinterland. Distance allows the writer uncluttered communion with this inner self, and the result is a freer play of the imagination. This is an argument that sees the writer as a self-sufficient cosmos, best left to work in isolation. An old-fashioned idea, you might think, a nineteenth-century romantic self-dramatization of the author, but it is one that still has appeal and endures in a variety of ways.

If one way of seeing distance as helpful to the writer pictures him or her as a closed world, another sees distance as liberating a critical imagination. This second argument even suggests that such a displacement is necessary, that the writer produces work of value in isolation because he or she is then free from responsibilities and intimacies that mute and dilute the truth of what needs to be said, the writer as hero, as truth-seer.

If the first way of seeing the writer's relationship to place has echoes of nineteenth-century romanticism, the second recalls modernists of the early to middle decades of the twentieth. Many of the major writers of English modernism wrote far from home in order to write more truthfully as they saw it, to escape a cultural climate they saw as deadening.

There is also an argument the other way: that in isolation among strangers, the writer loses a sense of balance, loses a sense of people and of the relevance and weight of his or her perceptions of them. This is said to be especially true in our post-imperial times, and of writers from territories that were former European colonies. Colonialism legitimized itself by reference to a hierarchy of race and inferiority, which found form in a number of narratives of culture, knowledge, and progress. It also did what it could to persuade the colonized to defer to this account. The danger for the postcolonial writer, it seems, is that it might have worked, or might come to work, in the alienation and isolation of a stranger's life in Europe. That writer is then likely to become an embittered émigré, mocking those left behind, cheered on by publishers and readers who have not abandoned an unacknowledged hostility, and who are only too happy to reward and praise any severity on the non-European world. In this argument, writing among strangers means having to write harshly to achieve credibility, to adopt self-contempt as a register of truth, or otherwise to be dismissed as a sentimental optimist.

Both arguments—distance is liberating, distance is distorting—are simplifications, although that is not to say they do not contain traces of truth. I have lived my entire adult life away from my country of birth, settled among strangers, and cannot now imagine how I might have lived otherwise. I sometimes try to do so, and am defeated by the impossibility of resolving the hypothetical choices I present to myself. So to write in the bosom of my culture and my history was not a possibility, and perhaps it is not a possibility for any writer in any profound sense. I know I came to writing in England, in estrangement, and I realize now that it is this condition of being from one place and living in another that has been my subject over the years, not as a unique experience that I have undergone, but as one of the stories of our times.

It was also in England that I had the chance to read widely. In Zanzibar, books were expensive, and bookshops were few and undernourished.

Libraries, also few, were meager and dated. Above all, I had no knowledge of what I wanted to read, and took what turned up in its haphazard way. In England, the chance to read seemed limitless, and slowly English came to me to seem a spacious and roomy house, accommodating writing and knowledge with heedless hospitality. This, too, was another route to writing. I believe that writers come to writing through reading, that it is out of the process of accumulation and accretion, of echoes and repetition, that they fashion a register that enables them to write. This register is a delicate and subtle matter, not always a method that can be described, although literary critics are dedicated to doing so; not an instrumental program that advances a story, but when it works, it is a complex of narrative moves that is appropriate and persuasive. I do not wish to make a mystery, to suggest that writing is impossible to speak about or that literary criticism is a self-delusion. Literary criticism educates us about the text and about ideas that go far beyond the text, but I don't think that it is through criticism that the writer finds the writing register of which I am speaking. That comes from other sources, central to which is reading.

The school education I received in Zanzibar was a British colonial one, even though by the last stages of it we were briefly an independent, even a revolutionary, state. It is probably true that most young people go through school acquiring and storing knowledge that has no meaning for them at the time, or that seems institutional and irrelevant. I think it was probably more puzzling for us, and so much of what we learned made us seem incidental consumers of material meant for someone else. But as with those other schoolchildren, something useful came out of it all. What I learned from this schooling, among many other valuable things, was also how the British looked at the world and how they looked at me. I didn't learn this at once, but over time and on recollection, and in the light of other learning. But that was not the only learning I was doing. I was learning from the mosque, from Qur'an school, from the streets, from home, and from my own anarchic reading. And what I was learning in these other places was at times flatly contradictory to what I was learning at school. This was not as disabling as it might sound, though it was sometimes painful and shaming. With time, dealing with contradictory narratives in this way has come to me to seem a dynamic process, even if by its very nature it is a process first undertaken from a position of weakness. Out of it came the energy to refuse and reject, to learn to hold on to reservations that time and knowledge will sustain. Out of it came a way of accommodating and taking account of difference, and of affirming the possibility of more complex ways of knowing.

So when I came to write, I could not simply shuffle myself into the crowd and hope that with luck and time my voice would perhaps be heard. I had to write with the knowledge that for some of my potential readers, there was a way of looking at me which I had to take into account. I was aware that I would be representing myself to readers who perhaps saw themselves as the normative, free from culture or ethnicity, free from difference. I wondered how much to tell, how much knowledge to assume, how comprehensible my narrative would be if I did not. I wondered how to do all this and write fiction.

Of course, I was not unique in this experience, although the details always feel unique as one frets at them. It is arguable that it is not even a contemporary or particular experience in the way I have been describing it, but one that is characteristic to all writing, that writing begins from this self-perception of marginality and difference. In that sense, the questions I am raising are not new questions. If they are not new, however, they are firmly inflected by the particular, by imperialism, by dislocation, by the realities of our times. And one of the realities of our times is the displacement of so many strangers into Europe. These questions, then, were not only my concern. While I was worrying away at them, others who were similarly strangers in Europe were working on problems just like these at the same time and with huge success. Their greatest success is that we now have a more subtle and delicate understanding of narrative and how it travels and translates, and this understanding has made the world less incomprehensible, has made it smaller.

UNIVERSITY OF KENT

Abdulrazak Gurnah (b. 1948) was born in Zanzibar, Tanzania, and is the author of several highly acclaimed novels, including *Paradise*, which was shortlisted for the 1994 Booker Prize. His latest book, *Afterlives*, appeared in 2021, and he was also awarded the Nobel Prize in Literature that year. Gurnah teaches at the University of Kent in Canterbury.

GENTLY, PLEASE

(2008)

HAVIVA PEDAYA

Translated from the Hebrew by Peter Cole

Gently, please
please, with force
release my soul
bound, now,
please, longing and sighing
I need more than what exists
so that I'll yearn
though nothing come
but let me not stop asking
please, restore in me
words you gave me purely once—
and I will say have pity, please
today, today and not tomorrow
declare, please, that even if
I linger I will surely come
and give myself to things, remember, please
for I have wished for you for me and not
for I am but a mortal being
because the body's walls are struck
by a soul that seeks to be
uprooted and strikes itself and wails
blessed one, please
bless us, please
and fathom that I'm barren
and do not have a soul to whom
I might reveal my plight
and did not understand in time
that my body is me
and when I understood was lost
and found no outlet for my weeping

when it struck, since none exists—
understand that I need time
to calculate the flowering's prospects
whether more devastation will come
as, in terror, I wither
and morning by morning vomit
as night threatens to touch night
and knowledge of the world below
stretches toward the world below
and I no longer know
how to fashion words
in my own image and blood
and send spirit through them
just one thing have I asked—
and that is all I seek:
your dwelling within me
your sending soul into me
I wailed for just one thing,
remembering myself,
for when, then, I prayed
nothing was lacking
and now that I desire nothing
all within me is beaten down
be gracious, please, to me, have mercy
bless my days with purity
raise them like a daughter weeping
over the apple of her eye
if you're able, gently, please

Born in Jerusalem, Haviva Pedaya (b. 1965) is the award-winning author of more than a dozen books of poetry and prose. She is a professor of Jewish history at Ben-Gurion University in Be'er-Sheva, Israel.

An NEA, NEH, Guggenheim, and MacArthur Fellow, American writer Peter Cole (b. 1957) is the recipient of a National Jewish Book Award for Poetry and a PEN Translation Award for Poetry.

THE SWORD OF POETRY

CLARIBEL ALEGRÍA

Translated from the Spanish by David Draper Clark

THROUGHOUT MY LIFE, I have made incursions into many literary genres, but ever since my childhood, poetry has been and continues to be my passion. From before I knew how to read, my parents had me memorize poems by Rubén Darío, the great Nicaraguan poet who founded the modernist movement that transformed the Spanish language and whose work I recited with pleasure to whoever was naïve enough to ask me to do so. The rhythm of Darío's poems fascinated me. Often—and even alone—I would recite his work out loud. Understanding the meaning of his verse didn't matter, for the music of his poems was the most important thing. It was like the voice of the wind, the pounding of rain on windows, or the eternal roar of the ocean waves. As I grew older, I became more and more enamored of words. I wanted to know the meaning of each one of them and to memorize the dictionary.

Words are sensual. They seduce us and spark our imagination, but they also express intelligence and logic in constructing towers of ideals and culture. The Bible tells us that "In the beginning was the Word, and the Word was with God, and the Word was God." The word is our sword, our strength, the magic force that is given to things in order to name them. Having already entered into adolescence, I wanted to express myself through words. I evoked them, was delighted by them, but at times I also came to hate them, to come to blows with them when they didn't respond to me. As a poet, I like to invent and conjure up words, watch them fly, remain in flight, and many times fall and rise again bruised and wounded. There are words that reveal and others that conceal and still others that steal our sleep. Words are often empty, and we know not what to do with them, and they make us want to throw them to the floor and stomp on them to see what might emerge.

From very early on, I was quite fond of reading poetry. It is a habit of mine. At night, whenever possible, I read at least one poem before going to sleep. There have been good and bad influences on me as a poet. I have written many imitations of whatever I might be reading at any given time. I learned numerous tricks, some of which are quite useful and still serve me well. The Bible has greatly influenced me: the Book of Job, the Psalms, Ecclesiastes, the Song of Solomon. And poetry, as Percy Shelley observed, is like a great river into which thousands of tributaries flow. In essence, all poets contribute to writing the great endless poem.

The poet celebrates humankind, the universe, and the creator of the universe. It is impossible for one to remain indifferent to the turbulence that our planet and its inhabitants suffer through: war, hunger, earth-quakes, misery, racism, violence, xenophobia, deforestation, AIDS, and childhood affliction, among others. In the region from which I come, Central America, we love poetry, and at times we use it to denounce what is happening around us. There are many fine testimonial poems. The poet, especially where I'm from, cannot and should not remain in an ivory tower.

To be a female poet was very difficult for me as an adolescent. I began writing relatively early. At the age of fourteen, after reading *Letters to a Young Poet*, by Rainer Maria Rilke, I knew that this vocation was for me. My parents never voiced opposition to the idea, but I used to write virtually in hiding. Except for my parents, I showed my poetry only to my literature professor; to Salarrué (Salvador Salazar Arrué), a great Salvadoran short-story writer; and to Alberto Guerra Trigueros, a Nicaraguan/Salvadoran poet. If my women friends had been aware that I was writing poetry, they would have made fun of me, and no young man would want to approach me, not even to dance. Among my generation in Central America, women of the leisure class had the option of marrying or controlling their hus-band's purse strings or of remaining chaste and virtuous, baking cakes for their nieces and nephews.

Just a few years ago, one could easily identify the women in all of Latin America who stood out in literature. Names like Gabriela Mistral, Alfonsina Storni, Juana de Ibarbourou, Delmira Agustini, Claudia Lars, not to mention the greatest of them all, Sor Juana Inés de la Cruz, who, five hundred years ago, took off her feminist gloves when she wrote, "Stupid men, who, without cause, accuse women," words proclaimed rather shockingly. I suspect that Sor Juana opted to become a nun in order to have the opportunity to receive an education, without which she would have been veiled in silence.

In my particular case, after finishing secondary school, I had to spend two years learning to sew, cook fine cuisine, and play "Für Elise" on the piano before I could rebel. My father in no way wanted me to travel abroad to study or to attend the university in El Salvador. He said that there were hardly any women there and that I would be the object of disrespect. Finally, with the complicity of my mother, along with threats of my own, I succeeded in convincing my parents to allow me to travel to the United States to continue my studies. In spite of the fact that my father was *machista*, he never opposed my pursuing a career as a poet. On the contrary, I believe deep down that he was pleased that I did, for he loved poetry.

Soon before traveling to the United States, my parents invited me and my younger sister to gather in the living room. There, my father showed an upright Steinway piano to my sister, who had great musical talent, and told her, "This is your instrument. Take advantage of it." In turn, he brought me a wooden case with a felt-lined interior that housed a Parker fountain pen: "This is your instrument. Use it as a sword," he instructed. My father was intuitive. I'm sure he feared his own words, but he had to speak them to me, nevertheless. Quite often I have used my poetry as a sword, and I have brandished it against my internal and external demons. . . .

MANAGUA, NICARAGUA

Nicaraguan/Salvadoran poet, essayist, novelist, and journalist Claribel Alegría (1924–2018) received many honors over the course of her career, including Cuba's Casa de las Américas Prize (1978) and the Premio Reina Sofía de Poesía Iberoamericana (2017). Awarded the 2006 Neustadt Prize, she delivered this acceptance speech at the University of Oklahoma.

An accomplished translator and lifelong bibliophile, David Draper Clark was the editor in chief of *World Literature Today* from 2002 to 2008.

SILENCED? FEAR AND COURAGE IN AN ERA OF BOOK BANS (2025)

MARGARITA ENGLE

WRITERS IN THE UNITED STATES are currently suffering through a barrage of hostile attacks against our books. This repression strikes me as the most drastic assault on expressive freedom since the blacklists of the McCarthy era, and the range of targeted books truly astonishes. In a predictable twist, books written for children and teenagers face the most scrutiny, with BIPOC and LGBTQ authors especially vulnerable. Onlookers who shrug and claim the bans will help sell books fail to understand the landscape of literature for young readers. Book bans benefit no one and harm everyone.

Unfortunately, diverse authors aren't always featured in chain bookstores; we depend upon schools and libraries. We care about our readers, the children and teens who might not have enough money to buy books. These children require a wide variety of reading materials in classrooms, school libraries, and public libraries. They deserve to choose what they read, with the guidance of their parents, teachers, and librarians. They don't need rules set by their classmates' parents or, in many cases, by fanatics who aren't directly involved with schools, other than when acting as self-appointed censors.

How will the resulting chaos affect writers? Will we censor ourselves to avoid being attacked? Will we omit sensitive topics from our writing, even though many children and teens need stories about those exact topics? Will publishers begin rejecting potentially "high-risk" manuscripts for fear of outrage? Do reviewers and award committees shy away from giving stars and prizes to books that might offend extremists? Will libraries, schools, and bookstores opt to carry titles that seem likely to become controversial? Will our society revert to shelves full of nothing but antiquated "classics" written by white men? These threats even lurk outside the realm of creative fiction: how can biology teachers be expected to present the truth when ignorant individuals target anatomy and physiology textbooks, simply because they show how the human body works?

As you can see, I have more questions than answers. Such is the job of a poet. We ask. We wonder. We praise or we rage, but we rarely waste energy pretending that we know more about the mysteries of existence than other equally wonderstruck poets.

What I do know is this: Freedom is a muscle. It atrophies whenever fear reaches into the mind of a writer, resulting in self-censorship or—even worse—total silence.

I know that writers are often the first targets of dictators. In times of uncertainty all over the world, poets, novelists, and journalists alike have been imprisoned or silenced. At this very moment, creative individuals languish in prison at the behest of various nation-states and their repressive ideologies. Why? Because we ask and we wonder while authoritarians propagandize, pretending to know what's best for everyone else.

Pretense remains the essence of book bans. Extremists usurp spheres of power to dictate which types of poetry, fiction, and nonfiction deserve to be read. They demand this privilege, and although such acts thoroughly violate the treasured First Amendment of our shared Constitution, they maintain their dogmatic ignorance.

Extremists pretend. They claim to have read every disputed library book, just as they claim to be infallible judges, dictating what *is* and *is not* age-appropriate. If they weren't pretending, they would leave that task to professional librarians and teachers. Instead, librarians like Amanda Jones have received death threats for speaking up against book bans. Has fear caused Amanda Jones to be silenced? No. After being targeted with threats and insults, she wrote *That Librarian: The Fight against Book Banning in America*. She is not alone; many authors follow her courageous example. All over the United States, grassroots organizations have surfaced, formed by librarians, teachers, parents, and writers to protect the right to read freely. PEN America, PEN International, and other established organizations continue their long-standing tradition of defending our freedom to write. Publishers are speaking out, lawsuits have been launched, and above all, there is hope—because the McCarthy blacklists are not forgotten. Those imprisoned poets in other countries are not forgotten. We know what is "at stake," a term that makes me think of the Inquisition and all the poets who, along with their verses, burned at the stake.

One might assume that banned books for young readers would all be sexually explicit or otherwise shocking. Nothing could be further from the truth. The lists of banned children's and young adult books are long and absurd. They include famous authors and newcomers alike. Many are BIPOC and LGBTQ authors, with the subjects and genres being as varied as literature itself. Fantasy, romance, history, science, social justice, and biographies—all have been targets of self-appointed censors.

Ironically, my own potentially controversial young adult verse novels such as *Wild Dreamers* and *Wings in the Wild* are not yet targets, even though they include social and environmental justice issues. Instead, my most challenged children's book is *Drum Dream Girl*, a biography of Millo Castro Zaldarriaga, who became a famous drummer in Cuba at the age of ten. Growing up in the 1930s, she was faced with the challenge of overcoming a cultural bias against female drummers, so it's a story about equality and perseverance, intended to be inspiring.

Why is *Drum Dream Girl* viewed as dangerous by extremists? Tragically, the answer is obvious: racism. Millo was the daughter of an Afro-Cuban mother and Chinese Cuban father. Diversity lists used by school districts often include *Drum Dream Girl*, with book ban fanatics in parts of Florida, Ohio, Pennsylvania, and Michigan challenging those entire lists. I doubt they've read all the stories. I suspect that they simply don't want white children to see brown faces on book covers.

The United States has been a sanctuary for my Cuban refugee relatives, and for anyone who treasures the freedom to read freely, write freely, and speak freely. The line between banning books and arresting poets is as fragile as a strand of mist. Every time a reporter uses the phrase "culture wars," I feel nauseous. This is not about culture. It's about racism, sexism, homophobia, transphobia, and xenophobia. When I read a book like *Worm*, Edel Rodriguez's powerful new graphic memoir, I am reminded that freedom of speech, freedom to write, and freedom to read are all muscles. If we don't use them, they will atrophy, and we won't be able to defend children against tyranny.

So, there is no choice. We have to speak, write, and read about liberty and equality. We have to set our fears aside and choose courage. We won't be silenced.

CLOVIS, CALIFORNIA

A Cuban American poet and writer, Margarita Engle (b. 1951) won the 2019 NSK Neustadt Prize for Children's and Young Adult Literature. Reminding us that "freedom is a muscle," Engle urges readers to set aside fear and to speak, write, and read about liberty and equality.

ASSIA DJEBAR

Translated from the French by Joanna Goodman

I liberated the day
from its emerald cage
like a rapid spring
it slipped from my fingers.

I liberated the night
from its grave of water
like a cloak of rain
it fell back on me.

I liberated the sky
from its bed of amaranths
in a flash of pride
it was carried off like a king.

I flung the sun
on the stage of the world
the shadow was so vast
it became an outlaw.

The first woman to be accepted into the École Normale Supérieure in Paris and the first member of the Académie Française from the Maghreb, Algerian novelist, filmmaker, translator, and historian Assia Djebar (1936–2015) was awarded the Neustadt International Prize for Literature in 1996.

Joanna Goodman has been awarded the Iowa Poetry Prize, the "Discovery"/The Nation Prize from the 92nd Street Y, and an NEA poetry fellowship.

VILMA'S STORY

MARYSE CONDÉ

Translated from the French by Richard Philcox

I WISH I WERE my Indian grandmother who would have followed him to the funeral pyre. I would have thrown myself onto the flames licking over his body, and our ashes would have mingled as our souls never did. I wish I were my Indian grandmother who would have died for him. That's what I wish I were.

Our happiness did not have time to bud. Perhaps if he had lived beyond his allotted time, I would have managed to nurture that fragile plant which heat withers and rain devastates. Such as it is, our story is a sad one. He took me in; you could say he kept me out of pity because I had come to seek refuge and he was not the type of man to leave a dog out in the rain.

Yes, I wish I were my Indian grandmother who would have followed him to the funeral pyre. Our ashes would have mingled and rained down on the Ganges.

If you want to know why I took refuge with him, a disreputable man, who one wretched morning loomed up in the middle of Rivière au Sel, you'll have to go back far, far into time to the day I was born, when the midwife shouted:

"A girl, Madame Ramsaran! The Good Lord has taken pity on you."

She never held my hand.

When she soaped me down as I stood naked under the sun, the palm of her hand was rough. When she took me to school, she walked three paces in front, and I'd stare at her black braid twisted into a chignon, held in place by a long tortoiseshell pin, while she presented me with her back under the black calico dresses that she wore every day the Good Lord made, in mourning for my sister Shireen. Shireen, dead at the age of three months, suffocated by the worms that had crawled up her insides to her mouth.

There was never any room for me in her heart. Nor for the boys either. Not even for Alix, the youngest, so handsome people called him "pitite a Bon Die" (the Good Lord's child). But the boys had their Papa who, as soon as school was out, took them across the fields, to soccer matches on Saturday, and to the beach at Viard on Sunday, where they hunted for grey clams in the grey sand.

I had nobody. I had nothing. Only my books.

"Where did she get all that intelligence from?" the schoolmistress marveled.

The other children refused to play with me. Out of jealousy they called me "Kouli malaba." Yes, all I had was my books. As soon as I got back from school I would lie down under my mosquito net and read and read until her rough voice found me where I had gone and brought me back to earth.

"Can't you hear when I'm calling you?"

That's why I can remember as if it were yesterday the day my father took me out of school, and I think I shall remember it until the day I die. For me it was the beginning of the end. It was a few weeks before school was due to start again. September had been fine, relatively dry for our region, smitten with the wind and the rain. The leaves glistened green under the golden rays of the sun. The fireflies danced in the dusk. The nights were humid with the dampness of our sweat. One of my cousins from the Grands Fonds had spent the holidays with us and we'd been walking in the woods, going as far as the pond at Bois Sec whose waters, it is said, turn to blood when the sun goes down and where the spirits come to drink.

That day we were finishing lunch. She was fussing around Father, as she'd been doing for years and years, peeling a juicy, sticky brown sapodilla. Then she cut it into pieces and arranged them on a white saucer edged with blue. Without taking the trouble to thank her, Father stopped me as I was getting up from the table.

"Let me tell you: you're not going back to school. It's a waste of time, I've got other plans for you!"

Nobody looked surprised, as if it were perfectly natural. I was speechless.

I ran out to my room, threw myself on my bed, and started to cry. Leaving school for me was tantamount to dying! After a while she came in and sat down on the bed.

"Listen," she said. "Your Papa knows what he's doing. A woman is like an orange tree or a litchi. She's made to bear fruit. You'll see how happy you'll be when your belly swells out firmly in front of you and your child starts to kick in its haste to come out and warm itself in the sun."

Her eyes contradicted her words. You could sense she didn't believe a word, that she was reciting a lesson.

"I'm not interested in having children," I replied. "I don't want to get married."

She shrugged her shoulders and her mouth curled up in spiteful joy.

"But that's what's going to happen to you. I'm telling you so that you know, your father's made an arrangement with Marius Vindrex."

My tears dried instantaneously.

"What!"

Marius Vindrex is a sad-looking yellow man, as long as a rainy day, whose languishing eyes have not let me alone ever since I've been able to walk on my own two feet. He's got money, that's for sure! After having studied something or other in Canada, he started up his family's sawmill again. The logs arrive from Guyana, since our forests have been decimated, and all day long his machines whine, sawing wood, blackening the air with their smoke. He's Carmelien's good friend. Always talking politics with him. Last year, when a bomb killed that American, he was in seventh heaven; you'd think he'd placed it himself.

"Marius Vindrex?" I screamed. "But I don't love him!"

She sighed, then said in a tired voice:

"You watch too much *Dallas* and *Dynasty*. What does that mean: 'I don't love him'? Do you think I loved your Papa when I married him? And in India, in our country, don't you know that husband and wife didn't meet each other until they slept in the same bed, under the same sheets?"

I couldn't sit there listening to all her silliness. I went out. It was two o'clock in the afternoon. The sun was hammering down on my head. I felt madness running behind me, about to grab hold of me. I ended up on the Saint Charles forest path, and at a turn I stumbled into the gully that was always cool and inviting with its dark, almost invisible waters singing their little song under the ipecacs and the ferns.

Sye bwa
Legowine kase
Sye bwa.

(Saw the wood / The handsaw is broken / Saw the wood.)

A man was sitting on a rock watching the water. On hearing me, he stood up and stammered:
"Is it you? Is it you?"
Then his face closed up again.
"I'm sorry! I mistook you for someone else."
Considering how long I'd been hearing about the color and state of his clothes I had no trouble recognizing Francis Sancher and needed no introduction. I knew he'd just given a belly to Mira and that everyone was out for his blood. Personally, I don't like Mira Lameaulnes and I'm not afraid of her either. People believe her green eyes can turn them into dogs. People also believe that she can give hernias as big as banjos and erysipelas as heavy as yam seedlings. I just think her heart inside her breast is hard and grey as a rock. When she was at school, before they ended up expelling her, even though she was Loulou Lameaulnes' little darling, she used to arrive late after having roamed God knows where, sit down in her place, and while the other children recited their multiplication tables, she'd hum the weirdest songs that nobody had ever heard before.

Chobet di paloud
Se an Ian me
An ke kontrew.

(The whelk said to the clam / I'll see you / In the sea.)

What she had in her belly wasn't my problem.
"Who were you waiting for?" I asked Francis Sancher.
He stuck his bakoua hat on his hair that looked as though it hadn't seen a comb for months, and disappeared without even bothering to answer.

It was the wind. Blame it on the wind.

In the dark the mountain was sound asleep and the wind was lying at its feet. Suddenly, it shook itself and got up. It pressed up against the candlewood trees, then with one leap it rushed down to the savannah, overturning everything in its way. In its fury it blew into our house, throwing open doors and windows. She got out of bed to close them, and I heard father order her to go and check the gate.

I felt anger and revolt boil up inside me. What's the point of a mother if she doesn't temper a father's egoism and cruelty? But for her, only Shireen counted. I could be sold like the last lot of hog plums in the market for all she cared! I had to make her ashamed, I had to hurt her, take my revenge. But how?

Then, laughing like a madman, the wind whispered me the idea. Blame it on him! Blame it on the wind!

When I arrived at his house, the ferocious Dobermans, with their red muzzles, were fighting over a carcass. They left off to run towards me. But he made them lie down. He was sitting behind his typewriter.

"What do you want?" he asked, not in the least bit agreeable.

"Would you have a little job for me? Cooking or washing?"

He laughed. But even when he laughed, his eyes were as black as mourning.

"Here you are looking like an apsara,* and you want to work for me? It's the world upside down!"

I went closer.

"What are you doing?"

He laughed again.

"You see, I'm writing. Don't ask me what's the point of it. Besides, I'll never finish this book because before I've even written the first line and known what I'm going to put in the way of blood, laughter, tears, fears and hope, well everything that makes a book a book and not a boring dissertation by a half-cracked individual, I've already found the title: 'Crossing the Mangrove.'"

I shrugged my shoulders.

"You don't cross a mangrove. You'd spike yourself on the roots of the mangrove trees. You'd be sucked down and suffocated by the brackish mud."

---

*   An Indian nymph or temple maiden.

"Yes, that's it, that's precisely it." He gave me the smaller of the two bedrooms. For a whole week I heard him scream and struggle with invisible spirits, call for help and cry. I prayed the Good Lord would help him. Finally, at first light, he came to find sleep in my bed.

I didn't expect to love this man I had chosen in the great wind of madness. Love took me by perfidy. It crept stealthily into my heart and took possession of it . . .

But Francis Sancher was never mine. He was never Mira's either, that I know. The creature he belonged to was hiding in the shadows amidst the sounds of the night.

The days were spent more or less peacefully. He wrote pages upon pages on the veranda. When he was tired of tearing them up, he went off into the woods, sometimes with the dogs who returned with their tongues hanging out and their coats soaked. He didn't speak to me, he ignored me.

But as soon as darkness fell, everything changed. He drew close to me as if I could protect him.

Shaking, he would ask me:

"Can you hear him? Can you?"

I shrugged my shoulders and answered:

"Yes, I can hear the laughter of the wind that the night cannot keep under lock and key as it scours the countryside. Yes, I can hear the cavalcade of mangoes in a hurry to sink their stones into the belly of the earth so that they in turn can become eternal. I can hear the sea there in the distance endlessly quarrelling with the rocks."

He found no consolation in these words. He went up to the window, peered into the night, and said:

"Can you see him? Can you? He's standing there under the ebony tree. He's waiting for me. He's counting the days."

I went up to stare into the night over his shoulder and I could see nothing but high, dark smooth walls.

"Come to bed," I begged him. "Doesn't my body taste nice?"

He wouldn't listen to me and went off to Chez Christian to search for solace in rum. I stayed alone praying that one day he would find peace. When he returned he lectured me in a hollow and meaningless way. He told me about towns, he told me about all sorts of places, and I tried to find my way through his words without a guide.

"When we left Balombo it was dark. We had been fighting over this village for months. We had finally cleaned out the rebels. I had this smell of fresh blood in my nostrils that I couldn't get rid of. I had the death rattle in my ears of all those whom I let pass over to the other side without being able to provide comfort. There was this young girl, this child I should say, with her legs torn off, who at the height of her suffering kept repeating: 'Long live the Revolution!' But I was past believing in it. I couldn't take it any longer. It was that evening I put one foot in front of the other and became a deserter. The desert was white like salt under the moon."

I wanted to ask him questions. But he dozed off without even thinking of waiting for what I had to say. I watched him with his eyes closed and his mouth open, and I wondered through what wretched, arid lands this man's mind was roving. He never told me anything about himself, and I wouldn't know what truth there is in all those stories the people of Rivière au Sel tell.

When I was pregnant, I told him. He didn't say a word. Over our heads the rain continued to drum on the iron roof that the branches of the trees scraped every time the wind breathed. I touched his shoulder.

"Did you hear what I just said?"

He turned his back to me in answer and faced the wooden wall. From the shaking of his shoulders I realized he was crying. From that day on, he no longer took me in his arms, and we lived like father and daughter. When I was alone I made up sentences to soften his heart: "Why are you angry because my womb is fertile? For someone who is so afraid of death, don't you know that a child is the only cure?"

But when he returned, my words took fright at his impenetrable face, as hard as a rock, and flew away.

And now he's dead! All I have left is the memory, cold as ashes, of a little pleasure and a lot of pain. I confuse the past and the present.

I think I've never been closer to Francis Sancher than tonight, now that he has nothing left to say, now that he has gone and will never come back. Our ancestors used to say that death is nothing but a bridge between humans, a footbridge that brings them closer together on which they can meet halfway to whisper things they never dared talk about.

Amidst the patter of the rain on the roof, the scraping of the trees, the rustling of the grass, and the whistling of the wind as it steals between the badly joined planks of this house, I seem to hear his voice speak mysterious words I never heard before, lifting the enigma of who he was.

I wish I were my Indian grandmother who would have followed him to the funeral pyre. For then we would have gone on talking and talking.

VAUCLUSE, FRANCE

Born in Pointe-à-Pitre, Guadeloupe, award-winning writer Maryse Condé (1934–2024) was a French novelist, playwright, scholar, and critic. She was honored as the Puterbaugh Fellow at the University of Oklahoma in 1993.

Richard Philcox was Maryse Condé's longtime translator and husband. His translation of her final book, *The Gospel According to the New World*, was shortlisted for the International Booker Prize in 2023.

BRICEIDA CUEVAS COB

Translated from the Spanish by Jonathan Harrington

The owl arrives.
It crouches on the wall
and meditates.
Whose death should it announce
if no one lives in this village?
The fossils of the people
have never been moved.
The moon paints the graves
of the overgrown cemetery.
The owl calls out a song to life,
refusing to foretell its own death.

Briceida Cuevas Cob (b. 1969) is a Yucatecan Maya poet and cultural promoter whose work has appeared in many journals and anthologies.

Jonathan Harrington is a graduate of the Iowa Writers' Workshop. He has lived in Yucatán, Mexico, since 2002.

LITERATURE AND CIVILIZATION (1933)

ALBERT GUÉRARD

Editor's note: The article which follows is the prospectus of a forthcoming book [*Preface to World Literature* (1940)] by Albert Guérard, to be published under the title given above. In the course of the correspondence following our request for the article, Professor Guérard made the following suggestion: "If you want to justify its inclusion in *Books Abroad*, you may mention the fact that I am a teacher (i.e., a student) of General and Comparative Literature; and that, although I have never lost sight of American conditions, I have been almost compelled to borrow many of my examples from 'books abroad.' It would be difficult to deal with the influence of Courts and Academies strictly in American terms."

We are complying with the author's suggestion to the extent of reproducing his "justification"; but it seems to us that our pages are the most natural place in the world for a discussion of this type, and we agree entirely with a phrase which occurs later in his letter: "I could not think of a better public for my work than the one which is reached by *Books Abroad*." [Roy Temple House]

ART IS THE EXPRESSION of a unique personality; yet there is no literature, not even the wildest Prophetic Books of Blake, that is not, in some measure, the joint production of author and public. He who "voyages through strange seas of thought alone" is not acclaimed as a poet until he returns. How could the critic of literature take cognizance of "the mute inglorious Milton"? As Martial said nineteen centuries ago, he does not write at all, whose poems are read by none. Shakespeare exists for us because he is acknowledged. If he were not, his most fervent admirers today would have had no chance of coming across his works. Literature may be the reflection of Eternal Beauty: empirically, it is, first of all, the reflection of Public Taste. For the pragmatist, the Corpus, the Canon of literature is determined by recognition. To say: "This man is great" means:

"He is accepted by the right people." And who are the right people? This is the question that the present book will attempt to answer, concisely, in about a hundred thousand words.

On this pragmatic basis, literature is a social product. It implies language, a means of communication: the One can express himself only in terms accessible to the Many. Language itself is a set of symbols which embody, beyond their plain, literal meaning, all the customs, feelings, beliefs of the group. *King*, for instance, has a different connotation for the seventeenth-century absolutist, for the eighteenth-century liberal, for the nineteenth-century democrat. The word may evoke a throng of images, from the Vicar of God to a comic-opera puppet. A language is not an algebraic code: with the best dictionaries at your command, you literally cannot understand an author if you are wholly out of touch with his civilization. This conception is hoary with age. It was already clear in Madame de Staël's work *On Literature Considered in Its Relations with Social Institutions*, which appeared in 1800. Its application was codified by Taine, in his *Introduction to the History of English Literature*, with the magic formula *Race, Environment, and Time*. Taine himself may be antiquated: his method is still with us. It does not tell the whole truth, nor perhaps the essential truth: but the truth that it tells is far from negligible. Race, it seems, cannot be exorcized from the literary field. Even today, reputable critics will speak of "Latins," "Celts," and "Slavs," as if the words had some bearing on the interpretation of masterpieces. Mrs. Gertrude Atherton tells us that human nature is largely a matter of the cephalic index; that *The Scarlet Letter* is incompatible with brachycephaly; and that our dismal naturalism is due to a resurgence of the Alpine. If a critic has never indulged in such racial fantasies, let him cast the first stone.

The concept of Race is somewhat enfeebled at present—the nemesis of its own excesses; that of Environment is as lusty as ever. Environment means more than the physical climate, the geographical habitat: it includes political, social, economic conditions. When Irving Babbitt ascribes to a false conception of democracy the low state of our culture, he is using the method of Taine, just as much as the Critics of the Extreme Left when they interpret literary history in the light of Karl Marx's Communism.

It might be interesting, therefore, to restate Taine's famous principles in terms of modern experience; and, as we restate them, to submit them to the most searching criticism. We have no desire to explode Race, Environment, and Time; we only want to understand. We all feel that there is "something" to them: but what is that "something," and how much of it is there? We have no faith whatever in the holiness of the vague; and we have but scant respect for prejudice camouflaging as pseudoscience.

Race, Environment, and Time are, roughly speaking, common to author and reader, and affect them very much in the same fashion. They account for folklore, "floating literature," or, in the parlance of today, "folkways" and "folksay." They *explain* Jack Brown and his pulp magazines even more than they *explain* James Branch Cabell. But literature in the stricter sense, literature as conscious craft, implies a dissociation: the few who are vocal, the many who listen. Authors are, in very definite respects, different from the mass; the laws of civilization do not apply to them with exactly the same incidence. We shall have to consider a series of problems about the Man of Letters as such, the natural gifts which constitute his vocation, the deformations, the aberrations which are his professional risks. Coal miners are exposed to melanosis, white-lead workers to necrosis, writers to various forms of graphitis. A psychological and social study of *Homo litteratus* may yield curious results. The dissociation, however, is never complete. The author remains linked with his public—else the Ivory Tower would be his tomb. Every book is a dialogue in which the silent interlocutor, the Reader, cannot be ignored. Literature is written for a public, large or small, even when it is written for the express purpose of exasperating that public. It is a reflection, however distorted, of the public mind; and the works that survive for posterity are a fairly accurate reflection of the best public taste. But that common word *public* is as hard to define as it is convenient to use. Is there such a thing as a clear, spontaneous *vox populi*? Is not "the public mind" a myth? In literature, as in politics, the public mind is made up by conscious, vocal, energetic minorities. The masses are offered merely a choice between the small groups which assume leadership and claim authority.

If we could determine what these centers of influence are, many problems of literature would be elucidated. But we should bear in mind that the "Phantom Public" is evolving: the solutions of yesterday fail to meet present conditions. In the classical age, whose shadow lingers in Europe, and even, very faint but unmistakable, in our Western world, these active minorities were essentially emanations of Society in the narrower sense: the Court as the supreme drawing room, the Salon as a miniature private Court, the tavern or the café as an impromptu Bohemian salon, the Academies as the most exclusive of clubs, the Universities as those places where "gentlemen" were trained. Literature ranked with horsemanship, dancing, and table manners among the possessions and distinctive marks of a social elite. This "genteel tradition," as Santayana called it, is no longer "at bay": it is gone. The Neo-Humanists are mourning over a tomb. The disruption of the ancient social hierarchy has destroyed the old scale of literary values. We shall restore "standards" if we restore to their primacy the Monarchy, the Church, the Aristocracy. In spite of such prophets as Charles Maurras and T. S. Eliot, the chances for such a restoration are dim.

In our pluto-democracy, literature may be roughly defined in terms of the book industry. Manuscripts that cannot possibly sell are not printed; if printed, they are stillborn. But this affords no key to our problem: the book industry does not know the rules of its own game, and publishers are the first to realize that their trade is a gamble. They do not know enough about our civilization to "give the public what they want." In their own interest, they are eager to know more about "the laws of public taste." They would like to possess the infallible recipe for a bestseller; and they dream, not only of the short-lived bestseller, but of the perennial good-seller, i.e., the *classic*. How can classics be told? Forecasting is the test of science as well as the key to successful production. In literature, forecasting is Criticism. The critic should be able to tell: "Such a book will appeal to such a class of readers, in such numbers." He should be: but he is not, to the despair of authors, publishers, and public alike. The chaos of our competitive economics is reflected in the chaos of our literary mart.

How can literature transcend such a chaos—the road back to yesterday being irremediably closed? How can it supply the needs of the general public without the waste, surfeit, and spiritual starvation which we are experiencing to-day? And especially, what chance of life is there, under the present dispensation, for the unpopular but adventurous, subtle, cryptic, or simply unobtrusive and gentle? Now that the elites no longer have a common center and a consolidated prestige, how can the scattered lovers of things rare and delicate be integrated into a *public?*

Literature as one of the elements in civilization—conditioned, if not determined, by social life as a whole, reacting upon social life in its turn: such is the problem which we propose to discuss in this book. We do not claim that this is the sole possible approach to literature. As a matter of fact, much of our work will consist in marking the limits of the sociological method: this work, not committed to materialistic determinism, will never be used as a textbook in the schools of Soviet Russia. All aspects of civilization, whilst they are parts of an organic whole, enjoy a measure of autonomy; and in no case is this autonomy larger than in the case of literature. This other side of the question—the refusal of the artist to bow down, to conform, to serve; the defiant assertion of the Unique against the laws of the herd—we hope to study in a companion volume on *The Doctrine of Art for Art's Sake.*

STANFORD UNIVERSITY

A prominent French-born literary scholar, Albert Léon Guérard (1880–1959) was renowned in his lifetime for publishing numerous works on European civilization, world literature, and international languages. After studying at the University of London and the Sorbonne, he immigrated to the United States in 1906 and taught at Stanford University for many years.

ISMAIL KADARE

Translated from the Albanian by Ani Kokobobo

THERE IS NO SHORTAGE of questions about literature. We hear questions such as, Does the world need literature? This question would call to mind clichéd TV-show questions, trying to stir up debate, had it not been already raised thousands of years ago. There have obviously been two parties lobbying over this question, for and against literature.

Literature was born along with a denial, a barrier. Even if at first this seems strange, if we think about the questions, we will reach the conclusion that this negation is somehow befitting of literature, and it is even quite natural. Literature and negation are one and the same. Rather than being born of angels, literature is the handiwork of demons.

Let's look at things more simply. Literature, in the form of early oral poetry, has often had as its subject matter the return from long travels: telling of what happened there, at the far border of a country, the desert, or death itself. The first travelers coming from afar were practically the first writers. Walking back to their countries, in the solitude of the road, their minds reconstructed events in such a way that they would be most interesting to listeners. Thus, along the way, dialogues emerged, events became more exciting, colors grew brighter, and something was emphasized while something else erased.

Although the travelers brought with them stories, their heroes stayed mostly far away. They were absent, always from beyond, either on the other side of state lines or on the other side of life—meaning they were dead. In this way, since its beginnings, death and absence assumed a special place in literature. But literature entered death's domain not to curry favor but as an equal. In the majestic *Epic of Gilgamesh*, literature, fully knowing the power of death, still assumes the right to censor it. Gilgamesh is defeated by death, but for the sake of literature, part of him still escapes the grip of death. In other words, using contemporary verbiage, we might call this a contract. Only great art could engage in such contracts with the impossible. Literature continued to feed off of death and its subsidiaries: nighttime, sleep, dreams, guilt.

From its very beginnings, literature was bound up with sacrifice. Troy was the first victim on its altar. Subsequently, there were hundreds of events, subjects, characters, and scenes drenched in blood and grief that fed the literary repertoire. When the Albanian poet Fan Noli translated Victor Hugo's *Waterloo*, he noted at the end that after all the tragedy between the pages, he had a single consolation, that he himself was alive, and the poem had been reborn through him.

Literature was used to commanding this kind of sacrifice. Over the years, we have paid this tribute in one way or another.

Death, sleep, and guilt remind us of nighttime. Night has always been connected with negation in human thought. But we say such things in a lighthearted fashion, without considering what terror there would be in this world if we were irrevocably separated from the night, if our calendars merely reflected an endless day. Until now, no one has bothered to carry out a research study on the role that the night plays in softening humanity. Without her intervention, without that restraint and interruption, human evil, anxiety, and anger would march forward at a catastrophic pace.

During its nascent stages, literature only knew about those dangers that threatened human life: erasure and oblivion. The rhapsodists sang, people heard them, and new rhapsodists emerged to sing new songs that died away with their singers or shortly thereafter. In this sense, literature confronted some of the same natural dangers as human life. Later on, literature was also confronted with dangers that came from another sphere, from society and the state. It was the theater, likely due to its ability to gather people in the center of cities, that first helped conjure the practice of censorship. Official censorship was thus born, over two thousand five hundred years ago, and it was so powerful that it created many problems for the literary giants of the time, the great tragedians.

Censorship is bound up with writing. Before the Akkadian-Sumerians invented writing, efforts to control oral poetry were inexact and not very persistent. At the most, a nonconformist rhapsodist would not be invited to sing at the gathering of a prince, and that was the end of the matter.

When writing appeared on the cultural horizon, it was like an unimaginable earthquake. Writing carried out a dual project. On the one side, it opened a new horizon for literature, while on the other hand, it suffocated, killed, and mummified it.

Prior to a new phase in its development, literature, in accordance with its stringent legal codes, always sought a heavy tribute from writers. They had to give up part of their spontaneity, to pass their thought through the wheels and banners of the heavy machinery of syntax. They could not criticize literature on any given day if they were in the mood to do so. Writing was thus a dual form of control. The control that derived from a kind of consciousness, prescient for its time, but also an official form of control. The history of writing is, above all, the history of the dangers confronting writers.

Some contemporary expressions that are connected to this, such as "this literary work can burn you" or "let's hope this work doesn't land on your head like a misfortune," become surprisingly clear when we think about the clay tablets on which Sumerians recorded their thoughts. When the baked tablets were taken out of the oven carelessly, the writer could burn his hands. Or a literary work, let's say a long narrative, could have been placed in the writer's studio so as to cover an entire wall, and one day, either because it had been placed poorly, or because it had not been baked properly, or due to an earthquake, the tablet would fall on the writer and trap him underneath.

Like every new initiative, literature brought along many such dangers. These early possibilities were simple compared to the horrors that would follow, which have become well known.

The departure of Aeschylus from Athens was the first of many such departures. Aeschylus and Homer were humanity's greatest writers until the fifth century BCE. At least one of these two great writers was obliged to abandon their home. (I say at least one, because we cannot exclude the possibility that Homer, as a traveling rhapsodist, could have been traveling so much that for him the notion of departure would have lost all meaning altogether.)

The departure or the banishment of writers was thus tied to literature, becoming part of its genetic code from early on. But the departure also changed over the centuries. Even as the weather in the world grew milder, its position vis-à-vis literature only grew harsher.

The departure of Ovid from Rome seems like the most painful, because unlike the departure of Aeschylus, where it was the anger of writers that assumed a deciding role, Ovid was sent away by the state. The repression of writers that continues to our time began with him.

In the case of Ovid, we have all the makings of future totalitarianism: condemnation with no known cause. The kind of suppression of the totalitarian state, where you yourself don't even know why you're being condemned. This unexplained terror, a blind strike, would remain one of the key devices of terror until the twentieth century, when communism, after having perfected its own devices, just like Kafka's machine, would crumble along with it.

With their departure, great writers like Aeschylus and Dante Alighieri seemed to have been looking for a way to return to that zone, that climate, and that chaos in which literature was born. In other words, they sought to experience the status of a semideath, if not the depths of death itself. It was, perhaps, an internal order of art, of the same great ritual that suggested to Dante that before he started describing his journey into the inferno, he had to somehow separate himself from life.

At the same time, it must be said that up until Dante, writers, even in cases of misfortune, were generally treated as a seigneurial group. It was later dictatorships that understood that in order to attack writers better, they had to have their status lowered. So they made a habit of what had previously not been a habit: the imprisonment of writers, their placement in communal cells, their internment, their dishonoring, their movement by train from one camp to another, their insult, their reeducation through physical labor, and so on and so forth.

In no other dictatorial regime has there been such a telepathic exchange between the tyrant and the people as under communism. Suffocating, irritating, terrifying, sleep-inducing, and intoxicating, the psychic echoes encompassed all this, and it was dominant.

The communist regime was one that more than any other regime took its battle against literature seriously. Communism and literature simply had no means of joint coexistence. The negative stance toward literature was not a later manifestation; it was inherent to communism. The shallow paragraphs by Marx about ancient literature or about Shakespeare were a mere alibi to cover up later crimes. There is no room for literature in the Marxist vision of the future world. Lenin's seminal article, "Party Organization and Party Literature," was as brutal in its effects as some of the fury of Genghis Khan. There is a red thread among communists that connects their treatment of literature, from Lenin's articles, to Stalin's executions, to Mao's pathological hatred for writers, to the massacres of both writers and their readers by Cambodia's Pol Pot.

Totalitarianism likewise surmised early on that it could not merely destroy literature through terror alone. It understood that a massacre alone would not do, that a suicide of sorts would also be needed to completely solve the problem of literature. Self-censorship, this long-standing, century-old disease, which literature confronted but overcame, communism attempted to turn into a real plague.

And it managed, in one way or another, to do so. Thousands of writers, most of them mediocre ones, surrounded literature's temple from all sides. Their number grew daily, just as the number of true writers, who sought to keep alive the holy fire, decreased by the same measure.

Never has the literature of half the globe been confronted with such a danger. In totalitarian regimes, literature and the arts were tested cruelly, in a manner unknown in world history until then. We know about the punishment of writers even before: the censors, the prisons, and the camps were well known. But Stalinism went further. It did not satisfy itself with simply repressing well-known works, the ones sometimes called artistic cathedrals. It attempted to forever bury the possibility of their creation too. In other words, that system sought to destroy the raw materials whereby such cathedrals are built. It attempted to create a new race of writers, who would eagerly take upon themselves the destruction of literature. Stalinism achieved this in a way. Those of us who remained faithful to the temple were in the minority in that endless and hopeless desert known as socialist realism.

Writers were thus broken into two groups: those who betrayed the temple and those that stayed faithful to it. The divine question that could be posed to writers of the East—"What did you do, Adam?"—would have two possible answers. The first answer was: I degraded myself and literature according to communist law. And the second was: I continued to write normally, as though communism didn't exist. When I hear questions like the ones frequently posed to writers of the former communist empire (namely, How did you continue to write normally, during a time and place when this seemed impossible?), my answer has been precisely this: we had faith in literature. It rewarded our faith and devotion with this blessing and protection.

To believe in literature means to believe in a higher reality. To believe in literature means that your country's dark regime seems pale compared to the majestic literary funerary rites. To believe in this art means you always know that the government which dominates you, the police that surveil you, that the parliament, the bosses, the administration, tyranny itself, are a passing nightmare, dead matter, compared to the great order of which you have become initiated as a member.

So as not to drag on, let me repeat something that I have said elsewhere in connection with an episode of Dante's *Divine Comedy*. While traveling through hell, Dante Alighieri is frightened for one moment by an approaching storm, and his master, Virgil, says: "Do not be afraid, it is a dead storm."

Within these words we can find the explanation of what I mention above. To view the storms of the regime as dead storms is an unusual skill. And only writing can afford a writer this skill. It has never been easy for the writer to feel alive amidst all the surrounding death.

It has been said multiple times that to think normally in the mad communist world is an incredible stance. To speak normally is outright heroic.

Communism fell without fully realizing its perverse dream. We arrived at the end of this millennium without it. Our literature has lived in the world for three thousand years. Its first millennium was wealthy and bright. The second one was unfortunately less rich; it seemed as though humanity wanted to rest a bit during that time. And then the third millennium arrived, the one we are living in, which gave new life to literature. Let us hope that the new millennium, the fourth one, will not repeat the second, as though in a fatal symmetry.

During these difficult days, when the whole planet is experiencing the distress of a global pandemic, I want to express my regret that I cannot be present among you for a beautiful celebration that coincides with the fiftieth anniversary of this prestigious prize. Due to the impossibility of reaching you from my native Albania on the Adriatic, I wish to express my appreciation to the jury. I am honored that you have chosen me from among the most well-known authors in the world. [*Edited by David Bellos*]

TIRANA

Ismail Kadare (1936–2024) was an Albanian writer of novels, plays, screenplays, poetry, and essays. After defying and outwitting strict censorship laws during the long rule of dictator Enver Hoxha, Kadare defected to Paris in the 1990s. During the Covid-19 pandemic, the 2020 Neustadt Prize ceremony was broadcast to a worldwide Zoom audience; David Bellos read the English-language version of Kadare's acceptance speech.

Ani Kokobobo is dean of the College of Liberal Arts at the University of Louisiana at Lafayette. Her writings have appeared in the *Washington Post, LARB,* and *Chronicle of Higher Education.*

APPENDIX

25 BOOKS FOR THE 21ST CENTURY, 2000–2025

In spring 2021 the editors of *WLT* invited twenty-one writers to nominate a single book, published since the year 2000, that had had a major influence on their own work, along with a brief statement explaining their choice. We published the longlist, invited readers to vote on their favorites, and published the results in June 2021 (the top six are indicated by an asterisk). To augment the list with titles from 2021 to 2025, we polled the same twenty-one writers, published the longlist in the March 2025 issue, then had readers vote on their favorites. Below, the top four new titles have been added to the twenty-one from the original list.¶

¶ Mosab Abu Toha, *Things You May Find Hidden in My Ear* (2022)
   Meena Alexander, *Atmospheric Embroidery: Poems* (2018)
   Aharon Appelfeld, *Days of Astonishing Brightness* (2014, in Hebrew)
* Roberto Bolaño, *2666*, trans. Natasha Wimmer (2008)
   Mia Couto, *Sleepwalking Land*, trans. David Brookshaw (2006)
   Boris Cyrulnik, *Resilience: How Your Inner Strength Can Set You Free from the Past* (2011)
¶ Percival Everett, *James* (2024)
* John FitzGerald, *The Mind* (2011)
   Amitav Ghosh, *The Glass Palace* (2000)
   Jack Gilbert, *Refusing Heaven* (2005)
* Yaa Gyasi, *Homegoing* (2016)
¶ Samantha Harvey, *Orbital* (2023)
¶ Fady Joudah, *[. . .]* (2024)
   John Keene, *Counternarratives* (2015)
* Deborah Levy, *Things I Don't Want to Know: On Writing* (2014)
   Audre Lorde, *The Selected Works*, ed. Roxane Gay (2020)
   Dulce María Loynaz, *A Woman in Her Garden: Selected Poems*, trans. Judith Kerman (2002)
   Ian McEwan, *Atonement* (2002)
   W. S. Merwin, *The Essential W. S. Merwin*, ed. Michael Wiegers (2017)
   Haruki Murakami, *Kafka on the Shore*, trans. Philip Gabriel (2005)
* M. NourbeSe Philip, *Zong!* (2008; rev. ed. 2024)
* W. G. Sebald, *Austerlitz*, trans. Anthea Bell (2001)
   William Trevor, *Selected Stories* (2011)

Mario Vargas Llosa, *The Feast of the Goat*, trans. Edith Grossman (2001)

Helen Vendler, *Dickinson: Selected Poems and Commentaries* (2010)

Nominated by Chris Abani, Hélène Cardona, Margarita Engle, Aminatta Forna, Alisa Ganieva, Kimiko Hahn, Aviya Kushner, Claire Messud, Philip Metres, Dipika Mukherjee, Andrés Neuman, Felipe Restrepo Pombo, Shahilla Shariff, Mahtem Shiferraw, Naomi Shihab Nye, Samrat Upadhyay, Buket Uzuner, Luisa Valenzuela, Padma Viswanathan, Hope Wabuke, and Sholeh Wolpé

POSTSCRIPT:
WORLD LITERATURE TODAY AND WORLD LITERATURE

DANIEL SIMON

> *Magazines* do *world literature.*
>
> —Patricia Novillo-Corvalán & Francesca Orsini

AS NOTED IN MY INTRODUCTION, the democratization of the magazine form in the early twentieth century allowed modernism to flourish in some decidedly provincial backwaters. One such accident of geography—Norman, Oklahoma—might be the most unlikely place imaginable for starting a literary publication. Yet even before being officially proclaimed the forty-sixth state in 1907, Oklahoma had caught the imaginative attention of many who dreamed of the land during its earlier avatars as Indian Territory (1834–1906) and Oklahoma Territory (1890–1907). In Mark Twain's *Adventures of Huckleberry Finn* (1885), Huck has Indian Territory in mind when he "lights out" at the novel's end. A few years later, Cuban poet, journalist, and prophet of revolution José Martí reported on the 1889 Oklahoma Land Run:

> And at that same hour homesteaders wait impatiently on the distant prairie for the stroke of noon on Monday when they will invade the new Promised Land and stake their claims in the ancestral hunting ground of the Seminole. . . . Who will be the first to arrive? . . . From the four corners of that land besieged by settlers one cry goes up: "Oklahoma! Oklahoma! . . ." But they continue to pour in from near and far. Whole towns have migrated. In clusters, in straggling lines, in cavalcades they come, amid clouds of dust. The silent land stretches, virgin and green, with its grass-land and bluffs, surrounded on all four sides by human masses, fenced off only by the flanks of the mounted troops. Burning eyes peer between the flanks. This is how the wilderness has been

settled here, and how the wonder called the United States has come into being.

For Martí, despite the utopian vision evoked here, the imperial greed that fueled the 1889 land grab foreshadowed the Spanish-American War at century's end and a continuing clash of empires in the twentieth century.

By the early 1910s, Franz Kafka would also imagine "The Nature Theater of Oklahoma"—the closing chapter of his first novel, *Amerika*—as the land where "everyone is welcome." Written as he was discovering the thriving Yiddish theater in Prague, the Czech-Austrian writer never completed the novel, which was published posthumously in 1927 (the year of *Books Abroad*'s founding). After auditioning for the Nature Theater, the novel's immigrant protagonist, Karl Roßmann, and the other actors barely catch the train to Oklahoma on time, then dream about the promised land en route.

And in the mid-1920s, Roy Temple House—a young professor of German and chair of the Department of Modern Languages at the University of Oklahoma—nurtured another dream. House had grown alarmed as the United States retreated into political isolationism following World War I, embodied in such policies as the Immigration Act of 1924. The co-author of that legislation, newspaper editor and vigilante-turned-congressman Albert Johnson—who espoused eugenics, anti-Semitism, and supported the Ku Klux Klan—feared that American culture was being infected by a "stream of alien blood" from Asia, Africa, and southern and eastern Europe (especially nonwhites, Jews, and Catholics). The Red Summer of 1919, the terror campaigns of the KKK, and the Tulsa Race Massacre of 1921 were further signs of worsening racial violence and ethnic xenophobia, even as transatlantic literary modernism was flourishing. The history of Oklahoma itself, a crossroads of cultures and translation, embodies much of that tension as Spanish and French explorers, African American homesteaders, and white settlers—who believed Manifest Destiny entitled them to the land—all staked their claims to a territory that had been the domain of Native nations for centuries.

In the center of that contested landscape and against the grain of isolationism, Dr. House, who had assisted European orphans and refugees after World War I, believed that launching a literary periodical on the Southern Plains might "begin fostering contributions to the scholarly and cultural activities of the nation," as he wrote in a letter to the university's president,

William Bennett Bizzell (October 21, 1926). So, in January 1927, just twenty years after statehood and with a start-up budget of $150, House launched his venture, dubbed *Books Abroad*, as a modest thirty-two-page pamphlet. With a topsail schooner and the motto LUX A PEREGRE (Light from Abroad) emblazoned on the cover, the publication would come to represent a metaphorical "inland harbor" equidistant from the Atlantic and Pacific coasts.

House's decision to found a magazine in the hinterlands of literary geography also paralleled the 1920s vogue of publishing all-encompassing "outlines" of the world's knowledge systems: H. G. Wells's *Outline of History: Being a Plain History of Life and Mankind* (1922), J. Arthur Thomson's *Outline of Science: A Plain Story Simply Told* (1922), British poet and playwright John Drinkwater's *Outline of Literature* (1923), American editor and critic John Albert Macy's *Story of the World's Literature* (1925), and Clement Wood's *Outline of Man's Knowledge: The Story of History, Science, Literature, Art, Religion, Philosophy* (1929) all appeared in the same decade. Since then, *Books Abroad* (1927–76) and its successor, *World Literature Today* (*WLT*, 1977–present), have similarly attempted to sketch an evolving outline of world literature in their pages. By 1948, House would be nominated for the Nobel Peace Prize for his service as an "ambassador of international cooperation and goodwill."

House turned over the editorial ship to a succession of European émigrés, including Ernst Erich Noth (1949–58), Wolfgang Bernard Fleischmann (1959–61), and Robert Vlach (1961–66). When Vlach died suddenly at the age of forty-nine, House's longtime assistant editor, Bernice Duncan, took over as interim editor (1966–67). Duncan would play a key role in recruiting an Estonian poet, translator, and literary scholar as her successor: Ivar Ivask, born the year *Books Abroad* was founded, assumed the helm and eventually became the longest-serving editor (1967–91) of *Books Abroad* and *WLT*. Ivask inaugurated the famed Puterbaugh Conferences in 1968 and, in 1969, the award that would become the world-renowned Neustadt International Prize for Literature. By 1976, *Books Abroad*'s fiftieth year of continuous publication, Dr. Ivask—who was born on the Baltic coastline of Riga, Latvia—looked to both past and future:

What is *Books Abroad*, the international literary quarterly published for half a century by the University of Oklahoma?

It is not just another literary journal. It actually is a secret inland harbor which receives and registers cargoes of books from all over the world. It is not a proud, aesthetically exclusive island nor an ideologically self-assured promontory, but a wide-open port offering a place for the exchange of different literary ideas and the latest news. *Books Abroad* was invented by a scholar of vision from landlocked Nebraska, Roy Temple House. He devised as the journal's logo a full-rigged ship with the motto *Lux a peregre*—"Light from Abroad." He obviously thought of books as ships, filled with light from abroad, reaching the inland harbor of his journal. It is a rather poetic but nonetheless apt image. However, the image of the generous harbor must be coupled with that of a lighthouse which radiates the light received back abroad, since this has also been an essential function of the quarterly. . . .

Perhaps a more descriptive title for our journal may well be "World Literature Today" rather than *Books Abroad*. . . . The present editor, born and raised in a seaport, has no trouble identifying *Books Abroad* with the maritime imagery launched by its founder. Indeed, *Books Abroad* approaches its second half-century with every intention of continuing its proven mission of both harbor and beacon in Oklahoma.

The Mexican writer Octavio Paz would later characterize the Oklahoma plains as a "navigable sea"—evoking the so-called prairie schooners of the pioneers and reinforcing the lighthouse metaphor—and declare *Books Abroad* as his compass to world literature. By 2004, the Polish poet and essayist Adam Zagajewski pronounced Norman "an undeclared capital of modernity."

After Ivask's departure, three subsequent editors—Djelal Kadir (1991–1996), William Riggan (1996–2002), and David Draper Clark (2002–2008)—consolidated *WLT*'s international reputation in the 1990s and early 2000s. The magazine's current executive director, Robert Con Davis-Undiano, helped usher the magazine into the twenty-first century with his "Back to the Essay" manifesto in 1999. As of 2026, *WLT*'s one hundredth year of continuous publication, the magazine tallies 2.2 million annual readers and has received more than two dozen awards in the past quarter-century. The ship sails on.

ACKNOWLEDGMENTS

for my family

*and for all those dedicated to advancing
the cause of world literature*

IN MY MONNET HALL OFFICE on the University of Oklahoma (OU) campus, a single seven-foot-by-four-foot bookcase contains every issue ever published of *Books Abroad* and *World Literature Today*. My goal in this anthology has been to distill that bookcase—the work of more than 80,000 bylined contributors and nearly 11,000 pages—into a single volume that showcases one hundred years of international literary history. Between July 2002 and March 2026, I have had the privilege of working on 122 of those 423 issues. (*WLT*'s official centennial issue is forthcoming in September 2026.)

To thank those tens of thousands of contributors would require a book in its own right, had I world enough and time. With neither option in abundance, I must pare down my acknowledgments to the essentials. First and foremost, I'd like to express my profound gratitude to Ananda Devi for her enthusiastic support for the project. When I sent her the draft manuscript in fall 2024, she sent me, almost immediately, the following reply: "What I wanted to say is that, just looking at the table of contents and reading the first few essays, I feel as if all the answers, or possibilities of hope—as we face a world that seems to be heading to its own destruction and as we see the suffering of so many millions of people that we are powerless to save—are contained in these writings, that they offer us a beacon, a sense that salvation (a loaded word!) is possible. So, thank you for this immense work you have undertaken, dear Daniel, and for asking me to contribute to it" (August 16, 2024).

I'm also grateful to Pico Iyer, whose work I've long admired, for his luminous and generous foreword.

My academic background in comparative/world literature, modern languages, and translation studies owes much to the courses I took with several legendary faculty at the University of Nebraska–Lincoln (1985–90) and Indiana University Bloomington (1991–94), especially Robert Knoll, Warren Motte, Linda Pratt, and Susan Rosowski at UNL as well as Matei Călinescu, Eugene Eoyang, Breon Mitchell, and Ilinca Zarifopol-Johnston at IUB.

Since 2002, I have had the pleasure of working in close collaboration with Robert Con Davis-Undiano, *WLT*'s longtime executive director, whose tenure (1999–present) has marked a third golden age of the magazine, building on the successes of the two previous golden eras under Roy Temple House and Ivar Ivask.

In 2023 I was fortunate to receive a Faculty Investment Program grant from the OU Research Council, sponsored by then–Vice President for Research and Partnerships Tomás Díaz de la Rubia, for my work on the anthology. I'm indebted to my faculty colleagues Julie-Françoise Tolliver and Ron Martinez for providing invaluable feedback on my grant application. Dr. Tolliver also offered enlightened suggestions on subsequent stages of the project.

In 2025 I received additional funding from three additional sources at OU: Senior Vice President and Provost André-Denis Wright, Vice President for Research and Partnerships Matthew Wade Hulver, and Dodge Family College of Arts and Sciences Interim Dean Randall S. Hewes. I'm grateful for their generous support and also thank Associate Vice President for Research and Partnerships Ann H. West for facilitating the process.

For their professional guidance and courtesy in granting me access to *WLT*'s manuscript archives, I'm grateful to the staff of OU's Western History Collections, especially Todd Fuller, Lina Ortega, Jackie Reese, and Melissa Weiss.

For their kind assistance—as well as many decades of service to the field of comparative literature—I'm also indebted to David Damrosch and Zhang Longxi. Dr. Damrosch includes the theories of Goethe, Tagore, and Zheng in *World Literature in Theory* (2014). Dr. Zhang discusses Tagore's notion of *viśva-sāhitya* in *World Literature as Discovery* (2024). My thanks as well to Jing Tsu, who notes the influence of Drinkwater's and Macy's compendia on Zheng's *Wenxue dagang* (1924–27) in "Getting Ideas about World Literature in China," *Comparative Literature Studies* 47, no. 3 (2010): 290–317.

At OU and beyond, I would like to express my deep appreciation to Julia Luisa Abramson, Rea Amit, Rilla Askew, Amit Baishya, Douglas Clayton, Peter Constantine, Jonas Elbousty, César Ferreira, Carolyn Forché, Aminatta Forna, Pamela Genova, George Gömöri, Kyle Harper, Alamgir Hashmi, Sam Huskey, Emily Johnson, Ilya Kaminsky, Rita Keresztesi, Joseph Legaspi, Ryan Long, Idra Novey, Pádraig Ó Tuama, Mina Raminsabet, William (Bill) Riggan, Rhona Seidelman, Liran Yadgar, and Eric Ziolkowski. Anna Badkhen provided much-needed encouragement and advice at crucial stages of the project. Alice-Catherine Carls, *WLT*'s longtime contributor and current editorial board member, also offered steadfast counsel and enthusiastic support throughout.

OU students Amber Durst, Emily Holson, Hannah Morris-Voth, and Aliki Paisiou provided extensive assistance with the project while serving as *WLT* interns, as did James E. Fawcett, Dani Glidewell, and Karsyn Scruggs.

At Restless Books, my profound thanks to Ilan Stavans for his passionate endorsement of this project early on, not to mention his guidance throughout the drafting and revision process. Thanks as well to Jennifer Alise Drew, Paulina Ochoa-Figueroa, and Lydia McOscar for their superb engagement and assistance along the way.

To the past editors of *Books Abroad* and *WLT*—Roy Temple House, Ernst Erich Noth, Wolfgang Bernard Fleischmann, Robert Vlach, Bernice Duncan, Ivar Ivask, Djelal Kadir, William Riggan, David Draper Clark—I am mindful that I'm standing on the shoulders of giants. To *WLT*'s current staff, all dear colleagues—Kay Blunck, Parker Buske, Robert Con Davis-Undiano, Michelle Johnson, Terri Stubblefield, and Rob Vollmar—our many years of collaboration have offered the most enduring satisfaction of my professional career.

Finally, to *mi familia querida*, may my thanks to you outlive this book long into the future.

PERMISSIONS

The selections in this anthology all previously appeared in the pages of *Books Abroad* (1927–76), *World Literature Today* (1977–present), or worldlit. org. In the citations below, *Books Abroad* and *World Literature Today* have been abbreviated as *BA* and *WLT*, respectively.

Minor editorial changes for the sake of accuracy and consistency, including emendation of occasional typos and factual errors, have been made silently. Some generic titles have been replaced with descriptive titles. Substantive deletions are marked by bracketed ellipses. Full-text versions of every piece can be found as digitally archived facsimiles on JSTOR (1927–2023) and Project Muse (2009–present). Since 2010, *WLT* has also published its own full-text edition and weekly blog content at worldlit.org.

Due to limitations of space, when choosing the texts for this anthology, I have favored the inclusion of writers from Asia, the Middle East, Africa, the Caribbean, and Latin America, where possible, since modern and contemporary European and American—especially anglophone—literatures have received the most attention in previous critical studies and anthologies of world literature.

All texts are reprinted by permission of the author or the author's estate, except where otherwise noted. Every effort has been made to contact copyright holders. In case of inadvertent omissions, please contact Restless Books: publisher@restlessbooks.com.

PART I: BOOKS AS MAPS

Alareer, Refaat. "If I Must Die: A Bilingual Poem from Gaza." Trans. into Spanish by D. P. Snyder. *WLT*, December 2023, online.

Ancalao, Liliana. "The Silenced Language." Trans. Seth Michelson. *WLT* 92, no. 1 (January 2018): 59–61.

Bishop, Elizabeth. "Laureate's Words of Acceptance." *WLT* 51, no. 1 (1977): 12.

Carretta, Roberto. "Margherita." Trans. Stiliana Milkova. *WLT* 94, no. 2 (2020): 21.

Chu Yo-sop. "Imaginative Literature in the Age of Science." *BA* 36, no. 3 (Summer 1962): 277–78.

Couto, Mia. "Re-Enchanting the World: The 2014 Neustadt Prize Lecture." Trans. Paul Fauvet. *WLT* 89, no. 1 (2015): 50–53.

Danticat, Edwidge. "All Geography Is Within Me: Writing Beginnings, Life, Death, Freedom, and Salt." *WLT* 93, no. 1 (2019): 59–65.

Diaz, Natalie. *See* Shook.

Farrokhzad, Forugh. "Reborn," in *Sin: Selected Poems of Forugh Farrokhzad*, translated by Sholeh Wolpé (Fayetteville: University of Arkansas Press, 2007), 79–81. Reprinted in "Writing Beyond Iran," *WLT*, March 2015, online.

Frisch, Max. "Neustadt Prize Acceptance Speech." *WLT* 62, no. 1 (1988): 11–13.

Guillén, Jorge. "Al Margen de Borges." *BA* 45, no. 3 (1971): 386–87.

Harjo, Joy. "Bless This Land." *WLT* 93, no. 4 (2019): 34–35. From *An American Sunrise: Poems*, copyright © 2019 by Joy Harjo. Reprinted by permission of the author and W. W. Norton & Company, Inc.

Hirshfield, Jane. "Three Pebbles." *WLT* 93, no. 3 (2019): 59.

Kido, Shuri. "Wandering Birds." Trans. Tomoyuki Endo & Forrest Gander. *WLT* 95, no. 4 (2021): 20–21.

Le Clézio, J. M. G. "On Reading as True Travel." Trans. Julia Luisa Abramson. *WLT* 76, no. 2 (2002): 103–6.

Lee, Li-Young. "Seven Marys." *WLT* 80, no. 4 (July 2006): 27.

Masalha, Salman. "The City of the Walking Flower." Trans. Vivian Eden. *WLT* 95, no. 4 (2021): 46–50.

Miłosz, Czesław. "Gift." Trans. by the author. *WLT* 73, no. 4 (1999): 692. Copyright © 1988, 1991, 1995, 2001 by Czesław Miłosz Royalties, Inc.

Ocampo, Victoria. 1942. "Some Letters from Old Files (1931–1951)." *BA* 50, no. 4 (1976): 789–90.

Pamuk, Orhan. "Implied Writer." Trans. Maureen Freely. *WLT* 80, no. 6 (2006): 20–24.

Paz, Octavio. "Literature as a Compass on the Navigable Sea: The 1982 Neustadt Prize Lecture." Trans. Lowell Dunham. *WLT* 56, no. 4 (Autumn 1982): 598–600.

Roback, A. A. "Yiddish Writing in America." *BA* 8, no. 1 (Jan. 1934): 15–17.

Sforza, Carlo. "D'Annunzio, Inventor of Fascism." *BA* 12, no. 3 (Summer 1938): 269–71.

Shaw, George Bernard. 1931. "Some Letters from Old Files (1931–1951)." *BA* 50, no. 4 (1976): 785.

Shook, David. "Poetry as Wonder, Desire, Rage, and Memory: A Conversation with Natalie Diaz." *WLT* 94, no. 4 (Autumn 2020): 12–15.

Tranströmer, Tomas. "Oklahoma." Trans. May Swenson with Leif Sjöberg. *WLT* 64, no. 3 (Summer 1990): 436. From *Windows and Stones: Selected Poems*, © 1972. Reprinted by permission of the University of Pittsburgh Press.

PART II: FIRST TAKES ON MODERN CLASSICS (1926–1975)

Publication dates for each review follow the reviewer's name. Detailed bibliographical information about the books under review can be found in the original headers in the *WLT* archive at jstor.org (1927–2023) or worldlit.org (2012–present).

PART III: BOOKS AS SHIPS

Brathwaite, Kamau. "Newstead to Neustadt." *WLT* 68, no. 4 (1994): 653–60.

Carson, Anne. *See* Constantine.

Chaturvedi, Geet. "The Tongue of Kumārajīva." Trans. Anita Gopalan. *WLT*, October 2016, online.

Cheuse, Alan. "The Form Read Round the World: American Short Fiction and World Story." *World Literature Today* 84, no. 5 (September 2010): 24–27.

Constantine, Peter. "Ancient Words, Modern Words: A Conversation with Anne Carson." *WLT* 88, no. 1 (January 2014): 36–37.

Debeljak, Aleš. "In Praise of the Republic of Letters." *WLT* 83, no. 2 (March 2009): 25–27.

deNiord, Chard. "'Voices from the Debris Fields': A Conversation with Carolyn Forché" (*abridged*). *WLT*, January 2017, online.

Forché, Carolyn. *See* deNiord.

Forna, Aminatta. "Selective Empathy: Stories and the Power of Narrative." *WLT* 91, no. 6 (November 2017): 32–37.

Gunn, James. "Science Fiction around the World." *WLT* 84, no. 3 (May 2010): 27–29.

Haavikko, Paavo. "Laureate's Acceptance." Trans. Philip Binham. *WLT* 58, no. 4 (1984): 500–501.

Hikmet, Nâzım. "Yellow Geranium in a Tin Can," trans. Randy Blasing & Mutlu Konuk; qtd. in Joanne Leedom-Ackerman, "Introduction," *WLT* 83, no. 6 (2009): 40–41.

Hussein, Taha. "The Modern Renaissance of Arabic Literature." Trans. Ernst Erich Noth. *BA* 29, no. 1 (Winter 1955): 4–18.

Mann, Thomas. 1940. "Some Letters from Old Files (1931–1951)." *BA* 50, no. 4 (1976): 789.

Maranhão, Salgado. "Delirica X." Trans. Alexis Levitin. *WLT* 92, no. 5 (2018): 29.

Momaday, N. Scott. "When Dogs Could Talk: Among Words in a State of Grace." *WLT* 81, no. 5 (September 2007): 15–17.

Morejón, Nancy. "Toward a Poetics of the Caribbean." Trans. Alan West-Durán. *WLT* 76, nos. 3/4 (Summer 2002): 52–53.

Musil, Robert. 1938. "Some Letters from Old Files (1931–1951)." *BA* 50, no. 4 (1976): 788.

Nafisi, Azar. *See* Simon.

Neruda, Pablo. "Ode to an Actor." Trans. Ilan Stavans. *WLT*, online, July 2023.

Neuman, Andrés. "Translating Each Other." Trans. George Henson. *WLT*, July 2012, online. Copyright © 2012 by Andrés Neuman. Reprinted by permission of Casanovas & Lynch Literary Agency, SLU.

Ó Tuama, Pádraig. "Rite of Baptism." *WLT* 98, no. 3 (May 2024): 24

Pound, Ezra. "Correspondence," *BA* 9, no. 3 (1935): 347; rpt. in "Some Letters from Old Files (1931–1951)," *BA* 50, no. 4 (1976): 787.

Rao, Raja. "Laureate's Words of Acceptance." *WLT* 62, no. 4 (1988): 534–35.

Simon, Daniel. "A Republic of the Imagination: In Conversation with Azar Nafisi." *WLT* 97, no. 3 (2023): 30–36. Copyright © 2023 by Azar Nafisi and Daniel Simon. Reprinted by permission of the Wylie Agency, LLC.

Stavans, Ilan. "Is American Literature Parochial?" *WLT* 87, no. 4 (July 2013): 26–30.

Vargas Llosa, Mario. "La novela latinoamericana hoy." Copyright © 1970 by Mario Vargas Llosa / "The Latin American Novel Today." Trans. Nick D. Mills Jr. *BA* 44, no. 1 (Winter 1970): 7–16. Reprinted by permission of Agencia Literaria Carmen Balcells.

Wiesel, Elie. "A Vision of the Apocalypse." Trans. Joan Grimbert. *WLT* 58, no. 2 (Spring 1984): 194–97. Copyright © 1984 by Elie Wiesel. Used by permission of Georges Borchardt, Inc., on behalf of the author's estate. All rights reserved.

Zheng Min. "Golden Rice Sheaves." Trans. Ming Di. *WLT* 95, no. 4 (2021): 15.

PART IV: FIRST TAKES ON MODERN CLASSICS (1976–2025)

Publication dates for each review follow the reviewer's name. Detailed bibliographical information about the books under review can be found in the original headers in the *WLT* archive at jstor.org (1927–2023) or worldlit.org (2012–present).

PART V: BOOKS AS LIGHTHOUSES

Alegría, Claribel. "The Sword of Poetry." Trans. David Draper Clark. *WLT* 81, no. 3 (May 2007): 30–32.

Alexander, Meena. "What Use Is Poetry?" *WLT* 87, no. 5 (September 2013): 17-21.

Badkhen, Anna. "An Anatomy of Lostness." *WLT* 92, no. 6 (Nov. 2018): 36–40.

Cabral de Melo Neto, João. "Laureate's Acceptance Speech." Trans. Djelal Kadir. *WLT* 66, no. 4 (1992): 603–6.

Coetzee, J. M. "How I Learned about America, and Africa, in Texas." *WLT* 78, no. 1 (2004): 6–7.

Condé, Maryse. "Vilma's Story." Trans. Richard Philcox. *WLT* 67, no. 4 (1993): 700–703.

Cuevas Cob, Briceida. "Owl / Xooch' / El Búho." Trans. Jonathan Harrington. *WLT* 84, no. 1 (2010): 17.

Devi, Ananda. "Heavy Lies the World on the Pen" (2024). First publication.

Diop, Boubacar Boris. "How Do We Say 'Genocide' in Wolof? The 2022 Neustadt Prize Lecture." Trans. Bojana Coulibaly. WLT 97, no. 1 (2023): 50–53.

Djebar, Assia. "Poem to the Sun." Trans. Joanna Goodman. WLT 70, no. 4 (1996): 787.

Elytis, Odysseus. "Mozart: Romance." Trans. Kimon Friar. BA 49, no. 4 (Autumn 1975): 647.

Engle, Margarita. "Silenced? Fear and Courage in an Era of Book Bans." WLT 99, no. 1 (2025): 5–7.

Glavatskii, Sergei. "Buried Alive in an Instant." Trans. Ilya Kaminsky & Katie Farris. WLT 96, no. 4 (2022): 41.

Grace, Patricia. "Headlights." WLT 83, no. 3 (2009): 31–34.

Guérard, Albert. "Literature and Civilization." BA 7, no. 1 (Jan. 1933): 3–5.

Gurnah, Abdulrazak. "Writing Place." WLT 78, no. 2 (2004): 26–28.

Halman, Talât Sait. "Literatures of the Near East: A Generation of Renewal." BA 46, no. 2 (Spring 1972): 183–91.

Kadare, Ismail. "Dead Storms and Literature's New Horizon: The 2020 Neustadt Prize Lecture." Trans. Ani Kokobobo. WLT 95, no. 1 (2021): 44–48.

Lima, Conceição. "Archipelago." Trans. Shook. WLT 90, no. 1 (Jan. 2016): 47.

Malouf, David. "Reading Late at Campagnatico." WLT 74, no. 4 (2000): 713.

Mutis, Álvaro. "The Wanderer's Tale." Trans. Alastair Reid. WLT 77, no. 2 (2003): 17–18. Copyright © 2008 by the heirs of Álvaro Mutis. Translation copyright © 2003 by Alastair Reid.

Nettel, Guadalupe. "Writing with Light: The 2025 Puterbaugh Lecture." Trans. Rosalind Harvey. WLT 99, no. 4 (July 2025): 22–25.

Pedaya, Haviva. "Gently, Please." Trans. Peter Cole. WLT 82, no. 5 (2008): 52.

Polonskaya, Anzhelina. "The History Teacher." Trans. Andrew Wachtel. WLT 87, no. 6 (2013): 17–19.

Tannahill, Jordan. "Why Live? A Question for 21st Century Theatre." WLT 90, no. 1 (2016): 36–39.

Ugrešić, Dubravka. "A Girl in Litland: The 2016 Neustadt Prize Lecture." Trans. Ellen Elias-Bursać. WLT 91, no. 1 (January 2017): 58–60.

Wilder, Thornton. 1940. "Some Letters from Old Files (1931–1951)." BA 50, no. 4 (1976): 789. Reprinted by agreement with The Wilder Family, LLC, and the Barbara Hogenson Agency, Inc. All rights reserved. ThorntonWilder.com.

ABOUT THE EDITOR

An award-winning poet, translator, and essayist, Daniel Simon is assistant director and editor in chief of *World Literature Today* at the University of Oklahoma, where he also serves on the English, International Studies, and Judaic Studies faculty. His poetry has appeared in three verse collections, most recently *Under a Gathering Sky* (2024); three anthologies; been translated into six languages; and nominated for multiple awards. *Nebraska Poetry* (2017), his edited anthology, won a 2018 Nebraska Book Award and was included on NPR's "50 States" summer booklist (2022). More recently, he edited *Dispatches from the Republic of Letters: 50 Years of the Neustadt International Prize for Literature* (2020), named a *Publishers Weekly* starred pick. He has also served as consulting editor for the *Best Literary Translations* annual anthology and is a member of the Academy of American Poets, Nebraska Center for the Book, and the Norman Arts Council Roundtable. The grandson of Czech and Irish immigrants, Simon grew up in Nebraska, attended the University of Nebraska–Lincoln (BA 1990), and received graduate degrees in comparative literature from Indiana University Bloomington (MA 1994, PhD 2000). He and his wife currently live in Norman, Oklahoma, and have three daughters.

INDEX